Unless Recalled Earlier

DATE DUE

Demco, Inc. 38-293

Jews, Slaves, and the Slave Trade

REAPPRAISALS IN JEWISH SOCIAL
AND INTELLECTUAL HISTORY

General Editor: Robert M. Seltzer

Martin Buber's Social and Religious Thought:
Alienation and the Quest for Meaning
LAURENCE J. SILBERSTEIN

The American Judaism of Mordecai M. Kaplan
EDITED BY EMANUEL S. GOLDSMITH, MEL SCULT,
AND ROBERT M. SELTZER

On Socialists and "the Jewish Question" after Marx
JACK JACOBS

Easter in Kishinev: Anatomy of a Pogrom
EDWARD H. JUDGE

Jewish Responses to Modernity:
New Voices in America and Eastern Europe
ELI LEDERHENDLER

Russia's First Modern Jews: The Jews of Shklov
DAVID E. FISHMAN

Rabbi Abraham Isaac Kook and Jewish Spirituality
EDITED BY LAWRENCE J. KAPLAN AND DAVID SHATZ

The Americanization of the Jews
EDITED BY ROBERT M. SELTZER AND
NORMAN J. COHEN

The "Other" New York Jewish Intellectuals
EDITED BY CAROLE S. KESSNER

The Nations That Know Thee Not:
Ancient Jewish Attitudes toward the Religions of Other People
ROBERT GOLDENBERG

The Original Torah:
The Political Intent of the Bible's Writers
S. DAVID SPERLING

Jews, Slaves, and the Slave Trade: Setting the Record Straight
ELI FABER

ELI FABER

JEWS, SLAVES, AND THE SLAVE TRADE

Setting the Record Straight

NEW YORK UNIVERSITY PRESS
NEW YORK AND LONDON

NEW YORK UNIVERSITY PRESS
New York and London

Library of Congress Cataloging-in-Publication Data
Faber, Eli, 1943–
Jews, slaves, and the slave trade : setting the record straight
/ Eli Faber.
p. cm. — (Reappraisals in Jewish social and intellectual
history)
Includes bibliographical references (p.) and index.
ISBN 0-8147-2638-0 (alk pap)
1. Jews—Caribbean Area—History.   2. Jewish slave
traders—Caribbean Area—History.   3. Slavery—Caribbean
Area—History.   4. Caribbean Area—Ethnic relations.   I. Title.   II.
Series.
F2191.J4 F33 1998
972.9'004924—ddc21   98-9051
CIP

New York University Press books are printed on acid-free paper,
and their binding materials are chosen for strength and durability.

Manufactured in the United States of America

10 9 8 7 6 5 4 3 2 1

For Lani

Contents

All illustrations appear as an insert following p. 86.

Acknowledgments

This study of the extent to which Jews in the British empire participated in the African slave trade and owned slaves originated in the
fourth annual Sonia Kroland Coster Memorial Lecture at Hunter
College of The City University of New York. Delivered in May 1994
at the invitation of Professor Robert Seltzer, director of Hunter College's Jewish Studies Program, the lecture examined allegations that
attributed domination of the slave trade and a preponderance of slave
ownership to Jewish financiers and colonists. Shortly after the lecture,
published subsequently as "Slavery and the Jews: A Historical In-
quiry," Professor Seltzer proposed a fuller study of the role played
by Jews in the institution of slavery in the western hemisphere. He
presented his views to New York University Press in his capacity as
editor of its series entitled Reappraisals in Jewish Social and Intellectual History. Mr. Niko Pfund, editor-in-chief and director of the
Press, enthusiastically endorsed Professor Seltzer's proposal and was
instrumental in making the project possible. I am indebted to both
for their interest and initiative, and for their continuing involvement
after the manuscript was completed.

At every stage of the book's development, many colleagues and
friends provided assistance and encouragement. The support and
advice of Dee Dee Aikens, Horace Banbury, Daniel Gasman, Mary
Gibson, Jack Jacobs, Thomas Litwack, Marilyn Lutzker, Jacob Ma-
rini, T. Kenneth Moran, Jane Mushabac, and Lydia Rosner, all of
John Jay College of Criminal Justice of The City University of New
York, began as early as the Sonia Kroland Coster Memorial Lecture

and proved invaluable thereafter in a variety of ways. Leo Hershkowitz guided me with his extensive knowledge of the history of New York City and its Jewish population during the eighteenth century, and made available copies of original sources in his care. Stephen Behrendt of the Charles Warren Center for Studies in American History at Harvard University graciously responded to my inquiries and generously shared his knowledge of the Liverpool slave trade after 1780. Carol Ruth Berkin's appraisal of the manuscript was inestimably important, as were the critiques by David Brion Davis, Henry Feingold, and Colin Palmer of a paper summarizing the findings, presented at the convention of the Association for Jewish Studies in December 1997. My appreciation of Professor Feingold's help extends to the inspiring part that he played in turning my attention more than ten years ago to the significance of the history of the Jewish people in colonial America.

I am grateful as well for the extensive assistance I received from the following individuals. In England: Abigail and Simon Fink, and Harriet and Charles Grace; in Jamaica: Cheryl Coote, Ernest De Souza, Valerie Facey, Ainsley and Marjorie Henriques, whose hospitality and responses to my inquiries for historical information were untiring, Donald Lindo, Jacqueline Ranston, and Derek Roberts; in Canada: Dr. Anthony Macfarlane; in Israel: Dr. Joseph Faber; in Lexington, Massachusetts: Sonia Reizes and Robert Bolleurs; and in New York: Michael Ben-Jacob, Kate Gluck, Robert E. Levine, Jonathan De Sola Mendes, and Elaine and Brian Rappaport.

The archivists, librarians, and staffs of research facilities are consummate professionals whose invariable willingness to provide assistance leads to important breakthroughs. I am profoundly grateful to the following research institutions, their archivists and librarians, and the members of staff who stand behind them. In New York City: the Jewish Division and the Rare Books and Manuscripts Division of the New York Public Library, Susan Rosenstein and the Hispanic Society of America, and Aviva Weintraub and the Jewish Museum; in Albany: Jim Folts and the New York State Archives; in Waltham, Massachusetts: Michelle Feller-Kopman, Ellen Smith, Holly Snyder, and the American Jewish Historical Society, with special thanks to its executive director, Dr. Michael Feldberg; in Cincinnati: Abraham Peck, Kevin Proffitt, and the American Jewish Archives; in Spanish Town: Ms. Elizabeth Williams and the Jamaica Archives and Record Center, whose efforts to preserve and make available the extremely important historical records of Jamaica are exemplary, and the Island Record Office; in Kingston: the Institute of Jamaica; and in London, Ms. Miriam Rodrigues Pereira and the Spanish and Portuguese Jews' Congregation, as well as the staff of the Public Record Office, an extraordinary group of public servants whose enthusiasm and helpfulness never flag, even after a day spent delivering literally thousands of documents to researchers.

I acknowledge the skill and helpfulness of Usha Sanyal, copy editor, and Despina Papazoglou Gimbel, managing editor, of New York University Press.

Travel to archives outside the United States was made possible by generous support provided by the American Philosophical Society, the Lucius N. Littauer Foundation, the Jacob T. Zukerman Fund of the Workman's Circle, and the Center for American Jewish History at Temple University.

I am indebted to Kenneth W. Rendell, Inc., for permitting me to examine its collection of Aaron Lopez, Jacob Rodrigues Rivera, and Nathaniel Briggs papers at its gallery in New York City in December 1995, and for permitting me to make reference to them.

Last, but really first, I am grateful to my wife, Lani, for her steadfast support in this as in all other endeavors. It is with deep gratitude that I dedicate this book to her.

Tables

Abbreviations

AJA	American Jewish Archives (Cincinnati)
AJHS	American Jewish Historical Society (Waltham)
BL	British Library (London)
CSP	W. Noel Sainsbury et al., eds., *Calendar of State Papers, Colonial Series, America and West Indies,* 43 vols. (London: H.M.'s Stationery Office, 1860–1963)
IJ	Institute of Jamaica (Kingston)
IRO	Island Record Office (Spanish Town, Jamaica)
JA	Jamaica Archives and Records Center (Spanish Town, Jamaica)
PRO	Public Record Office (Kew)

A Note on Spelling and Dating

The spelling of Sephardic Jewish names varies from one original source to another and often within the same source. The spellings followed here usually conform to those in the index to the published marriage contracts of the Spanish and Portuguese Jews' Congregation of London, the parent congregation of Jews in the British empire. However, in instances where spellings in the index differ from those that are generally employed in secondary historical accounts, the latter have been followed. For example, Gomez and Lopez are used, rather than the index's Gomes and Lopes. Other exceptions are names that appear in quotation marks as direct citations from original sources.

Years are given in New Style.

Introduction

In recent years interest regarding the extent to which Jews participated in the institution of slavery in the Americas has stemmed from allegations that they predominated in the slave trade and that they owned slaves well in excess of their proportion among the white population. This study argues that they did neither. To the contrary, their participation in the slave trade and in the ownership of slaves was quite small. When compared with their non-Jewish contemporaries, their involvement was one that had little impact.

Despite assiduous efforts by historians since Philip D. Curtin published his seminal study of the size of the slave trade in 1969, we shall probably never know, in all its grim and cruel enormity, how many men, women, and children on the continent of Africa were trapped in the net of the Atlantic slave trade. Wrenched from their homes and their families, marched in chains to the coasts and transported across the seas during an era that lasted well over three centuries, millions were condemned to spend the remainder of their lives in servitude and to witness the enslavement of their children. Many more did not survive the Atlantic crossing, perishing instead on vessels swept by disease or from a profound depression that the historical record tells us frequently seized many of the captives in its grip. Still others died within a few years of arrival, toiling on the plantations and in the mines of Europe's colonies in the western hemisphere.

Estimates vary as to the number of people carried from Africa to the Americas between 1502, the beginning of the transatlantic traffic in African slaves, and the late nineteenth century, when at last it ended. Historians who in recent decades have endeavored to calculate the size of the slave trade have proposed totals that range from nine million to fifteen million. Within that spectrum, scholars continue to offer new estimates and to make further adjustments, as new sources of information are discovered and as refinements in methods of measurement and estimation are developed.[1]

Procuring slaves in Africa and conveying them to the Americas was the work of both Africans and Europeans. African merchants brought caravans of slaves to the coast for sale, while African governments not only went to war in order to obtain captives to sell into slavery but also established the trading regulations, dictated the terms, and set the prices under which the Europeans were required to operate.[2] Backed in turn by their own governments and by investors in their homelands, European merchants, shipowners, captains, sailors, and ships' doctors made up the other half of a nefarious commerce whose repercussions still resound today.

Four western European nations, Portugal, England, Holland, and France, accounted for the bulk of the African slave trade. A fifth, Spain, barred in 1494 by the Treaty of Tordesillas from establishing a presence in Africa, relied on the others to supply the slave labor it required in its vast American empire. In 1595, Spain inaugurated the asiento, the exclusive contract it granted to first one nation or foreign business firm, then to another, to supply its colonies with slaves. Portugal held the asiento, often the object of high diplomacy and of no small intrigue, until 1640. During the late seventeenth and early eighteenth centuries, it bounced among Italian, Dutch, Portuguese, and French hands, until it eventually fell under English control from 1713 to 1744.[3]

That Jews participated in the slave trade, sometimes by investing in companies engaged in it, sometimes as the owners of slave ships, and that they owned slaves when they settled in the Americas, are matters that have long been known from a substantial body of works produced by Jewish historians. The oldest, a history commissioned by the elders of the Jewish community of Suriname, dates back more than two centuries to 1788. Writing in order to prove that the Jewish population had always contributed to the Dutch colony's welfare, the author recounted how Jewish settlers had provided leadership and manpower for expeditions into the interior to suppress runaway slaves. A sizable segment of the colony's Jews entered plantation agriculture and therefore owned slaves, whose labor their owners often contributed to public works. The author estimated that Jewish colonists owned more than nine thousand slaves in 1690, although modern scholarship has demonstrated that this figure is impossibly high. And while their involvement in agriculture diminished by the middle of the eighteenth century, shrinking to a shadow of what it once had been, plantation ownership continued, guaranteeing that slave ownership also lasted.[4]

In our own era, Salo Wittmayer Baron, one of the twentieth century's most prolific Jewish historians, cautioned against avoiding historically unpleasant truths, and noted the existence of slaveownership not only among crypto-Jews who resided in Mexico but also in Jamaica, where, as in Curaçao, they may have participated in the slave trade.[5] Indeed, the authors of a two-volume history of the Jewish inhabitants of the Dutch colony of Curaçao, one of them the rabbi of its Jewish community, the oldest in the western hemisphere, confirmed that the island's Jewish residents participated in the institution of slavery. Curaçao's Jews, they wrote, relied on slave labor from the time they settled in the colony during the 1650s. Late in the seventeenth century, nearly all of them owned between one and nine slaves, while in 1754 one owned more than four hundred. At least a dozen sold slaves between 1686 and 1710, purchasing them for resale from the Dutch West India Company, which held the monopoly on the importation of slaves from Africa. They continued to own slaves until emancipation in 1863, when they still held 1,851, amounting to 27.4 percent of the island's 6,751 slaves. Moreover, the authors compiled a list of Jewish colonists who owned plantations, gardens, and corn patches between 1660 and 1896 that runs to fifty-five published pages, in which they included, where known, the number of slaves each owned. Finally, they published the slave-tax list of 1765. Explaining that it was the most complete one available for the island, they identified each Jewish entry and reported that, of a total of 5,534 slaves in the colony, Curaçao's Jewish population owned 867.[6] (We may note, incidentally, that the latter figure, 15.6 percent of all slaves, was a substantially smaller proportion than the 28.8 percent of the entries on the tax list that were Jewish. Furthermore, non-Jewish slaveowners held an average of 11.9 slaves each, while Jewish slaveowners owned a much smaller average of 5.4 each.)[7]

Like his counterpart in Curaçao, the rabbi of the oldest synagogue in the United States included evidence that the Jews of colonial New York City owned slaves in his biographical sketches of them in the early 1950s. The author relied on the early New Yorkers' last wills and testaments for this purpose, citing bequests of slaves they made to their beneficiaries.[8] Much of this information had been available since 1915, when the American Jewish Historical Society published wills written by New York's eighteenth-century Jewish inhabitants. The Society did so a second time in a fully annotated version that appeared in its journal over the course of two years during the 1960s.[9] It reproduced the material yet a third time, when it published the wills in a single volume in 1967.[10]

Nor were these the only published wills that demonstrated that Jewish colonists in the Americas owned slaves. In Great Britain, the Jewish Historical Society of England in 1936 published the wills written by Barbados's Jews between 1676 and 1739. The subsequent discovery of still more Jewish wills for the same period in Barbados resulted in their publication too, this time in a festschrift in honor of Jacob Rader Marcus, the preeminent student of American Jewish history in the mid-twentieth century. In his analysis of the contents of the new wills, the author of the essay about them reported what they revealed about slaveholding among Barbados's Jewish population.[11]

Marcus, the founder and director of the American Jewish Archives had, for his part, documented Jewish activity in the slave trade in his extensive synthesis of American Jewish history during the colonial era, while one of his students, Stanley F. Chyet, described the participation of Aaron Lopez of Rhode Island in the slave trade with Africa.[12] Moreover, Bertram Wallace Korn, the editor of the festschrift in Marcus's honor and the author of the contribution on the additional Barbados wills, had written what remains the definitive essay on involvement by Jews in slavery in the United States between 1789 and 1865. Korn published his essay in 1961 during the centennial observance of the Civil War, after delivering it as the president's address at the annual meeting of the American Jewish Historical Society. In it, he demonstrated that Jews had owned slaves, that they had functioned in the South as slave traders, and that "Jewish opinions about and relationships to the system of slavery were in no appreciable degree different from those of their non-Jewish neighbors."[13]

Knowledge that Jews had participated in slavery was not, however, restricted to a small circle of scholars writing esoteric monographs for a professional audience. Solomon Grayzel's history of the Jewish people, widely used as a text in colleges and Jewish religious high schools for at least three decades, made the point that Jews who settled in the South before the Civil War adhered to prevailing social norms, and cited the first Jewish member of the United States Senate, David Yulee of Florida, as an example of a slaveowner.[14] Then too, the *Encyclopaedia Judaica* contained a lengthy entry by Bertram Korn under the heading "Slave Trade," with more than one-third of it devoted to Jewish participation in the slave trade in the western hemisphere. "Jews appear to have been among the major retailers of slaves in Dutch Brazil (1630–54)," wrote Korn. He identified Jewish slave traders in Curaçao in the late seventeenth century, in Jamaica during the eighteenth century, and still others in colonial Philadelphia, Newport, and Charleston. Later in the United States, Southern merchants, auctioneers, and commission agents who sold slaves included two leaders of the Jewish communities of Mobile and Columbia during the 1850s, for "at no time did Southern Jews feel tainted by the slave trade." To provide perspective and balance, however, Korn noted that the total activity of all Southern Jews engaged in the slave trade "probably did not equal the turnover of the largest single non-Jewish firm which specialized in slaves," a statement he had made in his earlier essay.[15]

The Civil War centennial exhibit organized by the Jewish Historical Commission, a consortium comprised of eight American Jewish organizations, likewise presented information about involvement by Jews in slavery in a form that was readily accessible to the public. The plan formulated by the Commission's Technical Committee called for an exhibit divided in six segments, including one entitled "Jews and Slavery." Visual materials were to include enlargements of advertisements placed by Jews in the slave trade and coverage of Rabbi Morris Raphall of New York City, who preached in defense of slavery, counterbalanced by Rabbi David Einhorn, an opponent of slavery in Baltimore who was forced to leave the city because of his views. The exhibit went forward as originally envisioned; when it opened at the Jewish Museum in New York City early in December 1960, the *New York Times* reported that it explored "attitudes toward slavery" among American Jews during the era of the Civil War. Displays included examples of Jewish slaveowners and slave traders, along with space devoted not only to Rabbi Raphall but also to Senator Judah Benjamin and his speech defending slavery before the Senate in March 1858. On the other hand, the exhibit also included evidence of abolitionist activity among Jews, as well as the antislavery views of Rabbi Einhorn.[16]

Many more studies could be cited to demonstrate that Jewish historians have neither overlooked nor denied the fact that members of the Jewish faith participated in the institution of slavery. Insofar as Jewish historians were concerned, there never had been anything "secret" about the "relationship" between blacks and Jews during the era of slavery, contrary to what the title of the tract that appeared in 1991 that indicted the Jewish people for their involvement in the enslavement of Africans implied. Written by the Historical Research Department of the Nation of Islam, *The Secret Relationship between Blacks and Jews* charged that Jews had financed and dominated the slave trade, owned slaves well in excess of any other group, and inflicted cruelty with abandon on slaves.[17] During the same year, the chairperson of the Black Studies Department at City College of The City University of New York attracted national attention because of comments he delivered during a public address about the role played by Jews in the suppression of blacks, which included the allegation that wealthy Jews had been instrumental in financing the slave trade.[18] And in 1994, the leader of the Nation of Islam endorsed the statement by one of his senior advisers that Jews had not only financed the slave trade but also owned fully 75 percent of all slaves in the South prior to the American Civil War.[19]

These views quickly attracted a following, as Henry Louis Gates, Jr., the chairperson of Harvard University's Afro-American Studies Department, noted with grave concern in 1992, in an essay in which he decried the rise of anti-Semitism among African Americans. Gates described the Nation of Islam's publication as one that "may well be one of the most influential books published in the black community in the last 12 months," and wrote that its conclusions were "in many circles, increasingly treated as damning historical fact. . . . Among significant sectors of the black community, this brief [that Jews were inordinately responsible for the enslavement of Africans] has become a credo of a new philosophy of black self-affirmation."[20] At City College, students supported the professor who proclaimed that Jews had financed the slave trade. An editor of the campus newspaper declared that the assertion that Jews bore responsibility for the slave trade was not anti-Semitic; it was factually correct. " 'When I think about the Jews,' another stated, 'I'm constantly reminded of the fact that they funded a huge amount of the slave trade. That's not anti-Semitism; it's just the historic truth.' "[21]

The book published by the Nation of Islam relentlessly singled out the Jews, with no mention of the many thousands of Portuguese, Spanish, Dutch, French, and British merchants, shippers, and colonists who were slave traders and slaveowners. Nor did it mention the Danes, Swedes, and Germans who participated in the slave trade to a smaller extent, or the Africans who sold slaves to European slave traders.[22] It highlighted cruelties committed by Jews against slaves, as if the brutalities that occurred under slavery had been perpetrated by them alone. It listed example after example of Jewish slaveowners and the number of slaves each possessed, without ever providing such data for the non-Jews who owned slaves. This was one of the book's most egregious distortions, for the omission of comparative information about non-Jewish participants in the slave system implied that Jewish domination could simply be assumed; it did not have to be proved empirically.

Henry Louis Gates, Jr., characterized *The Secret Relationship between Blacks and Jews* as "the bible of the new anti-Semitism."[23] As such, the volume represented a new if not wholly original contribution to the corpus of anti-Semitic ideas.[24] To the litany of Christ killer, well poisoner, usurer, unscrupulous businessman, ruthless banker, conspirator bent on world domination, and racial polluter was now added the label of slave trader. The late twentieth century thus bore witness to the creation of a new myth regarding Jewish malevolence, as well as Jewish responsibility for mankind's suffering.

In the public controversy that ensued after publication of *The Secret Relationship between Blacks and Jews*, the Council of the American Historical Association, the organization's elected governing board, adopted a resolution in which it labeled as "false any statement alleging that Jews played a disproportionate role in the exploitation of slave labor or in the Atlantic slave trade." Scholars produced reviews examining the allegations, and essays were published by way of refutation.[25] But while many of the reviews and essays were of substantial merit, their authors could not cite much in the way of data that measured the actual size and scope of involvement by Jewish merchants and colonists. Historians who had written in the past on participation by Jews in the institution of slavery had provided little such information. They had not endeavored to examine the questions of extent and impact, undoubtedly because such matters had never been at issue.

The present study addresses this gap in our knowledge. The purpose here is not to establish degrees of guilt or blame nor, conversely, to exonerate. It is, rather, to ascertain what the historical record provides by way of empirical evidence regarding the degree to which Jews and their non-Jewish contemporaries participated in slavery as investors, traders, and owners.

Had the scale of participation by Jews in slavery not become a matter of contemporary controversy, the extent of such activity would be a matter of interest in its own right. Slavery underlay a large part of the economy of the Atlantic region in the early modern era. It bound five continents together. It fueled European settlement and expansion in the western hemisphere. Greater knowledge of the role played by Jewish merchants and colonists in the institution of slavery can only enhance our understanding of the development of the Atlantic economy and the emergence of an Atlanticwide perspective in the early modern world. For that matter, greater knowledge of any other ethnic, national, or religious group's impact on the slave trade or on slaveownership would be of equal interest and value.

The British empire has been selected for examination here because of its preeminent position in the slave trade during the eighteenth century, when British vessels transported more slaves from Africa to the western hemisphere than any other European nation. Britain established its lead during the second decade of the eighteenth century, and retained it until Parliament abolished the slave trade from Africa in 1807.[26] During the era of Britain's dominance, Jewish communities existed in England, in several of the empire's colonies on the North American mainland, and in Jamaica and Barbados, both of which were plantation colonies with large slave populations. Combined with Britain's leadership in the slave trade, the presence of Jewish merchants and settlers at the empire's center and in a number of its colonies permits assessment of the role of Jews in a setting that was of signal importance in the history of slavery in the Americas.

Jews also resided simultaneously in the Netherlands and in the Dutch colonies of Curaçao, Suriname, and St. Eustatius, but the Dutch lagged far behind the British as slave traders. As one historian of the slave trade estimated in 1981, the Dutch transported 498,000 slaves from Africa between 1625 and 1803, while the British carried off 2,807,100 over the course of the substantially shorter period between 1690 and 1807.[27] And while a small Jewish population also resided in France, Catholic merchants dominated the slave trade there, followed by Protestant businessmen. A small number of Jewish merchants at Bordeaux participated in it, but their cumulative share was of very minor proportions.[28] As for Spain and Portugal, the two had expelled their Jewish populations shortly before the end of the fifteenth century, forbidding them to return or to reside in their overseas empires. Although some Jews remained in Spain and Portugal and others settled in their colonies, secretly practicing Judaism while living outwardly as Christians, differentiating them from true Christians is fraught with difficulty because of their common surnames. Furthermore, individuals arrested and tried for secret adherence to Judaism may, in fact, have been sincere Christians who were denounced by personal enemies who sought their ruin and the acquisition of their property. In short, measuring the number of people in the Spanish and Portuguese empires who were truly Jewish and who participated in slavery encounters what probably are insurmountable obstacles.

Far fewer difficulties encumber the process of identifying Jewish merchants and colonists in Britain's empire during the seventeenth, eighteenth, and early nineteenth centuries. Most encountered in the course of this study had family names that originated in Spain and Portugal, for they were the descendants of men and women who had been forced to flee from the Iberian Peninsula. As the bearers of Spanish and Portuguese surnames, they are readily distinguishable from their non-Jewish contemporaries, thereby permitting assessment of their involvement in slavery, which, as argued here, was of very small proportions when viewed within the overall scope of slavery in the British world.[29]

Saul S. Friedman, *Jews and the American Slave Trade* (New Brunswick: Transaction Publishers, 1998) appeared after production of the present work had already commenced. Regrettably, therefore, it was not possible to cite it in the course of this study.

CHAPTER I

England's Jewish Merchants and the Slave Trade

After an exile from England that had lasted almost four centuries, Europe's Jewish inhabitants learned in the middle of the 1650s that they could once again reside in that nation. Expelled in 1290, they had been forbidden to return until Oliver Cromwell's government quietly gave them permission to reenter the country after receiving a delegation sent by the Jewish community of Amsterdam to argue the case for readmission. Although a handful of Jews had previously entered and taken up residence in England during the 1630s, their presence was illegal until Cromwell gave the nod to Jewish settlement in 1656, thereby inaugurating what is known in Anglo-Jewish history as the Resettlement. Whether prompted by economic calculation or by the Puritan belief that the conversion of the Jews would precede the advent of the millennium, the government disregarded opposition among the merchants of the City of London and unofficially assented to the return of the Jews.[1]

By 1663, approximately 220 of them resided in London. Some, in flight from the Inquisition, came directly to England from Spain and Portugal. Others originated in the Canary Islands, France, and the German port of Hamburg, while still others came from Holland, a center of Jewish settlement dating only to the end of the previous century.[2] Virtually all traced their origins to the Iberian Peninsula, as descendants of the thousands of Jews who had remained in Spain and Portugal after those nations had expelled their Jewish populations, Spain in 1492 and Portugal in 1497. Jews who decided to remain after the expulsions could do so only if they accepted Christianity. Those who stayed and converted comprised a distinct social group in the two Iberian nations called the New Christians, a category first created in Spain at the end of the previous century following a wave of massacres and forced conversions in 1391.

The New Christian label proved to be a term of opprobrium that passed from one generation to the next. Because many New Christians prospered as merchants, achieved eminence in the professions and in public office, or served as tax collectors, they frequently became targets of vilification. More terribly, many were accused of secretly adhering to Judaism and of transmitting it to their children. To root out the heresy of crypto-Judaism, the Office of the Holy Inquisition periodically unleashed fierce campaigns in both Spain and Portugal during the sixteenth, seventeenth, and eighteenth centuries. Arrest as a New Christian automatically meant the loss of one's property and, frequently, torture by the Inquisition as it sought to extract confessions. Some went mad in the Holy Office's dungeons, while hundreds were delivered after their examinations to the civil authorities for a public death by burning at the stake.[3]

The objects of public obloquy and of Inquisitional terror, New Christians in the 1590s began to emigrate from Spain and Portugal (combined under a single crown at that juncture) to the Netherlands, then in the midst of its eighty-year rebellion against Spanish rule. Once safe in Holland, many New Christians reverted to Judaism. A thriving Jewish community consequently established itself in Amsterdam. Before long it grew to be Europe's largest, expanding from approximately two hundred individuals in 1609 to about two thousand at midcentury. While Holland's rigid Calvinist clergy opposed the Jews, Amsterdam's civil authorities were tolerant toward them. Although they were barred from retail trade and the artisan crafts, had to wait almost fifty years for the right to worship publicly in Amsterdam, and even longer to settle in many of Holland's towns, the prevailing atmosphere in their new home proved to be one of mildness and benevolence.[4]

It was from the Jewish community in Holland that the Resettlement in England began. Coping at midcentury with a surge in Jewish refugees from Spain, Portugal, Brazil, the German states, and Poland, the leaders of Amsterdam's Jewish community dispatched an emissary to London to propose to Oliver Cromwell that Jews be permitted to settle in England. The Resettlement was the result of his mission.[5]

As descendants of Jews who had originated on the Iberian Peninsula, the Jews of the Resettlement in England belonged largely to the Sephardic branch of Judaism, one of the two major subdivisions of the Jewish people. Members of the other branch, the Ashkenazim, originated in central and eastern Europe, and they too contributed to the Resettlement, although in much smaller numbers. Pushed by poverty and by persecution, Ashkenazim had begun to migrate westward before 1648 from Lithuania and Poland to the German states, to the lands of the Hapsburg monarchy, and to the Netherlands. The numbers on the move increased at midcentury because of war, growing oppression, and deadly Cossack assaults. Ashkenazim reached England for certain by the middle of the 1680s and at first worshiped together with the Sephardim in their congregation. By 1690, however, traditional rivalries triumphed, and the Ashkenazim separated from the Sephardim and established their own congregation. Combined, the two groups in 1695 numbered between 751 and 853, roughly 70 percent of them Sephardim and 30 percent Ashkenazim.[6]

Despite the community's small size and the poverty in which many of its members lived, the Jews of the Resettlement claimed that they contributed significantly to England's international commerce. When a proposal to impose a special tax on them surfaced in 1689, they drew up a petition for submission to Parliament in which they protested against discriminatory taxation by arguing that the English nation benefited from their mercantile activities. They "drive a considerable Trade," the petitioners wrote, with Jewish merchants responsible for "exporting great Quantities of the Woolen manufactures of this Nation, and importing vast Quantities of Gold and Silver, and other Foreign Staple Merchandizes, which do greatly Enrich the Nation, and encrease the Revenue of the Customs. . . ." Moreover, they had eliminated the Portuguese as a factor in the diamond trade with India:

The Market for Diamonds in the *East Indies* was formerly at *Goa* (belonging to the *Portugueze*) and by the means and industry of the *Jews* the Market hath been brought to the English Factories, and by that means *England* has in a manner the sole management of that precious Commodity, and all Foreigners bring their Monies into this Kingdom to purchase the said Diamonds.

While underscoring their contributions to the country's commercial life, the petitioners pointed out that not all of England's Jews were successful merchants. If one-quarter had accumulated "Moderate Estates," another quarter had only "very indifferent Estates." The remainder, workers, consisted in part of "indigent poor people." The latter did not burden the English, for, as the petitioners were careful to point out, the Jewish community provided them with support and assistance.[7]

At virtually the same moment that Jews received permission to resettle in England, the English government undertook to carve out a place for Britain in the slave trade as part of a policy to supplant Holland in international commerce. Openly challenging the Dutch in Africa, England established a series of forts along the coasts of West Africa during the early 1660s, and in 1663 dispatched a military force to capture the fortifications and trading posts held by the Netherlanders. Dutch counterattacks undid the initial successes of the British, in turn precipitating the second of the three Anglo-Dutch Wars the two nations fought between 1652 and 1674.[8]

England relied not only on military action but also on its merchants to achieve its goals. In 1660, four years after the Resettlement commenced, Britain chartered the Company of Royal Adventurers Trading into Africa. Obtaining gold was initially its primary purpose, but in 1663 the slave trade became one of the Company's aims when the government revised its charter. It subsequently delivered slaves to Barbados and contracted to supply slaves to Spain's colonies. By 1669, however, it was clear that the Company's finances were in disarray, and plans to salvage it gave way to the creation of a new company. Continuing to count on private capital, the government established a successor by chartering the Royal African Company in 1672, endowing it with a monopoly to all commerce between England and the western parts of Africa, including the slave trade. Although the new company proved incapable of earning profits on a sustained basis, plunging toward bankruptcy by the early 1700s, it did succeed in penetrating the slave trade, transporting in excess of an estimated ninety thousand slaves to the Caribbean between 1673 and 1711.[9]

Because many of them were merchants who resided in the City of London, the country's commercial and financial center, where they participated in international commerce, the Jews of the Resettlement might well have been regarded as likely to invest in the two slave-trading companies, although in the Iberian Peninsula, the region where many of them (or their ancestors) had originated, they had barely participated in the enslavement of Africans. As Salo Wittmayer Baron wrote of New Christians in Spain and Portugal who were accused of surreptitious adherence to Judaism,

> We rarely hear of Negro slaves in the households of secret Judaizers. The inquisitorial records frequently offer the testimony of servants from the defendants' households, but these witnesses evidently were for the most part free Spanish or Portuguese proletarians. Nor did the great Marrano international traders appear to have played an independent role in the growing slave trade. . . . Occasional references like that to the purchase of a boatload of slaves by Manuel Rodriguez Lamego (a brother of the Rouen Jewish leader) are too rare to be typical.[10]

Jewish law had certainly not precluded their involvement (no more than Christian theology precluded the involvement of non-Jews), nor would it have prevented their descendants who were now in England from investing in it. Biblical, Talmudic, and medieval Jewish law, the latter in the instance of Moses Maimonides, recognized slavery by prescribing regulations applicable to slaves and their owners.[11] *Shulhan Arukh,* the definitive work of Jewish law compiled by Joseph Caro in the sixteenth century and accepted by the seventeenth century throughout the Jewish world as fully authoritative, recognized the existence of slavery and listed the rules that were to govern relations between slaves and masters.[12] Furthermore, a variety of contemporary developments in which Jews in Holland and in the Americas participated in the enslavement of Africans also existed, serving as precedents for the Jews of the Resettlement.

Such precedents included New Christians from Portugal who reverted to Judaism when they settled in Holland during the 1590s. Some brought slaves to Amsterdam and tried to sell them prior to 1596, the year in which the city's authorities decided to bar the development of a slave market. Others must have owned slaves thereafter, for the city's Sephardic congregation made provision for the burial of servants and slaves in its cemetery in a regulation adopted in 1614. Between 1608 and 1621, a handful of ships chartered by Jewish merchants in Amsterdam transported slaves from West Africa to the Americas. And during the second half of the seventeenth century, Sephardic merchants in the Netherlands played a part in the transit of slaves to Spain's colonies, although the scope of their involvement is unknown.[13]

Overseas, Jewish settlers became involved in slavery in Holland's colonies, beginning in Brazil. Seized by the Dutch West India Company from Portugal in 1630, Brazil attracted Jewish settlers in relatively substantial numbers. By the middle of the 1640s, approximately fifteen hundred Jewish inhabitants resided in the areas of northeastern Brazil controlled by the Dutch, where they established two congregations and employed the first rabbi in the Americas. Their numbers began to decline in 1645 when the Portuguese colonists rose in rebellion, raising the specter of renewed control by Portugal and the return of the Inquisition. Nine years later, in 1654, a Portuguese expeditionary force recaptured Recife, forcing the Dutch to abandon Brazil. When the Dutch left, the remaining Jewish population, approximately 650 in number, also departed, some returning to Holland and others emigrating to the Dutch colony at New Amsterdam or to the English one at Barbados.[14]

While in Brazil between 1630 and 1654, a few of the Jewish settlers acquired sugar plantations and mills, and it is entirely reasonable to assume that they consequently employed slave labor. However, their contributions to the sugar industry were far more significant when it came to providing capital, exporting sugar, and advancing credit for slaves. As creditors, according to the historian of the Brazilian Jewish community, "they dominated the slave trade." To be sure, all slave imports from Africa were in the hands of the Dutch West India Company, which under the terms of its charter held the monopoly to the slave trade. But the Company sold the slaves it transported to Brazil at auctions where Jewish purchasers predominated, purchasing slaves and then selling them to plantation owners and others on credit.[15] For the brief time that they resided in Brazil, therefore, Jewish settlers were an essential part of the fabric of the slave trade, although the actual number of slaves they might have purchased and then sold as middlemen amounted to a minute fraction of the huge number of Africans brought to Brazil over the course of more than three centuries.[16]

Their communal regulations acknowledged their participation in slavery. The taxes the Jewish community imposed on its members included a levy of five soldos for each slave purchased from the Dutch West India Company. The regulations even made provision for slaves who converted to Judaism. (Later records of the Portuguese Inquisition suggest that conversions probably did occur.)[17] The community decreed that they must first be freed before undergoing circumcision, in order to make it impossible for an owner to sell a slave who had converted. As the congregational minutes stated,

A slave shall not be circumcised without first having been freed by his master, so that the master shall not be able to sell him from the moment the slave will have bound himself [to Judaism].[18]

Despite the Dutch debacle in Brazil in 1654, interest in settling in the northeastern part of South America remained high among Holland's Jews. In 1657, a group among them obtained a charter from the Zeeland Chamber of the Dutch West India Company permitting them to settle on the Wild Coast, a region defined as lying on the mainland between one and ten degrees north of the equator. The charter presumed that the settlers would use slaves to work the lands distributed to them by the new colony's commander, for it offered tax abatements as an inducement to settle, with the greatest reductions in rates going to settlers who established plantations with slaves:

> The settlers shall be free from all taxes, customs, duties or any other similar fee for the space of seven years; those who establish a plantation of sugar with fifty negroes shall have twelve years of the same freedom; those who will establish a plantation of oxen, with thirty negroes, nine years, and if it be less, accordingly. . . .

Moreover, the charter modified the Dutch West India Company's monopoly rights in the slave trade by permitting settlers to send their own vessels from Holland to Africa, to acquire slaves there, transport them to the Wild Coast, and reship them elsewhere, subject only to a payment for each slave to the Company.[19]

Efforts to establish a colony at Essequibo, the site apparently chosen under the charter issued by the Zeeland Chamber, faltered and quickly failed, but a Jewish presence did take root almost simultaneously on the nearby island of Cayenne.[20] The Dutch seized Cayenne in 1656 or 1657, a French possession vulnerable to attack because of incessant internal bickering. In 1659, the Amsterdam Chamber of the Dutch West India Company issued a charter to David Nassy, formerly a Jewish settler in Brazil, authorizing him to establish a colony there. Under Nassy's leadership, a fairly large Jewish colony arose on Cayenne, with slightly more than 150 settlers emigrating to it from as far away as Italy. Like the earlier charter for the Wild Coast, Cayenne's made provision for slaves, with leeway for the settlers to engage in a piratical slave trade:

> In regard to the slave trade, the aforesaid colonists, insofar as the need of the colony may [require], shall have such rights as are granted by the Council of the Nineteen. Their accommodations at all times shall be estimated as those allowed to the colony in [nearby] Essequebo under the Chamber of Zeeland. . . .

They shall also be provided by the Company with such a number of slaves as shall from time to time be needed there . . . but the slaves who are captured by the colonists on the sea may be brought into the colony, and they may transport them to any place that they see fit, on payment of a tax. . . . [21]

David Nassy's tenure as a colonial entrepreneur did not last long. In 1664, the French reconquered Cayenne, forcing its Jewish population out.[22] Jews had been present in nearby Suriname as early as 1652, and it was to that destination that Nassy led his fellow colonists and their slaves. The colony was then in British hands, but in 1667 the Dutch acquired it in exchange for New Netherland, which the English had seized in 1664 and renamed New York.[23] With the advent of the Dutch, some of Suriname's Jews left for Jamaica in 1677, preferring to live under the British flag. Ten Jewish families with 322 slaves reportedly did so, with individual holdings that ranged from a low of 2 to a high of 74, or an average of 32.2 per family.[24] The names of the 10 who were willing to remove to Jamaica with their slaves had been reported to the English government in 1675, along with the name of a Jewish emigrant who actually did depart from Suriname that year for Jamaica with 33 slaves in tow. The name of another Surinamese Jewish slaveowner was also known in England, but his 15 slaves were transported to Jamaica by a Christian family.[25]

It was in Suriname, nonetheless, that a Jewish presence on the South American mainland at last took permanent form. In 1669, the Dutch governor confirmed the privileges that Jewish settlers had enjoyed under the English, including permission for them and their slaves to work on Sunday. An all-Jewish town, Joden Savane, began to rise in 1682, and only three years later the new community erected a large brick synagogue. By 1690, Jews also resided in the town of Paramaribo. Around that year, 92 families and approximately 50 single men comprised the colony's Jewish population, estimated at between 560 and 575 individuals. Those who settled in Paramaribo turned to commerce, while others elsewhere turned to agriculture, relying, as we have already seen, on slave labor.[26] Suriname's Jewish population therefore comprised another precedent for English Jews.

An even larger Jewish community than that in Suriname had already been established on the island of Curaçao, a Dutch possession since 1634, and its members, too, utilized slave labor. The first dozen Jews to attempt settlement on Curaçao did so in 1651, and at least one of them arrived with a slave. Inasmuch as this initial effort did not succeed for long, the establishment of a permanent Jewish community on the island did not occur until the end of the decade, when approximately seventy individuals emigrated to the colony from Amsterdam, including several who had fled from Brazil in 1654. The privileges granted to them by the Dutch West India Company included the right to purchase slaves, along with a directive to the colony's governor to sell them horses, land, and slaves. For approximately fifteen years, however, the Company sold them only sickly slaves, not permitting them to acquire healthy ones until 1674.[27]

The most relevant precedent of all for Jewish merchants in London who may have contemplated investing in England's new slave-trading companies was the Jewish community in Amsterdam. There, the Dutch West India Company offered the opportunity to purchase stock in a slave-trading enterprise. When the Company was established in 1621 to challenge Spanish and Portuguese hegemony in the Atlantic, its charter empowered it to attack Spanish shipping, control the Caribbean salt trade, undertake military conquest of Spanish and Portuguese possessions in the western hemisphere, establish and administer new colonies there, and to monopolize the slave trade. During the 1620s, the Company consequently sent out privateering expeditions, established the colony of New Netherland with its headquarters at New Amsterdam on Manhattan Island, and attacked Brazil in 1624 in its first attempt to seize it from the Portuguese. The Company did not, however, enter the slave trade during its formative decade.[28]

It began to do so after its successful effort in 1630 to seize northeastern Brazil, followed in turn in 1637 by the capture of Elmina, a major slaving station in Africa. Brazil's settlers required slave labor from Africa in order to produce the great sugar crops that the colony exported to Europe. The Company's rule in Brazil lasted for twenty-four years, during which time it invoked its monopoly power over the slave trade to supply the colony with more than 26,000 Africans. After its expulsion from Brazil in 1654, the Company subsequently turned to supplying slaves to its colonies at New Netherland and Curaçao. While New Netherland took few slaves, Curaçao, seized from Spain by the Company in 1634, developed into a major entre-pôt in the seventeenth-century slave trade. Too arid for significant agriculture, it became a way station for the supply of slaves to the Spanish mainland. The Company transported at least 24,555 slaves to Curaçao between 1658 and 1674, accounting for approximately 55 percent of the slaves it delivered to the western hemisphere during those years.[29]

Because of setbacks in its other enterprises—the transfer of its privateering functions to another organization in the early 1640s, the loss of certain trading monopolies, the loss of Brazil, the conquest of New Netherland by the English in 1664—the slave trade emerged as the Dutch West India Company's primary underpinning.[30] Few of Holland's Jews, however, invested in the Company. When chartered in 1621, Amsterdam residents purchased stock in it in the amount of 3 million florins; of this, the 18 Jews who participated invested 36,000 florins, or 1.2 percent.[31] The percentage of stock owned by Jews thereafter is unknown, but the number who invested is. They remained a distinctly small presence. In 1656, when the Company had already been deeply committed to the slave trade for at least twenty years, 7 out of 167 of the stockholders, or 4 percent, were Jewish, rising to 11 out of 169, or 6.5 percent, in 1658. In 1671, Jewish investors numbered 10, or 5 percent of the Company's 192 shareholders. Three years later, 11 of the Company's "main partici-pants," or 10 percent of all such shareholders, were Jewish.[32] The 11 Jewish investors comprised substantially less than 1 percent of Am-sterdam's Jews, who in 1674 are thought to have numbered approx-imately 7,500.[33]

Deposits in the Amsterdam Exchange Bank reveal that an appre-ciably greater number of Holland's Jewish inhabitants did have capital and therefore could have invested in the Dutch West India Company. The Bank, an indicator of economic activity for twentieth-century historians, provided evidence of financial stature to seventeenth-century contemporaries. "To acquire prestige as a merchant or man of affairs in Amsterdam," according to Violet Barbour, "it was almost indispensable to have an account in the bank. The list of depositors is in the nature of a roll-call of Amsterdam capitalists."[34] During the 1620s, when 18 Jews invested in the Dutch West India Company, Jewish depositors in the Exchange Bank ranged between 76 and 114. In the 1650s, when between 7 and 11 Jewish investors owned Dutch West India Company stock, the number with assets in the Exchange Bank fluctuated between 197 and 243. And in 1674, when 11 Jews invested in the Dutch West India Company, 265 deposited funds in the Exchange Bank.[35]

Such, then, were the precedents and contemporary developments that served to inform the community of the Resettlement about involvement by Jews in slavery and the slave trade. Would they, however, choose to invest in the companies that England established as it sought to carve out a presence in the slave trade? Unlike the charter of the Levant Company, a corporation that traded in the eastern Mediterranean, the charter of the Company of Royal Adventurers Trading into Africa did not prohibit Jews from purchasing its stock. The Levant Company limited membership to the nobility, to gentlemen who had never been apprenticed or otherwise employed in commerce, and to the freemen of London. The Jews of the Resettlement did not qualify on any of these grounds, for they clearly did not belong to the nobility or the gentry, while admission to freemanship in the City required a Christian oath and Communion in the Anglican church. In contrast, the 1660 charter of the Company of Royal Adventurers Trading into Africa authorized the transfer of shares by the original stockholders "to any other person." Under the slightly altered name of the Company of Royal Adventurers of England Trading into Africa, its revised charter in 1663 permitted shareholders to transfer stock "to any person or persons whatsoever."[36]

Jewish investors, however, did not elect to invest in the Company, whose stockholders numbered 32 in 1660, twice as many in 1663, and 112 in 1667. Members of the royal house, the nobility, and the City's merchant community figured in the roster of shareholders. Not a single Jewish individual was among those who acquired stock.[37]

Nor were Jewish investors among the early stockholders of the Royal African Company, the corporation that replaced the Company of Royal Adventurers of England Trading into Africa at the end of 1671. The new corporation's charter, issued in 1672, did not preclude participation by them; in this it was identical to the revised charter of 1663 of the Company of Royal Adventurers of England Trading into Africa, which had permitted the transfer of stock "to any person or persons whatsoever."[38] Nonetheless, the list of shareholders on July 1, 1674, two and a half years into the Company's existence, reveals that London's Jews continued to shun investment in the African slave trade. At that point, the Company's 203 shareholders held stock valued at £111,600, in amounts that ranged from the high of £4,000 subscribed by Robert Vyner and the £3,000 subscribed by the King, to the low of £100 invested by each of fifteen individuals. But the investors did not include any Jews.[39]

Two years later, when the Company paid a return to its investors on September 21, 1676, a total of 194 individuals received dividends. Transfers of stock had occurred during the intervening two years, but Jewish investors had still not shown any interest in acquiring Royal African Company stock and therefore were not among the recipients of the dividends that were paid out.[40]

The stock-transaction records for the subsequent fourteen years reveal that Jewish investors continued to refrain from investing any of their capital in the Royal African Company.[41] The Company's books disclose, for example, that on January 4, 1677, Humphrey Edwin sold his stock to Benjamin Coles for £300; that on April 25, 1681, "the Right honble George Earle Berkeley of Berkeley" purchased part of Richard Nicholl's stock for £300; and that John Bull, a frequent dabbler in Royal African Company shares, sold £1,000 of his stock to Thomas Heatly on October 2, 1684.[42] Women, too, purchased shares, as when the Earl of Berkeley sold part of his holdings to Widow Priscilla Baylie on September 22, 1687 and another part on January 11, 1688. A year later, on January 10, 1689, from exile in France, the deposed King James II divested himself of his holdings in the Company, valued at £3,000.[43] But for nearly the first full twenty years of the Company's existence, no Jewish investors stepped forward to acquire shares.

It was not a lack of financial resources that inhibited them, for members of London's Jewish community possessed sufficient capital for investment during the Royal African Company's first two decades. Fourteen accordingly purchased shares in the East India Company, well before the first investment by a Jewish businessman in the Royal African Company.[44]

Nor was it as if the Royal African Company could not attract the interest of the investing public. Few opportunities for investment existed in late-seventeenth-century England, where joint-stock companies were few in number, small in size, and did not seek much capital. The East India Company, the largest by far, did not offer new shares between 1657 and 1693, preferring instead to take loans when it needed additional funds.[45] Perhaps these limitations on the acquisition of shares in corporations help explain why trading in Royal African Company stock was brisk from the Company's inception. Of the £111,100 initially subscribed at the end of 1671, £18,700 worth of stock, approximately one-sixth of all outstanding shares, changed hands in 1672. An average of £16,291 of stock changed hands annually over the course of the next eighteen years, ranging from a low of £9,250 in 1685 to a high of £24,500 in 1675. And during the first seven months of 1691, Royal African Company stock transfers skyrocketed to £82,350.[46]

It was during this last period of heightened activity in the Company's stock, a period of increased activity in stock trading in general, that a Jewish investor joined the ranks of the Royal African Company's shareholders for the first time. On May 26, 1691, Alvaro Da Costa purchased £500 worth of its stock. Born in Lisbon, Da Costa had arrived in England in the early 1660s as a refugee from the Portuguese Inquisition. Fashioning a career as a merchant, Da Costa became one of the small Jewish community's leading importers and exporters, sending woolen cloth abroad and importing, among other items, bullion, olive oil, indigo, and wine. An act of Parliament in 1667 made him England's first naturalized subject of the Jewish faith.[47] Naturalization required that he take an oath as a Christian and receive Communion, but Da Costa appears to have floated between Christianity and Judaism, a not unfamiliar course of action for a refugee from the Inquisition who maintained trading ties with the Iberian Peninsula. It was a strategy followed by others as well, for this was an era in which agents of the Inquisition spied on Sephardic merchants.[48] The latter consequently often employed aliases, including Da Costa, who used the Hebrew name of Jacob within the synagogue and Alvaro outside.[49] As Alvaro, he never submitted to circumcision, but as Jacob he was buried in London's Sephardic cemetery, while all his children married Jews and lived openly as members of the Jewish community.[50]

Da Costa had the wherewithal to invest in the Royal African Company well before 1691. That he possessed both the capital and the inclination to take risks is evident from the records of the East India Company. In contrast to his late entry into the Royal African Company, waiting twenty years before he bought any of its stock, Da Costa acquired shares in the East India Company within several years of his arrival in England. Presenting evidence of his naturalization by act of Parliament, he purchased £1,000 worth of East India Company stock in 1668. In 1674 he invested another £1,200, and in 1675 £1,800. Between 1675 and 1678, when the East India Company's records referred to him as "an adventurer in the General Joint Stock," Da Costa sold off £2,700 of his shares.[51] Clearly, therefore, Da Costa could have invested in the Royal African Company long before he did so.

Subsequent to his initial investment in the Company, Da Costa acquired additional stock during the late spring and summer of 1691. Three other Jewish investors soon followed his lead, purchasing shares during the summer.[52] Other members of the Jewish community later followed suit, and by April 20, 1693 the Company had 11 Jewish shareholders. Eight invested as individuals, 2 did so in partnership, and the remaining shareholder was the estate of a deceased individual who had purchased stock prior to his death. As a group, they comprised a small minority within the Company, which had a total of 301 shareholders and a general stock valued at £438,850. The 11 Jewish newcomers amounted to 3.6 percent of the whole, and their £19,500 in holdings to 4.4 percent of all outstanding shares.[53] After 1693, their presence in the Company continued to increase, rising by March 1699 to 29 shareholders out of 423, or 6.8 percent, whose holdings were worth £135,000, or 12.2 percent of the entire stock.[54]

Between 1691 and 1701, the number of Jewish investors who all told acquired Royal African Company stock totaled 31, with possibly 1 more.[55] The 31 investors represented roughly 10 percent of the Jewish households of England, which were comprised in 1695 of approximately 185 families and 114 single lodgers.[56]

But while 31 members of the Jewish community joined the ranks of the slave-trading company's stockholders during the 1690s, most English Jews with capital to invest did not. A total of 80 members of England's Jewish community invested in various enterprises during the decade; the 31 who bought shares in the Royal African Company therefore comprised a minority of 38.7 percent of their number. At least 73 Jewish investors acquired shares in the Bank of England, more than twice as many as the 31 who invested in the Royal African Company.[57] The number who acquired Bank stock may have been even higher, with perhaps as many as 10 additional investors.[58]

Like their counterparts in Holland in earlier decades, England's Jews clearly preferred other investment vehicles to the Royal African Company, for slightly more than two-thirds of those who invested in the Bank (49 of the 73) did not own Royal African Company stock. Refusing to commit all their investments to the Royal African Company, the remaining 24, or about one-third, split their capital between the two corporations. In all, therefore, fewer than 10 percent of England's Jewish investors chose to entrust their capital exclusively to the Royal African Company. Of the 79 investors[59] known to have purchased shares in either the Company or the Bank, or in both, only 6, or 7.5 percent, invested solely in the Royal African Company. The remainder, 73 individuals, or 92.4 percent, either invested nothing in the Royal African Company or lodged only part of their capital with it.

Still other investment opportunities absorbed more of their capital during the 1690s. Six Jews subscribed to the Tontine in 1693, the first long-term loan floated by the British government. At least two others, and possibly a third, invested in the East India Company between July 1691 and April 19, 1695, emulating the fourteen who had done so in earlier years.[60]

In truth, the Royal African Company was a losing enterprise, which may (apart from moral considerations) account for the judiciousness the majority of London's Jewish investors exhibited by either dispersing their capital among more than one investment possibility or by avoiding the Company altogether. War, low prices for the sugar that it carried from the West Indies to Europe, and, above all, illegal slave trading by interlopers, the term for private merchants who persistently violated the Company's monopoly between 1672 and 1698, undermined its ability to earn a profit. According to K. G. Davies, historian of the Royal African Company, it was unable to do so even during the years of its unmodified monopoly, the quarter-century between 1672 and 1698. As Davies wrote, the 1690s, the decade in which Jewish investors first acquired stock in it, were "years of unmitigated disaster for the company."[61]

Investment by London's Jews in the Royal African Company began, in fact, *after* the Company had attained its peak in the slave trade. While cautioning that data for the number of slaves it brought to the western hemisphere cannot be regarded as definitive, Davies calculated on a tentative basis that the Company delivered 90,768 slaves to the West Indies between 1673 and 1711. Sixty-five percent of those deliveries occurred before Alvaro Da Costa purchased his stock in 1691, for the Company conveyed 59,091 slaves to the West Indies in the eighteen years between 1673 and 1690. Deliveries fell by 54.3 percent during the subsequent seventeen years (1691–1707) to 26,975, which represented only 29.7 percent of all the Company's slave deliveries through 1711.[62] In sum, Jewish investors appear to have invested capital in the Royal African Company as it relinquished its position in the English slave trade to the private traders who emerged as the dominant force. Between 1698 and 1708, for example, such merchants are reputed to have delivered 76,062 slaves to Britain's colonies in the Caribbean and North America, in contrast to the Company's 18,943.[63] According to one contemporary account, the private traders delivered 35,718 slaves to Jamaica alone between 1698 and June 14, 1708, far in excess of the 6,854 delivered by the Royal African Company.[64]

Not surprisingly, the number of Jews who invested in the Company declined as its prospects deteriorated, falling from 29 in 1699, to 16 (and possibly 2 more) in early 1708, still hovering at 16 or 17 at the beginning of 1713.[65] The Company's records for early 1708 indicate that the relative amount of stock held by Jewish investors also declined from the 1699 level, although modestly. As noted previously, they held 12.2 percent of the Company's stock in 1699, but by 1708 their share had fallen to 9.3 percent. The latter was somewhat in excess of their 6.6 percent presence among the Company's shareholders, just as their ownership of 4.4 percent of the stock fifteen years earlier in 1693 had exceeded their 3.6 percentage of the shareholders.

The fact that Jewish investors owned proportionally more stock in 1693, 1699, and 1708 than their percentage as shareholders does not indicate any unusual interest on their part in the slave trade or any rush by them to own Royal African Company stock. The same occurred in connection with other contemporary opportunities for investment, and therefore appears to have characterized their activity as investors. Data compiled by P. G. M. Dickson show that Jewish investors between 1707 and 1709 exhibited the same tendency when subscribing to ventures in other companies (Table 1.1).[66] Moreover, the factor by which their proportion of shares exceeded their proportion as shareholders in those ventures was higher in every case than it was in the Royal African Company in early 1708.[67]

The tendency between 1691 and 1701 of most Jewish investors either to avoid the Royal African Company altogether or to refrain from committing all their investment capital to it continued, and characterized the strategies of new shareholders between 1702 and

TABLE 1.1
Jewish Investors in English Stock, 1707–9

Investment Vehicle	No. of Investors	% of All Investors	% of Total Stock
Annuities, 1707	17	2.4	6.9
Bank of England subscription, 1709	13	1.2	4.9
Bank of England stock, 1709	49*	2.6	9.4
East India Co. stock, 1709	65*	4.3	12.2

*For the need to reduce these figures slightly, see the discussions at ns. 57, 69, and 72.

SOURCE: P. G. M. Dickson, *The Financial Revolution in England: A Study in the Development of Public Credit, 1688–1756* (London: Macmillan, 1967), 268.

the end of 1712. During the course of that period, at least 86 Jewish investors acquired stock for the first time in the Company, in the Bank of England, or in both.[68] Twenty-six, or 30.2 percent, acquired shares in the Royal African Company, a decline from the 31 between 1690 and 1701 (or 38.7 percent of all Jewish investors then) who did so. As in the earlier period, most Jews making investments preferred other avenues to investment in the Company. At least 72 individuals invested for the first time in the Bank of England over the course of the later period.[69] This was 2.76 times as many as the number of those who acquired shares for the first time in the Royal African Company—a somewhat greater margin of difference between acquisitions in the two corporations than in the 1690s, when the difference was 2.35 times. Fully 83.3 percent of the new Bank investors (60 of the 72) did not purchase Royal African Company stock; and virtually none of them had owned any of it in the previous decade. As before, others refused to commit all their investments to the Royal African Company, for the remaining 12, or 16.6 percent of the 72, apportioned their capital between the two enterprises.

Only 14 of the 86 individuals who invested for the first time in one or both companies, or 16.2 percent, invested exclusively in the Royal African Company. Half, however, had invested earlier in the Bank of England, and they continued to hold its stock between 1702 and 1712. Another 2 had invested in the Bank during the previous period, but whether they continued to hold its stock in the later period is not known. In all, therefore, only 5 of the individuals who invested for the first time in either company between 1701 and 1712, or 5.8 percent, can be said to have invested exclusively in the Royal African Company when the entire period between 1691 and 1712 is examined.[70] Why those 5 did so, in view of the fact that the Company failed to pay dividends, "plumbed the depths of joint-stock finance" during the first decade of the eighteenth century, was essentially bankrupt by 1708, and four years later collapsed in "a state of moribund somnolence" is not known. And matters did not improve after 1712. The Company continued to limp along, functioning in a tubercular fashion, defaulting, for example, when it contracted to deliver slaves to the South Sea Company in the mid-1720s.[71]

As in the years between 1691 and 1701, Jewish investors from 1702 through 1712 turned not only to the Bank as an alternative to the Company but also to other investment opportunities, as indicated by the data in Table 1.1. By 1706, new investors in the East India Company included such individuals as Isaac De Valencia, Daniel De Mattos, Anthony Mendes, Moses Barrow, and Alvaro Da Fonseca. In early 1709, Jewish investors in the newly reorganized East India Company numbered at least 62, a group almost four times greater than the 16 who, less than a year before, had held Royal African Company stock.[72]

A new opportunity to earn profits in the slave trade presented itself in 1714 with the assignment of the asiento to the recently established South Sea Company. England acquired the much coveted contract in 1713 in the Treaty of Utrecht, thereby obtaining the exclusive right to deliver slaves to Spain's colonies. Early the following year the Crown assigned the asiento to the South Sea Company, bypassing the nearly bankrupt Royal African Company. Established in 1711 as a vehicle for funding the government's growing debt, the South Sea Company held a monopoly to all commerce with Spain's American colonies; its charter empowered it alone to trade in the South Seas. It was therefore logical to designate the new company as the one to implement the asiento for the next thirty years, the duration of Spain's concession to England at Utrecht.[73]

In unfortunate contrast to the Royal African Company, stock-transaction records for the South Sea Company no longer exist.[74] There is, however, a published list of the voting shareholders, defined as those who held at least £1,000 worth of stock, on December 25, 1714, a date early enough to reflect the degree to which the investing public had some measure of confidence in the new company.[75] Ominously, its first directors had no experience in commerce with the West Indies or Spanish America. On the other hand, its recurring difficulties with the Spanish government, war between the two nations, scandal, and its inability to earn a profit in the asiento trade all lay in the future.[76]

The South Sea Company had a total of 2,039 voting shareholder groups on Christmas Day in 1714. Nearly all were individuals; only a very small number were either partnerships, in the main comprised of two or three people, or corporate entities like the Master and Wardens of Trinity House or the "Governour and Company for making hollow Sword-blades." The religious identity of two shareholders is unknown. Of the remaining 2,037 shareholder groups, 34, or 1.6 percent, were made up of Jewish shareholders. Thirty-three of these owned their shares as individuals, while the remaining Jewish shareholder group was a partnership consisting of three men, two of whom also owned shares on an individual basis.[77]

The 34 Jewish individuals who were willing to invest in the South Sea Company at the end of 1714 in amounts large enough to qualify as voting stockholders were double the 16 or 17 who owned stock in the Royal African Company at the beginning of 1713, indicative of greater confidence in the new company than in the bankrupt older one. Yet they were fewer than the approximately 49 who, five years before, had held shares in the Bank of England and the 62 with investments in the East India Company. The prospects of the South Sea Company, predicated in part on the transport of slaves to Spain's colonies, evidently did not inspire as much confidence as the other two great corporations did.

On the other hand, Jews who chose to invest in the new enterprise were more likely to take greater risks than their non-Jewish counterparts. Five of the 34 Jewish stockholding groups, or 14.7 percent, each possessed four votes, indicating that each owned at least

£10,000 worth of stock.[78] Of the 2,003 non-Jewish stockholding groups, 132, or 6.5 percent, did. Six of the Jewish investors, or 17.6 percent of the Jewish shareholding groups, each qualified for three votes, indicating holdings ranging from £5,000 to £9,999. The corresponding figure for non-Jewish shareholders was 237, or 11.8 percent. With holdings between £3,000 and £4,999, 5 Jewish shareholding groups, or 14.7 percent, could each cast two votes. Non-Jewish shareholding groups with two votes totaled 296, or 14.7 percent of all non-Jewish shareholding groups, precisely the same percentage as the Jewish investors in this category. Finally, 18 of the Jewish investors, or 52.9 percent of the Jewish shareholding groups, could each cast one vote, for they owned at least £1,000 in stock but not more than £2,999, while the non-Jewish investors who qualified for one vote apiece were 1,338 in number, or 66.7 percent of the non-Jewish shareholding groups.

If Jewish investors comprised a small segment of the stockholders of the Royal African Company and of the voting members of the South Sea Company, all available evidence leads to the conclusion that they had as little or perhaps even less interest in establishing direct commercial ties with Africa. This pattern was apparent by 1700, when thirty-nine merchants with interests in the African trade who petitioned the House of Lords included only one Jewish individual, Abraham Mendes.[79] It persisted through the course of the eighteenth century.

England's Jewish spokesmen took credit in 1689, as described previously, for exporting woolen goods, importing gold, silver, and other foreign products, and for capturing the diamond market in India. They traded during the late seventeenth century with Spain, Portugal, and their American colonies, and with Holland, Italy, Flanders, the German States, France, the Canaries, the Azores, Jamaica, Barbados, and India.[80] Whether they also had at least some commercial ties with Africa cannot be determined definitively, for interlopers, Jewish or otherwise, who violated the Royal African Company's trade monopoly with Africa obviously did so in secrecy. On the other hand, none of the interlopers involved in the slave trade whose identities are known was Jewish.[81]

In 1698, the identities of the private traders became a matter of public record. Acknowledging the porousness of the Royal African Company's monopoly, Parliament that year authorized private merchants to trade with Africa upon payment to the Company of 10 percent of the value of all goods they exported to Africa, and 10 percent on goods imported from specified regions. Gold, silver, and slaves were exempted, no matter where they were procured in Africa. No fee had to be paid for these three commodities, thereby ending the Company's monopoly rights to them. This new arrangement, to remain in force until July 1712, gave a new name, ten-percent men, to merchants who until then had been dubbed interlopers. Time would prove that the Ten Percent Act of 1698 was actually the first step in the termination of the Royal African Company's monopoly rights. When the act lapsed as scheduled in 1712, Parliament chose to throw open all commerce with Africa to free trade rather than continue the arrangement or reestablish the Company's monopoly. Henceforth, English merchants who wished to trade with Africa were entirely at liberty to do so; they were no longer required to pay anything to the Royal African Company.[82]

The identities of the merchants who traded with Africa under the terms of the Ten Percent Act are known from the records of their payments to the Royal African Company. In all but one case, the forty-one largest private traders with Africa between 1702 and July 1712 were conclusively not Jewish. The remaining one, Joseph Martin, had a name that could have been either English, French Huguenot, or Jewish. Martin was probably the prominent East India merchant of that name who served as English consul in Moscow between 1702 and 1705, as a director of the South Sea Company between 1711 and 1715, and as a member of Parliament between 1710 and 1715. On the other hand, the London Jewish community included a Jose [sic] Nunes Martinez, who married in the Sephardic synagogue in 1712.[83]

Payments by private merchants other than the top forty-one to the

Royal African Company under the Ten Percent Act demonstrate that Jewish merchants played a minuscule part in trade with Africa from 1698 to mid-1712. Of the many hundreds of cargoes imported from there into England, only six belonged to Jewish merchants, including one credited in 1701 to Abraham Mendes, signatory to the petition presented to the House of Lords during the preceding year by individuals involved in commerce with Africa. Export cargoes totaled only four, again out of many hundreds, with the largest of the four belonging to Abraham Mendes in 1712. The value of the exports by Jewish merchants totaled £2,573–7–0 (Table 1.2). With the value of all sworn exports by private merchants to Africa between 1702 and July 1712 amounting to £295,144, the Jewish merchants' component amounted to less than 1 percent (eight-tenths of 1 percent).[84] By contrast, Jewish merchants were far more active in the commerce conducted by the East India Company. Unlike their near invisibility in the ten-percent accounts of the Royal African Company, the records of the East India Company document a greater Jewish presence in the commercial affairs of that company.[85]

The paucity of exports sent to Africa by Jewish merchants under the terms of the Ten Percent Act suggests, in turn, that in the early eighteenth century England's Jewish community played hardly any part in the slave trade. Africa's rulers and merchants were paid in European and Asian goods for the people they brought to the coasts for sale as slaves.[86] The negligible presence of London's Jewish merchants among the ten-percent men implies that they conducted little business exchanging European merchandise for slaves, with the exception of Abraham Mendes, who, as will be seen, is known to have participated in the slave trade between 1715 and 1719.

With the advent of unrestricted trade between England and Africa in 1712, Jewish merchants did not shift over to commerce with the African continent. No Jewish names appeared on the list of 48 "Merchants of London Tradeing [sic] to the Coast of Africa," who responded in 1726 to questions put to them by the Board of Trade about the advantages arising from free trade with Africa and the condition of the English trading posts there.[87] By contrast, Jewish

TABLE 1.2
Jewish Ten-Percent Men, April 24, 1699–July 8, 1712

Date	Merchant	Merchandise	Value
Exports:			
November 10, 1702	Moses Francia	Wine	26–0–0
December 15, 1702	Moses Francia	Wine	26–0–0
October 20, 1709	Moses De Medina	Cowries	100–0–0
June 17–19, 1712	Abraham Mendes	Cowries, beans, calico, sheets, tobacco, iron, tallow, coral, carpets, gunpowder, spirits, blankets, pewter, knives	2,421–7–0
Imports:			
November 8, 1701	Abraham Mendes	Ivory	
December 31, 1701	Moses Francia	Redwood	
November 26, 1703	Isaac Dias	Ivory	
October 17, 1710	Elias Abenaker [Abenatar]	Ivory	
October 24, 1710	Abraham Franco	Ivory	
December 13, 1710	Abraham Franco		

SOURCES: PRO, CO 388/10, H121, H122; PRO, T 70/1198, 70/1199.

merchants appeared as signatories on petitions regarding trade with Jamaica. In 1722, a protest signed by 51 merchants against prevailing practices in Jamaica's courts included at least 7 Jews.[88] When 92 "Traders to Jamaica and others" submitted a petition to the Crown in the mid-1730s against discriminatory taxation imposed by Jamaica's legislature on the colony's Jewish inhabitants, at least 41 London Jews, along with at least 49 non-Jews, were among the signers.[89] Similarly, a 1723 petition submitted by 56 London merchants who traded with Portugal included 13 Jews, while another one nine years later, again from businessmen in the Portugal trade, contained 10 Jewish signatures among a total of 25.[90]

At midcentury, Jewish merchants still did not figure in the African trade. In 1753, the anonymous author of a pamphlet published in connection with the bitter public debate that erupted when Parliament considered a bill to naturalize foreign-born Jews listed the contributions made by Jews to English commerce, but he included neither the general trade with Africa nor the slave trade in his discussion.

If ever an occasion presented itself for England's Jews and friendly supporters to argue that the nation benefited from Jewish participation in the slave trade, this was it, for the controversy that swirled around the so-called Jew Bill required every possible argument to defend the reputation of England's Jews and their position in English society. Had it been possible to do so, the writer would no doubt have cited such trade by Jews as conducive to the "national advantage," the terminology he employed when describing their significance in the Spanish trade.[91] The author of the pamphlet in question, whose title page assured readers that "the Utility of the Jews in Trade [would be] . . . fully considered and proved," claimed that Jewish merchants handled 5 percent of the nation's trade, citing their activities as bullion importers, silk and cotton middlemen, insurance brokers for foreign shipping, and discounters of foreign bills of exchange. As for geographic regions, the writer specified that England's Jewish merchants traded with the East Indies, Jamaica, and Spain's American colonies.[92]

Owing to their disinterest in commerce with Africa, Jewish merchants did not join the Company of Merchants Trading to Africa, established by Parliament in 1749 to assume the responsibilities of the Royal African Company for British forts and trading posts there. Outpaced by free traders, displaced by the South Sea Company as the supplier of slaves to Spain's colonies, the Royal African Company had limped along as best it could after 1712. By 1730, the debilitated corporation required an annual subsidy to run the forts and trading facilities it operated in Africa, ironically for the benefit of the free traders who had always been its bane. Parliament allocated £10,000 annually beginning in 1730, but by 1746 the Company's debts were so high, its credit so low, and the forts in such a state of deterioration that other arrangements had to be made. The Company of Merchants Trading to Africa was the result.[93]

Under the terms of its charter, nine directors were to administer the new company, three from each of the English ports that traded with Africa. It was not to issue stock; membership required payment of a mere 40 shillings rather than the purchase of shares.[94] Under these terms, 480 merchants residing in the three English cities that traded with Africa joined its ranks by June 1758. London members numbered 146, while Bristol accounted for 245 and Liverpool for 89. None of the 480 was Jewish.[95]

Almost thirty years later, in 1787, the number of Londoners who belonged to the Company of Merchants Trading to Africa had sky-rocketed to 1,086, among whom were eleven Jewish individuals, or 1 percent of the total.[96] Several of the eleven may have been the owners of vessels whose ships were listed in Lloyd's shipping registers for 1776 and 1790, although none gave Africa as the destinations of their vessels.[97] Whether the eleven were actually involved in commerce with the African continent is not at all clear, for, as a pamphleteer who identified himself as "an African Merchant" wrote in the early 1770s, the Company's membership lists had long been padded with the names of hundreds of Londoners who had nothing whatsoever to do with the Africa trade. In 1771, 1,425 Londoners were members of the Company, and yet, he asserted, everyone knew that at most only fifty traded with the African continent. Since the Company's inception approximately twenty years before, no more than a hundred had ever been engaged in African commerce, yet hundreds of new members had enrolled in 1768 and 1770. The same occurred in 1771, when 274 individuals paid their 40 shillings and became members, but not even ten of them traded with Africa. The newcomers included barbers, cheesemongers, weavers, and shoemakers, and many were underage clerks who were enrolled as members without their knowledge. The reason for all this? To influence the election of company officers, although letters sent by the candidates in 1771 to approximately two hundred of the members went undelivered because they were not to be found at the addresses where they allegedly resided.[98]

Uninvolved in the general trade with Africa, marginal at best to it at the beginning of the eighteenth century, Jewish merchants in England did not participate in the slave trade, with only a few known exceptions.

One, Andrew Lopez, is known to have been involved in the slave trade to Mexico in the late seventeenth century. Furthermore, he contracted in the late 1690s with Portugal's Royal Guinea Company, the holder of the asiento at that juncture, to deliver slaves to Spain's colonies. In fulfillment of his obligation, Lopez engaged two London Jewish shipowners to convey slaves from Africa across the Atlantic. But Jews who momentarily entered the slave trade through the doorway of the asiento proved to be a detriment. When the contract with the Portuguese company expired in 1701, the Spanish refused to renew it, in part because of the presence of Jewish merchants in its activities.[99] In view of this, the assertion by one Isaac Pereira in 1703 on behalf of the small Jewish community at Jamaica that "the Jews before the present war by their industry and interest had procured the Assiento of Negroes to be established at Jamaica" is inexplicable.[100]

At least one of London's Jewish merchants and quite possibly a second participated in the slave trade between 1715 and 1719. In 1715, Abraham Mendes received authorization from the South Sea Company to transport slaves to Jamaica and from there to the Spanish mainland on his ship, the *King Solomon*. The vessel subsequently carried 289 slaves from Jamaica to Porto Bello and, while it still clearly belonged to Mendes, 295 slaves on July 1, 1719 to Jamaica.[101] Mendes, it will be recalled, had signed the African traders' petition to the House of Lords in 1700 and had functioned in the commerce between England and Africa during the ten-percent era. In the second case, Isaac Fernandez Nunes, one of the larger investors in the South Sea Company at the end of 1714, petitioned the Company in 1715 on behalf of the owners of the *May Flower,* a slave ship that had been seized by the Spanish in the West Indies with 200 slaves on board. Whether or not Nunes himself had a share in the vessel is, however, not known.[102]

Two Jewish merchants who resided in London are known to have participated in the slave trade during the 1720s and 1730s. The number of slaves traceable to their efforts indicates, however, a negligible impact on the slave trade, one that was far below the capacity of the London slave fleet in 1726. One, Rodrigo Pacheco, had resided in New York as early as 1711, where in partnership with two non-Jewish and one other Jewish merchant he imported a slave from

Curaçao in 1716. Returning to London in the late 1720s or early 1730s, Pacheco was involved between 1727 and 1739 in the transport of 25 slaves to New York from various locations in the western hemisphere, 21 of them in partnership with non-Jewish investors.[103] The second of the two, Isaac Levy, imported 117 slaves from Africa to New York in 1721 in partnership with three other merchants, two of whom were not Jewish. His remaining partner, Nathan Simson, was a Jewish merchant who at the time resided in New York.[104] Simson returned to London by the summer of 1722, where he died in 1726. In the interim, he is not known to have participated again in the slave trade.[105]

One additional Jewish individual in England, Gabriel Lopez Pinheiro, is known to have had a form of contact with the slave trade during the 1720s. An officer of the London Sephardic community, Pinheiro was a refugee from Portugal in 1706 who, using various aliases, traded primarily with his homeland after he fled to England, but also as far afield as Vienna, to which he exported diamonds. Pinheiro became involved in 1726 in a transaction involving the sale of 51 slaves as attorney for the Marquis Govia, a Portuguese aristocrat. The owner of the island of St. Antonio off the coast of West Africa, the Marquis leased it to several Englishmen for a period of twenty-seven years, and subsequently permitted them to acquire 100 slaves on the island at a cost of £10 per person, payable in London. The lessees refused to pay, arguing that, inasmuch as only half the slaves had been delivered, the contract had not been fulfilled. Because the Marquis had meanwhile left London, the lessees found themselves dealing with his attorney.[106]

Toward the end of the eighteenth century, when London's West Indian houses functioned as bankers to merchants and planters in the colonies, one of London's Jewish firms is known to have provided financial backing in the slave trade. In keeping with the dependence of colonial slave factors, or retailers, on London's West Indian houses, the company of Lindo, Aguilar & Dias provided credit for two shipments of slaves sold in Jamaica in 1789 by Alexandre [sic] Lindo, a leading Jewish slave factor there.[107] Lindo, Aguilar & Dias, later known as Aguilar, Dias & Son, provided "Guarantees" for

Lindo, Lake & Co., a partnership in Jamaica that between 1796 and 1802 marketed slaves arriving from Africa. By extending such "Guarantees," the London house provided credit to the firm in Jamaica for slave cargoes. Aguilar, Dias & Son of London also provided support to Alexandre Lindo after he moved to England in the mid-1790s, where, along with his enterprises in sugar, coffee, cotton, and insurance, he lent funds to firms and individuals who participated in the slave trade.[108]

With the eclipse of the Royal African Company, private traders in London, Bristol, and Liverpool consolidated their hold on the slave trade, with London playing the predominant role during the first quarter of the eighteenth century.[109] Britain's slave fleet numbered 171 vessels in early 1726 and was capable of transporting somewhat in excess of 49,000 slaves. Liverpool, its dominant position in the slave trade still a quarter-century in the future, had the fewest: 21 vessels, with a capacity of 5,200 slaves. Bristol had 63 vessels, able to carry 16,950 slaves. London, not yet overtaken by its rivals, had the most, with 87 vessels capable of loading slightly more than 26,990 slaves.[110] Approximately 50 merchants were the primary owners of London's 87 slave ships. Thirty-three owned 1 vessel, 11 owned 2, 2 owned 5, 1 owned 6, and 2 owned 7, while the names of the owners of 2 vessels are not known. None of these owners of London's slave fleet in 1726 was Jewish.[111]

However, lists of primary owners account for only part of the story. Although shipping in eighteenth-century England was at times owned by individual entrepreneurs, the more usual form of maritime ownership occurred through partnerships formed for a particular venture. Shares were at times divided as minutely as sixty-fourths; and the greatest shareholder usually acted as ship's husband, the term for the organizer and agent of the undertaking, who was therefore the individual usually listed as the vessel's owner.[112]

It is highly unlikely, however, that Jews figured in any consequential manner as small investors in slave ships. The important pamphlet published in 1753 describing the contributions of England's Jews to the nation's trade made no mention, as we have seen, of participation by them in either the general commerce with Africa or in the slave trade. Nor was there any trace of them in the Company of Merchants Trading to Africa until late in the century, when their presence may in fact not be indicative of trade with Africa. Then too, Jewish merchants in England are known to have purchased shares in shipping, 39 of them doing so in 85 ventures between 1693 and 1798, but overwhelmingly in voyages bound for India and other locations in the Far East.[113] Accordingly, the 1753 pamphlet emphasized the role they played in commerce with those regions.[114] Finally, and most tellingly, the surviving Naval Office records of slave ships that arrived at New York between 1715 and 1765, at Georgia between 1754 and 1767, and at Barbados between 1782 and 1805 identify all the investors in such ventures. The records for these colonies therefore make it possible to retrieve not only the names of the primary owners but also those of smaller shareholders; and save for several instances in New York, the minor investors as well as the primary owners were overwhelmingly non-Jewish.[115]

Ship registers compiled by Lloyd's beginning in the 1760s indicate that London's Africa fleet remained in the hands of the City's non-Jewish merchants after midcentury, lending support to James A. Rawley's assessment that, despite the "rich ethnic mix of the [London] commercial community . . . native Englishmen, West Indians, and Scots seemed to preponderate in the slave trade sector."[116] Lloyd's register for 1764, the first published, listed 74 London vessels with Africa as their destination; none of the primary owners listed therein was Jewish.[117] The registers for 1776 and 1790 respectively listed 72 and 69 vessels, again with primary owners whose names were not Jewish.[118]

Bristol edged ahead of London during the 1730s for leadership in the slave trade, and in the early 1740s it ranked first among England's three slave-trading ports.[119] There, 124 merchants and 74 shipowners invested in the slave trade between 1698 and 1729. From 1730 through 1745, when Bristol led its rivals in the British slave trade, 68 merchants and 72 shipowners did so.[120] None in either period was Jewish.[121] But then, Jews did not yet reside in Bristol. They did not settle there until the 1750s, and when they did they functioned as modest artisans and shopkeepers; apparently not a single international merchant was to be found among them.[122] Subsequently, none appeared among the 112 merchants and 74 shipowners who invested in the slave trade between 1746 and 1769.[123] And after one to two generations of residence in Bristol, its Jewish inhabitants (nor London Jews with funds to invest) still did not participate in the port's slaving ventures. None of the primary owners of the approximately 520 slave ships between 1770 and 1807 that belonged to Bristol was Jewish, nor were any of the lesser investors in 134 of those vessels.[124]

By the middle of the eighteenth century, Liverpool surpassed both Bristol and London, achieving and maintaining an unassailable position of supremacy until the abolition of the British slave trade in 1807.[125] Here too, Jews did not begin to settle until the 1750s, and when they did so they made their livings as peddlers and small shopkeepers. Weak and inconspicuous, the congregation they established around 1750 faded away soon thereafter, and they proved incapable of organizing a permanent community or erecting a synagogue until the 1780s. In 1790, only nineteen recognizably Jewish inhabitants were listed in the Liverpool directory for that year, out of a population of 54,000. In marked contrast to their marginal position, the merchants of Liverpool who participated in the slave trade were usually men of wealth and, in James A. Rawley's phrase, individuals of "high standing."[126]

As in London and Bristol, the Jews of Liverpool did not own ships in the slave trade. Peddlers and petty shopkeepers, none were on the list of 101 Liverpool merchants who belonged to the Company of Merchants Trading to Africa in 1752, nor, as noted previously, among the 89 who belonged to it in 1758.[127] Nor were Jews to be found among the 66 primary owners of the 88 Liverpool vessels trading with Africa in 1752 that carried 24,730 slaves, or among the owners of the 80 Liverpool vessels listed by Lloyd's as trading there in 1764.[128] Twenty-six years later, in 1790, the Liverpool slave fleet of 141 vessels was owned by forty firms, none of which was Jewish. And in 1807, the year in which Britain terminated the slave trade throughout its empire, none of Liverpool's seventy-odd companies trading to Africa was Jewish.[129]

Further verification that England's Jewish merchants did not own the ships that procured and transported approximately three million slaves from Africa to the Americas during the eighteenth century comes from the ports where the vessels delivered their human cargo. Naval Office records reporting the arrival of slave ships survive to varying degree for such colonies as Barbados and Jamaica, Nevis and Dominica, Grenada and St. Vincent, New York and Virginia, South Carolina and Georgia. Between 1710 and 1720, the information entered by the officials of the Naval Office began to include the names of the vessels' owners. In case after case, for ship after ship, ceaselessly, relentlessly, until the abolition of the slave trade in the British empire in 1807, slave vessels registered in London, Bristol, and Liverpool belonged to the non-Jewish merchants of those cities who were their primary owners and, as noted before, to the smaller investors who, where known from the Naval Office records, were in almost every case not Jewish.[130] It is to two of the major destinations of their slave ships in the Caribbean, where Jewish communities developed, that we turn next.

CHAPTER 2

Jews and Slaves in Seventeenth-Century Barbados and Jamaica

British settlement on the island of Barbados began in 1625, and within five years the new colony's population numbered 1,800 inhabitants. It increased rapidly thereafter, growing to 30,000 by 1650. At first the colony's residents endeavored to raise tobacco as their cash crop, but by the middle of the century they shifted to sugar. Sugar made Barbados England's wealthiest colony during the seventeenth century, which meant, accordingly, that the island relied extensively upon slave labor. It accounted, according to one estimate, for as much as 53.3 percent of all slave imports to Britain's Caribbean possessions during the 1600s.[1]

As in England, where a small number of Sephardic Jews had established residence prior to the readmission permitted by the government in 1656, Barbados became a destination for Jewish settlers in advance of the Resettlement. Some may have appeared on the island during the late 1620s. Shortly before midcentury, a Jewish inhabitant was thought to have discovered how to make bricks using local clay, problematic until then because of the quality of the island's soil. Dutch Jews may have helped introduce sugar cultivation between 1645 and 1654. Finally, Jewish refugees from Dutch Brazil made their way to the colony by November 1654, and in January 1655 its Council (the upper house of the legislature and the governor's closest advisors in the British colonial system) directed that they be permitted to settle on the island.[2]

Not long after the readmission of Jews to England, the Crown granted patents of endenization to Jewish settlers in Barbados, thereby encouraging the development of a permanent Jewish community on the island. Thirty-one such patents went to Jews who settled between 1661 and 1671. A synagogue existed by 1664, when one of the boundaries of a piece of property in Bridgetown, the colony's main port, was identified as "the Jewes Synague & burying place."[3] Before long, for certain by 1680, Barbados's Jews employed a haham, the Sephardic term for a rabbi, who emigrated to the island from Amsterdam and remained for twelve years, perhaps as many as eighteen. But while the community had the resources to support a haham, not all its members prospered. In 1676, Barbados's governor reported that many were poor, and in 1681 a grand jury complained to him of "the evil done to the island by vagrant and poor Jews."[4]

Many of Barbados's non-Jewish settlers greeted the development of a Jewish community with dismay, and traditional canards depicting Jews as disloyal surfaced in the middle of the 1660s. Analyzing the colony's vulnerable condition then, one writer claimed that they were "very Treacherous to the Island." Specifically, he charged, they had acted in league with foreign enemies, hatching "designes . . . to discover when the English were ready to Embarque ag[ains]t the French and Dutch and in the matter [of], the reliefe of Antiga." Fortunately, the number of ships riding in the harbor at Bridgetown seduced the Jews into believing that English forces were stronger than actually was the case. The assumption that they were a dangerous internal threat led to their quarantine, for "the Jewes were confined to theire respective Townes," as the writer concluded. The claim that they were disloyal surfaced anew in 1681, coupled with an assertion that they were guilty of "barbarous inhumanity." The "subtle conspiracy of the Jewish nation in general against all Christendom, and particularly against England," wrote several petitioners, made their presence "inconsistent with the safety of Barbados; they have already given, as there is too much reason to believe, intelligence to her enemies, and will do the same again."[5]

From the outset, Barbados's Jewish inhabitants settled in the colony's towns, choosing to concentrate on commerce rather than on plantation agriculture. By the middle of the 1660s, at least 23 Jewish

merchants exported sugar, rum, and other produce through the Barbados customs house.[6] In 1680, 54 Jewish households resided in
Bridgetown. Of the 16 households that resided elsewhere, 14 were to
be found in the parish of St. Peter, and because none of them owned
land there it is apparent that they resided in the town of Speightstown.[7] Only 2 of the 70 Jewish households on the island, which
amounted in all to approximately 260 individuals, appear not to have
resided in one of the colony's four towns.[8] And while some of Barbados's Jews did own land outside the towns, concentration in the
latter, hence in commerce, meant that the Jewish population was
destined to own few of the island's slaves.[9]

Not all welcomed this new community of merchants. Although the
island's plantation owners did, citing the benefits they derived from
competition between Jewish and English merchants, non-Jewish businessmen feared the consequences. "The Jewes are a People soe subtile
in matters of Trade," they informed the Crown as early as 1661,
"that in a short time they will not only ingrosse Trade among themselves; but will bee able to direct the benefit hereof to other
places. . . ."[10] Twenty-one years later, one of their number stood
accused of importing and passing devalued Spanish coin, threatening
the value of the currency that circulated in the colony. Still later,
early in the eighteenth century, the Council asserted that the colony's
Jews were ruinous to its trade, for they allegedly refused to buy its
produce, preferring instead to export the money they acquired.[11]

Given such attitudes, along with the prevailing view in contemporary European thought that the Jews comprised a separate nation, it
could hardly have surprised Barbados's Jews that they were taxed
separately in parish assessments.[12] Nor were they treated in other
situations as the equals of Englishmen under the law. In 1669, for
example, they complained to the Crown that, despite endenization,
they were not permitted to give evidence in court in cases involving
non-Jews. Five years later, legislation enacted by the colony excluded
them from testifying except in cases related to commerce. In 1675,
an order issued by the colony's Council accorded them the right to
sue in matters related to trade, but they found that in practice they
were barred from obtaining redress in the courts. They were therefore

forced to appeal in 1681 for the right to sue "for their protection as traders and the right to trade."[13]

Efforts to curtail the island's Jewish population extended to restrictions on their right to own slaves and to conduct commercial transactions with them. Late in 1679, when the island's non-Jewish merchants and traders protested against the "great injuries and inconveniencies to the English nation by the great number of Jews inhabiting and trading in Barbadoes," the Assembly (the lower house of the legislature in the British colonial system) responded by approving "An Act to restrain the Jews from keeping and trading with negroes."[14] Nine years later, in 1688, the island's legislature acted to limit the number of male slaves that Jews could own. Jews who resided in seaport towns and who had not been endenized could henceforth own no more than one. Those who possessed letters of endenization could do so only after receiving authorization by the Lieutenant Governor and by both houses of the legislature. This restriction, one that remained in force until its repeal in September 1706, was necessary, the legislation specified, because the growing number of slaves on the island posed a danger to public safety.[15] The law did not apply to non-Jews who resided in the seaports, making it evident that this was not the real reason for the prohibition. Rather than an attempt to curtail the alleged danger to Barbados's white population, the law obviously gave non-Jewish merchants in the towns an economic edge over their Jewish competitors. That it was indeed a weapon against the Jewish merchants became explicit in 1705, when the Council, declaring that "the Jews in this Island are very prejudicial to Trade," directed the colony's legal officers to draw up a list of all slaves owned by Jews in the colony in order to revive the prohibition. And a year later, when the act was repealed, the legislature specified that because the colony's Jewish inhabitants "are become considerable Traders," they were "obliged to employ a greater number of Negroes and Slaves. . . ."[16]

Barbados's Jews did not, in any case, exhibit any ability or inclination to acquire many slaves. A detailed census conducted in 1679–80 found a total of 37,495 slaves on the island.[17] Of these, 300, or less than 1 percent (eight-tenths of 1 percent) belonged to Jewish owners.[18] Almost 71 percent of the slaves owned by the colony's Jewish inhabitants resided in towns, 163 of them in Bridgetown and another 49 in Speightstown.[19] The remaining 88 slaves belonged to 4 owners, 3 of whom were landowners who presumably were involved in agriculture utilizing slave labor. Two of the 4 also owned slaves in Bridgetown.[20]

The census taken in Bridgetown reveals that the Jewish population there did not acquire slaves out of proportion to their presence among its white households, and that they owned fewer slaves on average than did non-Jews in the town. Of the 404 white households in Bridgetown in 1680, 54, or 13.3 percent, were Jewish. They owned 163 of the town's 1,439 slaves, or 11.3 percent, a figure slightly below their proportion among the town's families. Bridgetown's 350 non-Jewish families, or 86.6 percent of its households, owned 1,276 of its slaves, or 88.6 percent, placing the proportion of the slaves they owned slightly above their proportion among the town's families. Jewish slaveowning households, numbering 49, owned an average of 3.3 slaves, while non-Jewish families owning slaves, totaling 318, owned an average of 4.0. Finally, Bridgetown's Jewish families were no more likely to own slaves than those that were not Jewish. Of its 350 non-Jewish households, 318, or 90.8 percent, possessed slaves; and of the 54 Jewish households, 49, or 90.7 percent, did.[21]

In St. Peter's parish, the average and the proportional differences between non-Jewish and Jewish households were even greater, owing to the fact that the census there combined the results for the parish's town, Speightstown, with those for its plantations. Of the parish's 246 households, 14, or 5.6 percent, were Jewish, but they held 49, or 1.6 percent, of its 3,017 slaves. Conversely, St. Peter's 232 non-Jewish households, or 94.3 percent of the total number of households, owned 2,968 slaves, or 98.3 percent of all slaves. The parish's non-Jewish slaveowning families, a total of 189, owned an average of 15.7 slaves each, while its 14 Jewish households averaged 3.5. According to the criteria of proportionality and averages, therefore, Jews in St. Peter were less apparent as slaveowners than were its non-Jewish inhabitants. On the other hand, the parish's Jewish households were more likely to hold slaves. Each of the 14 Jewish families, or 100 percent, did, while among the parish's 232 non-Jewish households, 189, or 81.4 percent, owned slaves.[22]

The island of Jamaica quickly became a second destination for Jewish colonists who desired to settle within the British orbit in the Caribbean, after an English naval expedition seized it from Spain in 1655. The new prize eventually surged ahead of Barbados as a plantation colony, surpassing it during the last quarter of the seventeenth century as Britain's largest importer of slaves. By the 1720s, Jamaica almost always exceeded the older colony in sugar exports to Great Britain.[23] The colony offered opportunities for merchants who supplied its developing planter class as well as its fabulous buccaneers, the swashbuckling pirates who preyed upon Spanish shipping and Spain's colonies with official approval at least until the 1680s, when Jamaica's governors undertook to suppress them.[24] Opportunities to conduct business also arose from Jamaica's important role as an intermediary for trade between England and Spain's colonies. Although officially an illicit commerce, the English government conveniently looked the other way and even permitted Spanish traders to call at Jamaica because of the profits that accrued to the empire from this trade, notably in flour, cloth, iron goods, alcohol, and slaves, as well as from the silver bullion that flowed to Britain from the mines of Spanish America.[25]

As in Barbados, a Jewish presence took shape in Jamaica during the 1660s, eventually growing to become the largest Jewish community in any single British colony during the eighteenth century. Settlement apparently began in 1663 with the arrival of six Jewish settlers from London, followed a year later by others after the Jewish colony at Cayenne collapsed. Early in 1672, the colony's governor reported that twenty-nine Jews resided in Jamaica, thirteen of them settlers, the others their servants. By 1683, the island's Jewish community employed a haham.[26]

Jamaica's Jewish inhabitants gravitated to Port Royal, the colony's premiere town and one of England's wealthiest and most strategically placed ports in the western hemisphere.[27] Opportunities for trade drew Jewish settlers to it, as did no doubt the toleration extended to dissenters and to non-Protestants. As John Taylor, a visitor to Jamaica in 1687, observed, the town had "a Romish Chappell, a Quackers meeting House, and a Jewe's Sinagog. . . ." Taylor reported, furthermore, that Port Royal was home to "many Jewes, verey wealthy merchants, haveing free commerce with our English Factory," and that "many wealthy Jewes Merchants" resided likewise at Carlisle Town, a site thirty-five miles to the southwest.[28] Jamaica's Jews, on the other hand, informed the Crown after the great earthquake that devastated Port Royal in 1692 that many of them were impoverished. Twentieth-century research utilizing estate inventories compiled during the 1690s supports their assessment for some.[29]

Mirroring the animosities that prevailed in Barbados, Port Royal's Jewish merchants rapidly incurred the hostility of their non-Jewish counterparts. As early as 1672, thirty-one of Port Royal's English merchants protested against "the infinite Number of Jewes wch daylie resort to this Island & Trade. . . ." They conduct their commerce, the petitioners complained, in violation of a Parliamentary law prohibiting retail sales by aliens, by importing merchandise from Holland (where they would undoubtedly return after having taken advantage of their stay in Jamaica), and by underselling non-Jews. Before long, the non-Jewish merchants asserted, they will have succeeded in capturing all business for themselves.[30] In 1684, the colony's legislature enacted a measure against "engrossing and forestalling," aiming it in part against the Jewish merchants. As the act explained, it was "designed to prevent small traders and Jews at Port Royal from bringing up goods from ships before the inhabitants who live at a distance have time to come down and make their own bargain with the master of this ship. . . ."[31] Port Royal's non-Jewish merchants continued thereafter to denounce the Jewish population, eventually enlisting the colony's Council in their cause. In 1692 the Council wrote to the Lords of Trade in London that,

> The Jews eat us and our children out of all trade, the reasons for naturalising them not having been observed; for there has been no regard had to their settling and planting as the law intended and

directed. We did not want them at Port Royal . . . and though told that the whole country lay open to them they have made Port Royal their Goshen, and will do nothing but trade. . . . Had we not warning from other Colonies we should see our streets filled and the ships hither crowded with them. This means taking our children's bread and giving it to Jews.[32]

The references in the Council's statement to "the reasons for naturalising them not having been observed" and to their malfeasance at not "settling and planting as the law intended and directed" referred to the fact that Jamaica's Jewish inhabitants did not restrict themselves to plantation agriculture. To attract settlers to the colony, the Crown in 1661 had offered grants of thirty acres to anyone who would settle in Jamaica within two years, together with all the rights and privileges of Englishmen to any children born there.[33] Six Jewish newcomers received land during the 1660s, as did fifteen more during the following decade.[34] But rather than establish plantations and raise sugar, complained their opponents, most of the Jewish newcomers had taken up residence in the colony's port.

To counter the charge that they had violated the terms of their immigration by not becoming planters, Jamaica's Jews in 1692 supplied the Crown with the names of twelve Jewish plantation owners.[35] Non-Jewish Jamaicans continued nevertheless to protest that the Jewish population pursued commerce in preference to agriculture. As the governor and Council explained to the Crown in 1700, in answer to complaints against the practice of imposing discriminatory taxation upon the colony's Jewish inhabitants,

Their first introduction into this Island was on condition that they should settle and plant, which they do not, there being but one considerable and two or three small settlements of the Jews in all the Island [on the land], but their employment generally is keeping shops and merchandising. . . . [36]

Several of Jamaica's Jews in the late seventeenth and early eighteenth centuries identified themselves as planters in their wills, but whether their primary interest really lay in agriculture or merely in cultivating a protective fiction because of the allegations made during the 1690s cannot be determined.[37] Indeed, the wills of three of the individuals listed in 1692 as plantation owners contain clear evidence of association with Port Royal or of involvement in commerce.[38] The future for Jamaica's Jews, in any case, lay overwhelmingly in town life and commercial activity; and this in turn meant that they would own but a fragmentary part of the colony's slaves.

A detailed census conducted in Port Royal in 1680 permits assessment of their ownership of slaves there. As non-Jewish colonists repeatedly complained, this was the site where most if not all resided. Although several manuscript defects and omissions of data make it necessary to treat some of the totals that can be computed from the census as approximations, such problems are so few in number that the results provide a close picture of the town's demography in 1680. Fortunately, none of the manuscript's few defects or omissions occur in conjunction with the census's Jewish entries.

Approximately 2,883 individuals resided in Port Royal in 1680, of whom 2,069 were white and 814 were black.[39] The town contained 523 households, of which 499 (including the prison keeper's; as was typical of jails in the colonial era, he apparently resided in it), or 95.4 percent, were not Jewish. Twenty, or 3.8 percent, of the households were Jewish.[40] They owned 48 slaves, or approximately 5.8 percent of Port Royal's enslaved inhabitants (Table 2.1). Port Royal's Jewish population, therefore, owned about half the percentage of slaves owned by their counterparts in Bridgetown, where the total for Jewish owners stood at 11.3 percent of all slaves.

In contrast to Bridgetown, where the proportion of slaves owned by Jewish households was somewhat less than their proportion among the town's total number of households, Jewish households in Port Royal owned somewhat more of the town's slaves (approximately 5.8 percent) than their proportion among its families (3.8 percent). Then too, unlike Bridgetown but as in Speightstown, the Jews of Port Royal were more likely than their non-Jewish counterparts to own slaves. Among the 499 households known to have been non-Jewish, 258, or 51.7 percent, owned slaves, while 18 of the 20

TABLE 2.1
Population of Port Royal, 1680

	Households		Whites		Slaves	
	No.	%	No.	%	No.	%
Non-Jewish	498	95.2	@1,962	@94.8	@739	@90.7
Jewish	20	3.8	75	@ 3.6	48	@ 5.8
Religion Not Certain	4	0.7	3§	@ 0.1	2+	
At Prison	1*	0.1	29	@ 1.4	11	@ 1.3
Parish Property					14	@ 1.7
Totals	523	99.8	@2,069	@99.9	@814	@99.5

@Approximately

*The prison keeper's household; included with the non-Jewish population in the discussion in the text.

§Probable figure

+Perhaps more; manuscript defective in two places

NOTE: For the Jewish inhabitants and the number of slaves each owned, as well as for those whose religion is not certain and their slaves, see Appendix V, Table 1.

SOURCE: PRO, CO 1/45, 96–107.

known Jewish families, or 90 percent, did. On the other hand, the town's non-Jewish slaveowning households held a slightly higher average number of slaves, 2.8, than its Jewish slaveowning households did, 2.6. The average owned by non-Jewish families remains the same whether or not the prison keeper and the 11 slaves in his care, some of whom he may in fact have owned, is included in the calculation.

The forty-eight slaves owned by Port Royal's Jewish residents comprised a minute fragment of Jamaica's total slaves. If the recent estimate by one historian that the colony's slave population numbered 21,500 in 1680 is correct, then those in Port Royal who were owned by the town's Jewish population would have amounted to less than 1 percent (two-tenths of 1 percent) of the colony's enslaved inhabitants.[41] Slaves on the few plantations actually owned and worked by Jews could not have raised that percentage by much.

Settlement in towns and careers in commerce did not predispose the Jewish inhabitants of Barbados and Jamaica to serve in any significant manner as factors, the term for the retailers who received consignments of slaves from the ships that imported them, and then sold them. The Royal African Company appointed two or three factors in each colony between 1672 and 1698, selecting highly placed officials because of the political edge that the Company consequently gained. The appointees, for their part, received a 7 percent commission on all sales, making factorage a highly lucrative enterprise. As K. G. Davies has observed, "An agency for the Royal African Company must, therefore, have been amongst the best remunerated private employments in the English colonies. . . ."[42] But none of the Company's appointees to this lucrative position was Jewish, if for no other reason than the fact that Jews in this era were barred from public office and therefore would have provided no political benefit to the Company had they been appointed.[43]

Like non-Jews who resided in Barbados and Jamaica, a portion of the Jewish inhabitants of the two colonies purchased slaves from the Royal African Company through its factors, but in both locations they acquired a small percentage of its imports. In Jamaica, the Company reportedly sold slightly more than 16,636 slaves between November 1674 and the end of 1700; of these, 15,421, or 92.6 percent, were purchased by non-Jewish colonists, while 1,193, or 7.1 percent, were acquired by Jewish individuals. Of the remaining 22 slaves, 18 were bought by Jews and non-Jews acting in partnership, and 4 were bought by parties whose religion is not certain.[44] In Barbados, the percentage of slaves acquired by Jewish individuals was still smaller. Of the 23,072 slaves known to have been sold by the Company between March 1673 and December 1700, 22,226, or 96.3 percent, were acquired by non-Jews, and 811, or 3.5 percent, by Jews. Of the remaining 35, 32 were bought by Jewish and non-Jewish partners, while 3 were acquired by parties whose religion is not certain.[45]

While most of the Jewish purchasers in the two colonies bought slaves infrequently and in very small numbers, others did so repeatedly, in quantities large enough to indicate that they were purchasing them for resale.[46] They were, in other words, engaged in the business of buying and selling slaves. In Jamaica, this included the purchase of "refuse," the term applied to newly imported slaves whose poor health precluded reexport to the Spanish empire and who consequently were retained for sale within the colony.[47] Jamaica's planters frequently assailed the Royal African Company for skimming off the healthiest slaves for reexport and selling only the sickliest on the island. In one such protest to the Crown in 1689 against the practice of siphoning the best slaves to the Spanish colonies, the colony's legislature complained that "in one parish . . . it can easily be shewn that £4000 has been lost by buying refuse negroes of Jews and [other] beggarly subbrokers. . . ."[48]

Significantly, Jamaicans, the planters in particular, are not known to have complained that Jews participated in the export of slaves by private merchants. Jamaica's important role as an entrepôt for the sale of slaves to Spain's empire engaged not only the Royal African Company but also Port Royal's merchants, one of whom observed in 1688 that buying slaves from the Company and reselling them to the Spaniards "was 'a much easier way of making money than making sugar.' " In reaction to this source of pressure on the supply of slaves in Jamaica, the planters did not merely complain; they sought relief in the form of a tax on the exports.[49] But while non-Jewish Jamaicans were quick to raise a host of diverse charges against the colony's Jewish population, draining slaves to the Spanish empire was not among them.[50] The silence in this matter suggests the possibility that, if Jews were involved in the export of slaves from Jamaica, they played only a small part in such commerce.

Nor are interlopers known to have been among Jamaica's or Barbados's Jewish population. The right to import slaves from Africa belonged exclusively, of course, to the Royal African Company until 1698. Interlopers who violated the Company's monopoly obviously operated in secrecy, limiting our knowledge as to who they were. However, of the few whose identities are known, none was Jewish.[51]

In neither Barbados nor Jamaica, therefore, does the Jewish population appear to have carved out much of a role in the institution of slavery during the late seventeenth century. We may note, finally, that a minute Jewish presence developed on the island of Nevis during the last quarter of the seventeenth century. Their involvement in slavery was unremarkable. In 1678, Nevis had 8 Jewish inhabitants out of a total white population of approximately 3,600. They did not own any of the colony's 3,849 slaves in that year.[52] Nor did they purchase many of the slaves offered for sale by the Royal African Company; they acquired 102, or 1.5 percent of the 6,736 slaves the Company sold at Nevis between 1674 and the end of 1700.[53] The colony's Jewish population was destined to grow somewhat during the early eighteenth century, but, as will be seen, it never became a significant Jewish community in the Caribbean, had little stake in the colony's slave population, and did not participate in its factoring enterprises.

CHAPTER 3

Jews and Slavery in Jamaica, 1700–80

The ground at Port Royal began to heave and writhe in wavelike fashion shortly before noon on June 7, 1692, heralding a massive earthquake that in an instant destroyed much of the town. While many of its buildings toppled and crashed to the ground, others simply slid into the sea, sinking in thirty or more feet of water. Within minutes, a great tidal wave coursed over the devastation, raising the death toll to approximately two thousand, more than half the town's population. As if to confirm Port Royal's reputation as the Sodom of the western hemisphere, a wave of looting, robbery, and violence followed hard on the heels of the natural disaster, as survivors sought to grab what they could from the wreckage that remained.[1]

New Jewish settlements arose elsewhere in Jamaica as a consequence of the earthquake, one in Spanish Town, the colony's capital, and another in the new town of Kingston, established to replace the destroyed port. Although some of the Jewish population remained in the shattered town, others departed for Spanish Town where a congregation had apparently been established earlier that year. Still others began to settle in Kingston, as it slowly began to rise across the water from Port Royal on the northern side of the magnificent harbor they both shared. Several acquired lots there and constructed homes by 1702, as indicated on the map drawn in that year by the surveyor who laid out the new town. Kingston's development surged after 1703 when Port Royal was again leveled, this time by fire, and it quickly grew to eclipse the hapless older town as the colony's commercial center. The Jewish community that took root in Kingston congregated in its western swampy region, where a sufficient number resided by 1707 to establish a synagogue.[2]

Kingston's Jewish population overshadowed Port Royal's before long, just as Kingston quickly surpassed the older port in most ways. The poll tax for Port Royal in 1740 contained just 29 Jewish entries, in contrast to the 188 Jewish entries on Kingston's tax list in 1745. Then too, the Kingston Jewish community outpaced Spanish Town's. In 1769, Kingston's tax list included 197 Jewish entries, while three years later the capital's numbered 76.[3] Spanish Town's Jewish population at that juncture reportedly included 300 individuals, making it probably the third-largest Jewish community in the English-speaking world, exceeded only by the Jewish populations of London and Kingston.[4]

Unfortunately, this is the only figure to have come down to us for the population of any of the individual Jewish communities in eighteenth-century Jamaica. Otherwise, no more than three general estimates by contemporaries appear to exist for the colony's Jewish population as a whole. At the beginning of 1703, in a petition to the Crown for relief from discriminatory taxation imposed by the colony's legislature, the Jewish community's spokesmen declared that they were a group of no more than eighty families.[5] Second, Benjamin Bravo, a Jewish merchant who returned to London after residing in Jamaica for eleven years, estimated early in 1736 that the colony's Jewish population was "about seven or eight hundred, reckoning men, women and children." Finally, *The North-American and the West-Indian Gazetteer* reported in 1776 that "800 or 900 Jews" resided in Jamaica. If correct, this would mean that the Jewish population had increased as much as twelvefold since 1680 when, it will be recalled, it had numbered seventy-five at Port Royal.[6]

As Jamaica's Jewish population increased, it inevitably attracted the attention of non-Jewish Jamaicans. "Some of them are men of Probity," wrote James Knight during the 1740s in his history of the island, praising their "Industry, Moderation and Oeconomy. . . ." A merchant who had resided in Jamaica for more than twenty years, Knight regarded the Jews as people worthy of emulation, noting especially their tendency to abstain from alcohol as well as their "Regular manner of living."[7] Edward Long, perhaps the most knowledgeable of all Jamaican observers during the middle of the eighteenth century, also commented favorably, when he wrote around 1770 that "the chief men among the Jews are very worthy persons," explaining that they provided relief for their poor and did what they could to ensure that the less affluent members of their community earned honest livelihoods. As for Spanish Town's Jewish inhabitants, Long commented that some were "good men" who performed "many benevolent actions to Gentiles as well as their own fraternity" and who did not use alcohol, one of the factors that accounted for their "good health and longevity, as well as their fertility. . . ." Furthermore, Long portrayed Jewish commercial activity as beneficial to the entire colony.[8]

Both Knight and Long, on the other hand, attributed highly undesirable characteristics to the Jews who resided in Jamaica. Some may have been honest, Knight believed, but the majority were not. "The generality of them," he explained, "Trade and subsist on Credit, and have so many little Roguish Tricks, as are detrimental to the Country they live in and a Scandall and Reproach to their own Nation." According to an allegation that enjoyed wide currency among Knight's contemporaries, they purchased houses in order to cheat their creditors, for under the island's laws dwellings could not be attached to satisfy debtors' obligations.[9] They cheated blacks by using false weights and measures and by engaging in "other vile Practices" that Knight did not specify. Echoing the charge made during the previous century, Knight claimed that Jewish merchants deprived Christians of decent livelihoods by surpassing them in business. Moreover, they were useless in time of war, for a handful of stout invaders could easily drive off twenty-five times as many Jews.[10]

Edward Long disagreed with the last point, hearkening back to the military service Jews had performed during the French invasion of 1694, when "they opposed the enemy with great courage," a view with which Jamaica's Jews of course concurred.[11] Otherwise, Long subscribed to the view that the Jews were crafty businessmen. "The rascally tricks, for which both antient and modern Jews have always been distinguished" served for Long to explain why so many people disliked them. The less affluent were a "lower rabble," whose short-comings included "fraudulent bankruptcies" that "now and then happen among the poorer and more knavish tribe." While some of the Jews in Spanish Town were honest men, the majority were "very selfish and tricking, fraudulent in their trade, and rigid in their trans-actions, not only with Christians, but with one another." Especially reprehensible was their practice of mixing a deadly alcoholic bever-age, selling the concoction to lower-class whites and soldiers who fell victim to the harmful brew. And the Jews in general, not just those who resided in the capital, declined to appear at militia musters on their Sabbaths and religious festivals during the slave rebellion that scourged the island in 1760, while continuing to conduct their busi-nesses. "It was well known," Long alleged, "that they never scrupled taking money and vending drams upon those days; others wilfully absented themselves, and paid the fine [for missing muster], which came to much less than their profits amounted to by staying at home, and attending their shops."[12]

Failure to report for militia duty on holy days was not a fanciful story. The issue was sufficiently troubling to merit inclusion in an appeal sent by the island's Jewish leaders to the officers of London's Sephardic community, in which they asked the Londoners to inter-cede for them with the colony's newly appointed governor before he departed from England. In their response, the Londoners counseled against asking for exemptions from militia service, and they informed the Jamaicans that they could violate the Sabbath when martial law was in force.[13]

In a lengthy analysis of the adverse consequences of the island's perennial shortage of hard currency, Long repeatedly singled out Jewish businessmen for blame. Because Jamaica did not have an adequate supply of hard money, Jewish moneylenders, he asserted, charged extremely high interest rates, ones that were in fact illegal. By doing so, they ruined many who stood highest in the island's social hierarchy, planters who found themselves compelled to "take up loans in the island of some rich Jew." Hoping to avoid economic collapse, a trapped planter would find himself further enmeshed when "the remedy for him is pointed out by the Jew, who, from pretended motives of lenity, or friendship, consents to make up the matter, on his entering into a fresh bond. . . ." Non-Jews on the middle rung of the social scale such as soldiers and tradesmen also suffered, thanks to Jews who specialized in converting Jamaican dollars into rials. Paid in dollars, the soldiers and craftsmen "were obliged to lay them out immediately in the purchase of small necessaries, chiefly among the Jewish shopkeepers, who have made very considerable sums by the exchange." As for the blacks at the bottom of Jamaica's social hierarchy, the shopkeepers with whom they dealt were mostly Jews who took payment from their customers in depreciated currency "with design to profit upon them." As depreciated coin continued to plummet in value, "the Negroes are unable to carry on their traffic; and a general confusion ensues. . . . A Negroe with the whole of his weekly pay or acquisition, could then purchase scarcely half as much as before." The indelible impression conveyed by Long was one of rapacious moneylenders and shopkeepers, even as he admitted that not all of the latter were Jewish and, more important, let slip the fact that the island's shopkeepers were themselves subject to the importers from whom they bought their merchandise, who would not accept payment in excessively depreciated coin.[14]

On balance, therefore, contemporary observers regarded Jamaica's Jews unfavorably, even if they conceded that some were honest individuals who were of decent character. A similarly complex picture emerges from their descriptions of attitudes toward the Jews among the black population. Knight reported that, because the Jews used false weights and measures (although he alleged that non-Jews did so too), the blacks despised them so thoroughly that, had they the power to do so, they would have expelled them from Jamaica. In Knight's words, "They have conceived so implacable a prejudice to the Jews, that were they not protected by our Laws, the Negroes would soon Root them out of the Island."[15] Long, on the other hand, recounted "a little anecdote" that evoked the possibility that a community of interest existed between the two groups. During the slave uprising of 1760, a leader of the rebellion awaiting trial attempted to suborn a

Jewish guard by arguing that Jews and slaves shared a common enemy:

> You Jews, said he, and our nation (meaning the Coromantins), ought to consider ourselves as one people. You differ from the rest of the Whites, and they hate you. Surely then it is best for us to join in one common interest, drive them out of the country, and hold possession of it to ourselves.

Long noted, as well, that slaves owned by Jews had more time to themselves than those owned by non-Jews. Christians annually gave their slaves approximately 86 days of free time, while the Jews gave theirs about 111, the difference arising from the Jews' practice of giving their slaves not only Sunday but all of Saturday, the Jewish Sabbath, off. Christian owners, in contrast, required their slaves to work a half-day on Saturday. The additional time meant, further, that slaves owned by Jews could earn more during their free time than those owned by Christians could: 11–2–0 as opposed to 8–12–0.[16]

The roster of anti-Jewish sentiment in Jamaica included the belief that Jews connived with slaves at illegal activity by encouraging them to steal from their masters. This view was well established by the beginning of the eighteenth century, for in 1700 the governor and Council could write that,

> It is likewise too plain that the meaner sort of that nation buy anything from our negroes, by which they encourage them to steal from their masters or any else, that they may sell it to the Jews . . . this trade being driven on most at night or Sundays, when people are at Church, and hereby the ignorance of the negroes gives advantage to the Jews to buy anything of them for much under its real worth, which the sooner sets them on to stealing more.[17]

The charge of collusion with larcenous slaves enjoyed a long life. To an unidentified Jamaican who attempted in 1738 to justify the imposition of discriminatory taxes on the Jewish population, "their way of business [includes the sale of] . . . provisions to the Negroes with whom they traffick for Commodities often stolen from their Masters." To Knight, it was "well known, that they Corrupt the Negroes, and Encourage them to Steal, by Receiving, Concealing, and Purchasing Stolen goods of them. . . ." Several decades later, Long wrote that "some Jews . . . [were] known to accumulate several casks of sugar in a year, purloined, in small quantities at a time, by the Negroes, who were handsomely rewarded for robbing their masters."[18]

The Jewish population came in for even more serious criticism during the Maroon uprising of the 1730s, when they were accused of selling powder to the blacks.[19] In 1733, the island's governor informed his superiors in London that a rebel courier named Quashee had entered Kingston and sought out "Jacob a Jew in Church Street" in order to obtain powder. Later investigation ascertained that it was not Quashee but an individual named Cuffee who contacted a Jew residing in Jew Alley, rather than in Church Street. The accusation persisted, so that in 1738 it could still be said that "they have even lain under great Suspicions of selling powder to the Negroes, by which means the Rebels have been supplied," but because testimony by blacks against whites was not admissible in court it was not easy to convict the alleged Jewish suppliers. Knight, adding arms to the powder, repeated the charge in the mid-1740s, although he later deleted it from his manuscript history of the colony when reminded that, after the uprising had ended, the leader of the rebellion denied having received any supplies from the Jews.[20]

During the 1730s, Jamaicans also voiced allegations that the Jewish population smuggled, an accusation that added the specter of criminality to crafty business techniques. "The Jews with us know very well how to land goods at our wharfes in the night time, without any Notice being taken of them," wrote the agent of the South Sea Company in 1737. A year later, in his justification of the discriminatory taxes imposed upon the Jewish population, the president of the colony's Council charged that most of the cocoa and indigo they imported from Hispaniola was smuggled by them in order to avoid payment of required duties.[21]

Finally, more traditional anti-Jewish ideas were also current in the colony, ones that were not rooted, as were most of the allegations made by Knight, Long, and other non-Jewish Jamaicans, in the economic and social circumstances peculiar to the colony. Ancient canards surfaced with vigor in 1750 when Abraham Sanches petitioned the Assembly for the right to vote on the grounds that he owned a large tract of land and that he had been naturalized. The Christian inhabitants of Kingston counterpetitioned that the Jews had "renounced their right of government to the governor, Pontius Pilate, in favour of the Roman emperors, in order to destroy, and put to the most cruel and ignominious death, Jesus Christ, the lord and saviour of mankind." And in another counterpetition, the Christian residents of the parish of St. Catherine alluded to yet another well-established charge: that Jews were not loyal to the societies in which they took up residence. They always remained aliens, antagonistic not only to Christianity but also to the law of the land. As the protestors wrote, "The Jews are a foreign nation . . . and pay no voluntary obedience to our laws; but, on the contrary, abhor both them and our religion. . . . To admit a nation, under such circumstances, to exercise a share in the legislature . . . might be destructive to our religion and constitution." So disturbing did several of Jamaica's Jews find these imputations of disloyalty that they felt compelled to respond:

> The petitioners, and the Jewish nation, are well known to profess no opinions destructive of civil society, or prejudicial to the constitution and laws of their country, and have ever manifested an unalterable attachment to the present happy establishment, under a protestant and most gracious prince, and shown a dutiful obedience to every act of government.

The legislature, it should be noted, rejected Sanches's petition, and Jamaica's Jewish population did not receive the right to vote until the early 1830s.[22]

Residing almost entirely in towns, few of Jamaica's Jews earned their livelihoods from plantation agriculture, the basis of the colony's importance as a sugar producer and the reason for the accumulation of extensive slaveholdings. In 1736, Benjamin Bravo estimated that there were approximately 15 Jewish plantations in a population of 700 to 800 Jewish inhabitants. Non-Jewish observers offered even smaller estimates. Richard Mill, president of the Council, reported in 1738 that the number of Jews who owned sugar plantations had never exceeded five or six. In the mid-1740s, James Knight wrote that "very few [of the Jews] have any Notion of Planting; so that they have not amongst them all more than Eight or ten Plantations, of which three or four are Sugar Works." Three or four sugar works represented less than 1 percent of Jamaica's sugar plantations, which in 1745 numbered 455.[23] And of the 1,671,569 acres across the island in 1754 on which quitrent payments to the Crown were required, roughly 1.5 percent belonged to Jewish landowners. Non-Jews with large holdings in 1754 far outnumbered Jewish ones; of those who owned plots of a thousand or more acres, 458 were non-Jewish and 5 were Jewish.[24]

While acquiring relatively little land in the countryside, Jamaica's Jews readily invested in urban real estate, acquiring many houses, stores, and vacant properties, a development that attracted the attention of contemporary observers.[25] From poll-tax records in which tenants can be matched to landlords, it appears that the Jewish inhabitants of the major towns owned approximately 20 percent of all lots: slightly more so in the case of Port Royal in 1740, and slightly less so in Kingston in 1745 and 1769 and in Spanish Town in 1772 (Table 3.1). Not counting the Jewish town of Joden Savane in Suriname, this might well prove to have been the highest rate of urban real estate ownership by Jews anywhere in the world at the time.[26] Jamaican non-Jews, as we have seen, viewed the situation with hostility, including it in their antagonistic evaluations of the Jewish population. Curiously, however, they did not fault Jewish landlords as rent gougers, but confined their critical judgments to the allegation that the Jews accumulated houses in order to cheat their creditors.

As town dwellers, most of the colony's Jewish inhabitants earned their livelihoods as merchants and shopkeepers. That was how they usually identified themselves in their wills, except for the few who

TABLE 3.1
Urban Real Estate Ownership in Jamaica*

| | Lots Owned by | | | | | | | |
| | Non-Jews | | Jews | | Public Bodies | | Religion Not Certain | |
	No.	%	No.	%	No.	%	No.	%
Port Royal, 1740	283	76.2	79	21.2	2	0.5	7	1.8
Kingston, 1745	739	77.8	175	18.4	0	0.0	35	3.6
Kingston, 1769+	1393	77.9	345	19.3	7	0.3	41	2.2
Spanish Town, 1772	185	78.0	45	18.9	2	0.8	5	2.0

*Lots for whom no owners were entered are not included in the totals here, viz., 2 in Port Royal; 97 in Kingston in 1745; 41 in Kingston in 1769-70; and 5 in Spanish Town.

+King Street, East Division, missing in the 1769 tax list, is derived from the 1770 tax list, for a total of 69 lots.

SOURCES: JA, 2/19/1 for Port Royal; 2/6/5 for Kingston, 1745; 2/6/5 for Kingston, 1769 and 1770; and 2/2/22 for Spanish Town, under the designation "Town Precinct."

called themselves craftsmen or planters.[27] That was how they portrayed themselves to the Crown in 1721, describing themselves as "for the most Part trading People, and great Promoters towards the Enlargement of Business, as may appear from the Increase thereof. . . ."* One observer specified in 1738 that "their way of business is chiefly in disposing of Dry Goods & in keeping of Shops, [and] in retailing out spirituous Lickors & provisions to the Negroes . . . ." In Kingston, Jewish businessmen in 1769 comprised about 20 percent of the town's merchants and on average paid about the same in trade taxes as the town's non-Jewish ones. Three years later in Spanish Town, Jewish shopkeepers amounted to approximately 44 percent of the town's businessmen, and they paid on average substantially more in trade taxes than their non-Jewish counterparts (Table

* Surviving records yield many indications that Jamaica's Jewish residents were economic leaders among the Jews of the western hemisphere during the eighteenth century, perhaps even surpassing Curaçao's large Jewish community. The degree to which they prospered, and the impact on London's Jewish community by Jews who moved there from Jamaica, are matters worthy of study. This comment does not necessarily mean that Jamaica's Jews had a profound impact on the general economy. There were many more non-Jewish merchants in the colony engaged in the same economic activities, as well as in other enterprises from which Jewish merchants were largely absent, notably slave factoring.

3.2). Spanish Town, according to Edward Long, had a section called "the Jew-market," where Jewish merchants sold a variety of provisions. Finally, Jewish merchants who resided outside Spanish Town, Kingston, and Port Royal inhabited country villages, as James Knight attested, where they kept shops that supplied the planters and their slaves.[28]

Not just shopkeepers who sold to the local market, some of Jamaica's Jewish businessmen functioned as merchants engaged in international commerce. The transactions conducted by Benjamin and Manasseh Pereira of Kingston in 1715 and by Diego and Abraham Gonzalez of Port Royal between 1719 and 1726 illustrate the range of merchandise with which they dealt and the extent of their transatlantic connections. The Pereiras imported flour and pork from New York and pipes of cocoa, the latter apparently from Curaçao. They transmitted "weighty Money," or bullion received from the Spanish colonies, to London. The Gonzalezes imported wooden staves, flour, bread, pork, and onions from New York and woolens from London. They exported woolens and flour to the Spanish empire, receiving

TABLE 3.2

Taxes on Trade

	Kingston 1769*	Spanish Town 1772
Non-Jews		
No. of Entries	205	50
Average Tax (£)	2.0	4.16
Jews		
No. of Entries	58	41
Average Tax (£)	2.01	5.60
Religion Not Certain		
No. Of Entries	4	2
Average Tax (£)	1.62	4.0

*Does not include King Street, East Division, missing in the 1769 tax list. Probable loss is fifteen entries (13 non-Jewish and 2 Jewish), the number of households and companies assessed for trade taxes there in 1770, but at a different rate than the previous year.

SOURCES: JA, 2/6/5 for Kingston, and 2/2/22 for Spanish Town, under the designation "Town Precinct."

silver in exchange. The bullion they obtained went to London, along with bills of exchange and exports of indigo.[29] Perhaps they acquired the latter from Moses Mendes, another Jewish resident of Kingston, who imported the dye from the island of Hispaniola during the 1720s.[30]

Jamaica's Jewish merchants, according to Richard Mill, continued to import small amounts of indigo as well as cocoa during the 1730s. They concentrated, however, on importing cloth from Jewish merchants in London for sale on the island or for export to the Spanish colonies, for as the colony's Assembly stated in 1741, "such of them as are engaged in trade, seldom import any but dry goods."[31] Woolens and linens of all kinds were the island's leading import from England, according to the colony's governor in 1730, who explained that commerce with the Spanish Coast accounted for the volume of such imports to Jamaica.[32] Five years after Governor Hunter had provided this information, William Wood, representing a group of ninety-two Jewish and non-Jewish merchants in London who petitioned the Crown against discriminatory measures imposed by Jamaica's legislature on the Jewish population, described the contribution by Jewish merchants in England and Jamaica to the British cloth trade:

> The Jews, here [at London], are almost the only persons that send any dry, fine goods to Jamaica, at their own risk, and on their own account, and the Jews, in Jamaica, the only persons almost that have any large quantities of all kind of goods lying in their houses, warehouses, or shops, for the supply of the inhabitants of the island, and for making proper sortments of goods for the Spaniards. . . . These are the reasons that induced so many Gentlemen, not Jews, to join in signing the petition with them, and in their behalf; for should the Jews, by any hardship, be discouraged from continuing to send such quantities of dry, fine goods to Jamaica, as they have generally done for a great number of years past, they would, proportionably, have their dealing with the Jews lessened, consequently be, greatly, sufferers by it . . . as well as the nation in general. . . .[33]

Ties to London's Jewish merchants were one of the advantages that gave Jewish merchants in Jamaica an edge, for membership in a transatlantic religious and ethnic network contributed to commercial success in the eighteenth-century trading world.[34] The experience of Port Royal's Diego and Abraham Gonzalez, father and son, is illustrative. The daughter of the one, hence the sister of the other, was married to Moses Lamego, who had gone to London "some time ago from this Island this being the Needful att presentt," as the Gonzalezes informed Nathan Simson in London during the summer of 1722. Six months later, they suggested to Simson that he send them woolens, then in great demand in the colony, but that he first confer with Lamego, "my Son and Brother," who could advise on "all the goods and Colours . . . proper for this Island." Diego Gonzalez, moreover, had a brother in Bayonne, further extending the family's commercial ties.[35] Nor were the Gonzalezes unusual. The wills of Jamaica's eighteenth-century Jews demonstrate that many who identified themselves as merchants had family ties not only in London but also in Amsterdam, Bordeaux, Bayonne, and even Leghorn.[36]

Facility with foreign languages also contributed to commercial success. In addition to English, Sephardic Jews all over the British empire used Portuguese and Spanish in commercial correspondence, in the synagogue, and on tombstones, and they taught the two languages to the next generation of Jewish merchants, bookkeepers, and clerks in the schools attached to the synagogue. On occasion, they served as official interpreters.[37]

Jamaica's Jews were no exception. James Knight claimed that they spoke no other language but Portuguese among themselves. They sometimes wrote their wills in Spanish and Portuguese, including Isaac De Mella, whose 1768 will, filed in both Portuguese and an English translation, reveals that adherence to the Iberian languages had more than commercial reasons behind it. De Mella left the rents from his houses in Kingston to his wife during her lifetime and to his niece thereafter, "until such time some one of my Nephews Sons to my Brothers and Sisters who reside in the Kingdom of Portugal or Spain shall come and Embrace Judaism," whereupon the niece was to share the inheritance with the refugees.[38] The advantage that their adeptness with other languages bestowed, together with their ties to Jews who resided in other locations, prompted Edward Long to comment that "their knowledge of foreign languages, and intercourse with their brethren, dispersed over the Spanish and other West-India colonies, have contributed greatly to extend the trade, and increase the wealth, of the island; for they have always been the chief importers of bullion."[39]

The bullion to which Long referred originated in trade with Spain's empire in America; and in Long's judgment the Jews who resided in Kingston dominated the Spanish trade.[40] Sources earlier in the century suggest, however, that the Spanish trade was hardly a Jewish preserve, for many non-Jewish merchants also participated in it. In 1713, 42 Jamaica merchants involved in commerce between the island and the Spanish colonies presented a petition to the government, but none of them was Jewish.[41] Between 1712 and 1715, of the 39 supercargoes and captains of vessels who traded between Jamaica and the Spanish empire, only 3 were Jewish.[42] And from September 29 to December 25, 1742, 28 of the 31 vessels that sailed from Jamaica to Spanish ports were owned by non-Jews and 3 by Jews.[43]

Despite their participation in international commerce, few of Jamaica's Jews owned vessels that went to sea. "Nor are they concerned in shipping," wrote Richard Mill, the Council's president in 1738, while an unidentified writer in the same year repeated that "they are concerned in no shipping." In 1741, the Assembly echoed both, when it declared that "the Jews . . . are not at all concerned in shipping."[44] In the absence of Naval Office listings of multiple owners, primary owners alone having been recorded, these comments by contemporaries suggest that Jews in Jamaica did not invest in ships as minor partners, or at least not to any significant degree.

The surviving records of the Naval Office in Jamaica indicate that a handful of the vessels that entered the colony's ports did, in fact, belong to Jewish owners, but because the number of such ships was so small the generalization made by Mill and the others has considerable merit. Early in the century, of the 57 vessels registered at the Naval Office as ships belonging to Kingston or Port Royal between April 2, 1703 and April 25, 1705, 53 (92.9 percent) belonged to non-Jewish owners. Two were owned by non-Jewish and Jewish partners, and only the remaining 2 were owned by Jews alone. A total of 99 individuals participated in the ownership of these vessels, of whom 4 (4 percent) were Jewish.[45] In the year between June 24, 1719 and June 25, 1720, of the 164 vessels that entered Jamaica at either Kingston or Port Royal, 3 (1.8 percent) were owned by Jews, and 140 (85.3 percent) by non-Jews. Owners' names were not listed for 20 of the remaining vessels (12.1 percent), while the religion of 1 whose name is known cannot be determined. Significantly, none of the 3 Jewish owners resided in Jamaica. Two were from New York, while the third was from London.[46]

In 1745, 6 out of 263 vessels that entered Jamaica's ports, or 2.2 percent, were owned by 5 Jewish individuals; 2 resided in Jamaica, 2 did not, while the place of residence of the fifth is not known.[47] Thereafter, the proportion of vessels entering Jamaica owned by Jews declined. In 1755, it stood at 1.2 percent (6 out of 484), at least 1 of which was not owned by a Jamaican Jew.[48] In 1765, fewer than 1 percent of the ships that entered Jamaica (6 out of 657) belonged to Jewish merchants. At least 2 of these vessels belonged to Jews who were not Jamaican.[49]

Records for the vessels that sailed from Jamaica confirm that the Jewish population's investment in shipping was quite small. In 1745, 2.7 percent (9 out of 333) of the vessels that departed from the colony were owned by Jews.[50] As with vessels entering in, the proportion owned thereafter by Jews declined. In 1755, it stood at 1 percent (5 out of 470).[51] In 1765, fewer than 1 percent (5 out of 620) belonged to Jewish merchants.[52]

Jamaica's demand for slaves was insatiable, and not just because of its importance as a sugar producer. The island functioned as the British empire's premiere transit point for slaves destined for the Spanish empire. Moreover, mortality among the slave population in the British Caribbean was high, while the reproductive rate was low. In a 1745 tract on slavery attributed to the governor of Jamaica, the author noted that "it is notorious that in most Plantations more [slaves] die than are born there." Much later in the century another observer asserted that, if any charge were to be directed against plantation owners, it would be their constant need to replenish their labor force with new imports from Africa in order to replace slaves who had perished, for "the natural encrease . . . in the sugar islands, is insufficient for this purpose."[53]

Jamaica's leading position as an importer of slaves had become apparent by the beginning of the eighteenth century. In 1708, in answer to a request by the British government for an estimate of the number of slaves annually required in the colonies, a group of merchants who traded with Africa put the number at 25,000 and placed Jamaica's needs far ahead of all the others. While Virginia and Maryland together required 4,000, the Carolinas and New York 1,000, Barbados 4,000, and the Leeward Islands another 4,000, Jamaica, they reported, required 12,000 slaves a year, some for the colony itself and the rest for transportation from Jamaica to the Spanish colonies.[54]

Figures supplied to Parliament at the end of the 1780s demonstrate that Jamaica's preeminence in slave importation continued after 1708. From the beginning of 1723 through the end of 1734, Jamaica reputedly imported 101,119 slaves, while Barbados received just under one-third that number, 33,344. In the three years encompassed by 1756–58, Jamaica imported 22,506 slaves, while Barbados received 6,556. In the nine-year period between 1764 and 1772, Jamaica's slave imports reached 58,430, while Barbados's stood at 37,574. Because of Jamaica's higher level of imports, and despite the outward flow arising from exports to Spain's colonies, more than half of all the slaves in 1789 in England's Caribbean colonies were to be found there. Of the estimated 461,684 slaves reported that year, 256,000 or 55.4 percent resided in Jamaica. Of the rest, 62,115 (13.4 percent) were in Barbados, and 143,569 (31 percent) were distributed among Britain's other possessions in the West Indies.[55]

Because many made their living in commerce, whether as shopkeepers, as merchants in international trade, or in a combination of the two, it would have been plausible for Jamaica's Jewish inhabitants to have participated extensively in the slave trade. Opportunities for enrichment ranged across its three distinct components: the importation of slaves from Africa; service as factors; and the export of slaves to other colonies in the Caribbean or on the American mainland.

Despite the obvious advantages, Jewish merchants, according to Jamaica's Assembly in 1741, played no role in the importation of slaves, while no more than five or six of them participated in the export side of the slave trade. For that matter, the lower house of the legislature added, no more than five or six owned plantations, the greatest employer of slaves in the colony. As the Assembly noted in 1741,

> The duty imposed by the Bill on the importation of negroes they are entirely free from, not one of them being concerned in any such importation, [and] not above five or six of them pay the duty on the exportation of negroes, and the planters among them do not exceed that number. . . . [56]

The surviving records of ships that entered into and cleared out of Jamaica compiled by the Naval Office at Jamaica permit assessment of the degree to which Jews participated in the slave trade as the owners of the ships that sailed to Africa, purchased slaves there, and then transported them to the colonies. A vital organ of the British government in each of its colonies, the Naval Office first began to function in 1676 in Barbados and in Jamaica, where the earliest surviving records date to 1680. The Office registered each vessel that entered in and cleared out, recording the date of entry and clearance, the name of the vessel, its master, tonnage, number of guns, number of sailors on board, where and when built, where registered, where bond was given, and the cargo on board. Most significant of all for the purpose here, the Naval Officers began to record the names of vessel owners between 1710 and 1720, doing so in Jamaica in 1719.[57]

Naval Office records for vessels that entered Jamaica survive for eighteen and a quarter years of the twenty-seven and a quarter-year period between September 1742 and December 1769, or for 66.9 percent of that time span. According to the information supplied to the British government in the late 1780s, the colony imported 204,233 slaves from the beginning of 1742 through the end of 1769.

The Naval Office lists account for 149,705 of those slaves, or 73.3 percent.[58] For the period under examination, therefore, it is possible to identify the owners of the vessels on which approximately 73 percent of the slaves, during slightly more than two-thirds of the years involved, reportedly arrived in the colony.

Of the 149,705 slaves recorded by the Naval Office, 148,725, or 99.3 percent, arrived in Jamaica on vessels owned by non-Jews. Slaves who arrived on vessels owned by Jews numbered 665, or less than 1 percent (four-tenths of 1 percent). Finally, 315 slaves, or again less than 1 percent (two-tenths of 1 percent), arrived on vessels whose owners' names were not recorded or whose religion is not certain.

Five Jewish individuals or firms owned the vessels that delivered the 665 slaves. Four did not reside in Jamaica. The earliest of these, Benjamin Massiah, brought 35 slaves to Jamaica late in 1753 on the *David*. Massiah's vessel was registered in Barbados, where, according to the engraving on his tombstone, he was a merchant.[59] The three remaining non-Jamaicans were all from Newport, Rhode Island, home of the largest number of slave-ship owners in any of Britain's thirteen mainland colonies. Naphtali Hart's *Camelion [sic]* delivered 55 slaves from Africa in mid-1755, and his *Osprey* brought 80 approximately ten years later, again from Africa.[60] In 1766, three ships belonging to Aaron Lopez, Newport's leading Jewish merchant, brought a total of 142 slaves from Africa on the *Spry*, the *Betty*, and the *Africa*. The *Africa* returned during the following year with 69 slaves. And in early 1767, the *Greyhound*, belonging to Moses Levy & Co., entered Jamaica with 84 slaves on board.[61]

The remaining shipowner, David Orobio Furtado, is the sole Jewish merchant of Jamaica who is known to have delivered slaves on his vessel, one of the few that was owned by Jamaican Jews. His cargo, however, did not originate in Africa. Furtado participated in the trade between Jamaica and the Spanish colonies. Late in 1742, his vessel, the *Abraham and Sarah*, returned from the Spanish Coast with two hundred unsold slaves and a load of unsold dry goods. Whether or not Furtado had been the original exporter of these slaves from Jamaica is not known; but he is known to have exported slaves from the colony to the Spanish Coast three years later.[62]

The fact that Jamaica's Jewish merchants did not venture to Africa to return with slaves mirrors their reluctance to become shipowners. But then, non-Jewish Jamaican shipowners also did not carry slaves from Africa. Edward Long succinctly summarized the situation when he wrote that "the Negroe slaves are purchased in Africa, by the British merchants. . . ."[63] That this was already long and well established by the 1740s, when the colony's Assembly stated that no Jewish individuals were involved in the importation of slaves, is evident from the records of the Naval Office. Almost all the 38 ships that delivered slaves to Jamaica between March 25, 1743 and March 25, 1744 were owned by English merchants. Fourteen vessels hailed from London, 10 from Liverpool, 6 from Bristol. Of the remainder, only 2 belonged to Jamaicans, while the home ports of 6 more were not listed. The 2 vessels owned by Jamaicans, not incidentally, did not bring slaves from Africa but, rather, returned with slaves that had been exported from the colony to South America, where they could not be sold.[64] Similarly, of the 42 vessels that delivered slaves from March 25, 1748 to March 24, 1749, 18 were from Liverpool and 17 from Bristol, while the home ports of 5 were not listed. One vessel, owned like the others by a non-Jewish firm, returned with slaves from the Spanish Coast, while the remaining ship had no named owner.[65] And between December 25, 1753 and March 25, 1754, 11 slave vessels arrived at Kingston and Port Royal, 5 of them from Liverpool, 4 from Bristol, and 2 from Newport, Rhode Island.[66]

Noninvolvement in the importation of slaves extended to service as factors, the merchants who received consignments of incoming slaves and arranged for their sale. Not serving in that capacity, Jamaica's Jewish merchants did not derive earnings from what was a major source of income for the eighteenth-century colonial merchant, for as Richard Sheridan has pointed out, "the dealers in slaves were the big businessmen in the colonies." Indeed, in the Kingston poll tax for 1769, Hibbert & Jackson, Kingston's largest factoring firm between 1764 and 1774, paid the town's highest tax on trade, £20, an amount twice as high as the next largest trade assessment.[67]

Contemporary observers of the Jews in eighteenth-century Jamaica who described their economic activities did not link them to the slave-factoring business. In the mid-1740s, James Knight, eminently informed about matters related to the slave trade because of his extensive experience as a slave factor, described them as shopkeepers in the countryside, warehouse owners in Kingston and Port Royal, and importers of goods supplied by the Jewish merchants of London.[68] Edward Long, whose account provides the most ample picture of all of life in eighteenth-century Jamaica, wrote that they had always been the island's leading bullion importers. Externally, they traded extensively with Spain's empire as well as with other Caribbean colonies, with Kingston's Jews predominating in the trade with the Spanish colonies. Within Jamaica, they continually bought and sold real estate and traded extensively with the black population, selling them mainly salted fish, butter, and inexpensive wares imported from Jewish manufacturers in England. The advantage they enjoyed in their contacts with the black population arose from the fact that the bustling markets at which slaves sold the produce they raised on their own account were held on Sundays, when Jewish merchants did not have to compete with their Christian counterparts.[69]

Few of the factors who operated in Jamaica prior to the middle of the century have been identified, but none of those who are known was Jewish, including the agents of the South Sea Company, who by the mid-1720s began to purchase slaves in Jamaica so that the Company could fulfill its obligations under the terms of the asiento, and beginning in 1730 from the London, Bristol, and Liverpool ships that transported slaves from Africa.[70] The Assembly's statement in 1741 that no Jews were involved in the importation of slaves may be regarded as encompassing factoring. The eleven firms that received 9,124 of the nearly 9,200 slaves imported between September 22, 1752 and December 22, 1753 all belonged to non-Jewish factors (Table 3.3). And in the 1750s and 1760s, no Jewish factors were to be found among the ten enterprises in Kingston that received slaves carried to Jamaica on ships owned by Bristol merchants. Bailey, Elworthy & Co.; Bright, Hall & Co.; Bright, Whatley & Co.; Du-Common & French; Edward & John Ford; Peter Furnell; Hibbert &

TABLE 3.3
Kingston's Slave Factors,
September 22, 1752–December 22, 1753

Firm	Consignments	No. of Slaves
Bailey, Elworthy & Co.	1	500
Bright, Whatley & Co.	2	479
Henry Levingston	3	278
Hibbert & Spriggs	15	3,401
John & Alexander Harveys	4	441
John & Edward Ford	1	170
Peter Furnell	5	1,148
Peter Woodhouse	1	36
Richards & Gordon	7	1,629
Watson, Swymmer & Co.	5	898
William Gordon	1	144
"Sundry Persons"		73

SOURCES: PRO, CO 142/16, 1–1a; and for numbers partially obliterated in the latter, CO 142/15, entries for September 29–December 25, 1753.

Jackson; Hibbert & Spriggs; Richards & Gordon; and Watson, Swymmer & Co. were the non-Jewish factors to whom the Bristol vessels made their deliveries at Kingston.[71]

Between 1767 and 1780, two of Jamaica's Jewish merchants are known to have functioned as slave factors, each, however, on a single occasion, while a third expressed interest but does not appear to have succeeded in doing so. The first, Abraham Pereira Mendes, was the son-in-law of Aaron Lopez, described before as Rhode Island's most important Jewish merchant. In 1767, Lopez sent him back to Jamaica from Newport with the hope that he would serve as his trading representative on the island, an aspiration that quickly proved beyond the young man's capabilities. Shortly after Mendes reached Kingston, he reported to his father-in-law that the *Africa,* one of Lopez's slave ships, had arrived in port before him, but that Captain Abraham All was having difficulty selling the slaves who were on board because of their condition. Mendes offered to take charge, but All declined, explaining that Mendes's proposal was contrary to his orders. Several weeks later, however, Captain All relented because he had to sail from Jamaica, leaving Mendes to try to sell the cargo.[72]

Four years after this episode, a second Jewish merchant in Jamaica,

Abraham Lopez of Savanna la Mar, who is not known to have been related to Aaron Lopez, offered the latter his services as a slave factor.[73] While expressing regret that Aaron Lopez had suffered setbacks owing to "the Bad state of Marketts on the Coast of Africa," he appears to have proposed to serve as the Newport merchant's slave factor, writing in April 1771 that "Should you Incline to Try ours [i.e., the Jamaica market], with respect to the sale of Cargoe Slaves That Your Utmost Expectations may be Answered Towards which I Can any ways Contribute I shall think myself Happy." A little more than a year later, short of capital because he had recently assembled a dowry for his eldest daughter, he declined the Newport merchant's invitation to join in a venture to Africa, but offered to serve as his factor. As the Jamaican Lopez wrote in June 1772,

> I have often Consulted Your Proposels relative to the Guinea [African] Concern. I own the Scheme laid down by you very good . . . but just now tis Entirely out of my Power to join you . . . . Should you proceed on your own bottom on that trade & choose to Consign them to my House on Commissions[,] depend on our using every Method in our power to render you Satisfactory Sales & Returns.[74]

Aaron Lopez, however, preferred to consign his cargoes of slaves to non-Jewish merchants. As of 1765, he dealt with Phillip Livingston, Jr., of Kingston for that purpose, directing two of his captains to deliver their African cargoes to him.[75] And late in 1772, only five months after Abraham Lopez had expressed his readiness to serve as his factor, Aaron Lopez bypassed him, instead ordering Captain William English of the *Ann* to deliver his cargo of slaves either to Mr. Thomas Dolbeare of Kingston or to Captain Benjamin Wright of Savanna la Mar—the very same place where Abraham Lopez resided and conducted his business. The *Ann* subsequently delivered its cargo of 104 slaves to Dolbeare at Kingston, but Wright, rather than Abraham Lopez, functioned on other occasions as Aaron Lopez's consignee at Savanna la Mar, located on Jamaica's southwestern coast.[76]

Aaron Lopez relied, as well, on his non-Jewish factors for intelligence regarding the market for slaves in Jamaica. "The planters here are much disgusted," Dolbeare informed him in October 1773, because the governments of England and Spain had reached an agreement fixing the price of slaves sold at Kingston to the Spanish at £60 apiece for five years. "Negroes continue in demand, the Spaniards are now here on purchase," he wrote in November. And the following month, Dolbeare conveyed the news that two ships had arrived from Africa laden with seven hundred slaves.[77]

In addition to Livingston and Dolbeare, the names of a number of other factors in Kingston during the 1760s and 1770s are known, and, with one exception, none was Jewish. Beans & Cuthbert, succeeded by Bean [sic] & Cuthbert; William Brown; William Boyd & Co.; Peats & Westmorland; John Westmorland & Co.; Edward Ford; William Dalhouse & Co.; Dick & Co.; Dick & Milligan; Smith, Leigh & Co.; Papley & Wade; Sydebotham & Perry; Watt & Allardyce; Winde & Allardyce; and Hibbert & Jackson: all these were non-Jewish firms that functioned alongside Phillip Livingston and Thomas Dolbeare.[78] The single Jewish factor was Abraham Aguilar, who did not operate alone but conducted business in partnership with one or more non-Jewish merchants in the firm of Coppells & Aguilar.[79]

Largest of all of Kingston's slave marketers was the non-Jewish firm of Hibbert & Jackson, which received and sold a total of 16,254 slaves between 1764 and 1774, an amount equivalent to 18.7 percent of all slaves reportedly delivered during that period. The scale of the firm's activity prompted a committee of the Assembly to describe it as one of the five "most considerable African factors residing in this island" during the even lengthier period between 1764 and 1788. To Peleg Clarke, a highly experienced ship's captain in the slave trade, the company was the "surest of any house here." Several members of the Hibbert family, which enjoyed a prominent position in London's merchant community, worked in Jamaica as factors. Thomas Hibbert was described after his death in 1791 as having been the " 'most eminent Guinea factor in Kingston' " for a period that had lasted forty or fifty years, a chronology borne out by the number of slaves received by Hibbert & Spriggs between September 1752 and December 1753 (Table 3.3). Two of his nephews were in partnership with him, and later became partners in Hibbert & Jackson.[80]

Hibbert enterprise extended to the northern side of the island, where the firm had an outlet in Montego Bay that sold slaves under the name of Barnard & Montague.[81] None of the other factors known to have functioned in Montego Bay was Jewish, where five or possibly six Jewish merchants resided according to a census conducted in 1774.[82] In 1775, the slave sellers operating there included a Mr. Clarke, who "Sells as many As any hous in the Island," a Mr. Jackson & Co., and a Mr. Moger, while notices in the town's newspaper at the end of 1776 and in early 1777 announced that new arrivals from Africa would be sold by the firms of William Brown, Malcolm & Nevinson, Parkinson & Hill, and "Hibberts, Bernards & Mountague."[83]

In summary, Jamaica's Jewish merchants participated to a negligible extent as factors in Jamaica before 1780. They may, however, have played a more significant part in one niche connected with slave imports from Africa, the purchase and sale of slaves who arrived in sickly condition, the so-called "refuse negroes," an activity that had drawn adverse attention to them in 1689. The evidence for this rests, however, on only one statement, one that is not to be found among the assessments of Jewish economic enterprise made by the likes of Richard Mill, the Jamaica Assembly, James Knight, or Edward Long. In a letter to a Bristol slaving firm in 1729, two non-Jewish factors in Kingston wrote that they had received a cargo of a hundred and fifty sickly slaves, few of whom the island's plantation owners would purchase. They had therefore sold two-thirds of them to the Jewish firm of Lamego & Furtado. As the factors, the firm of Tyndall & Assheton, wrote,

> They are the worst Cargoe of negroes [that] have been imported for severall Years past. . . . They were so badd Could not sell Tenn to the planters. We yesterday sold one hundred and five to Messrs. Lamego and Furtado, at eighteen pounds Ten shillings per head, Which Considering the Condition the Negroes were in, is the greatest price have

been given. The remainder are so very bad, Cannott gett £8 per head for them. Wee shall be oblig'd to sell them at Outcry for the most they will Yield.[84]

Perhaps the firm of Lamego & Furtado purchased sickly slaves for export to Spain's colonies, for merchants in Jamaica after 1730 purchased "refuse" slaves for that purpose.[85] Slaves had comprised part of the trade between the colony and the Spanish empire ever since the previous century. As one leading West Indian trader urged the Lords of Trade in 1703 (even as he apologized for his note's hastily scribbled condition), "I do humbly presume it might be worthy your Ldshps Consideration about the Conniving at a trade betwixt our People at Jamaica & the Spaniards; for we Exchange our Goods with 'em for nothing but Gold & Silver, & the Goods we traffick with are onely wearing Apparell & negros for their Mines."[86] Slave exports to the Spanish colonies continued thereafter, although they were not restricted to those destinations; many were also sent to Curaçao and to England's North American colonies.[87]

Jewish merchants are known to have participated in the export trade in slaves prior to 1741, the year in which the Assembly specified that five or six were engaged in it. In 1728, the South Sea Company, examining evidence against one of its agents who had been accused of privately trading with the Spanish, learned that he had done so in the early 1720s together with one Bravo, a Jewish merchant in Jamaica. Following the conclusion of one deal, Bravo "made him another proposel to be concernd in Negroes," but the agent rejected it as contrary to the interests of his employer.[88] And in 1736, the Company's agent in Jamaica, advising his employers in London that the export of slaves by private traders did not really amount to much, recounted that he had been "surprised to see a Jew one of the top supercargoes in the illicit trade for negroes, and dry goods" apply for and receive a reduction in his taxes on the grounds of poverty.[89]

Measuring the involvement of Jewish merchants in the export of slaves is possible for the period between September 1742 and December 1769, for Naval Office records for exports from the colony survive for nineteen of the twenty-seven and a quarter years, or 69.7

percent, of that time span. According to the data supplied to the British government during the late 1780s, the colony exported 35,191 slaves from the beginning of 1742 through the end of 1769. The Naval Office lists account for 25,728 of those slaves, or 73.1 percent.[90] For the period under examination, therefore, it is possible to identify the owners of the vessels on which 73 percent of the reported slaves, during approximately 70 percent of the years involved, were exported for sale.

Of the 25,728 slaves recorded by the Naval Office, 24,199, or 94 percent, departed from Jamaica on vessels owned by non-Jews. Slaves carried on vessels owned by Jews numbered 1,523, or 5.9 percent. Only 6 were carried on a vessel whose owner's religion is not known. Clearly, therefore, Jews in Jamaica participated in the slave trade before 1780 as exporters more than they did as importers or as factors, although the scale of their activity was dwarfed by that of non-Jewish exporters.

Jamaica's Assembly, it will be recalled, pegged the number of Jewish slave exporters in 1741 at five or six. During the 1740s, six Jewish individuals appear as such exporters in the records compiled by the Naval Office, four of whom for certain were inhabitants of Jamaica. A fifth resided in New York, while the residence of the sixth is not known.[91] The six are known to have exported 996 slaves on the vessels they owned, making the 1740s the high point, in absolute numbers as well as proportionally, of slave exports by Jewish merchants between 1742 and 1769 (Table 3.4).

Owning hardly any plantations, Jamaica's Jews consequently owned few of the island's slaves. Several poll-tax lists for the towns in which they resided permit guarded conclusions regarding the scope of their ownership of slaves in the colony during the eighteenth century.

Local parish taxes paid by the inhabitants of Jamaica were based on their holdings in real estate, cattle, carriages, merchandise in shops and warehouses—and slaves. The number of slaves that were owned was therefore included with each entry on the poll-tax lists. An entry is defined here as the equivalent of either a household, a business firm, the estate of a deceased individual, or the owner of a vacant lot.

TABLE 3.4
Jamaica's Known Slave Exports, 1742–69

	On Vessels Owned by Non-Jews		On Vessels Owned by Jews	
	No. of Slaves	Percent	No. of Slaves	Percent
9/29/1742– 6/25/1749	9,799	90.7	996	9.2
12/25/1751– 6/25/1757	6,219	98.9	68	1.0
12/25/1761– 12/29/1769*	8,181	94.6	459	5.3

*Six slaves on a vessel whose owner's religious identity is not known have been added to the grand total that is the basis for computing the percentages reported for this period.

NOTE: For all Jewish exporters and their individual totals, see Appendix IV, Table 3.

SOURCES: PRO, CO 142/15, 142/16, 142/17, 142/18, passim.

In some instances, a family or a company appears more than once in the same tax list but has been counted each time in the analysis here as a separate entry, because of the possibility that more than one individual had the same name.

Identifying the Jewish entries on the tax lists is possible because of the distinctive family names of the largely Sephardic Jewish population of mid-eighteenth-century Jamaica. Wills, tombstones, naturalization records, and personal correspondence provide additional identifications, and assist as well in determining that in a few cases individuals with names that appear to have been Jewish were, in fact, Christian. In addition to categorizing entries as non-Jewish or Jewish, entries whose religious affiliation cannot be determined with certainty have been placed in a separate category.[92]

More problematic than determining the religious identities of entries is whether or not the people whom the entries represent reported all the slaves they owned to the tax assessors. Late in the century, a committee of the Assembly indicated that it was customary in many parishes to exempt the owners of fewer than seven slaves from the assessment on slaves, and, further, that many individuals misrepresented the number of slaves they possessed.[93] On the other hand, in its highly critical statements in 1741 about the Jewish population,

Jamaica's Assembly did not include underreporting the number of slaves they owned among their many faults, which is of pertinence to two of the tax lists examined here, Port Royal's in 1740 and Kingston's in 1745. Then too, in 1745, Jamaica's governor, the apparent author of a tract on slavery, does not appear to have questioned the accuracy of the tax records compiled five years before, when he cited them to estimate that the colony's slave population was ten times larger than the number of its white inhabitants.[94] Edward Long utilized the tax lists to calculate the colony's entire slave population in 1768 but, of significance because of his general reliability, did not question their completeness. This consideration is relevant to the other two tax lists analyzed here, Kingston's in 1769 and Spanish Town's in 1772.[95] The issue, however, remains an open one, and therefore requires guarded acceptance of the results. The qualification that the latter are based on *reported* numbers of slaves in the poll-tax records must prevail.

Port Royal in 1740 provides the earliest known tax list in the eighteenth century for a town with Jewish inhabitants. They numbered 29 entries, or 9.7 percent, and held nearly the same proportion of the reported slave population: 9.5 percent (Table 3.5). The non-Jewish population amounted to 87.5 percent of the entries, and owned 89.2 percent of all reported slaves. Port Royal's non-Jewish slaveowners owned only slightly more on the average than the Jewish ones did, the former holding 9.2 each, the latter 9.0. Each group was about as likely as the other to own slaves, for 52.8 percent (137 out of 259) of non-Jewish entrants did, compared with 51.7 percent (15 out of 29) of Jewish entrants.

Five years later in Kingston, site of the colony's largest Jewish community, the Jewish inhabitants there comprised approximately 17.4 percent of all entries on the tax list for that year, and held nearly the same proportion of all reported slaves: 18 percent (Table 3.6). The non-Jewish population amounted to 76.5 percent of all entries, and owned 78.9 percent of all reported slaves. Both groups, therefore, appear to have owned approximately the same proportion of slaves as their respective proportions in the town's white popula-

TABLE 3.5
Ownership of Slaves in Port Royal, 1740

Poll-tax Entries:	Total: 296	
Non-Jewish:	No.	%
Slaveowners	137	46.2
Non-Slaveowners	122	41.2
Jewish:		
Slaveowners	15	5.0
Non-Slaveowners	14	4.7
Religion Not Certain:		
Slaveowners	3	1.0
Non-Slaveowners	2	0.6
Public Bodies:		
Slaveowners	0	0.0
Non-Slaveowners	3	1.0
Slaveownership:	Total: 1,427*	
Owned by:		
Non-Jews	1,273	89.2
Jews	136	9.5
Religion Not Certain	18	1.2
Average Number of Slaves:		
Non-Jews	9.2	
Jews	9.0	
Religion Not Certain	6.0	

*Number of slaves held by two non-Jewish owners missing from poll-tax list.

NOTE: For Jewish inhabitants and for those whose religion is not certain, see Appendix V, Table 2.

SOURCE: JA, 2/19/1, Port Royal poll-tax list for 1740.

tion, insofar as those proportions are reflected as entries on the poll-tax list.

Two other comparisons, however, yield a more complex picture. In one, the data for 1745 suggest that Kingston's Jews were more likely to own slaves than the town's non-Jews, for 82.9 percent of the Jewish entrants owned slaves (156 out of 188), while 73.3 percent

TABLE 3.6
Ownership of Slaves in Kingston, 1745 and 1769

Poll-tax Entries:	1745 Total: 1,075		1769* Total: 1,389	
Non-Jewish:	No.	%	No.	%
Slaveowners	604	56.1	518	37.2
Non-Slaveowners	220	20.4	630	45.3
Jewish:				
Slaveowners	156	14.5	95	6.8
Non-Slaveowners	32	2.9	102	7.3
Joint Ownership:				
Partnerships	1	—	0	0.0
Religion Not Certain:				
Slaveowners	40	3.7	9	0.6
Non-Slaveowners	22	2.0	35	2.5
Slaveownership:	Total: 7,740		Total: 5,721	
Owned by:				
Non-Jews	6,111	78.9	4,602	80.4
Jews	1,397	18.0	1,045	18.2
Jointly	0	0.0	0	0.0
Religion Not Certain	232	2.9	74	1.2
Average Number of Slaves:				
Non-Jews	10.1		8.8	
Jews	8.9		11.0	
Religion Not Certain	5.8		8.2	

*King Street, East Division, mutilated in the 1769 tax list, is derived from the 1770 tax list, for a total of 168 slaves.

NOTE: For Jewish entries and for entries whose religion is not certain, see Appendix VI, Tables 1 and 2.

SOURCES: JA, 2/6/1 for 1745, and 2/6/5 for 1769 and 1770.

of the non-Jewish entrants did (604 out of 824). In the second comparison, on the other hand, non-Jewish entrants owned more slaves on the average, 10.1 each, while Jewish entrants averaged 8.9.

Between 1745 and 1769, slaveholding among the Jews of Kingston appears to have increased. In 1769, Jews in the town's population comprised 14.1 percent of all entries on the tax list for that year, but owned 18.2 percent of all slaves reported for the town (Table 3.6).

1. The Jewish town of Joden Savane in Suriname. Established in 1682, the settlement at its height had fifty to sixty families, each reportedly owning four to six slaves. Its brick synagogue was thirty-three feet high, ninety feet long, and forty feet wide. With the decline of Suriname's Jewish population in the eighteenth century, much of Joden Savane lay abandoned. In 1788, twenty-two impoverished families remained. *Publications of the American Jewish Historical Society* 9 (1901). Courtesy of the American Jewish Historical Society.

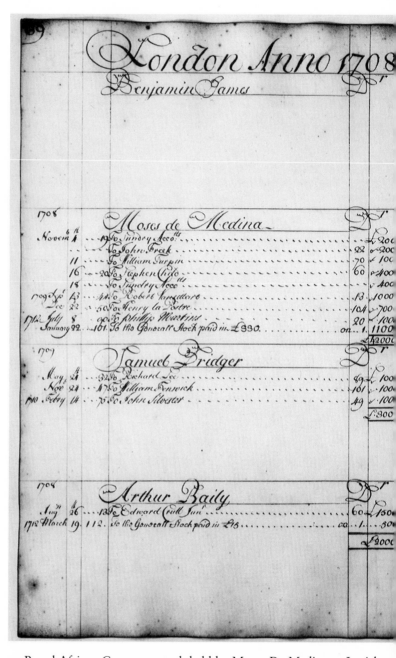

2. Royal African Company stock held by Moses De Medina, a Jewish shareholder, and by three non-Jewish shareholders. Entries on the right list the value of the shares held by each at the beginning of May 1708, followed by subsequent stock purchases. Entries on the left list sales, and conclude with the value of shares owned by each at the

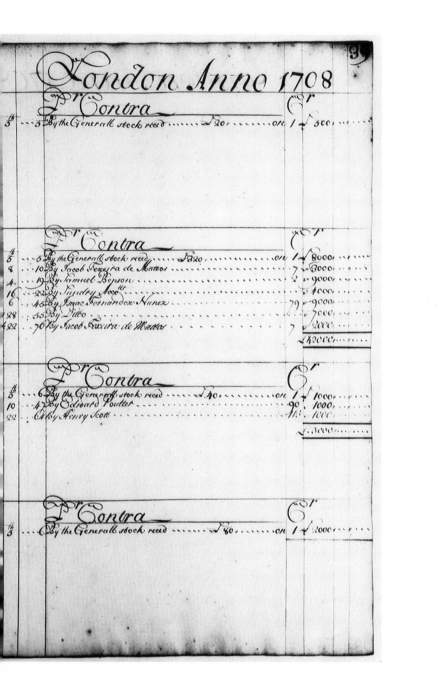

London Anno 1708

beginning of 1713. De Medina and other Jewish investors comprised a small minority of the Company's stockholders. PRO, T 70/196. Reproduced by permission of the Public Record Office, Kew.

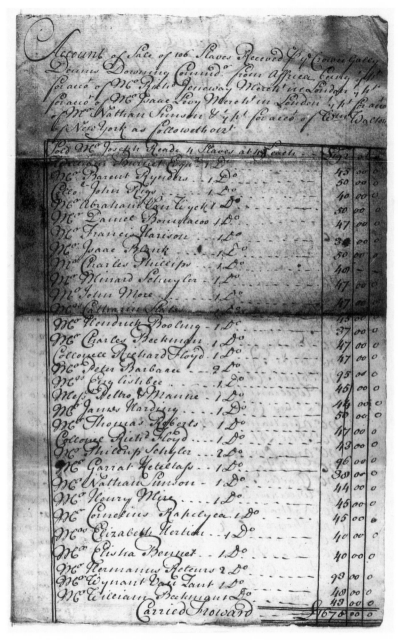

3. Purchasers of slaves imported on the *Crown Galley* and sold in New York in 1721. The vessel, owned in partnership by two non-Jewish merchants and two Jewish merchants, was one of the small number of ventures in which Jewish inhabitants of the British empire participated in the slave trade from Africa. PRO, C 104/13, Part 2. Reproduced by permission of the Public Record Office, Kew.

4. Moses Levy (1665–1728), a Jewish merchant in New York. Despite his widely-ranging commercial ventures in the Caribbean, Levy imported few slaves from the islands. Courtesy of the Museum of the City of New York. Artist unknown. Bequest of Alphonse H. Kunsheedt.

IT is agreed between the Mafter, Seamen and Mariners of the *Brigantine Africa* whereof *Abraham All* is Mafter, now bound from the Port of *Newport, Rhode-Ifland*, to *the Coaft of Africa* and from thence to *Rhode Ifland*

THAT in Confideration of the Monthly or other Wages, againft each refpective Seaman and Mariner's Name hereunder fet, they feverally fhall and will perform the abovementioned Voyage. And the faid Mafter doth hereby agree with, and hire the faid Seamen and Mariners for the faid Voyage, at fuch Monthly Wages, to be paid purfuant to the Laws of *Great-Britain*. And they the faid Seamen and Mariners doth hereby promife and oblige themfelves to do their Duty, and obey the lawful Commands of their Officers on board the faid *Brig* or the Boats thereunto belonging, as becomes good and faithful Seamen and Mariners: And at all Places where the faid *Brig* fhall put in, or anchor at, during the faid Voyage, to do their beft Endeavours for the Prefervation of the faid *Brig* and Cargo, and do not refufe nor neglect their Duty by Day or Night, nor go out of the faid *Brig* on board any other Veffel, or on Shore, under any Pretence whatfoever, without Leave firft obtained of the Captain or Commanding Officer on board: That in Default thereof, they will not only be liable to the Penalties mentioned in an Act of Parliament made in the Second Year of the Reign of King *GEORGE* the Second, entituled, " *An Act for the better Regulation and Government of Seamen in the Merchants Service,*" but will further, in Cafe they fhould on any Account whatfoever, leave or defert the faid *Brig* without the Mafter's Confent, 'till the abovementioned Voyage be ended, and the *Brig* difcharged of her Loading, be liable to forfeit and lofe what Wages may at each Time of their Defertion be due to them, together with every their Goods, Chattles, &c. on board, renouncing by thefe Prefents, all Title, Right, Demand and Pretenfion thereunto forever, for them, their Heirs, Executors, and Adminiftrators. And it is further agreed by both Parties, that Forty-eight Hours Abfence, without Leave, fhall be deemed a total Defertion, and render fuch Seamen and Mariners liable to the Penalties abovementioned: That each and every lawful Command, which the faid Mafter fhall think neceffary hereafter to iffue, for the effectual Government of the faid Veffel, fuppreffing Immorality and Vice of all Kinds, be ftrictly complied with, under Penalty of the Perfon or Perfons difobeying, forfeiting his or their whole Wages, or Hire, together with every Thing belonging to him or them on board the faid Veffel. And it is further agreed on, That no Officer nor Seaman belonging to the faid *Brig* fhall demand, or be entitled to his Wages, or any Part thereof, until the Arrival of the faid *Brig* from the abovementioned Port of Difcharge. That each Seaman and Mariner, who fhall well and truly perform the abovementioned Voyage (provided always that there be no Plunderage, Embezzlement, or other unlawful Acts committed on the faid Veffel's Cargo, or Stores) be entitled to the Wages or Hire that may become due to him, purfuant to this Agreement. That for the due Performance of each and every of the abovementioned Articles, Agreements, and Acknowledgements of their being voluntary, and without Compulfion, or any clandeftine Means being ufed, agreed to, and figned by us. IN TESTIMONY whereof, we have each and every of us under affixed our Hands, the Month and Day againft our Names affixed, in the Year of our Lord One Thoufand Seven Hundred and Sixty Six

Time of Entry.	MEN's NAMES.	Quality.	Wages per Month	Advance Wages before failing.	Wages taken on the Voyage.	Whole Wages.	Wages due.
1766					When difcharged		
Aug 22	Abraham All	Mafter	£60	60	1768 Jan 15 £1008		£948
Octor 6th	Thomas Briggs	Chief Mate	60	74. 10	1768 Jany 15 918		243. 10
13	John Fox	2d Do	70	80	1768 in Jany		
Sept 30	George Hearper	Seaman	50	107. 8	1767 Aug 20		
Do	Robert Jersey	Do	50	68. 10	not returned		
Octor 9	William Salisbury	Do	56	227. 18			30. 10
15	James Willson	Do	50	434. 12 1767 June 30		192. 12. 6
Octor 21	Ceafar Bannister	Do	50	50			705. 12. 6
				802. 18			92. 18. 4
1767 Nov 15	Benmin Lambeth	Do	50 Jannuary		1768 Jan 15		96. 5
28	Richard Gray	Do	56 Do		1768 Jan 15		78. 15
Decr 30	Thomas Odell	Do	50 Do		1768 Jan 15		113. 10
Nov 15	James Milley	Do	50 Do		1768 Jan 15	Charged Brig £3110. 13. 4	

N.B. If any Demands are made by the Hands not returned in ye Brig. ye Owners then to be charged if paid

I acknowledge the above to be an exact copy of the Brig Africa dodge Bull

Abrm All Jun

Printed and fold by *Samuel Hall*, in *Newport*.

5. Crew of the *Africa*, captained by Abraham All, Jr., which sailed from Newport for the African coast in October 1766 and arrived in Jamaica in January 1768. The vessel belonged to Aaron Lopez and his father-in-law, Jacob Rodrigues Rivera. Aaron Lopez Papers. Courtesy of the American Jewish Historical Society.

6. Jacob Rodriguez Rivera (1717–1789). Rivera inaugurated participation by Newport's Jewish merchants in the African slave trade in 1753, when he joined in partnership with one of the town's prominent non-Jewish merchants in a venture to Africa. All told, Jewish merchants in Newport participated in approximately 3.6 percent of the slaving voyages to Africa known to have been launched by Rhode Island's inhabitants. Courtesy of the Redwood Library and Athenaeum, Newport, Rhode Island. Attributed to Gilbert Stuart.

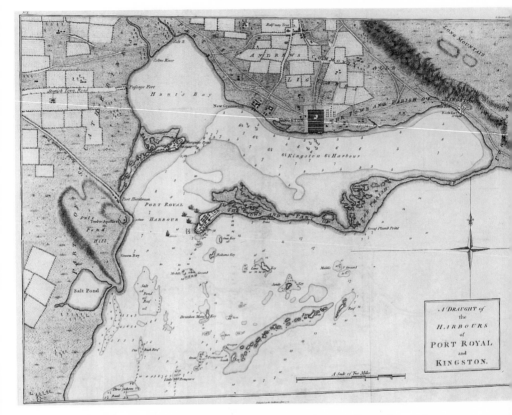

7. Port Royal and Kingston in 1774. Although a small number of Jews remained at Port Royal after the great earthquake of 1692, most of Jamaica's Jewish inhabitants settled in Kingston, site of the British empire's largest Jewish community outside London during the eighteenth century. The Jewish population resided primarily in the town's southwestern section. The colony's oldest Jewish cemetery, dating to 1672, was located on Hunt's Bay. Courtesy of Rare Books Division, The New York Public Library, Astor, Lenox and Tilden Foundations.

Kingſton, March 29, 1786.

FOR SALE,

ON BOARD THE

SHIP ELLIOT,

Captain *John Clemenſon*,

From WHYDAW,

On *Monday*, the 17th *April*.

898 Choice Gold Coaſt, Whydaw, Logos and Benin

SLAVES,

By ALEXANDRE LINDO,

8. Handbill advertising the sale of a large consignment of slaves received by Alexandre Lindo, one of Kingston's leading slave factors during the 1780s. The sole Jewish slave factor of note in the British empire, Lindo remained active during the following decade, most of the time in partnership with a non-Jewish factor, Richard Lake. JTB Photo. Courtesy of the National Library of Jamaica, Kingston.

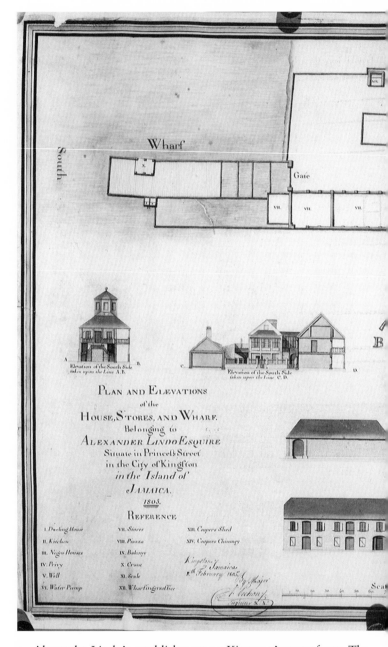

9. Alexandre Lindo's establishment on Kingston's waterfront. The size of the living quarters, warehouses, wharf, and other structures underscores Lindo's position as Kingston's leading Jewish mer-

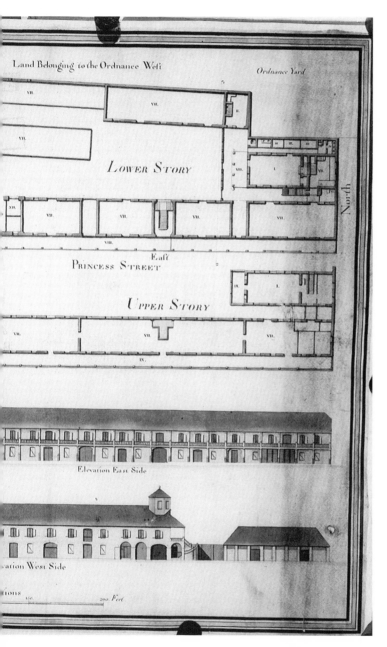

Land Belonging to the Ordnance West
Ordnance Yard

LOWER STORY

North

VII.
VII.
II.
VII.
I.
VI.
XII.
VII.
VII.
VII.
VII.
VIII.

East
PRINCESS STREET

UPPER STORY

IX.
I.
VII.
VII.
VII.
IX.

Elevation East Side

Elevation West Side

ions

200. Feet

chant at the end of the eighteenth century. PRO, MPH 512. Reproduced by permission of the Public Record Office, Kew.

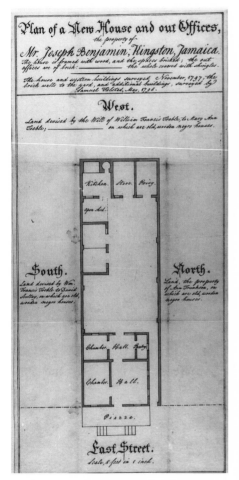

10. *Left:* Plan of the home and office belonging to Joseph Benjamin of Kingston in 1797. Smaller by far and therefore more typical of housing and working quarters in Kingston than Alexandre Lindo's establishment (previous illustration), Benjamin's property dramatizes Lindo's success. Benjamin, whose religion is not known, owned three slaves in 1795 according to Kingston's poll tax list for that year. PRO, C 114/40. Reproduced by permission of the Public Record Office, Kew.

11. *Below:* Abraham Rodrigues Brandon (1766–1831). A resident of Barbados, Brandon owned 168 slaves in 1817, the largest number held by any of the colony's Jews. Cumulatively, however, the island's Jewish population owned less than 1 percent of its slaves. Courtesy of the Museum of the City of New York. Painted by John Wesley Jarvis. Gift of Julian Charles Levy.

Non-Jewish entries amounted to 82.6 percent of all entries, and owned 80.4 percent of the reported slaves. In 1745, the Jewish population had owned almost exactly the same proportion of the town's slaves as their proportion among entries for the white population, the difference between the former proportion and the latter being less than 1 percent (six-tenths of 1 percent). In 1769, however, the difference between the two proportions had widened to 4.1 percent. Moreover, the average holding among Jewish entrants, 11 slaves per slaveholding entry, had not only increased since 1745 but was also now larger than the 8.8 average per slaveholding entry of the town's non-Jewish residents, thereby reversing the results for 1745. Finally, Jews in Kingston in 1769 were still more likely to own slaves than non-Jews, although by a smaller margin than had been the case in 1745. In 1769, 45.1 percent of the non-Jewish entrants (518 out of 1,148) owned slaves, while 48.2 percent (95 out of 197) of the Jewish entrants did. The spread between the two groups in 1745 had been on the order of 9.6 percent, but by 1769 it had diminished to a difference of 3.1 percent.

Three years later in nearby Spanish Town, slaveholding patterns differed from those evident in Kingston in 1769. In 1772, the Jewish inhabitants of Spanish Town comprised 17.3 percent of all entries on that year's tax list, but they held 10.7 percent of all reported slaves. The non-Jewish population equalled 81.2 percent of all entries, and held 89 percent of all slaves (Table 3.7). By every other measure, too, Spanish Town's non-Jews were more visible as slaveholders than the town's Jewish population. Whereas 83.4 percent of the non-Jewish entries on 1772's tax list (297 out of 356) owned slaves, each holding an average of 13.7 slaves, 60.5 percent of the Jewish entries (46 out of 76) had slaves, each with an average of 10.7 slaves.

Combining the figures for Kingston in 1769 and Spanish Town in 1772 yields a total of 1,540 reported slaves owned by the members of the two largest Jewish communities in Jamaica around the year 1770. According to Edward Long, the total slave population of Jamaica in 1768 stood at 166,904.[96] If Long's total—based on the tax lists whose accuracy he did not question—was more or less correct,

TABLE 3.7
Ownership of Slaves in Spanish Town, 1772

Poll-tax Entries:		Total: 438	
Non-Jewish:	No.		%
Slaveowners	297		67.8
Non-Slaveowners	59		13.4
Jewish:			
Slaveowners	46		10.5
Non-Slaveowners	30		6.8
Religion Not Certain:			
Slaveowners	5		1.1
Non-Slaveowners	1		0.2
Slaveownership:		Total: 4,602	
Owned by:			
Non-Jews	4,096		89.0
Jews	495		10.7
Religion Not Certain	11		0.2
Average Number of Slaves:			
Non-Jews		13.7	
Jews		10.7	
Religion Not Certain		2.2	

NOTE: For Jewish entries and for entries whose religion is not certain, see Appendix VII, Table 1.

SOURCE: JA, 2/2/22; entries for Spanish Town in 1772 appear under the designation "Town Precinct."

then the reported slaves possessed by the Jewish inhabitants of Kingston and Spanish Town would have amounted to less than 1 percent of the island's slave population (nine-tenths of 1 percent).

Slaves owned by Jews elsewhere in Jamaica could not have significantly altered this percentage, for few of the colony's Jews resided outside Kingston and Spanish Town and even fewer engaged in plantation agriculture. Port Royal still had a small Jewish population, but, as revealed by its poll tax in 1740 and Kingston's in 1745, the number of Jews there was markedly smaller than Kingston's already before the middle of the century; and there is no reason to expect anything but stasis or even further decline thereafter.[97] Small numbers were scattered about in other locations, in some of the towns and hamlets in the predominantly agricultural parishes. In addition to Abraham Lopez, encountered before as offering to serve as Aaron Lopez's factor, a few resided in Savanna la Mar in the parish of Westmoreland, as well as in Lucea in the parish of Hanover, both of which had synagogues in the 1760s. The hamlet of The Cross in the parish of Clarendon contained around ten houses in the late 1760s, most of them inhabited by Jews and mulattoes. And in Lacovia, a hamlet in the interior of the parish of St. Elizabeth, between twelve and fourteen houses were to be found at the same date, occupied mostly by Jewish inhabitants.[98]

By the early 1770s, a small number of Jews also resided in the town of Montego Bay, St. James Parish, drawn to it as it developed into the island's leading port on the northern coast and a harbor for the delivery of slaves from Africa.[99] At least six Jewish households were to be found there in 1774 according to a census conducted that year. Two were headed by merchants and three by shopkeepers, while the remaining one consisted of several orphans whose father had been a merchant. (A seventh possibly Jewish family was headed by a shopkeeper and held nine slaves.) In all, the six families owned forty-six slaves.[100] None, as we have seen, are known to have been slave factors, despite their careers as merchants and shopkeepers.

The 46 slaves owned by Montego Bay's Jewish families amounted to less than 1 percent (two-tenths of 1 percent) of the 16,656 slaves in the parish of St. James. Not unexpectedly, 12,557 of these slaves, or 75.3 percent, belonged to the owners of the parish's seventy-four sugar plantations, all of which were owned by non-Jews. An additional 3,044 slaves, or 18.2 percent, belonged to individuals who, in the social categories delineated by the census, stood "next in degree to sugar Planters," namely the "Smaller Settlers" who were the "[owners of] Pens, Coffee planters, [and] Jobbers, Millwrights, Carpenters, Masons & such like." Here too, none was Jewish. At the bottom of the parish's social hierarchy, labeled a "third degree of setlers" and lumped together under the designation "Housekeepers," stood those who resided in Montego Bay. Ninety-one householders with slaves, including the six aforementioned Jewish householders, were in this category, with such occupational designations as merchant, shopkeeper, wharfinger, blacksmith, carpenter, fisherman, doctor, and schoolmaster. This group owned a total of 1,055 slaves, or 6.3 percent of the parish's slave population.[101]

The six Jewish households in Montego Bay owned proportionally fewer of the town's slaves than their fellow townsmen. Comprising 6.5 percent of all households with slaves, they owned 4.3 percent of its enslaved population (46 out of 1,055). If the additional householder whose religion is uncertain is included among the Jewish households, the pattern remains unchanged: seven households, or 7.6 percent of all households with slaves, owning 5.2 percent (55 out of 1,055) of all slaves.[102]

The census of 1774 for the parish of St. James underscores the impact that plantation agriculture had on the size of slaveholdings. Because they did not engage in agriculture, Jewish residents of the parish owned a small fragment of its slave population. As shopkeepers and merchants, the occupations followed by most of Jamaica's eighteenth-century Jewish inhabitants, the Jews of Montego Bay in the mid-1770s exemplify why the colony's Jewish population did not participate in the ownership of slaves to any great extent. Coupled with their minute role as factors and the small part they contributed to the measurable dimensions of the export trade, it is impossible to argue that they dominated the institution of slavery in Jamaica, Britain's possession in the West Indies with the greatest number of slaves and the largest number of Jewish inhabitants.

CHAPTER 4

Jews and Slavery in Barbados and Nevis, 1700–80

Considerably less information is available for the Jewish population of Barbados in the eighteenth century than for Jamaica's. Nevertheless, Naval Office records, while sparser, do permit measurement of the extent of Jewish involvement in the import and export of slaves. A slave-tax list for 1729 documents the ownership of slaves in the parish in which the majority of the island's Jewish population resided. Finally, a report from the colony's governor to his superiors in England in 1727, a set of Treasury Office accounts, and records of slave deliveries by vessels from Bristol reveal the extent to which Jews served as factors.

In 1715, Barbados's Jewish inhabitants numbered between 52 and 92 households, with a population of between 228 and 336 individuals.[1] The Jewish population did not grow in any sustained fashion during subsequent decades; near the end of the century, the community's records listed only 44 "Yahidims," or members, while another 16 subsisted as pensioners supported by them.[2] Frequent disasters undoubtedly contributed to the community's eighteenth-century stagnation. Fires ravaged Bridgetown in 1756 and 1758. The great conflagration on the night of May 14, 1766 that consumed two-thirds of Bridgetown destroyed part of Swan Street, known also as Jew Street because of the Jewish population's concentration there. Fourteen years later, the great Caribbean hurricane of October 1780 devastated the island, compelling contemporary observers to doubt whether the colony would ever regain its former prosperity and wealth.[3]

Barbados's Jews resided in two of the colony's four towns, primarily in Bridgetown, the island's capital and commercial center, but also in Speightstown, which in 1710 reportedly had a population of 20 Jewish families out of the town's 125. As in Bridgetown, Speightstown's Jews were assessed separately from the non-Jewish population for tax purposes, and, again as in Bridgetown, Speightstown had a thoroughfare called Jew Street.[4] In 1739, Speightstown's non-Jewish inhabitants violently expelled the town's Jewish residents and destroyed their synagogue, in retaliation for an attack by several Jewish townspeople on a non-Jewish youth accused of theft.[5] At some later date, however, a Jewish presence again took hold at Speightstown, for when the colony's legislature imposed a tax in 1756 on the inhabitants of the island's towns, it levied a separate tax on the Jewish population there as well as in Bridgetown:

> And to the end that the Nation or People called *Jews,* dwelling in this Island, may also bear a just proportion . . . [they shall] pay . . . the sum of two hundred and ten pounds current money of this Island, that is to say, the *Jews* dwelling in *Bridge*-Town, shall pay the sum of one hundred and ninety; and the *Jews* dwelling in *Speight's*-Town, the sum of twenty pounds, over and above their Levies on Negroes, Mills, Kilns, and Houses. . . .[6]

Concentrated in the island's towns, Barbados's Jews earned their livelihoods as merchants and shopkeepers and, according to a visitor from New Jersey in 1741, "carry on a great trade."[7] Few, however, owned vessels that went to sea, mirroring patterns visible among the Jewish merchants of Jamaica. Surviving Naval Office records reveal that the overwhelming majority of the ships that entered and left Barbados belonged to non-Jews. Between March 25, 1718 and June 25, 1721, of 1,483 ships entering in and then clearing out, 1,458, or 98.3 percent, were owned by non-Jews (Table 4.1). Thirteen vessels, or less than 1 percent (eight-tenths of 1 percent), were owned by Jewish individuals, while an additional 12 vessels were owned by

TABLE 4.1
Ownership of Vessels Entering and Leaving Barbados, 1718–21

	No. of Vessels Owned by		
	Non-Jews	Jews	Jewish/Non-Jewish Partners
3/25/1718–6/24/1718	272	4	1
6/24/1718–9/29/1718	249	3	3
6/25/1719–9/25/1719*	88	2	1
9/25/1719–12/25/1719*	102	0	0
12/25/1719–3/25/1720	128	0	1
3/25/1720–6/25/1720*	157	0	1
6/25/1720–9/25/1720*	101	1	1
9/25/1720–12/25/1720*	111	1	1
12/25/1720–3/25/1721*	148	1	1
3/25/1721–6/25/1721*	102	1	2

*Other vessels also entered in or cleared out, but either insufficient data were listed for them or they were already listed in previous quarters.

SOURCE: PRO, CO 33/15.

combinations of Jewish and non-Jewish partners. The majority of the Jewish individuals involved, however, did not reside in Barbados.[8]

In subsequent years, even fewer of the vessels that docked at Barbados were owned by Jewish businessmen. Between March 25, 1735 and March 25, 1736, not a single vessel that arrived in the colony belonged to a Jewish merchant. Of the 345 that entered during that period, 344, or 99.7 percent, were owned by non-Jews. In the remaining case, the Naval Office did not record the name of the owner.[9] Later in the century, of 424 vessels that arrived in Barbados between January 1, 1774 and January 5, 1775, 420, or 99 percent, were owned by non-Jews. Two Jewish merchants were listed as owners in the remaining four instances, but both resided in Newport, Rhode Island.[10]

Almost entirely uninvolved in the ownership of maritime transport, Barbados's Jewish merchants played no part in the importation of slaves from Africa. While Naval Office records are thinner than for Jamaica, those that have survived do not provide any indication that Barbados's Jewish population had a hand in conveying slaves to the colony. In the sporadic returns that survive for the period between 1728 and 1780, 32,952 slave imports are recorded, of which 32,892, or 99.8 percent, arrived in Barbados on vessels owned by non-Jews. The remaining 60 slaves arrived on a ship owned by three partners, one of whom was not Jewish while the religion of the other two is not entirely certain.[11]

The colony's Jewish merchants played practically no part as slave factors, to judge from the rich documentation available for this aspect of the slave trade for the years between 1698 and 1739. Of 80,715 slaves delivered to the colony during that period, Jewish factors took consignment of 769, or less than 1 percent (nine-tenths of 1 percent).

The twelve firms that were the consignees of 14,562 slaves brought to Barbados between June 24, 1698 and 1707 included Isaac and Moses Mendes, who took delivery of 522, or 3.5 percent. Non-Jewish factors received the remainder, or 96.4 percent, and operated in most cases on a grander scale. Eight firms received larger shipments, ranging from 563 to 5,982, the latter being the number of slaves consigned to the firm of Bate & Steward by the Royal African Company. The eight also included John Grove, who received 1,362 slaves but refused to divulge his sales because he was a Quaker. The three remaining factoring operations handled consignments smaller than those delivered to Isaac and Moses Mendes, ranging in size from 173 to 226.[12]

In 1727, Barbados's governor provided his superiors in London with a compilation of all slave shipments to the colony between January 1713 and September 16, 1726, including in it the names of the factors who received them.[13] According to the governor's data, 46,004 slaves were delivered during that period, with non-Jewish consignees receiving 45,765, or 99.4 percent. The remaining 239, or less than 1 percent (one-half of 1 percent), were consigned to Mordecai Burgos, one of Bridgetown's Jewish residents. Burgos took delivery in two shipments, one of 151 slaves consigned to "Burges & Co.," and a second shipment of 88 slaves consigned to "Mordica Burgess." And while Burgos exceeded many others in the scope of his activity, such factors as Robert Harper, Thomas Harper, William Raymond, William Roberts, and Thomas Withers far surpassed his, dealing in thousands of slaves (Table 4.2).[14]

Finally, reports of the bonds posted in the colony's Treasury Office by factors for slave imports are available for the period between August 13, 1728 and December 13, 1739, save for three of those eleven and a third years.[15] These indicate that of the 20,149 slaves brought to Barbados during that period, only 8 were consigned to a Jewish factor, Abraham De Leon (Table 4.2).

Slave factoring was clearly not an economic activity in which Barbados's Jewish merchants played anything other than a minuscule role during the first forty years of the eighteenth century. Nor is there evidence that they became more active in it after 1740. Twelve business enterprises in the colony are known to have received consignments of slaves on vessels from Bristol between 1746 and 1780, but none belonged to Jewish merchants.[16] In the absence of Jewish factors, Aaron Lopez of Newport, Rhode Island, dealt with Daniel & Lytcott, one of the dozen non-Jewish firms, just as he relied on non-Jewish factors in Jamaica. In sailing orders in July 1770 to the master of the *Cleopatra,* bound for Africa, Lopez directed Captain Nathaniel Briggs to convey the slaves he acquired to Barbados, there to "value yourself on a good & safe house . . . [and to obtain] the best Terms[;] & we would Only mention that the House of Messrs. Daniel and Lyscott *[sic]* are warranted us at Philadelphia . . . we would choose to give that house the preference." Daniel & Lytcott subsequently informed Lopez in February 1771 that they had received Briggs's delivery, writing that it had "given us great pleasure to have disposed of his Cargo of Slaves . . . [although] we had neither profit nor loss in the Sale of them. . . ."[17]

As for the export of slaves, the third leg of the commerce in slavery, Barbados's Jewish merchants are not known, save for a single instance, to have participated in it any more than they did in the importation of slaves from Africa. While not as important an

TABLE 4.2
Barbados's Factors, 1713–39

| | No. of Slaves Imported | |
	1713–26	1728–39
Allen, William	98	
Alleyne, William	186	
Ball, Joseph		2
Baynes, Charles	104	
Bloome, William	1	
Blower & Cogan		313
Brown, Christopher		10
Burges & Co.	151	
Burgess, Mordica	88	
Butcher, William	161	
Byrch, Joshua	829	
Carney, Thomas & Co.	107	
Carter, Edwin	149	
Chearlney, Edward	104	
Cogan, John	5	
Cogan, William	503	
Colleton, John	161	
Corris, W. & Co.	13	
Crimble, Murray		201
Crocker, Benjamin	1	
Crowe, James	50	
Crump & Co.		804
Crump, Isaac	598	
Crump, Isaac & Co.	750	
Crump & Hasell	472	380
Curtis, Benjamin	1,070	
Curtis, Messr. & Co.	90	
Davies, John	130	
Day, William		2
De Leon, Abraham		8
Denney, John	94	
Dottin, Joseph	110	
Duez, Samuel	2	
Dundass, Alexander	219	
Fairchild, John		11
Fairchild, Jno.		66
Fenn, James	110	
Ferryman, John	67	
Fowler, Philip		2
Fowles, Joseph	109	
Frankland, William	100	
Freelove, Francis	1	
Freeman, Thomas	103	

	No. of Slaves Imported	
	1713–26	*1728–39*
Game, Samuel	127	
Gohair, James	614	
Greaves, Daniel	138	
Green, Thomas	242	
Haggatt, Othniel	118	
Hall, Benjamin		126
Hall, Hugh	176	
Hall, John	103	
Harper, Bleney	3	
Harper, Bleney & Co.		2,451
Harper, Messrs. & Co.	77	
Harper, Robert	2,317	
Harper, Robert & Co.	165	
Harper, Thomas	2,231	
Harper, Thomas & Co.	314	
Harper & Moore		1,981
Harris, Rice	11	
Harrison, Thomas	711	
Harthorpe, Robert		2
Hasell, James	252	
Hasell, James & Co.	1,046	
Haskins, William		3
Hill, Thomas	129	
Hole, Benjamin	204	
Hole, Henry	220	
Horsebrough, Alexander	90	
Howse, George	703	24
Jackson, Thomas	69	
Jasell, Samuel	89	
Johnson, Patrick		10
Jones, James & Co.		277
Jordan, Edward	370	
Kennedy, Oliver	72	
Lake, Thomas	189	37
Lake & Co.		290
Lascelles, George	222	
Lascelles, Henry	879	
Lawrence, Henry	231	
Levett, John		3
Lillington, George	121	
Lindal, Caleb	232	
Lochman, Otto Leonard	1	
Lynch, Anthony		23
Maddox, John	9	
Maxwell, George		1

TABLE 4.2 (*Continued*)

	No. of Slaves Imported	
	1713–26	*1728–39*
Maxwell, Robert		110
Merideth, Richard	30	
Minvielle, David		402
Molyneux, Richard	152	
Moore, Robert	82	
Moore, William	393	
Moore, William & Co.	141	
Morecroft, Richard	148	4,530
Morris, Thomas & Co.		137
Morris & Co.	6	924
Morris & Harper	294	
Neale, Thomas	205	
Newton, Henry	113	
Newton, Thomas	110	55
Peers, Col, & Co.	160	
Pemberton, James		133
Perrie, Samuel	5	
Ramsay, William	7	
Raymond, William	3,382	
Raymond, William & Co.	1,433	
Roberts, William	808	
Roberts, William & Co.	2,073	
Roberts & Co.	112	
Robertson, Robert	29	
Rowe, John	1	
Rowe, Thomas	7	
Ruddock, John	236	
Ruddock, Noblet		401
Ruddock & Co.		250
Salmon, Joseph	178	
Salmon, Samuel	395	250
Salmon & Co.		14
Salmon & Harris		75
Shaw, Thomas	311	
Shurland, John	809	
Shurland, John & Co.	151	
Shurland & Salmon		432
Sieuzae, John	329	
Sims, William		143
Stanford, John	80	
Stocker, Dedleston		120
Tarlton, John	288	
Thomas & Sterling		400
Thompson, Patrick	573	
Tuder, Thomas	110	

	No. of Slaves Imported	
	1713–26	*1728–39*
Wadsworth, John	861	
Ward, Thomas	335	
Warner, Henry	127	
Webb, Nathaniel	95	
Webster, William	1	45
Werden, William	6	
Whitesides, William	132	
Withers, James	153	
Withers, Thomas	2,451	
Withers, Thomas & Co.	5,292	
Withers & Co.		3,538
Withers & Harrison	154	1,163
Woodbridge, Dudley	3,786	
Worrell, Richard	167	
Young, Joseph	82	
Totals	46,004	20,149

SOURCES: PRO, CO 28/18, 321–25, for January 1713–September, 1726; CO 28/22, 26–28, 31–33, and 45–46, for November 27, 1728–February 27, 1729, May 26–November 26, 1729, and February 27–May 17, 1730; CO 28/25, 136b–137 and 139b–140, for June 13–September 13, and September 13–December 13, 1739; CO 33/30, for August 13–November 27, 1728; and Elizabeth Donnan, ed., *Documents Illustrative of the History of the Slave Trade to America,* 4 vols. (Washington, D.C.: Carnegie Institution of Washington, 1930–35), II, 427–31, for December 1, 1730–June 3, 1737.

exporting island as Jamaica, slaves were transported from Barbados to other British islands in the Caribbean, to British North America, to the Dutch possessions of Suriname, Curaçao, and St. Eustatius, and to Caracas and Demerara in South America.[18] Exports recorded by the Naval Office survive for almost twelve of the fifty-one and a half years between June 25, 1728 and January 1, 1780, or for approximately 23 percent of that period of time. Imprecise postings by the clerks of the Naval Office make calculation of the exact number of slaves exported during those years impossible, but the total fell somewhere between 7,600 and 9,500 slaves. None, however, was shipped out of Barbados on a vessel owned either outright or in partnership with other venturers by a Jewish individual.

Examination of surviving Naval Office lists for other colonies reveals only one instance in which a Jewish merchant from Barbados exported slaves. As described previously, Benjamin Massiah shipped thirty-five slaves on his vessel, the *David,* to Jamaica in 1753.[19]

For the most part shopkeepers and merchants who dwelled in towns, the Jews of Barbados undoubtedly owned few of the colony's slaves. Poll-tax records for the eighteenth century incorporating slave numbers, however, are not available for Barbados, precluding the kind of analysis of slaveownership that is possible for Jamaica.[20] There exists, on the other hand, a list compiled in 1729 of the men and women who came forward as required by law to report how many slaves they owned for tax purposes.[21] To avoid the levy on slaves, the overwhelming majority of the islanders failed to register their holdings, a problem about which the colony's governor alerted London.[22] In St. Michael, on the other hand, where most of the colony's Jewish population resided in Bridgetown, slightly more than three-quarters of the parish's Jewish slaveowners complied with the requirement to register slaveholdings, thereby permitting some reckoning of the extent of slaveownership among the colony's Jewish inhabitants.

St. Michael's slaveholders, both those who reported and those who did not, numbered 938 in 1729. Of these, 870, or 92.7 percent, were not Jewish; 66, or 7 percent, were Jewish; and the religious identities of two, or less than 1 percent (two-tenths of 1 percent), are not certain (Table 4.3). Failure to report their holdings was far more in evidence among the non-Jews, for 85.1 percent of the 870 Christians

TABLE 4.3
Slaveowners in the Parish of St. Michael, 1729

	Reporting—No. of Slaves		Not Reporting
Non-Jewish	129	1,723	741
Jewish	51	402	15
Religion Not Certain	1	2	1
Totals	181	2,127	757

For the names of all Jewish owners (reporting and non-reporting) and for those whose religion is uncertain, see Appendix XI.

SOURCE: PRO, CO 28/21, 104–9, 165–209.

neglected to register their slaves, while 22.7 percent of the 66 Jews did not do so.[23]

The 181 who complied with the requirement to register their holdings owned a total of 2,127 slaves. Of these, 1,723 of the registered slaves, or 81 percent, belonged to the non-Jews of St. Michael who reported their holdings, each owning an average of 13.3 slaves. The parish's 51 Jews who registered their slaves owned 402, or 18.8 percent of the registered slaves, and an average of 7.8 each.

The evidence that is available suggests, therefore, that slaveownership was much more apparent in 1729 among St. Michael's non-Jewish inhabitants than among its Jews. In addition to the disparity in the average number owned, a far smaller portion of the parish's non-Jews—14.8 percent—reported their slaves but owned most of the reported slaves: 81 percent of them. In contrast, 77.2 percent of the Jewish slaveholders reported, but held 18.8 percent of all reported slaves.

Because most of the colony's Jewish population resided in Bridgetown, the returns for St. Michael account for most of the slaveowners of Barbados in 1729 who were Jewish. Among the much smaller group of Jews residing at Speightstown in the parish of St. Peter, only six Jewish slaveowners were to be found; but the number they owned went unreported, as did the slaves owned by 262 of the parish's non-Jewish slaveholders.[24] Finally, the 402 slaves reported by St. Michael's Jews amounted to less than 1 percent (eight-tenths of 1 percent) of the island's entire slave population, which in 1734 numbered 46,362, as the colony's governor reported to London that year.[25]

If Barbados's Jewish population showed little sign of expansion over the course of the eighteenth century, Nevis's at first grew slightly but then faltered and failed. Six Jewish households were on the island in 1708, numbering about 17 whites out of 1,104 white persons throughout the colony, or approximately 1.5 percent. They owned 46 slaves out of a total of 3,676, or 1.2 percent, therefore owning slaves in the same proportion of all slaves as their own in the white population.[26] By 1724, approximately 75 Jewish individuals resided in the colony's single town, but decline set in at some point thereafter.

The last known Jewish interment occurred in 1768, and after a hurricane in 1772 no further trace of a Jewish presence on the island was to be found. This pattern mirrored that of the white non-Jewish population, which also rose between 1708 and 1720 but then declined steadily thereafter, falling by 1775 to approximately a level last seen in 1708.[27]

Two of the island's six Jewish householders in 1708, Solomon Israel and Isaac Pinheiro, are known to have invested in agriculture, for Israel was referred to in court documents as a planter, while Pinheiro in his will bequeathed "a Certain plantation or parcell of Land" to his sons. Israel and Pinheiro, however, were also merchants. Pinheiro identified Israel that way in his will, while his wife, Esther Pinheiro, identified her husband as a merchant after his death in 1710 in New York, where he had perished far from home with "Divers goods, Merchandizes, wares, ready monies, [and] Debts due by bond" in his possession.[28]

Commerce, predictably, proved to be the primary activity of Nevis's small Jewish population. Esther Pinheiro, for one, became a merchant after her husband's death. Between 1720 and 1728, she owned the *Samuel,* the *Abigail,* the *William* in partnership with a non-Jewish merchant in Boston, and the *Esther* in partnership with non-Jewish merchants in Boston and Nevis. Her ships, according to the small colony's surviving Naval Office records, ranged over the Atlantic from Nevis to Barbados, Boston, Rhode Island, Madeira, and London.[29]

Esther Pinheiro was hardly alone in her commercial activity. The minister of the colony's town wrote in 1724 that, although the planters approved of Nevis's Jews, the competition they represented rendered them undesirable to its non-Jewish merchants and shopkeepers. As he attested, the Jews were "very acceptable to the Country Part of the Island, but are far from being so by the Town, by whom they are charged with taking the Bread out of the Christians' mouths." Their economic activity, he went on to report, was among the reasons invoked by many to explain the island's declining condition.[30]

Despite their involvement in commerce, Nevis's Jewish population did not function as slave factors during the 1720s, the apparent

TABLE 4.4
Factors in the Leeward Islands,
1720–26

	No. of Slaves Imported
Nevis:	
Baker, Roger	47
Baker, Roger & Co.	276
Curwin, Christopher	20
Emma, James	174
Lady, Thomas	114
Morton, John	129
Rogerson, John	21
Ruddock & Harris, Messrs.	85
Tarlton, Capt. Thomas	202
Woodley, John	199
Antigua:	
Baker, —	129
Baker, Capt. Henry	132
Barbottain, John & John Green	242
Barbottain, John, John Green & others	272
Burke, John & Ambrose Lynch	176
Byam, Governor Edward & others	70
Byam, George	226
Chester, Edward, Jr.	658
Green, John & others	205
Griffith, Capt. William	78
Kerby, Thomas, Esq.	1,729
Kerby, Thomas, John Burke & John Tomlinson	180
Tarleton, Capt. Thomas	180
Thomas, Messr. George & William	355
Montserrat:	
Baker, William & Robert Henvill	209
French, Martin	112
Goold, Patrick & Robert Sherrett	100
Webb, Nathaniel	1,355

TABLE 4.4 (Continued)

	No. of Slaves Imported
St. Christopher:	
Gallaway, Nichs.	207
Helden, John	312
Henvill, Robert	134
Henvill & Webb	1,137
Hill, Thomas	471
Hone, Timothy	174
Morey, Thomas	210
Ottley, Drewry	492
Pilkenton, Thomas	272
Roach, Andrew	113
Sherreld, George	156
Stear, James	32
Tarleton, Thomas	253
Ware, Timo, Esq.	200
Willett, John, Esq.	1,054
Withard, Stephen	170

SOURCE: PRO, CO 152/15, 332, 333, 390, 391b.

height of their presence in the colony. Nine individuals and firms are known to have done so; none was Jewish. Nor, incidentally, were any of the factors in the neighboring islands of Antigua, Montserrat, and St. Christopher, which, with Nevis, belonged to the Leeward Islands group. (Table 4.4)

In conclusion, therefore, Jews in the eastern reaches of the Caribbean during the eighteenth century showed almost no inclination toward involvement in the slave trade. With no role in the importation of slaves from Africa, almost none in the export trade from Barbados, and a minute one as factors, their part was even smaller than that played by Jamaica's Jews. And like their contemporaries in Jamaica, settlement in towns rather than on plantations kept the ownership of slaves among them to very small percentages and averages.

CHAPTER 5

Jews and Slaves on the Threshold of Abolition: Jamaica and Barbados, 1780–1820

The forty-year period between 1780 and 1820 was one of momentous change in Britain's Caribbean colonies. Growing sentiment in England against the African slave trade culminated in its termination in 1807 by an act of Parliament. In the years that followed, opinion in Britain against the existence of slavery built inexorably, leading to its abolition in 1834, again by Parliamentary action. The antislavery movement led as well to the enactment of laws in the colonies requiring the registration of all slaves on a triennial basis, a census that permits accurate measurement of the extent to which the Jewish populations of Jamaica and Barbados owned slaves in the waning years of the institution's existence in the British empire.[1]

Internally, Jamaica's Jewish community grew more complex during this period. Overwhelmingly Sephardic since its inception in the 1660s, few Ashkenazim settled in the colony prior to 1780, perhaps sparing it from the conflicts that usually engulfed relations between the two branches of the Jewish people when they encountered each other. However, Ashkenazic immigration increased after 1780, leading to the creation of separate communities and synagogues. In Kingston an Ashkenazic congregation coalesced in 1787, and it dedicated its own house of worship in 1789. In Spanish Town, Ashkenazim established their own congregation in 1790 and constructed a synagogue six years later.[2]

In nearby Port Royal, on the other hand, no separate Ashkenazic presence developed. As earlier in the eighteenth century, the Jewish communities of Kingston and Spanish Town far outshadowed whatever small Jewish presence remained there between 1780 and 1820.[3] Indeed, when Port Royal's synagogue burned down in 1815 during a general conflagration that engulfed the town, there were serious doubts whether it would ever be rebuilt, as a bequest by Ellis Wolfe, grateful to the congregation for the assistance it gave him at the time of his marriage, reveals.[4] Wolfe, an Ashkenazic individual who resided in England when he composed his last will and testament more than a year after the fire, left the sum of £500 to rebuild the town's Sephardic synagogue in the event of its reconstruction. That, in fact, never transpired; and Port Royal's last Jewish inhabitants disappeared from that locality during the course of the nineteenth century.[5]

Despite the development of an Ashkenazic community in Spanish Town during the 1790s, the Jewish population there declined markedly from what it once had been. In 1772, 76 entries for the capital's Jewish inhabitants appeared on the poll-tax list for that year, but almost half a century later less than half that number did, for the tax list for the parish of St. Catherine in 1820 contained just 32 entries that were definitively Jewish.[6]

For Kingston, a more complicated pattern is evident. The number of entries there on the poll-tax list of 1769 for people who were clearly Jewish had amounted to 197, but in 1795, a quarter of a century later, the number of such entries stood at 167, a decline of about 15 percent.[7] Unsettled economic conditions in the Caribbean traceable to the American Revolution, to natural disasters in the early 1780s, and to the conflict between England and France in the wake of the French Revolution induced some of Jamaica's Jews to emigrate.[8] But with the passage of another quarter-century, Kingston more than regained the Jewish population it had lost. Jewish entries on the city's poll-tax list for 1819 rose to 212, an increase of almost 27 percent since 1795.[9]

Kingston's and Spanish Town's Jewish inhabitants continued to pursue livelihoods as shopkeepers and international merchants. In 1795, Kingston's Jewish businessmen paid one-sixth of the trade

TABLE 5.1
Slaves and Trade Taxes: Kingston, 1795

	Slaves		Trade Tax	
	No.	%	£	%
Entries:				
Non-Jewish	4,928	83.4	1,158–7–0	82.3
Jewish	908	15.3	234–3–15	16.6
Religion Not Certain	71	1.2	13–15–0	0.9
Total	5,907	99.9	1,406–6–3	99.8

SOURCE: JA, 2/6/105, poll tax for 1795. For Jewish entries and for entries whose religion is not certain, see Appendix VI, Table 3.

taxes assessed that year (Table 5.1). A quarter of a century later, in 1819, they paid virtually the same percentage of the town's trade taxes—16.5 percent worth—and accounted for 20.5 percent of all the entries on which trade taxes were assessed.[10] The latter figure was almost the same as exactly half a century before, when approximately 20 percent of all the entries paying trade taxes had been Jewish, indicating that the balance between Jewish and non-Jewish merchants and shopkeepers in Kingston did not change between 1769 and 1819.[11] It did, however, in Spanish Town. In 1820, approximately 54 percent of all entries that were assessed trade taxes were Jewish, up from about 44 percent in 1772.[12]

Kingston's Jewish businessmen in the early nineteenth century attracted the attention of Bernard Martin Senior, a military officer who resided in Jamaica between 1815 and 1835. Senior observed that the "members of the Jewish persuasion are unusually numerous in Kingston." Many of its Jewish merchants were "not only wealthy, but highly respected members of society," who surpassed their non-Jewish counterparts in "taste, splendour, ingenuity, and management." To be sure, "a christian certainly must be clever to make *an advantageous dealing with a Jew*," yet non-Jews, he indicated in more positive terms, "will find the liberal and gentlemanly feeling predominate during the intercourse." Senior reported that, in international commerce, Jewish firms handled most of the colony's Spanish trade, but that some traded extensively as well with the United

States.[13] As shopkeepers, Jews and Christians coexisted on Port Royal Street in the city's commercial district (Kingston was incorporated as a city at the beginning of 1803), where visitors from the Spanish Main conducted most of their business. At the bottom of the commercial hierarchy, the peddlers who thronged the streets of Kingston's commercial district near the harbor, imploring passersby to purchase their goods, were "hawkers, principally of the Jewish tribe," who sold merchandise usually acquired at the sale of property belonging to insolvent debtors.[14]

Outside Kingston and Spanish Town, small numbers of Jewish inhabitants pursued careers as merchants and shopkeepers in several of the towns located in the colony's agricultural parishes. Some are known from the records of Kingston's Sephardic and Ashkenazic synagogues, others from their tombstones or their wills, and still others from the first triennial slave census in 1817.[15] From London, the firm of Moses Levy Newton corresponded for many years with Solomon Arnold at Falmouth and with Samuel Solomon at Montego Bay.[16] At the latter, nine Jewish merchants were among the fifty-seven businessmen who paid trade taxes assessed by the parish of St. James in 1817.[17] Overall, however, most of the colony's Jewish inhabitants resided in Kingston; as Bernard Martin Senior commented, "in people of this persuasion, Kingston abounds. . . ."[18]

In Barbados, the other English possession in the Caribbean with a Jewish presence, a much smaller Jewish population, described in 1789 by an observer as comprising less than one-twentieth of the colony's white population and owning less than 1 percent of its property, concentrated in a single location. Bridgetown was the only place on the island where Jews resided, according to an officer of the community in 1811, who fixed their number at " 'about 100,' " which meant that they comprised less than 1 percent of the colony's white population.[19] The figure of 100 may have been somewhat on the low side, for, a year before, 43 rate payers, most of them probably heads of households, had appeared on the *finta* list, the annual communal assessment imposed by Sephardic communities on their members, and an additional 7 individuals had received communal funds as pensioners. Whatever the population's precise size, the community was in a permanent state of decline; and successive *fintas* foreshadowed its gradual disappearance during the course of the nineteenth century. In 1798, 44 were listed; in 1810, 43; in 1815, 38; and in 1818, 35.[20]

Although Bernard Martin Senior characterized the Jewish merchants of Kingston as a prosperous group when he encountered them after 1815, the period under examination here did not begin auspiciously for them, nor for Jews elsewhere in Jamaica or at Barbados. The hostilities that commenced in 1776 between England and her North American colonies engendered severe economic dislocation throughout the Caribbean. American privateers prowled the Caribbean, inflicting losses on British shipping. Sugar exports to London fell sharply. In Jamaica, supplies and staples necessary for maintaining the colony's plantations could not be imported from the rebellious American colonies, nor could Jamaica, in turn, sustain the export of molasses to North America, its largest market for that commodity.[21] Slave shipments from Africa to the Caribbean declined dramatically, as vessels clearing England for Africa fell from 152 in 1775, to 101 in 1776, 58 in 1777, 41 in 1778, and 28 in 1779.[22] In Barbados, slave imports recorded by the Naval Office plummeted from 1,035 in 1775 to 312 in 1777 and to none in 1779.[23] In Jamaica, slave imports fell from 18,400 in 1776, to 5,607 in 1777, 5,191 in 1778, 3,343 in 1779, before bottoming out at 3,267 in 1780.[24] Slave exports from the port of Kingston likewise collapsed; the average declined from 2,581 per year between 1774 and 1776 to an average of 330 per year between 1777 and 1781.[25]

Hard on the heels of war, nature heaped her own afflictions upon the Caribbean during the early 1780s. The great hurricane of October 1780 devastated Barbados, killing more than 4,300 people before moving on to strike elsewhere, punching its way as far as Jamaica.[26] A second hurricane struck Jamaica less than a year later. From Kingston, David Pereira Mendes wrote to Aaron Lopez in Massachusetts in the summer of 1781 describing an island that was reeling from both war and natural disaster:

This land is farr from being exempt of troubles, we suffer much by a total Stagnation of Trade, and the exorbitant Price of all Kind of Commodities. Besides these evils, which are the common attendants of War, Providence has been pleased to inflict us with distresses of another Nature. We have suffered two severe Storms in the Space of Ten Months, one on the 3d of October last, and the other on the 1 of this Month, by which all Kind of Provisions of the growth of this Island having been destroyed, we are threaten'd with a famine, which would certainly have prevail'd had it not been prevented by the timely Arrival of our fleets. I pray Heaven to remove from us the horrors of war, and restore to us the blessings of Peace.[27]

Mendes's prayers were not to be wholly answered. Although overt hostilities between England and the United States ended not long after, hurricanes in 1784, 1785, and again in 1786 inflicted additional damage. Drought, famine, epidemic, and skyrocketing prices followed the great storms, causing more suffering and the deaths of thousands by starvation.[28]

Mendes, however, did not mention several events in Jamaica related to the war that must have further unnerved the colony's Jewish inhabitants. Charges of treason had been brought against two of their number in 1779, once again raising the specter of that disloyalty of which Jews had been accused over the ages, even in Jamaica.[29] On August 13, the British army arrested Isaac Bernal, a shopkeeper in Spanish Town, and accused him of conspiring with the French, who had been allied with the United States since 1778. According to the British, Bernal, fluent in French, had been in secret communication with French commanders in the Caribbean. Adding to his woes, all his assets were stolen or embezzled while he underwent interrogation in prison. Bernal was eventually released from jail after more than a month, thanks to intervention by the island's Deputy Marshall, but several days later the British detained a second Jewish individual, Moses Gomez, and accused him too of conspiring with the French. Arrested at Port Royal, Gomez was charged with high treason for allegedly piloting French privateers in search of plunder through

Jamaica's waterways. His subsequent escape from jail no doubt gave rise to even greater anxiety among Jamaica's Jewish population.[30]

Half a year before Mendes wrote to Lopez, worse had occurred at the hands of the British army on the Dutch island of St. Eustatius, where a small Jewish population had resided since the 1720s.[31] News of what transpired there in February 1781—that the Jews on the island had been expelled forcibly following a British invasion—had reached as far as Pennsylvania and Massachusetts by May, and it had been publicized in Jamaica by the time Mendes penned his letter.

Functioning during much of the eighteenth century as a depot for the dispersal of European merchandise throughout the Caribbean, St. Eustatius served as a neutral transit point for all kinds of goods bound for the United States during its struggle for independence, including arms and ammunition. When evidence of a projected treaty between the Dutch and the United States surfaced, Britain declared war against the Netherlands, seized the island at the beginning of February 1781, and confiscated the vast stores found there.[32] The island's new masters then proceeded to compile a census of its inhabitants, which revealed the presence of 607 non-Jewish burghers and 62 Jewish burghers, together with the number of slaves each owned. Because the Jewish burghers were listed separately from the non-Jewish ones at the end of each letter of the alphabet, all without exception can be identified.

The census of 1781 reveals that, as was the case elsewhere, the Jewish inhabitants held a small part of the colony's slaves: 86, or 6.4 percent of the total (Table 5.2). By one measure, they were more in evidence as slaveowners than the non-Jewish population, for 43.5 percent of the Jewish burghers owned slaves (27 out of 62), as opposed to 36.9 percent of the non-Jewish ones (224 out of 607). According to two other yardsticks, on the other hand, it was the island's non-Jewish residents who were more apparent as slaveowners. The Jewish burghers owned fewer on a proportional basis, for although they comprised 9.2 percent of all burghers, they owned 6.4 percent of the colony's slaves. Second, they averaged 3.1 slaves per slaveowner, in contrast to the average of 5.5 owned by their non-

TABLE 5.2
Slaveowners at St. Eustatius,
February 1781

Burgher Entries:		Total: 669*	
Non-Jewish:	No.		%
Slaveowners	224		33.4
Non-Slaveowners	383		57.2
Jewish:			
Slaveowners	27		4.0
Non-Slaveowners	35		5.2
Slaveownership:		Total: 1,337	
Owned by:			
Non-Jews	1,251		93.5
Jews	86		6.4
Average Number of Slaves Held:			
Non-Jews		5.5	
Jews		3.1	

*One entry not included, a non-Jewish burgher in fragmentary condition at the end of entries under "D."

NOTE: For the Jewish entries and the number of slaves each owned, see Appendix XIII.

SOURCE: PRO, CO 318/8, 61–82.

Jewish counterparts. Therefore, even in an environment in which agriculture was of little importance and commerce was king, two of three means of comparison indicate that the Jewish population did not stand out as slaveholders.[33]

Armed with this census, Admiral George Rodney announced the expulsion of all Jewish men on the island, giving them no more than one day's notice to prepare for their departures. British forces placed them under close confinement and seized whatever property they carried on their persons.[34] Some were carried away on February 13, with no knowledge of their destination, while still others were banished three days later together with Dutchmen and Americans found on the island. As reported in Martinique and in North America,

The British ordered, with the greatest inhumanity, the JEWS to be embarked seperate [sic] from their wives and children; they were searched at the sea side with the most mercenary avidity, and again, with great carefulness, on board the vessel in which they were heaped together. British officers, (men of the nicest honour and delicacy) were seen plundering in detail, shaking and searching the meanest article. . . . They wantonly destroyed every article they did not think worth taking away. On the 16th they were sent, with the Dutch and Americans to St. Christopher, where they were destitute of every succour their distressed situation claimed, and reduced to one quarter rations. . . . [35]

News of these events reached Jamaica as well, for certain by the late summer.[36]

Yet another event, this one in the autumn of 1783 at the commencement of Yom Kippur, the most solemn day of the Jewish year, undoubtedly also evoked feelings of vulnerability among Jamaica's Jews, although this occurrence bore no relationship to the American Revolution. With the entire Jewish community of Kingston assembled in the synagogue at sunset to inaugurate the Day of Atonement, a twenty-four-hour period of fasting, prayer, and penitence at the beginning of the Jewish religious year, a disorderly crowd gathered outside and began to behave disruptively. When an affray broke out and several peace officers moved in to suppress it, an unknown party shouted "FIRE!" causing considerable fright and confusion within the synagogue and interrupting the evening's worship for some time. Although the perpetrators would subsequently issue a public apology, one in which they attributed their behavior to "the effects of wine" and, as "Gentlemen" and "Christians," assured "the Elders of the [Jewish] nation" that they would not purposely disturb anyone's prayers to the "Supreme Being," the references in the Yom Kippur liturgy to the hostilities encountered by Jews on so many occasions during the course of their long history must have assumed ominous relevance as the colony's Jewish population ushered in a new Jewish year.[37]

Hurricanes notwithstanding, better economic conditions began to return to Jamaica after the American war for independence ended. Abundant crops, rising demand for them in Europe, improvements in agriculture, the sale of depleted lands by far-seeing planters, and increases in cotton and coffee crops marked the economy's upturn.[38] As hostilities in North America wound down, slave imports rebounded from their low of 3,267 in 1780 to 7,049 in 1781, 6,291 in 1782, 9,644 in 1783, 15,468 in 1784, and 11,046 in 1785.[39] Slave exports also jumped, from the average of 330 per year during the war years to an average of 2,792 between 1782 and 1784.[40] And the colony began to repair the damage inflicted by the hurricanes of 1780 and 1781, generating more economic possibilities. Savanna la Mar, for example, leveled in 1780, was partially rebuilt and may have had sixty to seventy houses a dozen years later.[41]

Participating in the economy's rejuvenation during the 1780s, Jewish merchants acquired a larger percentage of the ships that traded with the colony than before, although their share still comprised a very small segment of the colony's maritime activity. In 1745, fewer than 3 percent of the vessels that entered in or cleared out of the colony had belonged to Jewish merchants. By 1765, the number had declined to less than 1 percent of the entries and clearances.[42] In 1785, however, Jewish merchants owned 27, or 3.8 percent, of the 698 vessels that entered Jamaica. Of the remainder, 667, or 95.5 percent, belonged to non-Jews, while 4, or less than 1 percent (one-half of 1 percent), belonged to owners whose religion cannot be identified or whose names were not entered by the Naval Office. Vessels in the export trade showed similar growth in the proportion owned by Jewish entrepreneurs. Of the 615 vessels that sailed from Jamaica in 1785, 27, or 4.3 percent, belonged to Jewish merchants or firms, while 585, or 95.1 percent, belonged to non-Jews, and 3, or less than 1 percent (four-tenths of 1 percent), had owners who were not listed or whose religion is not known.[43]

In most instances, the Jewish merchants whose ships traded with Jamaica in 1785 resided in the colony. Altogether, ten merchants and firms owned the vessels in question. One for certain resided in London.[44] The residence of two others is not known.[45] The remaining seven were Jamaicans, and were the largest number of Jews residing in the colony who are known to have owned maritime vessels there at any point in time during the eighteenth century. All traded locally within the Caribbean with the exception of Alexandre *[sic]* Lindo, whose vessel, the *Esther,* sailed regularly between Kingston and London. Later in the decade, Lindo & Co. simultaneously owned a second vessel, the *Esther Lindo,* that, like the first, journeyed regularly between Jamaica and England.[46]

After the 1780s, the confidence that prompted Jamaica's Jewish merchants to invest in shipping subsided, perhaps because of the dangers on the high seas in the wake of renewed conflict between England and France. Consequently, in 1796 (for which Naval Office records survive for three-quarters of the year), of 587 vessels that entered Jamaica, 12, or 2.0 percent, belonged to Jewish owners, and of 699 that cleared out, 17, or 2.4 percent, belonged to them.[47] In 1805, 788 vessels entered the colony, of which 9, or 1.1 percent, were owned by Jewish merchants; and of the 861 that cleared out, 11, or 1.2 percent, belonged to them.[48] Moreover, many of the Jewish owners were not inhabitants of Jamaica. Of the fourteen Jewish individuals and firms owning vessels that entered and sailed from the colony in 1796 and 1805, seven for certain resided in the colony.[49] Five did not, and the remaining two probably did not.[50]

The return of peaceful trading conditions in the Caribbean basin after the American Revolution allowed for the restoration of the slave trade, which in turn presented great opportunities for shipowners and factors. But despite their increased participation in the ownership of ships during the 1780s, and despite the fact that several of them in Jamaica and in England accumulated experience in transatlantic commerce as the owners of vessels that could cross the ocean, Jewish merchants did not participate in the importation of slaves from Africa as shipowners. Surviving Naval Office records for thirteen of the years between 1780 and the middle of 1807, the year in which Britain abolished the slave trade from Africa, note the arrival of 109,380 slaves in the colony along with the names of the owners of the vessels on which they traveled. Of these slaves, 107,756, or 98.5 percent, arrived on slave transports owned by non-Jewish firms in London, Bristol, and Liverpool. The remaining 1,624, or 1.4 percent, were imported on vessels whose owners' names were not listed.[51]

In the export trade in slaves, on the other hand, the evidence points to greater involvement during the 1780s among the island's Jewish shipowners than earlier in the eighteenth century. Between 1742 and 1769, vessels owned by Jews had carried almost 6 percent of the slaves reportedly carried out of Jamaica. The level during the 1780s, according to the surviving Naval Office records, was more than four times as great. Between December 29, 1783 and June 29, 1788, 3,724 slaves are listed therein as having been transported from Jamaica to a variety of destinations, although figures submitted to Parliament in the late 1780s demonstrate that the actual total was considerably higher.[52] Of the 3,724 referred to in the Naval Office records, 995, or 26.7 percent, were carried on vessels owned by Jewish merchants or firms, while 2,697, or 72.4 percent, were shipped on vessels owned by non-Jews. The remaining 32, or fewer than 1 percent (eight-tenths of 1 percent), were exported on a ship whose owner's name was not listed.

After the 1780s, participation by Jewish shipowners in Jamaica's slave export trade subsided. A total of 6,074 slave exports appear in the Naval Office lists for the period between December 29, 1795 and June 29, 1807.[53] Of these, 211, or 3.4 percent, were carried on vessels owned by Jewish individuals or firms. Of the remainder, 5,497, or 90.5 percent, were exported on vessels owned by non-Jews, while 366, or 6 percent, went on vessels whose owners were either not listed or whose religious affiliations are not known. Clearly, the export trade in slaves reverted after the 1780s to the contours that had characterized it earlier in the century.

Nine Jewish individuals or firms are known to have exported slaves from Jamaica between the end of 1783 and mid-1807. Seven did so during the 1780s. Of these, six resided in the colony; the seventh may have. Mirroring the Jewish merchants' subsequent withdrawal from the export trade, of the seven, only one, Judah Phillips, continued to export slaves thereafter. The remaining two joined the export trade in slaves during the 1790s. By the early 1800s, Phillips remained the only one who appears to have continued to participate in it.[54]

If the decade of the 1780s marked the high point of activity by Jewish merchants as slave exporters (as well as shipowners), it also witnessed

TABLE 5.3
The Leading Slave-Factor Firms in Jamaica, 1779–88

Name	Sale Dates	No. of Slaves Sold
Alexandre Lindo	Feb. 1786–Aug. 1788	7,510
Messrs. Coppells	Nov. 1782–Jan. 1788	10,380
Mures & Dunlop	1781–86	6,039
Messrs. Rainfords	1779–88	8,952
(Rainford, Blundell & Rainford)		

SOURCE: *Two Reports (One Presented the 16th of October, the Other on the 12th of November, 1788) from the Committee of the Honourable House of Assembly of Jamaica on the Subject of the Slave-Trade* (London: B. White and Son, 1789), 11, 22–25.

the beginning of greater involvement by a few members of Kingston's Jewish community as slave factors, with one family in particular playing a leading role. At the beginning of the decade, the firm of Coppells & Aguilar, with Jewish partner Abraham Aguilar, advertised the sale of more than 600 slaves in 1781.[55] Far greater in impact, however, was the factoring activity of Alexandre Lindo, who between February 2, 1786 and August 19, 1788 took delivery of 7,873 slaves and sold 7,510 of them, the remaining 363 perishing before they could be sold. Lindo's extraordinary level of activity as a slave factor merited his inclusion among those the colony's Assembly in late 1788 designated as "the most considerable African factors residing in this island."[56] Four in number between 1779 and 1788, they collectively sold 32,881 slaves, with Lindo selling 22.8 percent (Table 5.3). An expert on the sale of slaves, he gave testimony to the colony's legislature at a later date when it sought information about the death rate on board slave transports making the crossing from Africa.[57]

Lindo, as noted before, owned two transatlantic vessels during the 1780s that sailed regularly between England and Jamaica. He appears to have begun life in more modest circumstances, for on Kingston's tax list in 1769, where he appeared as "Alexander Linder," he did not own slaves and did not pay a trade tax. His ascent thereafter must have proceeded quickly, for by 1780 Kingston's commercial district had a wharf called "LINDO's wharf." A year later, advertisers could post notices of auctions at "the usual place of sale of ALEXAN-

DER Lindo," obviously able to assume that potential customers knew its location.[58] Moreover, in 1781 he was among 150 merchants, nine of them Jewish, who announced that they would accept payment in certain Spanish and British coin in an effort to relieve hardships attributable to the colony's shortage of specie. And in January 1783, Lindo joined with thirty-five other Jewish merchants and firms in Kingston (and a larger number of non-Jewish ones) in subscribing to a fund established for the relief of Englishmen and their families who had been carried into captivity. However, he had not yet risen to the top, for among the sums *"Subscribed by the* JEWISH *Nation,"* Lindo contributed more than twenty-eight others, but less than four and the same as the remaining three Jewish subscribers.[59]

By the end of the decade, Lindo's standing was markedly higher. As the year 1790 began, 180 public officials, merchants, and other inhabitants of Kingston proffered expressions of appreciation to Jamaica's outgoing Lieutenant Governor as he prepared to return to England; and Alexandre Lindo's was the sole Jewish signature, a signal symbol of recognition, perhaps one that even indicated inclusion in the town's public life.[60] In that year, on the other hand, his factoring activity apparently slipped from its level in 1786–88, for several other factors advertised many more slaves for sale than he, as well as higher percentages of the total (Table 5.4). But three years later, in 1793, Lindo paid the highest trade tax assessed in Kingston, £20. This was an amount substantially larger than the next highest, 12–10–0, which was paid by each of two different firms, both of which conducted business as slave factors: Hibbert, Hall & Fuhr; and Lindo & Lake.[61] Lindo had joined with a non-Jewish partner, Richard Lake, to form the latter, which advertised the largest number of slaves for sale known for Kingston's factoring enterprises during 1793, or 37.4 percent of the total.

Two years later, Lindo & Lake still figured prominently among Kingston's slave-factoring companies. The firm again advertised the largest number of slaves for sale, although its proportion had fallen to 21.7 percent of the total advertised for the year. At this juncture, Lindo, who far surpassed all other members of Kingston's Jewish community in commercial activity, was on the verge of relocating to

TABLE 5.4
Slave-Factor Advertisements in Kingston Newspapers,
1781–1805

Firm	No. of Slaves Advertised
1781:	
Coppells & Aguilar	620
Hibbert, Robert	320
Mures & Dunlop	946
Smith, James Whitfield	—
Smith, Leigh & Co.	260
1783:	
Adlam, Thomas	400
Allans & Campbell	793
Coppell, John & William	14
Coppell & Goldwin	2,070
Hibbert, Robert & Thomas	1,090
Mures & Dunlop	847
Rainford, Blundell & Rainford	650
Thompson, William & John	600
1790:	
Allan, White & Co.	694
Aspinall & Hardy	959
Chisholm, Tho. & Co.	547
Coppell & Aspinall	164
Daggers, W. & Co.	778
Gibson, James & Co.	189
Hibbert, Hall & Fuhr	248
Holcombe, Thomas & Co.	242
Levy, Solomon	30
Lindo, Alexandre	629
Rainford, Blundell & Rainford	1,131
Ross, Wm. & Rob.	305
Shaw & Inglis	550
Taylor, John	1,745
Yates & Hinde	308
1793:	
Allan, White & Co.	230
Aspinall & Hardy	484
Barret & Parkinson	256
Daggers, W. & Co.	1,195
Hibbert, Hall & Fuhr	354
Holcombe & Co.	40
Lindo & Lake	2,500
Ross, William & Robert	217
Shaw & Inglis	446
Taylor, Ballantine & Fairlie	844
Thompson & Jackson	105

TABLE 5.4 (*Continued*)

Firm	No. of Slaves Advertised
1795:	
Aspinall & Hardy	2,282
Ballantine, Fairlie & Co.	995
Boggle & Jopps	295
Hibbert, Robert & Co.	474
Hinde, John	1,309
Jones, R.	40
Lindo & Lake	2,715
Rainford, Blundell & Rainford	1,330
Shaw, Inglis & Holt	1,693
Taylor, Ballantine & Fairlie	1,340
1800:	
Atkinson, G. and M. & Co.	598
Boggle, Jopp & Co.	1,370
Bryan, W. & B. & Co.	308
Dick, McCall & Co.	923
Donaldson, Forbes, Grant & Stewart	340
Gibb, Robert & Co.	337
Hardy, Pennock & Brittan	780
Henry, West & Co.	1,394
Hibbert & Taylor	500
Hill, Mair, Orr & Co.	294
Hinde, John	361
Jaques, Laing & Moulton	170
Kinkeads & Sproull	83
Lindo, Lake & Co.	4,994
Lodge, Jopp & Co.	487
MacFarlane, John	150
Shaw, Holt & Co.	1,258
Willis & Waterhouse	381
1805:	
Aspinall, Thomas	511
Boggle, Jopp & Co.	387
Burke & Harris	300
Crossman, Harris & Co.	1,630
Dick, McCall & Co.	370
Fairclough, Barnes & Wilson	307
Garnett, Hardy & Co.	266
Hynes, Thomas	238
Lake, R. & Nephew	332
Lindo, Henriques & Lindo	559
Shaw, Inglis & Mills	261

NOTE: Aggregate sales known from other sources for the period 1789–99 for several factors, all of whom were non-Jewish, are for John Taylor, 180 slaves imported on the *Eliza* in 1789, in *Report, Resolutions, and Remonstrance, of the Honourable the Council and Assembly of Jamaica, at a Joint Committee, on the Subject of the Slave-Trade, in a Session which began the 20th of October 1789* (London: B. White and Son, 1790), 15; Barrett and Parkinson, 6,935 slaves in 1789–92, Allan, White & Co., 464 slaves imported on the *Hero* in November 1792, and W. Daggers & Co., 360 slaves imported on the *Diana* in the same month, all in *Proceedings of the Hon. House of Assembly of Jamaica, on the Sugar and Slave-Trade, in a Session which began the 23d of October, 1792* (London: Stephen Fuller, 1793), 22–23; Aspinall and Hardy, and for Hardy, Pennock & Brittan, who sold a combined total of 17,323 slaves in 1793–99; in *Journals of the Assembly of Jamaica*, X, 436.

Other factors at Kingston or more generally at "Jamaica" between 1782 and 1793, all again non-Jewish, were John Fowler, Fitch, Stewart & Co., Francis Grant, Malcolm & Barton, John Perry, and Phipps & Lane; David Richardson, ed., *Bristol, Africa and the Eighteenth-Century Slave Trade to America*, 4 vols. (Volumes 38, 39, 42, and 47 of the Bristol Record Society's Publications) (Gloucester: Alan Sutton Publishing, 1986–96), IV, 80, 87, 109, 151, 157, 174, 206.

SOURCES: *Royal Gazette*, 1781, 1783, January 5–March 2, 1793, 1795, 1800, and 1805; and *Daily Advertiser*, 1790, and August 14, 1793.

England.[62] Another of its more prosperous members, Emmanuel Baruch Lousada, Esq., had named him as an executor of his will, but only, as a codicil added by Lousada in December 1795 prescribed, if Lindo continued to reside in the colony.[63] Lindo, however, sold his furniture, plate, horses, and carriages in 1795 and settled in England sometime before the end of 1796 with every intention of never returning to Jamaica, although he felt obliged to do so in 1802 because of looming trouble with his partner, Richard Lake.[64] In 1805, his home and large commercial establishment on Kingston's waterfront, complete with a wharf, crane, scale, cooperage, and several large warehouses, some of them two stories in height, were still identified as his property in a detailed rendering of the site drawn by a military engineer. By then, however, Lindo had returned from Jamaica to his home and countinghouse in London, for it was there that he composed his last will and testament on November 7, 1805. At his death in 1812, he owned several plantations back in the colony together with their large complements of slaves, and left much of his estate to his eldest son, Abraham Alexandre Lindo, who had remained in Jamaica.[65]

The younger Lindo had followed his father into commerce. In 1795, the two were partners in Lindo, Son & Co. With his father's departure for England, the son struck out on his own; in 1796 and 1797, the firm of A. A. Lindo & Co. owned two vessels that imported coffee, cotton, and dry goods from Jérémie on the island of Hispaniola and exported a small number of slaves there in return. Over time, his interests extended to direct trade with England and to Jamaica's commerce with the Spanish empire. By 1800, he headed the firm of A. A. Lindo & Brothers.[66] And, together with his absentee father, he was a partner in Lindo, Lake & Co., which replaced the firm of Lindo & Lake in December 1796 for the exclusive purpose of selling slaves.[67] Like Lindo & Lake in 1793 and 1795, Lindo, Lake & Co. advertised the largest number of slaves offered in 1800 by any Kingston factoring company, amounting to slightly more than one-third of the total (Table 5.4).

Lindo, Lake & Co. collapsed, however, in a major lawsuit in Jamaica's Court of Chancery early in 1803.[68] Richard Lake continued thereafter to sell slaves, but now in partnership with his nephew and on a much smaller scale than before, as indicated by advertisements in 1805 for the sale of slaves (Table 5.4). For his part, Abraham Alexandre Lindo formed a new company with a Jewish individual named Henriques. The new partnership of Lindo, Henriques & Lindo had diverse interests, which included ownership of a wharf, commerce with England, and a part in the Spanish trade.[69] Lindo, Henriques & Lindo also sold slaves in 1805 (Table 5.4), although, like R. Lake & Nephew, at a level much below that achieved in previous years when the Lindo name, even if usually in conjunction with a non-Jewish one, had figured among Kingston's largest slave factors.

One other Jewish individual in Kingston is known to have functioned as a slave factor after 1780, doing so in a minor capacity. In the autumn of 1790, Solomon Levy offered thirty slaves for sale, describing his undertaking in terms that were unique for a factor's advertisement: "A Private Adventure." Levy had obtained them from the *Mercury,* which had arrived with 278 slaves. The remaining 248 were sold by Hibbert, Hall & Fuhr; and unlike Levy's, Hibbert's, of course, was a long-established name in Jamaica for slave consignments.[70]

Outside Kingston, only one Jewish firm is known to have taken delivery of a slave shipment from Africa. At Falmouth on the island's northern coast, the partnership of Levein, Wolfe, Flash & Joseph Cohen received a consignment of 166 slaves in 1805.[71] West of Falmouth, the Jewish merchants at Montego Bay appear to have continued to avoid slave factoring, despite the town's continuing role as a port for the reception of traffic from Africa. During the 1780s, and thereafter until the abolition of the slave trade, the sale of slaves at Montego Bay is not known to have been in the hands of any but non-Jewish firms. The same is the case as well for sales at Black River, Lucea, Martha Brae, and Port Maria.[72]

In contrast to their greater visibility as slave factors during the late eighteenth century because of the Lindos, Jamaica's Jewish inhabitants continued, as before, to own a minute segment of the colony's slaves. Poll-tax lists for Kingston in 1795 and 1819, one for the parish of St. Catherine in 1820, and, above all, the first triennial survey of slaves in 1817 confirm that the Jewish population's role in slaveowning was not more substantial than it had been prior to 1780.

In Kingston, they owned 15.3 percent of all slaves reported in 1795 (Table 5.1), and in 1819, 17 percent (Table 5.5). In both instances, the percentage of reported slaves owned by the city's Jewish inhabitants was about the same as in 1745 and 1769, when their percentages had been 18 percent and 18.2 percent, respectively.[73]

The poll-tax lists for the late eighteenth and early nineteenth centuries, however, tell only part of the story, for the underreporting of slaves was by then for certain rampant. Acknowledgments to this effect late in the eighteenth century by the colony's Assembly and by Bryan Edwards have previously been cited here.[74] Underreporting continued thereafter, as Bernard Higman found in his recent study of the colony's slave population during the early nineteenth century. In the course of analyzing the six triennial slave registrations conducted between 1817 and 1832, Higman concluded that Jamaica's slaveowners responded accurately when it came to the triennial census, while failing to report all their holdings at poll-tax time. In 1817, for example, they reported 345,252 slaves during the first triennial registration, but only 316,082 slaves for poll-tax purposes.[75]

In addition to their accuracy, the triennial slave registers have the

TABLE 5.5
Slaveownership in Kingston, 1819, and in St. Catherine, 1820

	Kingston 1819		St. Catherine 1820	
Poll-tax Entries:	Total: 1,274		Total: 354	
Non-Jewish:	No.	%	No.	%
Slaveowners	782	61.3	276	77.9
Non-Slaveowners	215	16.8	35	9.8
Jewish:				
Slaveowners	178	13.9	29	8.1
Non-Slaveowners	34	2.6	3	0.8
Joint Ownership:				
Partnerships	3	0.2	—	—
Public Institutions				
Slaveowning	3	0.2	1	0.2
Non-Slaveowning	5	0.3	—	—
Religion Not Certain:				
Slaveowners	39	3.0	9	2.5
Non-Slaveowners	15	1.1	1	0.2
Slaveownership:	Total: 8,169*		Total: 7,570**	
Owned by:	No.	%	No.	%
Non-Jews	6,402	78.3	7,116	94.0
Jews	1,395	17.0	340	4.4
Jointly	32	0.3	—	—
Public Institutions	41	0.5	25	0.3
Religion Not Certain	299	3.6	89	1.1
Average Number of Slaves:				
Non-Jews	8.1		25.7	
Jews	7.8		11.7	
Jointly	10.6		—	
Public Institutions	13.6		25.0	
Religion Not Certain	7.6		9.8	

*Corrected total (total in original source is 8,178)

**Corrected total (total in original source is 7,561)

NOTE: For Jewish entries and for entries whose religion is not certain, see Appendix VI, Table 4, and Appendix VII, Table 2.

SOURCES: JA, 2/6/106 for Kingston; and JA 2/2/19 for St. Catherine.

virtue of documenting slaveownership throughout the colony. A complete picture of the extent to which the colony's Jewish inhabitants owned slaves shortly before the emancipation of the slave population in 1834 is therefore possible. The first registration in 1817 has been selected for this purpose, for the number of slaves consistently declined thereafter as slavery's end throughout the British empire approached.[76]

Of the colony's 345,252 slaves in 1817, the Jewish population owned 6,538, or 1.8 percent, while another 2,772, or less than 1 percent (eight-tenths of 1 percent), belonged to owners whose religion is not certain. In the event that all of the latter were in fact owned by Jews, the total for the Jewish population would have been 9,310, or 2.6 percent.[77] Otherwise, 335,942, or 97.3 percent, were owned by the colony's non-Jewish residents and absentee owners (Table 5.6).

The inhabitants of Kingston, site of the colony's largest Jewish population, owned a total of 17,954 slaves in 1817, of whom 2,653, or 14.7 percent, were owned by its Jewish residents. An additional 420, or 2.3 percent, belonged to owners whose religion is not certain, while 14,881, or 82.8 percent, belonged to non-Jews.

In the parish of St. Catherine, the location of Jamaica's second-largest Jewish community at Spanish Town, a total of 9,679 slaves were to be found. The parish's Jewish population owned 465, or 4.8 percent, while another 120, or 1.2 percent, belonged to owners whose religion is not certain. The remaining 9,094 slaves, or 93.9 percent, belonged to the parish's non-Jewish population, some of whom had large holdings as plantation owners.

In the neighboring parish of St. Andrew, Jews owned more than twice as many slaves as in St. Catherine. All told, the parish's slaves numbered 15,830, of whom 1,101, or 6.9 percent, belonged to Jewish owners. St. Andrew did not have a larger resident Jewish population than St. Catherine, but it did contain three plantations and one pen owned by Abraham Alexandre Lindo, complete with 893 slaves, or 5.6 percent of the parish's total slave population.[78] The remaining 208 slaves held by Jewish owners accordingly comprised 1.3 percent of the parish's slaves.

Lindo also owned a plantation with 242 slaves in the parish of Port Royal.[79] All told, that parish had 7,217 slaves, so that Lindo's share amounted to 3.3 percent. The very small number of Jewish inhabitants who still remained in the town of Port Royal owned

TABLE 5.6

Slaveownership in Jamaica, 1817

| | No. of Slaves Owned by | | |
	Non-Jews	Jews	Religion Not Certain
Parish			
Clarendon	19,113	230	54
Hanover	23,651	84	44
Kingston	14,881	2,653*	420
Manchester	14,663	112	302
Portland	8,182	0	2
Port Royal	6,779	310	128
St. Andrew	14,500	1,101	229
St. Ann	24,384	358	72
St. Catherine	9,094	465	120
St. David	7,731	12	15
St. Dorothy	5,220	82	3
St. Elizabeth	19,419	247	477
St. George	13,632	0	8
St. James	25,464	103	74
St. John	6,025	106	2
St. Mary	26,769	0	57
St. Thomas-in-the-East	25,804	361	257
St. Thomas-in-the-Vale	12,066	151	24
Trelawny	28,028	24	445
Vere	7,924	132	0
Westmoreland	22,613	7	39
Totals	335,942	6,538	2,772

*Three slaves jointly owned by Abraham Alexandre Lindo and John Campbell, a non-Jewish partner, are included here.

NOTE: Non-Jewish totals have been derived by subtracting the totals for Jews and for those whose religion is not certain from the cumulative parish totals listed by Higman.

For Jewish owners and for those whose religion is not certain, see Appendix XII, Table 2, infra.

SOURCES: PRO, T 71/1, 71/13, 71/19, 71/25, 71/33, 71/43, 71/51, 71/57, 71/65, 71/74–79, 71/119, 71/125, 71/139, 71/145, 71/151, 71/158, 71/164–66, 71/178, 71/190, 71/201–4, 71/224–29; and B. W. Higman, *Slave Population and Economy in Jamaica, 1807–1834* (Cambridge: Cambridge University Press, 1976), 256.

another 68, or less than 1 percent (nine-tenths of 1 percent) of the parish's slaves.

Few of Jamaica's Jews other than Lindo had interests in plantations or pens, which, as before 1780, sharply limited the number of slaves and the percentage thereof owned by the colony's Jewish inhabitants. In addition to Lindo, only six Jewish individuals and two partnerships appear to have owned slaves in numbers large enough to indicate that they were involved in the island's agriculture. Collectively, their agricultural investments included 1,394 slaves.[80] When combined with Abraham Alexandre Lindo's 1,135 plantation slaves, the total number of slaves owned in 1817 by this very small group amounted to 2,529, or fully 38.6 percent of the slaves owned by the colony's Jewish inhabitants. Some, in addition, also owned slaves in the colony's towns, as well as a small number in the parish of St. John.[81]

While the triennial registration conducted in 1817 demonstrates that Jamaica's Jewish population owned a very small part of the colony's slaves, it cannot be used to determine whether they owned slaves in excess of, the same as, or less than their proportion among the white population. The size of the latter is not known, for the colony did not conduct its first census of the white population until 1844.[82] Fortunately, the poll-tax lists for Kingston in 1819 and St. Catherine in 1820, the two locations in which most of the colony's Jews resided, shed light on the issue.

While incomplete because of underreporting, the percentages in the two poll taxes of reported slaves owned by non-Jews, by Jews, and by those whose religion is not certain closely mirror the triennial census of 1817 (Table 5.7). The similarities are especially congruent in the case of St. Catherine. They indicate, as well, that in Kingston

TABLE 5.7
Percentages of Slaves Owned in Kingston and St. Catherine

	by		
	Non-Jews	Jews	Religion Not Certain
Kingston:			
1817 Register	82.8	14.7	2.3
1819 Poll Tax	78.3	17.0	3.6
St. Catherine:			
1817 Register	93.9	4.8	1.2
1820 Poll Tax	94.0	4.4	1.1

SOURCES: See Tables 5.5 and 5.6.

the non-Jewish population underreported to a somewhat greater degree than the Jewish population did; according to the more accurate
triennial registration, its Jewish inhabitants owned a somewhat
smaller proportion of the city's slaves than indicated by the poll tax
two years later. Given the close correspondence between the more
complete triennial register and the poll-tax lists, the latter may be
regarded as generally reflective of proportional slaveowning patterns
within the two towns.

Kingston's Jewish inhabitants in 1819 comprised approximately
16.5 percent of all entries on the poll-tax list, and held nearly the
same proportion of all reported slaves: 17 percent (Table 5.5). The
non-Jewish population amounted to 78.1 percent of all entries, and
held 78.3 percent of all reported slaves. The two groups, therefore,
appear to have owned approximately the same percentage of slaves
as their respective proportions within the city's white population, as
those proportions are reflected as entries on the poll-tax list.

Two other comparisons yield a more complex picture. In the first,
the data for 1819 suggest that Kingston's Jewish inhabitants were
somewhat more likely to own slaves than its non-Jews, for 83.9
percent of all Jewish entrants (178 out of 212) owned slaves, while
78.4 percent (782 out of 997) of the non-Jewish entrants did (Table
5.5). On the other hand, non-Jewish slaveowning entrants owned a
somewhat greater average number of slaves. They averaged 8.1 each,
while Jewish slaveowning entrants averaged 7.8, thereby reversing
the pattern in 1769 and reverting to that in 1745.[83]

In St. Catherine, the non-Jewish population clearly predominated
as slaveowners. The parish poll tax in 1820 did not distinguish between its rural plantation areas and Spanish Town, where most if not
all its Jews presumably resided. Accordingly, while the Jewish population accounted for 9 percent of the parish's entries on the poll-tax
list, they owned 4.4 percent of its slaves (Table 5.5). Non-Jews comprised 87.7 percent of all entries and owned 94 percent of the parish's
slaves. And while each group was almost as likely as the other to
own slaves, with 88.7 percent of all non-Jewish entrants and 90.6
percent of all Jewish ones doing so, non-Jews on the average owned
more than twice as many because of their involvement in agriculture.

They averaged 25.7 slaves per entry, while the Jewish entrants averaged 11.7.

In sum, slaveownership among Jamaica's Jewish inhabitants shortly before the abolition of slavery differed little from what had prevailed in the eighteenth century before 1780. Inhabiting the towns rather than the island's plantations, they owned a minute part of the colony's slaves. Within the towns, they do not appear to have owned slaves in excess of the percentage of their presence in the white population. In Kingston, they remained somewhat more likely than their non-Jewish counterparts to own slaves, but the average number they owned was below that of the city's non-Jews.

As in Jamaica, the much smaller Jewish community of Barbados owned a minute share of the colony's slaves. They played almost no part in the importation of slaves from Africa, and occupied a small position in the export trade. As importers and exporters, they always acted in partnership with non-Jews rather than on their own, further diminishing their impact on the slave trade. And slave factoring was an area in the commerce in slaves in which they may not have participated at all.[84]

Barbados's surviving Naval Office records for almost nine of the twenty-four years between November 11, 1781 and January 31, 1806 list the owners of the vessels on which 12,460 slaves arrived from Africa.[85] Of these, 12,332, or 98.9 percent, arrived on vessels owned by non-Jews. The remaining 128, or 1 percent, arrived in 1798 on a vessel that belonged to seven partners, of whom two, Jacob Barrow and Joseph Barrow, were Jewish.[86]

The island's surviving Naval Office records indicate that Barbados exported 5,728 slaves during the same years.[87] Of these slaves, 5,337, or 93.1 percent, traveled on vessels owned by non-Jews. Another 291, or 5 percent, were transported on five occasions between April 1, 1797 and September 1, 1799 on vessels in which Jews were partners with non-Jews. The remaining 100, or 1.7 percent, were carried on vessels whose owners' names were not listed.

Jacob Barrow and Joseph Barrow joined in one such export venture with seven non-Jewish partners to ship 80 slaves to Demerara in

British Guiana. In three other enterprises, copartners Eliezer Montefiore and Thomas Ames sent out a total of 57 slaves to Demerara and neighboring Berbice. And in the remaining undertaking, Montefiore and a second Jewish individual, Lewis Cohen, were partners with four non-Jews in the export of 154 slaves, likewise to Berbice.[88]

Slaveownership among Barbados's Jews is measurable through the colony's first triennial slave registration, conducted as in Jamaica in 1817. A total of 77,493 slaves were registered in that year.[89] Of these, 506, or less than 1 percent (six-tenths of 1 percent), were held by Jewish individuals. Another 104, again less than 1 percent (one-tenth of 1 percent), belonged to parties whose religion is not certain. (If all of them were owned by Jews, the total belonging to the latter would have been 610, or seven-tenths of 1 percent.)[90] Among the Jewish slaveowners, two had holdings large enough to indicate that they had agricultural interests. Together they owned 227 slaves, or 44.8 percent of the slaves owned by Barbados's Jewish inhabitants.[91] Overall, however, Barbados's Jewish population had even less of a stake, proportionally, in the colony's slaves than their counterparts in Jamaica.

CHAPTER 6

Jewish Merchants and Slavery in the Mainland Colonies

Settling first at New Amsterdam in the middle of the seventeenth century, Jewish colonists on the mainland of British North America established five small communities of varying size before the outbreak of the American Revolution. The largest was in New York, which had an estimated thirty to forty Jewish families in 1773. In 1790, or shortly after the termination of America's colonial era, between thirteen and fifteen hundred Jews resided in New York, Newport, Philadelphia, Charleston, and Savannah, along with a scattering of individuals and families in locations such as Richmond, Baltimore, Lancaster and Easton, Pennsylvania, and Westchester County in New York.[1] Although few in number, far more is known about early America's Jewish inhabitants than is the case with those who settled in Barbados, Jamaica, and Nevis, thanks to a century of investigation by American Jewish historians.

Established in 1654 by refugees in flight from Brazil after the Portuguese recaptured it from the Dutch, the Jewish community at New Amsterdam, renamed New York ten years later when the British seized it, amounted to little during the course of the seventeenth century. There were only eight or nine taxable Jews in the town in 1695, rising to fourteen by 1699. A year later, a hundred to a hundred and fifty Jewish individuals were to be found in a population of about five thousand.[2] Approximately fifteen Jewish households appear on two tax lists compiled in 1703 and in a census taken around the same time, in contrast to the eighty Jewish families in Jamaica in the same year.[3] It was not until 1729 that the small group at New York could at last successfully undertake the construction of a permanent synagogue. Even then, however, the New York congregation did not employ a haham, in contrast to the communities at Barbados and Jamaica where ordained rabbinical leaders had presided since the 1680s. New York, in fact, would not have an ordained rabbi until 1840. When appointed, he was mainland North America's first.

The New York census compiled around 1703 listed a total of 818 families and 802 slaves inhabiting the town. The names of 7 families with 16 slaves are missing, leaving 811 families and 786 slaves for comparing slaveowning patterns among Jews and non-Jews. Six Jewish families appear among the 811, while the religion of 5 other families is uncertain.[4] Four of the Jewish families, or two-thirds, owned 7 slaves. Each slaveholding family therefore owned an average of 1.7. Of the 800 non-Jewish families, 329, or 41.1 percent, substantially less than the percentage of slaveholders among New York's small number of Jewish families, owned slaves. On the other hand, with 778 slaves, they averaged 2.3 per slaveowning family.

Like their counterparts in the Caribbean, New York's Jewish inhabitants were shopkeepers and merchants, some of them participating in the commerce that crisscrossed the Atlantic, seeking success by building on ties with Jewish merchants in England, Jamaica, Barbados, and Curaçao.[5] The business ventures of several extended to the small slave trade conducted at New York, which was, of course, minute when compared with the slave trade in the plantation colonies to the south and in the Caribbean.[6] Surviving Naval Office records for New York for most of the period between June 24, 1715 and June 24, 1743 document the arrivals of 4,049 slaves, while another 314 appear in fragmentary records for March 25, 1748 through January 5, 1765. Of the total of 4,363 slaves, Jewish shipowners participated in the delivery of 377, or 8.6 percent. Of the latter, 345, or 7.9 percent of the grand total, arrived on vessels owned by partnerships of Jews and non-Jews. Thirty-two, or less than 1 percent (seven-tenths of 1 percent), arrived on vessels owned exclusively by Jewish individuals. The remaining 3,986 slaves, or 91.3 percent, were imported on vessels owned entirely by non-Jews.[7]

Slightly more than one-quarter of the slaves recorded by the Naval Office—1,128, or 25.8 percent—arrived on ships from Africa. Of the seventeen ventures that were involved, two were partnerships between Jews and non-Jews, one in 1717, the other in 1721.[8] In the first, Nathan Simson, then residing in New York, joined with non-Jews William Walton of New York and Richard Janeway of London to import 100 slaves.[9] In the second, Simson, still a year or two away from his return to London, was again partners with Walton and Janeway as well as with Isaac Levy, a Jewish merchant in London, this time in the *Crown Galley*. The vessel began its voyage from Madagascar to New York with 240 slaves, but by the time it reached New York after calling at Brazil, where 3 were sold, then at Barbados because of a fatal disease on board, only 117 remained alive.[10] Combined, the two voyages therefore brought 19.2 percent of the slaves transported from Africa to New York who are reported in the surviving Naval Office records.

Other slaves shipped from Africa to New York are known from the manifests filed by the captains of the vessels that transported them, and from the records of payments of duties required for each slave. These records do not identify who owned the slave vessels, but, rather, who received the dutiable cargoes they carried. While deficient because of extensive destruction by fire early in the twentieth century, the Manifest Books and the Entry Books, as they are known, identify who was involved in the slave trade between Africa and New York during 1744–47, 1749–September 1751, 1756, 1758, and 1765, periods for which Naval Office records do not exist. They reveal the arrival of an additional 310 slaves from Africa and their delivery to twelve different individuals or firms, as well as the name of a thirteenth importer where the entry for the number of slaves was destroyed by fire. None of the thirteen was Jewish.[11]

With the exception of Nathan Simson's two ventures to Africa, Jewish merchants in New York who imported slaves did so primarily from the Caribbean. Of the 160 slave imports in the Naval Office records that remain after Nathan Simson's imports from Africa are deducted and in which Jewish merchants were involved, 138 came from Jamaica, Barbados, Curaçao, St. Thomas, Antigua, the Bahamas, Nevis, the Bay of Honduras, and Martinique.[12] Most of the 160 were imported by the members of just two families, one of them the leading Sephardic family of New York's small Jewish community, the other its leading Ashkenazic family. Both families were involved in commerce throughout the length and breadth of the Atlantic.[13] Sephardic Mordecai Gomez and two of his brothers, David and Daniel, imported 61 slaves, 55 of them in partnership with several non-Jews, and another 6 on their own. The Ashkenazic group, comprised of Moses Levy, his brother Samuel, and Levy's son-in-law, Jacob Franks, imported 71 slaves, 52 of them in partnership with non-Jews and an additional 19 on their own. The remaining 28 were imported by just three other members of the New York Jewish community, one of whom, Rodrigo Pacheco, returned to London in the late 1720s or early 1730s, from where he continued to invest in the importation of slaves into New York.[14]

The Gomez and Levy-Franks family groups did not stand out among the merchants of New York who imported and sold slaves. As indicated previously, more than 90 percent of the slaves documented by surviving Naval Office records arrived on vessels owned exclusively by non-Jews. Among the latter, certain families and individuals figured more prominently than most others. Abraham Van Horne was involved in the importation of at least 250 slaves; Cornelius Van Horne and Garrett Van Horne, 355; and William Walton, Sr. and Jr., 445. Others approximated the Gomez and Levy-Franks numbers, such as Philip Livingston with 80 imports, and Rip Van Dam with 67.

As with the recipients of slaves from Africa, the Manifest Books and the Entry Books for the port of New York identify individuals who received slaves from locations within the western hemisphere. Very few such slaves went to Jewish importers.[15] The latter included Abraham Rodrigues Rivera, his son Jacob Rodrigues Rivera, and his son-in-law Moses Lopez, three importers who would otherwise not be known, for they do not appear in surviving Naval Office records as the owners of vessels that brought slaves to the colony.[16] Abraham Rodrigues Rivera paid duties for 2 slaves in 1729 and for 1 in 1730, while Moses Lopez did so for a single slave in 1736.[17] Jacob Rodrigues Rivera, who in the future would participate in the African slave trade, took delivery of 16 slaves from Boston in 1746, 1 from Rhode Island in 1747, and 4 from Rhode Island in 1751.[18]

Abraham Rodrigues Rivera and Moses Lopez, both of them refugees from the Inquisition, had remade their lives in New York. Rivera had fled from Spain, eventually making his way to the colony by 1726. Lopez fled from Portugal in the early 1730s, going first to England before moving on to New York. In the late 1740s, certainly by 1750, the entire clan moved from New York to Newport, Rhode Island, one of the leading seaports in mainland North America during the colonial era. In 1752, the extended family welcomed yet another refugee from Portugal, Duarte Lopez, Moses's half-brother. Safe from the Inquisition in Newport, Duarte Lopez reverted openly to Judaism, underwent circumcision, and changed his name to Aaron. Following the death of his first wife ten years later, he married Jacob Rodrigues Rivera's daughter, thereby further solidifying the links between the Lopezes and the Riveras.[19]

A small Jewish presence existed in Newport as early as 1658, attracting additional numbers in the early 1690s from Curaçao. The group was of little consequence until the 1740s, and it is even doubtful that Jews resided in the town between the end of the seventeenth century and that decade.[20] As elsewhere, commercial ambitions drew Jewish merchants to it. In 1746, for example, Naphtali Hart, along with four non-Jewish Rhode Islanders, was named in a suit in Jamaica as the owner of a privateer.[21] In subsequent years, Hart continued to trade throughout the Atlantic, as did others such as Isaac Elizer and Aaron Lopez, whose commercial interests encompassed almost every conceivable product traded during the 1750s, 1760s, and early 1770s.[22] But despite the lure of commercial opportunity in Newport, the community always remained small, numbering approximately twelve families at the beginning of the 1760s, and between thirteen and twenty-two in 1774.[23] It took its members nine years to finance and erect a synagogue, and they were forced to turn to other

Jewish communities around the Atlantic for contributions toward its construction. Dedicated for use in 1763, the structure remained unfinished in 1768.[24]

Although it ran a distant fourth behind Liverpool, London, and Bristol, Newport was America's leading port in the African slave trade during the eighteenth century.[25] Shortly after his family settled in Newport, Jacob Rodrigues Rivera joined in partnership with William Vernon, a member of one of Newport's leading non-Jewish slave-trading families, in a venture to Africa. Sailing from Newport in 1753, their vessel, the *Sherbro,* made its way to Africa, from where it delivered a cargo to Suriname shortly before the end of 1754, although the number of slaves it carried there is not known.[26]

Rivera's partnership with Vernon inaugurated participation in the slave trade to Africa by the Jewish merchants of Newport, the only location in the British empire in which such activity by Jewish businessmen is known to have stretched over more than a handful of occasions. Two years after Rivera's initial venture, Naphtali Hart & Co.'s vessel, the *Camelion [sic]* arrived in Jamaica from Africa with fifty-five slaves on board.[27] However, the next known venture by Newport's Jewish merchants did not occur until 1761, when Rivera and his future son-in-law, Aaron Lopez, launched a voyage to Africa that resulted in the delivery of 134 slaves at Charleston at the beginning of 1763. Rivera and Lopez were subsequently partners on twelve more occasions between 1764 and 1774, while Lopez undertook eight additional ventures to Africa on his own, for a total of twenty-one during the course of his lifetime.[28] Finally, partners Isaac Elizer and Samuel Moses launched a slaving expedition in 1762, Naphtali Hart, Jr., sent out two in 1764, and Moses Levy accounted for one in 1765.[29]

In all, therefore, Newport's Jewish merchants organized and owned twenty-seven voyages in the African slave trade during the generation that preceded the outbreak of the American Revolution, comprising the largest involvement by Jews in the slave trade known for the British empire. Their ventures, however, represented a small part of the slave trade centered in Rhode Island. Jay Coughtry has identified 508 slave voyages from the colony to Africa during the period between 1709 and 1774, to which must be added one more, Naphtali Hart's undertaking in 1755 on the *Camelion*, for a grand total of 509 known voyages.[30] Over the course of the sixty-five years between 1709 and 1774, the twenty-seven expeditions mounted by Newport's Jewish merchants represented, accordingly, 5.3 percent of Rhode Island's known total. During the years encompassed by 1753, when Jacob Rodrigues Rivera first entered the slave trade to Africa, and 1774, when Aaron Lopez conducted his last venture, voyages from Rhode Island to Africa totaled 347. The twenty-seven launched by Newport's Jewish merchants during the twenty years in which they participated in the African slave trade therefore comprised 7.7 percent of the colony's efforts in that period.

The number of slaves known to have been transported from the coast of Africa by Rhode Island slave vessels between 1753 and 1774 was 16,043, in 145 of the 347 voyages conducted during those years.[31] Of the 145 vessels, 135, or 93.1 percent, were owned by non-Jews; they carried 14,643 slaves, or 91.2 percent of the entire 16,043. The remaining 10 vessels, or 6.8 percent, belonged to Newport's Jewish merchants, and they conveyed 1,400 slaves, or 8.7 percent. Hence, insofar as one can judge, during the years in which they participated in the slave trade, Newport's Jewish merchants were involved in fewer than 10 percent of Rhode Island's voyages to Africa and in fewer than 10 percent of the slaves the colony's businessmen carried away from Africa. Over the entire course of their colony's involvement in the African slave trade they were responsible for a still smaller percentage of slaves, for they did not participate in the slave trade prior to 1753. Projected forward to 1807, when the United States abolished the slave trade with Africa, the percentage falls even further, for among the 421 known Rhode Island voyages to Africa between 1784 and 1807, only 7 were mounted by Jewish merchants, in every case in partnership with non-Jewish merchants. All told, they participated in 34 ventures—a minute fragment of the entire British slave trade, which between 1698 and 1807 is currently known to have numbered in excess of 10,000 voyages.[32]

To Aaron Lopez, the merchant in the Jewish community who was the most frequently involved, the African slave trade represented a small part of his commercial activity. Lopez's bills of lading for September 3, 1771 through July 8, 1773 demonstrate that he had commercial interests in more than twenty-five different locations in continental North America, the Caribbean, South America, Europe, the Mediterranean, and Africa. Amidst a torrent of shipments during that period to New York, Philadelphia, Massachusetts, Jamaica, Barbados, Suriname, London, Bristol, Amsterdam, Madeira, Lisbon, and Gibraltar, he sent out six vessels to Africa.[33] In all, Lopez's twenty-one slaving ventures to Africa over the course of his commercial career represented approximately 10 percent of his trading expeditions.[34]

Within Newport, members of the Jewish community owned slaves, as did many of their non-Jewish neighbors. A total of 1,590 families resided in the town in 1774, of which at least 1,568 (98.6 percent) were not Jewish, 13 were Jewish (eight-tenths of 1 percent), and 9 were of uncertain religion (one-half of 1 percent). Of the 1,568 non-Jewish families, 493, or 31.4 percent, owned 1,200 of Newport's 1,246 slaves, or 96.3 percent of the enslaved population. Among the 13 Jewish families, 11, or 84.6 percent, owned 37 slaves, or 2.9 percent of the town's slaves. Jewish families in Newport, therefore, were more in evidence as slaveholders than non-Jewish ones, for with eight-tenths of 1 percent of the town's families, they owned almost 3 percent of its slaves, distributed among approximately five-sixths of their families. And while non-Jewish families comprised 98.6 percent of the town's families and held only slightly less than that proportion of its slaves, 96.3 percent, fewer than one-third of their families owned slaves. Furthermore, with 37 slaves in 11 families, the Jewish population averaged 3.3 slaves per family, while non-Jewish ones, with 1,200 slaves in 493 families, averaged 2.4.[35]

To the south, a new Jewish community began to form during the late 1730s when several Jewish merchants and shopkeepers from New York settled in Philadelphia. The newcomers included brothers Nathan and Isaac Levy, who at the end of 1737, the year they arrived in Pennsylvania, took delivery of an imported slave and placed a newspaper advertisement in order to sell their newly acquired property. During the following year, the two imported another slave, again placing an advertisement to sell. Nathan Levy placed yet another advertisement for a single slave in 1742, his third and last, and the last by any of Philadelphia's small Jewish population until 1761.[36]

In the absence of Naval Office or other customs records for Pennsylvania, newspaper advertisements reveal that a very small import trade in slaves existed in the colony prior to 1729, and that it increased in volume between 1729 and 1766, only to plummet in 1767 and fade away thereafter.[37] During what proved to be the heyday of the slave trade in the colony, David Franks, one of Philadelphia's Jewish merchants, participated with several non-Jewish partners in two ventures to Africa. Together with Thomas Riche and Daniel Rundle in the summer of 1761, Franks advertised the sale of a hundred slaves from Africa. A year later, this time in partnership with William Plumstead, he again advertised the sale of a hundred slaves from there.[38]

Growing hostility to the slave trade in Pennsylvania persuaded the colony's Assembly in 1761 to raise the duty on each imported slave from £2, the amount set in 1729, to £10.[39] Protesting against the threat to the slave trade, specifically that with the West Indies, twenty-four of Philadelphia's merchants submitted a petition to the colony's governor pleading for temporary relief; the group included David Franks and a second Jewish merchant, Benjamin Levy. Arguing that slave imports would reduce the high cost of labor in the colony, they requested that more time be permitted to elapse before the new duty went into effect—or at least until present orders were filled. But the die was cast: the governor notified the Assembly that he would sign the bill, and by 1767 Pennsylvania's import trade in slaves collapsed.[40] Philadelphia's Jewish merchants would never play any part in the slave trade comparable to that of their contemporaries in Newport.

Philadelphia's inhabitants owned 1,118 slaves in 1769, according to its proprietary tax list for that year. Entries for non-Jewish individuals who owned slaves were 618 in number, with a total of 1,106 slaves, or 98.9 percent of all slaves, each entry averaging 1.7 slaves each. Entries for individuals whose religion is uncertain were 3 in number, with 4 slaves, an average of 1.3 each. The remaining 6 entries were for Jewish residents of Philadelphia. With 8 slaves among them, or seven-tenths of 1 percent of all slaves, they averaged somewhat less than Philadelphia's non-Jewish residents at 1.3 slaves each.[41]

Naval Office records for the colony of South Carolina, where a small Jewish community took root in Charleston during the 1740s and 1750s, confirm once again that, with the exception of Newport, Jews in the British empire ordinarily did not participate in the slave trade. Records survive for roughly twenty-eight years of the period between October 29, 1716 and September 30, 1767, and document the importation of 34,677 slaves. Of these, 34,465, or 99.3 percent, arrived in South Carolina aboard vessels owned by non-Jews, and 24 on vessels whose owners' religion is not certain.[42]

The remaining 188 slaves, or one-half of 1 percent, arrived on three different vessels owned by Jewish merchants, one of whom resided in Charleston. Early in 1731, 5 slaves arrived in the colony from Jamaica on the *Patience,* a sloop owned by Rodrigo Pacheco, who has been encountered earlier as a minor slave importer located in New York and London.[43] In the second instance, Moses Lindo, a member of Charleston's nascent Jewish community, imported 49 slaves from Barbados on his vessel, the *Lindo.*[44] Finally, in 1763 the Naval Office recorded the arrival of the *Greyhound,* the property of "Aaron Loper [sic], Jacob Rod Rivera of NYork [sic]," with 134 slaves. This, of course, was Aaron Lopez's and Jacob Rodrigues Rivera's first partnership in the slave trade, and Lopez's first venture to Africa.[45]

Other than Moses Lindo, no Jewish colonists who resided in Charleston are known to have engaged in the importation of slaves as shipowners. Had there been any, their impact on the slave trade, like that of non-Jews in South Carolina, would have been negligible, for vessels from South Carolina engaged in the slave trade were few and far between before the American Revolution.[46] Nor did Jewish merchants in the colony figure significantly as factors. Of 389 cargoes of slaves advertised for sale in Charleston's newspaper between 1733 and 1774, 5 were advertised by firms that had Jewish members. In 1755, Solomon Isaacs advertised 3 cargoes, twice on his own and once with two non-Jewish partners. Five years later, the firm of Isaac Da Costa and his non-Jewish partner Thomas Farr announced the sale of 200 slaves, and in January 1763 the sale of the slaves imported on the *Greyhound,* the vessel that belonged to Aaron Lopez and Jacob Rodrigues Rivera.[47]

The 5 cargoes received by Solomon Isaacs and by Da Costa and Farr are known as well from the records of the import duties on slaves they paid in the office of the colony's Treasurer. Jewish individuals in South Carolina paid import duties on 6 additional cargoes of slaves between 1735 and 1776: once each by Isaac De Pass in 1752, Solomon Isaacs in 1755, Isaac Da Costa in 1765, Jacob Wolfe in 1769, Nathan Levi in 1772, and Jacob Aarons in 1772. In all, therefore, Jewish importers took delivery of 11 slave cargoes, amounting to less than 1 percent (nine-tenths of 1 percent) of the 1,108 cargoes on which South Carolina's importers and factors paid duties over the course of the forty-one-year period.[48]

In neighboring Georgia, no involvement in the slave trade is known for the minuscule Jewish population that resided there. Sixteen Jewish individuals in 1750 and perhaps six Jewish families in 1771 resided in Savannah.[49] None appear in the sparse Naval Office records that survive for the colony, with the possible exception of Issac De Lyon; in partnership with two other merchants, an Isaac Lyon imported eight slaves in 1763.[50] There is, as well, the case of James Lucena, who in 1767 imported one slave. Lucena was Aaron Lopez's cousin, but unlike his relative in Newport he did not profess Judaism when he departed from Portugal. Continuing to adhere to Christianity while he resided in North America, he apparently affiliated with the Anglican church, and upon his return to Portugal before the end of the American Revolution he rejoined the Catholic church.[51]

That Jews in the southern colonies owned a very small number of slaves may be inferred from the first national census, conducted shortly after the end of the colonial era in 1790 by the newly established United States of America. While Georgia's census returns no

longer exist, having suffered destruction in 1812, those for South
Carolina reveal that Charleston's Jewish population owned 93 slaves.
Elsewhere in South Carolina, the state's Jewish inhabitants owned
64.[52]

In the North, where slavery still existed, the census of 1790 enumer-
ated a total of 64 slaves owned by Jews who resided in New York
City, Westchester County, Boston, Philadelphia, Lancaster, and Newport. The New Yorkers led with 35, and the Rhode Islanders followed with 16, less than half of the 37 they had owned in 1774.[53]
But then, the Newport Jewish community was in a state of deterioration and decline, unable to reconstitute itself after the American
Revolution, gone entirely by the early 1820s. Aaron Lopez had died
by drowning in 1782. His father-in-law, Jacob Rodrigues Rivera,
returned to Newport after the Revolution, where he joined with
several non-Jewish partners in two slave ventures to Africa in 1785
and 1786, before dying in 1789. Although Rhode Island's slave trade
to Africa continued to flourish until 1807, his efforts were almost the
last by Newport's few remaining Jews.[54]

Conclusion

Jewish involvement in the institution of slavery in the British empire was thus exceedingly limited. Jews participated as investors, importers, exporters, factors, and owners, but in no segment of the business of slavery did they stand out, save for the exceptions of Alexandre Lindo in Jamaica and Jacob Rodrigues Rivera and Aaron Lopez in Rhode Island. However, even in those instances the overall impact of the Jewish population in the colonies was marginal. Lindo's activity as a factor occurred during fifteen of the last twenty years of the slave trade, two-thirds of the time with a non-Jewish partner, while Rivera's and Lopez's ventures in the slave trade comprised an infinitesimal part of the slaving expeditions undertaken by British merchants to the coasts of Africa.

In London, the Jews of the Resettlement never invested in the Company of Royal Adventurers Trading into Africa, and after its demise they waited twenty years before beginning to invest in its successor, the Royal African Company. When at length they did so, it was after the Company had already delivered the majority of the slaves it would ever transport to the western hemisphere, and they would always remain distinctly in the minority among its shareholders. Most Jews with capital to invest avoided the Company altogether, preferring investment in the Bank of England and the East India Company, while almost all those who did purchase its stock simultaneously apportioned their capital among other investment opportunities. The South Sea Company also attracted only a minority of England's Jewish investors when it was established, although, proportionally, they were more willing to risk larger amounts in the new enterprise than were non-Jewish investors.

Because England's Jewish merchants did not trade with Africa, almost none of them were drawn into the exchange of European goods for slaves. Nor are any known to have been among the primary owners of the slave fleets of London, Bristol, and Liverpool, and it is highly unlikely that they figured to any significant degree as minor investors in the slave ships of the three ports. A few instances of participation as the owners of ships engaged in the African slave trade are known, but the number of slaves transported to the Americas as a result of their activity added up to a minute fraction of the vast British slave trade.

Jewish merchants in Jamaica and Barbados did not participate in the slave trade from Africa to the western hemisphere. A small number in New York, Philadelphia, and Newport did, and they engaged as well in the import trade in slaves from the Caribbean. Cumulatively, their impact on the forced migration of approximately three million people from Africa to the Americas in Britain's eighteenth-century slave trade was minute in the extreme. In Jamaica, some of Kingston's Jewish merchants participated in the colony's export trade in slaves, but again much of the time they occupied a small place in that commerce. Briefly, during the 1780s their export activity increased markedly, but thereafter it fell back to the lower levels that had prevailed earlier in the century.

In factoring as well, Jamaica's Jewish businessmen became more apparent during the 1780s, but here their visibility did not diminish. Alexandre Lindo's commanding position as a factor lasted throughout the 1790s, although during nearly the whole decade he operated with a non-Jewish partner. Prior to the 1780s, Jamaica's Jewish merchants played at the most a minute role as factors, and in this regard they were comparable to their counterparts in Barbados and South Carolina.

As owners, Jews held a minute part of the slaves in the colonies in which they settled. Most gravitated to towns, where they pursued careers as merchants and shopkeepers; few accumulated property in the countryside or attempted to engage in plantation agriculture.

Indeed, their avoidance of plantation life proved to be a recurrent source of the criticism directed against them late in the seventeenth century in Jamaica. Within the towns in which they resided, they usually did not own a disproportionate number of slaves, and they usually owned fewer slaves on the average than their non-Jewish neighbors. On the other hand, they were usually more likely to own slaves than non-Jews were; and in Kingston in 1769 and Newport in 1774, Jewish slaveowners owned more slaves on the average than non-Jewish slaveowners.

Why the Jewish inhabitants of the British empire were not more deeply involved in the slave trade as investors, importers, factors, and exporters is not known. Their careers in commerce; their membership in an ethnoreligious trading network that spanned the Atlantic; their facility with foreign languages that, like the last, bestowed a competitive edge: all would seem to have led them to greater participation in what was one of the largest economic enterprises in the Atlantic world during the seventeenth and eighteenth centuries. Archival sources, particularly the extensive papers of Nathan Simson, Aaron Lopez, and Moses Levy Newton are silent on this issue. Ascertaining what motivated them must await future discoveries in other sources or, perhaps, the enunciation of a general theory of the paths selected and the niches occupied by different ethnic, religious, and national groups in the Atlantic trading community during the era of the slave trade.

Future research perhaps may also bring to light occasional instances of investment by Jewish individuals as minor shareholders in slave ships. The voluminous papers in England of the Court of Chancery, the records of bankruptcy commissions, and the papers of major slave-trading firms might add to our knowledge of this avenue for participation in the slave trade.

Finally, comparable study of participation by Jewish merchants in the Dutch slave trade is warranted, although its dimensions were far smaller than Britain's slave trade. In addition to the Jewish community in Amsterdam, Jewish merchants resided in Suriname, St. Eustatius, and Curaçao, which, like Jamaica, exported slaves to South

America. Comparing their activity with that of their counterparts in the British empire would establish whether the patterns observed for England and her colonies were unique, or whether they were typical of the paths taken by Jewish entrepreneurs who settled in other parts of the Atlantic region during the seventeenth and eighteenth centuries.

Appendixes

147

IV. Slave Imports and Exports
1. Slave Imports Recorded by the Naval Office in Jamaica, 1719–1806
2. Slave Exports Recorded by the Naval Office in Jamaica, 1719–1806
3. Slave Exports from Jamaica on Vessels Owned by Jews, 1742–1806
4. Slave Imports Recorded by the Naval Office in Barbados, 1728–1806
5. Slave Exports Recorded by the Naval Office in Barbados, 1781–1806
6. Slave Imports Recorded by the Naval Office in New York, 1715–65

V. The Jewish Population of Port Royal, Jamaica
1. Jewish Inhabitants of Port Royal, 1680
2. Jewish Inhabitants of Port Royal, 1738–40

VI. The Jewish Population of Kingston, Jamaica
1. Jewish Households and Companies in Kingston, 1745
2. Jewish Households and Companies in Kingston, 1769
3. Jewish Households and Companies in Kingston, 1795
4. Jewish Households and Companies in Kingston, 1819

VII. The Jewish Population of the Parish of St. Catherine, Jamaica
1. Jewish Households and Companies in Spanish Town, 1772
2. Jewish Households and Companies in St. Catherine, 1820

VIII. Jewish Slaveowners in Montego Bay, Jamaica, 1774

IX. Jewish Landowners in Jamaica, 1754

X. Jewish Inhabitants of Bridgetown, Barbados, 1798–1818

XI. Jewish Slaveowners in St. Michael, Barbados, 1729

XII. Slave Registers, 1817
 1. Barbados, 1817: Jewish Slaveholders
 2. Jamaica, 1817: Jewish Slaveholders

XIII. Jewish Burghers and Slaves in St. Eustatius, 1781

I. Determining Who Was Jewish

The distinctive family names of the Sephardic Jews who comprised the majority of the Resettlement in England and the Jewish communities of Barbados, Jamaica, and Nevis provide the most important clue for identifying nearly all the people studied here. Because virtually no Spanish or Portuguese individuals settled in England or the colonies, there is little if any risk in stating that the bearers of such surnames as Henriques, Belisario, Pinheiro, Melhado, Da Costa, Fernandez, Nunes, Lopez, and others that originated in Spain and Portugal were Jewish.[1] Conversely, few Sephardic Jews can have been missed because they had family names that were more typically English, Scottish, or French Huguenot than Jewish, such as Martin or Barrow. All surviving original sources that have been consulted indicate that hardly any did, and it is therefore unlikely that any with such names have been improperly omitted. In the few cases where uncertainty exists because of surnames that could have been either Jewish or non-Jewish, the bearers have been placed in the category of "Religion Not Certain" in the appendixes that follow and in the notes to the text.

Abundant original sources provide verification for the Jewish identities of individuals with Spanish and Portuguese names, and for establishing the religious identities of the few with family names that could have been either Jewish, English, Scottish, or French Huguenot. The sources include synagogue records for England, Jamaica, and Barbados; last wills and testaments for Jamaica and Barbados, in which Jewish testators frequently invoked the god of Israel, swore on the Five Books of Moses, left legacies to the synagogue, made donations to Jewish charities for the poor, or mentioned relatives whose Jewish identity is not in doubt; naturalization records for Jamaica between 1740 and 1750; tombstone inscriptions and baptismal and non-Jewish marriage records for Jamaica and Barbados; and a 1783 newspaper account of contributors in Kingston to a fund for English captives in which the names and amounts *"Subscribed by the* JEWISH *Nation"* are listed separately.[2] Similarly, the 1679–80 census for

Bridgetown contains a separate section entitled "The Jewes," while in the St. Eustatius census of February 1781 Jewish burghers appear at the end of each letter of the alphabet. Finally, the papers of Nathan Simson, Aaron Lopez, Moses Levy Newton, and Harmon Hendricks, as well as the diary of the Sheftalls of Savannah, establish Jewish identities in a small but important number of instances.[3]

Secondary works by twentieth-century historians and other writers are also of great value in determining who was Jewish, although not all the identifications in such studies have been accepted here.[4] The secondary literature is particularly rich for England in the late 1600s and early 1700s, and assists in identifying Jewish stockholders in the Royal African Company, the East India Company, and the South Sea Company. Considerably less is available for Jamaica and Barbados, but the one full-length study of the Jews of Jamaica that exists (which is less a history than a hagiographic chronicle) is invaluable for establishing several identities, notably of Ashkenazic individuals.

Identifying Ashkenazim is more problematic than identifying Sephardim, beginning with the fact that, while they often had family names like Wolfe, Franks, Lazarus, Isaacs, and Hyman, their patronymics were sometimes not as distinctive as the Spanish and Portuguese surnames of the Sephardim. Fortunately, however, Ashkenazim in the Caribbean colonies were far fewer in number than the Sephardim. Moreover, the surviving synagogue records of Jamaica and Barbados date to the 1780s, the decade when Jews who traced their origins to central and eastern Europe began to settle in the two colonies in larger numbers than before. As is true for the Sephardim, wills, tombstone inscriptions, personal papers, and the like add considerably to the information in the synagogue records. In one instance, a gravestone removed from its original location to the yard of the Kingston synagogue identifies an early Ashkenazic individual who was present in Jamaica by 1745, who might otherwise have been misclassified as an Englishman or as of uncertain religion.[5]

Non-Jewish family names current among the Ashkenazim complicate the process of identifying them. The major instances encountered in this study were Arnold, Duke, Elkin, Flash, Gates, Hart, Hatchwell, Jacobs, Lucas, Lyons, Phillips, and Rivers. The original sources mentioned above, particularly the synagogue records, but also the wills, tombstones, and the papers of Moses Levy Newton, were of critical importance in differentiating those with such names who were Jewish from those who were not. Doing so is necessary to avoid either undercounting or overinflating the number of slaves owned by the Jewish population.

Conversely, a handful of non-Jews had family names usually associated with Jews, such as Cohen, Levy, Benjamin, and Israel. Wills, tombstone inscriptions of non-Jews, and the baptismal and non-Jewish marriage records of Barbados and Jamaica were consequently combed in order to identify bearers of these names who were in fact not Jewish. While they were very few in number, counting such individuals as Jewish would incorrectly inflate the number of slaves actually owned by Jews.[6]

In an exceedingly small number of instances, assimilation left people who were non-Jewish with Jewish names. One such case in Jamaica is that of Ralph Bernal, Esq., whose 601 slaves in the triennial register for 1817 would make for a sizable mistake in the number of slaves owned by Jews were he incorrectly included among them. Bernal was a Sephardic family name; and Bernals figured among the Jewish merchants of Kingston during the 1780s and the Jewish inhabitants of Spanish Town and Montego Bay in the early 1800s. Ralph Bernal's father, on the other hand, married a Christian woman, making the child non-Jewish according to Jewish law. Raised as a Christian, Bernal attended an English university, entered one of the Inns of Court, and ultimately served as a member of Parliament.[7] But such cases are rare, for intermarriage was an unusual occurrence in the eighteenth and early nineteenth centuries, as a search of marriage records between 1800 and 1815 for Kingston, St. Andrew, St. Catherine, Port Royal, and St. James demonstrated.[8]

Care must also be exercised not to count free people of color with Jewish surnames as Jewish.[9] Some may have acquired their family names through concubinage or from Jewish fathers, and still others perhaps took the names of their former owners when they were manumitted.[10] Some among the population of free people of color owned slaves, but counting them as Jewish because of their names would, again, incorrectly inflate the number of slaves owned by Jews, for there is no evidence that these individuals belonged to the Jewish community. Poll-tax records and the triennial slave register for 1817 identify free people of color who owned slaves as free Negroes, free mulattoes, or free blacks, but whether they do so in every case is not known.[11] The figures presented here for Jews and the number of slaves they owned may therefore be slightly inflated.

The identification of Jews in the North American colonies is facilitated by the extensive historical and genealogical studies published during the course of the present century. The historical works of Jacob Rader Marcus and the massive genealogical compilation by Malcolm Stern are of particular value for this purpose, while local histories of the early Jewish communities of New York, Newport, Philadelphia, Charleston, and Savannah provide amplification.

The appendixes that follow list the individuals who have been identified as Jewish and those whose religion is uncertain. They are included here so that future researchers may, as necessary, refine the data presented in them and the results reported in the text.

Notes

1. White settlers in Jamaica were overwhelmingly English or Scottish, while considerably fewer than 1 percent were from Spanish America; Trevor Burnard, "European Migration to Jamaica, 1655–1780," 3d ser., *William and Mary Quarterly* 53 (1996): 781–82, 790.
2. An unusual example of the importance of wills in the identification process is that of Daniel Albuquerque Da Costa of Kingston in 1748; IRO, Wills, XXVII, 4. Da Costa appears on the Kingston poll tax of 1745 as the owner of three slaves, but only as "Daniel Albuquerque." His will, therefore, is the only way to establish that, as a Da Costa, he was Jewish.
3. For an important example of the importance of personal papers in the identification process, see the case of Henry Israel at n. 6, infra.
4. See Chapter One, n. 57, and Chapter Two, n. 18.
5. Joseph Polander, who is on the Kingston poll-tax list for 1745, and who died in 1752. I am indebted to Mr. Ainsley Henriques of Kingston for informing me of the collection of gravestones at the synagogue.
6. See, for example, the family of Grace Israel in the parish of Clarendon

in Jamaica. Israel invoked Jesus Christ in her 1779 will, and mentioned her sons William Hewitt Israel and Joseph Israel; IRO, XLVI, 18. The 1772 will of Thomas Moses of St. Thomas-in-the-East, Jamaica, shows no Jewish associations whatsoever; IRO, XL, 163. Bellevue Lions [Lyons] of Falmouth in Jamaica directed that he receive a Christian burial; IRO, CXX, 11.

In contrast to Grace Israel and her children, Henry Israel, who appears on the Kingston poll-tax list of 1745 as the owner of nineteen slaves, was Jewish, as is clear from a letter that he wrote to Aaron Lopez in 1770, in which he stated that he had lived in the parish of St. Ann for forty-two years; 7th ser., *Collections of the Massachusetts Historical Society* 9 (1914): 338. The assumption made here, in including him among the Jews of Kingston in 1745, is that if in fact he already resided in St. Ann, he could well have owned slaves in Kingston. On the other hand, the Henry Israel of St. Ann in the triennial register of 1817 has been classified as being of uncertain religion, in view of the fact that no original source confirms that he was Jewish. While he may have been the first Henry Israel's grandson, he may just as well have been a free person of color with a Jewish name, a problem in the identification process discussed below.

Non-Jews in Barbados with seemingly Jewish names included John Israel (married in 1794), Henry and Susanna Levine (baptized their daughter in 1722), and David and Mary Israel (baptized their son in 1735); Joanne Mcree Sanders, *Barbados Records: Marriages, 1643–1800*, 2 vols. (Houston: Sanders Historical Publications, 1982), I, 285, and Joanne Mcree Sanders, *Barbados Records: Baptisms, 1637–1800* (Baltimore: Genealogical Publishing Co., 1984), 334, 518.

7. *Royal Gazette*, October 27, 1781, Supplement; Jacob A. P. M. Andrade, *A Record of the Jews in Jamaica from the English Conquest to the Present Time* (Kingston: Jamaica Times, 1941), 170.

8. But for an early instance of intermarriage, see the lawsuit in 1743 brought by a Jewish woman, Sarah Mendes Gutteres of Kingston, who had married William Forbes despite her father's threats to kill him, preferring to be "hanged with honour than live with disgrace," as the father told Forbes; JA, Records of the Court of Chancery, 1A/3/13, 442–43. Also, in 1741, Rachel Cardozo, "A person professing the Christian Religion," was naturalized in Jamaica; J. H. Hollander, "The Naturalization of Jews in the American Colonies under the Act of 1740," *Publications of the American Jewish Historical Society* 5 (1897): 112.

Thomas G. August has concluded that "marriage between Jew and Christian was taboo and did not become commonplace until the late nineteenth and early twentieth centuries" in Jamaica; Thomas G. August, "Family Structure and Jewish Continuity in Jamaica since 1655," *American Jewish Archives* 41 (1989): 30.

9. See, for example, Daniel, Moses, Elias, Abraham, and Joseph Rodrigues of the parish of St. James, Jamaica, in 1774, all of whom appear on A List of Quarteroons, Mulattoes and Negreos *[sic]* who are Free and Able to bear Arms at BL, Long Papers, Add. Ms. 12,435, 6. For instances in Kingston, see the marriages of Robert Craswell Gabay on January 23,1804, Letitia Dunn Lindo on August 4, 1810, and David De Leon on March 1, 1813; JA, 1B/11/8/9/14. Examples in Barbados include Richard, Rachel, and Mary De Piza, Catherine, Edward, Susanna, and Esther Lindo, and Judith, Mercy, and William Nunes; in Sanders, *Baptisms,* 188, 208, 212, 228, 230, 235, 237, 240.

10. For slaves with Jewish surnames, see the marriages of Mary Mendes Pereira on July 2, 1808 in Kingston, and George Lindo to Ann Lindo on April 6, 1815. The two Lindo slaves resided in the parish of St. Andrew on Constant Spring Estate, the property of Abraham Alexandre Lindo. For Pereira, see JA, 1B/11/8/9/14, and for the two Lindos, 1B/11/8/1/2; for the owner of Constant Spring, see PRO, T 71/125. On concubinage, see August, "Family Structure," 38–39. For slave manumissions by both Jewish and non-Jewish owners, see JA, 1B/11/6/5 for 1747–55, and 2/6/277 for Kingston between 1761 and 1795. Examples of manumissions by Jews in the latter are numbers 93, 104, 113, 121, 134–36, 184–85, 224–29, 234, 237, 259, 435, 469, 478, and 539–41.

11. For examples of free people of color in Jamaica with Jewish surnames who owned slaves, see the triennial register for the parish of Westmoreland in 1817 for Leah Touro, Abraham Pessoa, and Aaron De Leon; PRO, T 71/178, 128, 344, 443. For Barbados, also in 1817, see the instances of Harriet Levi, Sarah Barrow, Eliza Brandon, and partners Isaac Cohen and Benjamin Brandon, all of the parish of St. Michael; PRO, T 71/520.

II. Jewish Investors in England

TABLE I

Jewish Investors in the Royal African Company and the Bank of England,
1691–1701

	RAC	BOE
Adolph, Jacob	*	*
Almanza, Joseph	*	
Almanza, Manuel De	*	*
Alvarenga, Isaac Da Costa		*
Alvarenga, Samuel Da Costa		*
Alvarez, Aaron	*	*
Alvarez, Isaac		*
Aranjo, Abraham Gomez De		*
Athias, Simson Da Costa		*
Barrow, Moses		*
Bernal, Abraham	*	
Carrion, Moses	*	*
Casseres, Francis De		*
Castro, Isaac De		*
Castro, Joseph De		*
Coutinho, Isaac Pereira	*	
Da Costa, Abraham		*
Da Costa, Alvaro	*	*
Da Costa, Anthony, Jr.		*
Da Costa, Anthony, [Sr.]		*
Da Costa, Isaac Telles		*
Da Costa, John Mendes, Sr.	*	*
Da Costa, Joseph Nunes	*	*
Da Costa, Moses Telles	*	
Da Costa, Philip Mendes		*
Dessa, Jacob		*
Dias, Isaac		*
Faro, David De		*
Faro, John Rodrigues		*
Fonseca, Alvaro Da		*
Francia, Moses		*
Francia, Simon	*	
Franco, Abraham de Moseh		*
Gomez Serra, Anthony		*
Gomez Serra, Phineas	*	*
Gomez, Isaac		*
Gonzalez, Jacques	*	*
Henriques, Elias Gabay(+)		*
Henriques, Isaac Senior	*	*
Henriques, Jacob Gabay(+)		*
Henriques, Peter, Jr.	*	*

	RAC	BOE
Henriques, Peter, Sr.	*	
Levy, Benjamin	*	*
Lindo, Alexander		*
Lindo, Elias	*	*
Lis, Francisco De, Jr.		*
Lopez, Joseph		*
Mattos, Daniel De		*
Mattos, Jacob Teixeira De	*	*
Medina, Moses De	*	*
Medina, Sir Solomon De	*	*
Mellado, Isaac Lopez	*	*
Mendes, Abraham, Sr.		*
Mendes, Dr. Ferdinando		*
Mendes, Menasseh		*
Mesquita, Peter Henriques Da		*
Miranda, Jacob Gabay		*
Miranda, Manuel Nunes		*
Mogadouro, Pantalio Rodrigues		*
Morenu, Jacob De Paz	*	*
Morenu, Solomon De Paz		*
Mussaphia, Joseph		*
Nunes, Isaac Fernandez	*	*
Nunes, Jacob Fernandez		*
Nunes, Moses Israel	*	*
Paiba, Abraham De		*
Paz, Elias		*
Paz, Samuel De		*
Penso, David	*	*
Pereira, Francis		*
Pereira, Manuel Lopez		*
Portello, Isaac		*
Rodrigues, Alphonso	*	*
Rodrigues, Simon	*	*
Salvador, Francis		*
Sasportas, Samuel	*	
Silva, Fernando		*
Silveira, Antonio		*
Sotto, Benjamin Del		*
Valencia, Isaac De	*	*
Religion Not Certain:		
Dirquez, Jacques		*
Duez, Abraham		*
Martins, Abraham		*
Martins, Philip		*
Veiga, William	*	*

	RAC	BOE
Stockjobbers: (§)		
Abarbanel, Ephraim		
Avila, David D'		
Da Costa, John Mendes, Jr.		
Hart, Moses		
Mendes, Solomon		

RAC   Royal African Company

BOE   Bank of England

(+) Of Amsterdam

(§) Stockjobbers in Bank of England stock who are not known to have possessed their own shares

SOURCES: PRO, T 70/187, 70/188, 70/189; [J. A. Giuseppi], "Early Jewish Holders of Bank of England Stock (1694–1725),"*Miscellanies of the Jewish Historical Society of England* 6 (1962): 143–74.

TABLE 2

New Jewish Investors in the Royal African Company
and the Bank of England, 1702–12

	RAC	BOE
Abarbanel, Ephraim	*	
Almeida, Gaspar De		*
Almeida, Mordecai D'		*
Alvarenga, Daniel Da Costa		*
Alvarez, Isaac	*	
Alvarez, Matthias		*
Arias, Abraham Nunes		*
Azulay, Moses		*
Barrow, Moses	*	
Cardozo, Abraham		*
Cardozo, Moses		*
Castro, Isaac De	*	
Castro, Joseph De	*	
Castro, Solomon De	*	*
Correa, Abraham	*	*
Correa, David	*	*
Da Costa, Abraham	*	*
Da Costa, Anthony, Sr.	*	
Da Costa, Anthony Mendes		*
Da Costa, Fernando		*
Da Costa, Jacob Mendes	*	
Da Costa, John, Jr.		*
Da Costa, John Mendes, Jr.		*
Da Costa, Joseph		*
Da Costa, Joseph Telles		*

	RAC	BOE
Da Cunha, Judica		*
Felix, Abraham Penso(+)		*
Ferreira, Domingo Lopez		*
Ferreira, Jacob Henriques		*
Fonseca, Rodrigo Alvares		*
Francia, Widow Isabel		*
Francia, Simon		*
Franco, Abraham Israel		*
Franks, Moses		*
Gabay, Jacob	*	
Gideon, Rowland		*
Gideon, Samson		*
Gomez, Isaac	*	
Hart, Moses	*	*
Hart, Solomon		*
Henriques, Joseph, Jr.		*
Henriques, Joseph, Sr.		*
Isaac, Benjamin	*	*
Jacobs, Issachar		*
Lobo, Daniel Jesur[u]n(+)		*
Marquez, Manuel		*
Mazahod, Jacob		*
Mendes, Anthony	*	*
Mendes, David Franco		*
Mendes, Jacob, Jr.		*
Mendes, James (Jacob)	*	*
Mendes, John, Jr.	*	
Mendes, Moses, Jr.		*
Mercado, Abraham De		*
Meza, Manuel		*
Miranda, Isaac		*
Mocatta, Abraham		*
Mocatta, Moses	*	
Nunes, Abraham Franco		*
Nunes, Abraham Israel		*
Pacheco, Isaac		*
Paiba, Isaac De		*
Paiba, Moses De		*
Paz, Dr. David De		*
Peixoto, Isaac		*
Penso, Raphael		*
Pereira, David Lopez		*
Pereira, Francisco	*	
Pereira, Solomon de Moses	*	*
Pinto, Paulo Jacome(+)		*
Portello, Isaac	*	
Porto, Jacob Do		*
Prado, Joshua(+)		*
Rocamora, Hester(+)		*

	RAC	BOE
Rocamora, Dr. Isaac(+)		*
Rocamora, Dr. Solomon De(+)		*
Rodrigues, Isaac		*
Rodrigues, Joseph	*	*
Salomon, Benedictus		*
Salvador, Daniel		*
Silva, Fernando Da, Jr.	*	*
Sotto, Benjamin Del	*	
Teixeira, Benjamin(+)		*
Teixeira, Manuel, Jr.(+)		*
Veiga, Jacob Da		*
Ximenes, Rodrigo	*	*
Religion Not Certain:		
Crueze, Solomon De La		*
Joseph, Benjamin, Jr.		*
Julien, Simeon		*
Martines, Philip	*	
Martins, Isaac, Jr.		*
Martins, Jacob	*	*
Stockjobbers: (§)		
Alvarez, Jacob, Jr.		
Julian (Juliao), Jacob Henriques		
Mendes, Alvaro		
Mendes, Jacob Roiz		
Mendes, Lewis		
Silva, Jacob Da		

RAC   Royal African Company

BOE   Bank of England

(+) Of Amsterdam

(§) Stockjobbers in Bank of England stock who are not known to have possessed their own shares

SOURCES: PRO, T 70/191, 70/196; [J. A. Giuseppi], "Early Jewish Holders of Bank of England Stock (1694-1725)," *Miscellanies of the Jewish Historical Society of England* 6 (1962): 143-74.

TABLE 3

Jewish Shareholders in the Royal African Company,
April 15–May 5, 1708

Shareholder	Stock Value (£)
Bernal, Abraham	6,000
Castro, Isaac De	4,500
Castro, Joseph De	250
Da Costa, Abraham	7,000
Da Costa, Anthony, Jr.	500
Da Costa, John Mendes	4,100
Gabay, Jacob	3,000
Gomez Serra, Phineas	1,200
Henriques, Isaac Senior	11,400
Henriques, Peter, Jr.	2,700
Mattos, Jacob Teixeira De	2,000
Medina, Moses De	8,000
Pereira, Solomon de Moses	2,500
Rodrigues, Alphonso and Simon	600
Silva, Fernando, Jr.	3,000
Ximenes, Rodrigo	3,500
Religion Not Certain:	
Martin, Jacob	1,000
Martins, Philip	1,500

SOURCE: PRO, T 70/196.

TABLE 4

Jewish Investors in the East India Company,
1668–March 25, 1709

	a	b	c
Abarbanel, Ephraim			*
Alvarez, Aaron			*
Alvarez, Jacob, Jr.			*
Athias, Simson Da Costa			*
Barrow, Moses			*
Bernal, Abraham			*
Bernal, Simon Francisco			*
Bravo, James			*
Cardozo, Abraham			*
Castro, Isaac De			*
Castro, Joseph De			*
Correa, David			*
Da Costa, Abraham			*
Da Costa, Alvaro		*	*

	a	b	c
Da Costa, Anthony, Jr.			*
Da Costa, Anthony, Sr.	*		*
Da Costa, Fernando			*
Da Costa, John Mendes	*		*
Da Costa, Joseph			*
Da Costa, Lewis			*
Da Costa, Philip			*
Da Fonseca, Alvaro			*
Ferreira, Domingo Lopez			*
Gabay, Jacob	*		*
Gomez Serra, Anthony	*		
Gomez Serra, Moses			*
Gomez Serra, Phineas			*
Hart, Moses			*
Henriques, Abraham Bueno	*		
Henriques, Anthony			*
Henriques, Isaac, Sr.			*
Henriques, Joseph, Jr.			*
Henriques, Joseph, [Sr.]			*
Henriques, Joshua Bueno	*		
Henriques, Peter	*		
Henriques, Peter, Jr.			*
Henriques, "Pierra"	*		
Juliao (Julian), Jacob Henriques			*
Levy, Benjamin		*	*
Lis, Francis De	*		
Magadouro, Pantolio Rodrigues			*
Marquez, Antonio Rodrigues	*		
Mattos, Jacob Teixeira [De]			*
Medina, Moses De			*
Medina, Sir Solomon		*	
Mendes, Abraham			*
Mendes, Anthony & James			*
Mendes, Dr. Fernando			*
Mendes, Jacob Rodrigues			*
Mendes, Menasseh			*
Mendes, Solomon			*
Nunes, Isaac Fernandez			*
Nunes, Jacob Fernandez			*
Nunes, Moses Israel	*		
Pacheco, Aaron			*
Paiba, Moses De			*
Paz, Elias			*
Peixoto, Isaac			*
Penso, Raphael			*
Pereira, Francis			*
Pereira, Manuel Lopez			*
Pereira, Solomon de Moses			*
Rodrigues, Alphonso	*		*

	a	b	c
Rodrigues, Joseph			*
Rodrigues, Simon	*		
Rodrigues, "Simon Alpho"			*
Salvadore, Daniel			*
Silva, Fernando, Jr.			*
Sotto, Benjamin Del			*
Valencia, Isaac De			*
Veiga, Jacob Da			*
Ximenes, Rodrigo			*
Religion Not Certain:			
Martines, Philip			*
Martins, Jacob			*
Veiga, William	*		

a Acquired shares 1668–May 26, 1691

b Acquired shares for the first time between May 27, 1691 and April 19, 1695

c Held shares on March 25, 1709

SOURCES: Ethel Bruce Sainsbury, *A Calendar of the Court Minutes Etc. of the East India Company,* 11 Vols. (Oxford: Clarendon Press, 1907–38), VIII, X, XI; BL, Records of the East India Company, Court Books, B/37, B/38, B/39, B/40, B/50A.

TABLE 5

Jewish Investors in the South Sea Company
Who were Qualified to Vote,
December 25, 1714

	4 Votes	3 Votes	2 Votes	1 Vote
Abarbanel, Ephraim				*
Alvarez, Aaron				*
Alvarez, Matthias				*
Barrow, Moses			*	
Cardozo, Abraham				*
Da Costa, Abraham			*	
Da Costa, Alvaro			*	
Da Costa, Anthony, Jr.	*			
Da Costa, John Mendes, Sr.	*			
Da Costa, Joseph		*		
Da Costa, Joseph Telles				*
Da Fonseca, Alvaro		*		
Francia, Mrs. Isabell				*
Gomez Serra, Mrs. Phineas		*		
Hart, Moses	*			
Henriques, Jos.				*
Lamego, Aaron				*

	4 Votes	3 Votes	2 Votes	1 Vote
Lindo, Elias			*	
Lis, Francis De				*
Mendes, Abraham, Sr.				*
Mendes, Dr. Ferdinando	*			
Mendes, Menasseh				*
Mendes, Moses, Jr.				*
Mendes, Moses de Solomon				*
Mogadouro, Widow Rachel				*
Nunes, Isaac Fernandez	*			
Paiba, Moses De		*		
Pereira, Francis		*		
Pereira, Solomon de Moses		*		
Rodrigues, Alphonso				*
Salvador, Francis, Jr.				*
Salvador, Francis, Sr.				*
Sotto, Mrs. Sarah Del				*
In Partnership:				
Da Fonseca, Alvaro, Jeoshuah Gomez Serra, and Isaac Fernandes Nunes			*	
Religion Not Certain:				
Martins, Isaac, Jr.				*
Molines, Mrs. Anna				*

SOURCE: *A List of the Names of the Corporation of the Governor and Company of Merchants of Great Britain Trading to the South-Seas, and Other Parts of America, and for Encouraging the Fishery* (N.p.: John Barber, [1714]).

III. Vessel Owners

TABLE 1
Ownership of Vessels Entering Jamaican Ports

	Non-Jewish	Jewish	Religion Not Known
12/25/1744– 12/24/1745 (Q4)	256	6	1
12/25/1754– 12/25/1755 (Q4)	477	6	1
12/25/1764– 12/25/1765 (Q4)	649	6	2
12/29/1784– 12/29/1785 (Q4)	667	27	4
12/29/1795– 12/29/1796 (Q3)	548	12	27
12/29/1804– 12/29/1805 (Q4)	739	9	40*

*Mostly foreign packets

(Q3) Three quarters of reporting year recorded

(Q4) All quarters of reporting year recorded

SOURCES: PRO, CO 142/15, 142/16, 142/18, 142/23, 142/24.

TABLE 2
Ownership of Vessels Entering Barbados Ports

	Non-Jewish	Jewish	Jewish/ Non-Jewish Partnerships	Religion Not Known
3/25/1735– 3/25/1736 (Q4)	344	0	0	1
1/5/1774– 1/5/ 1775 (Q4)	420	3	1	0
1/1/1800– 12/31/1800 (Q2)	143	2	2	2
2/1/1805– 1/31/1806 (Q4)	490	0	0	2

(Q2) Two quarters of reporting year recorded

(Q4) All quarters of reporting year recorded

SOURCES: PRO, CO 33/16, 33/18, 33/21; PRO, T 64/49.

TABLE 3
London Slave-Ship Owners,
March 30, 1726

Owner	No. of Vessels	Slave Capacity
Basnett	1	250
Billew	1	250
Blackwood	1	300
Bonham	2	650
Bridgen	2	600
Browne	2	1,100
Butler	1	200
Byam	1	250
Cary	1	200
Chamberlaine	5	2,100
Coleman	2	550
Curtis	1	150
Eyles	2	950
Fitter	1	250
Frye	1	250
Gerish	6	1,050
Godin	2	500
Harris	7	2,180
Hooper	1	250
Hudson	1	500
Hunt	1	300
Hyde	1	500
Jeffreys	1	250
Jones	1	500
Knipe	2	—
Lingwood	1	200
Lowe	1	370
Macham	1	170
Macket	1	200
Mainwaring	2	750
Miln	1	200
Morice	7	2,950
Noden	2	550
Panuell	2	920
Pearce	1	200
Radburne	1	350
Ridge	1	250
Roberts	1	200
Rone	1	230
Salter	1	300
Sandford	1	600
Satur	1	200
Saunders	1	370
Smith	2	450
Stoneham	1	300

Owner	No. of Vessels	Slave Capacity
Trahee	1	250
Travers	1	600
Trueman	1	250
Wragg	5	1,300
Names Not Given	2	750

SOURCE: PRO, CO 388/25, S74.

TABLE 4

London Vessels Trading to Africa, 1764

Vessel	Owner
Anamaboe	S. Smith
Beckmont	Oswell & Co.
Bence Island	R. Oswald & Co.
Betsey	Clark & Co.
Betsey	McClean
Betsey	Norton & Co.
Bird-in-Hand	John Watson
Bird's Eye	Wm. Wright
Black Prince	Wm. Hunter
Brittania	Johnson
Brittania	Mallas
Brotherly Love	E. Bell
Conway	Bacon & Co.
Co[untes]s of Sussex	Tho. Gray
Dalrymple	Dalrymple
Dispatch	Hutch. Mure
Dispatch	Mason & Sons
Distiller	W. Wright
Duke of York	Collins & Co.
Duley [?]	Green & Co.
E[arl] of Guilford	J. Vernon
E[arl] of Halifax	Touchett
Enterprise	Bacon & Co.
Experiment	Haymond
Fly	Ross & Mills
Four Sisters	John Stevens
Fox	Smith & Co.
Francis	Haymon & Co.

Vessel	Owner
Greenwich	Bacon & Co.
Gui[ne]a Witch	Stevens
Hilsborough	Bacon & Co.
Hope	Frs. Enshaw
Hussar	Henry Bird
Joseph	Davis
Juno	Oswald & Co.
King Bonny	A. Bacon
Lord Ligonier	James De Batt
Magpie	Bostwick & Co.
Mary	Bacon & Co.
Meridith	S. Smith
Minories	Bostock
Nancy	E. Jeney
Neptune	Wadham & Co.
New Phoenix	H. Mure
Oswego	Smith & Co.
Othello	G. Taylor
Otley Lads	Binley & Co.
Peacock	Wright
Peggy	Evan Lievesey [sic] & Co.
Peggy	J. M'Adam
Penge	Ross & Mills
Phoenix	H. Mure
Pitt	Townson
Queensbury	Rd. Oswell
Rebecca	Gumperk & Co.
Regis	Mich. James
Rock Hall	Ross & Mills
Sally	Paterson & Co.
Sally	T. Scott
Senegambia [?]	Graydon
Speedwell	Gumperk & Co.
Speedwell	Messinger
Squirrel	Hunter & Co.
St. George	African Co.
St. Louis	T. & S. Pole

Vessel	Owner
Success	Jno. Townson
Susannah	Belfour
Trial	M. James
Two Sisters	Baking & Co.
Union	Stubbs
Utfield	Mason
William & Mary	Hall & Fletch
Woodmanstn [sic]	Ben. Steed
Worge	Smith & Co.

SOURCE: *Lloyd's Register 1764* (London: Gregg Press, n.d.).

TABLE 5
London Vessels Trading to Africa, 1776

Vessel	Owner
Adventure	A. Christie
Africa	Bowes & Co.
Ambuscade	Oswald & Co.
Apollo	"Campdn" & Co.
Betsy (now *Nancy*)	Oswald & Co.
Camelia	Rt. Aynsley
Eagle	Mather & Co.
Elizabeth	C. Christie
Fanny	Js. Bradley
Felicity	M. M'Millan
Fly	Bradley & Co.
Fly	Geo. Burton
Fox	Clark & Co.
Friendly Adventure (now *Adventure*)	Bostock & Co.
Friendship	J. Shoolbred
Gascony	G. Burton & Co.
Grace	Jn. Sho[o]lbred
Grenvil[l]e Packet	Govr[-]negal [?]
Hannah	Capt. A. Dalziel
Harriot	Calvert & Co.
Hawke	J. Shoolbred
Heart of Oak	R. Pattison & Co.
Hope	Wm. Lang
Hope	Js. Mather
Hope	J. Shoolbred
Jamaica	G. Burton
Jean (now *Friendship*)	J. Shoolbred

Vessel	Owner
John	Tho. Pool
Kingston	Wm. Burnett
Kitty (now *Nancy*)	Eden & Co.
Little Archee	Tho. Copus
Lord Dartmouth	M. Brown
Lord North	J. Shoolbred
Mally (lost)	Oswald & Co.
Mary	Wm. Annan
Mary	Js. Bradley
Mary	Capt. Js. Barville
Mercury	Oswald & Co.
Nancy	M. Barrett
Nancy	M. Dalzell
Nancy	C. Hosier & Co.
Nancy	Js. Mather
Nautilus	Js. Bradley
Neptune	C. Duffield
Neptune	Harrison & Co.
Peggy	J. Shoolbred
Philip	M. Shepherd
Polly	H. Connor
Polly	Ben. Duley
Providence	J. Shoolbred
Roosilia	Js. Bradley
Rosseau	M. Brown
Sabina	M. Brown
St. George	M. Read
Sally	J. Clarke & Co.
Senegambia	J. Shoolbred
Shandea	Shepherd & Co.
Sophia	C. Court
Spy	Geo. Burton
Spy	M. Nollison
Swallow	Js. Mather
Swift	J. Shoolbred
Thames	Jn. Fletcher
Three Brothers	Js. Bradley
Trial	"Teneriffe" [sic]
True Love	Capt. Jn. Reid & Co.
Ulysses	Capt. W. Littleton
Unanimity	Burnell & Co.
Venus	Camden & Co.
Venus	Camden & Co. [sic]
Venus	Harrison & Co.
Woortmans	J. Shoolbred

SOURCE: *Lloyd's Register 1776* (London: Gregg Press, n.d.); ships' names beginning with the letters G and Y partially missing.

TABLE 6
London Vessels Trading to Africa, 1790

Vessel	Owner
Active	P. F[r]ench
Africa	Barnes & Co.
African Pack	Calvert & Co.
Alfred	T. Bolt
Andalusia	J. Carbine
Ann	Bullock & Co.
Betsy	Miles & Co.
Betsy	——
Boyne	A. Willock
Catherine	P. Morgan
Commerce	Calvert & Co.
Concord	Anderson
Dispatch	Collow, etc.
Dragon	J. Dawson
Elizabeth	F. De Tastet
Elizabeth	De Tastet [sic]
Elizabeth	Morse & Co.
Essex & Samuel	A. Crosbie
Experiment	Calvert & Co.
Fairy	Calvert
Favourite	De Tastet
Favourite	Howell & Co.
Fly	A. Calvert
Fly	W. Collow
Fox	Calvert & Co.
Fox	Sharpless
Fredrick	Miles & Co.
Friendship	J. M'Nabb
Gambia	Miles & Co.
Gosport & "Havr"	W. Collow
Hannah	Lyall & Co.
Hawthorne	Capt. W. Lester
Helena	Palmer & Co.
Hercules	Barrow & Co.
Iris	Miles & Co.
John	Calvert & Co.
Kitty	Capt. J. Glynn & Co.
Lapwing	J. Sharp
Lion	Merry & Co.
Lively	Capt. Ballingal & Co.
Lively	T. Newby
Maria	J. M'Na[bb]
Mary	Calvert
Mary	Collow, etc.
Mentor	Littleton
Mercury	——

Vessel	Owner
Mercury	S. Farmer
Miro	Capt. J. Good & Co.
Neptune	Calvert & Co.
Nymph	Parkinson
Olive Branch	J. Adams
Perseverance	Capt. G. Bolland
Queen	Collow & Co.
Recovery	Calvert
Recovery	J. Colmer
Restoration	De la Coeur
Royal	[Daws & Co.?]
Sally	J. Colmer
Sally	Sharpley
Sophia	Eden & Co.
Spy	Miles & Co.
Swallow	W. Collow
Thames	Shepard
Tho[mas] & Kitty	T. Johns
Union	——
Valentine	Anderson
Venus	A. Calvert
Vigilant	Miles, etc.
William & Betsy	Miles & Co.

SOURCE: *Lloyd's Register 1790* (London: Gregg Press, n.d.).

TABLE 7
Liverpool Vessels Trading to Africa, 1764

Vessel	Owner
African Queen	Pringle & Co.
Ann	Crosbies & Co.
Billy	Barber & Co.
Black Joke	Knight & Co.
Blakeney	Crosbies & Co.
Brittania	Crosbies & Co.
Cerberus	Gregson & Co.
Cleveland	Brown & Co.
Commerce	Witherhead & Co.
Cudyo	Pownall & Co.
Delight	Rumbold & Co.
Derbyshire	Green & Co.
Diligence	Pringle & Co.

Vessel	Owner
Dispatch	P. Holme & Co.
Dispatch	R. Oswald
Dove	M. Barber & Co.
Edgar	Crosbies & Co.
Elly	Barber & Co.
Esther	Pownall & Co.
Friendship	Earle & Co.
George	Wm. James & Co.
Hamilton	Barber & Co.
Hamilton	W. Saul
Hannah	Barber & Co.
Hannah	Haywood & Co.
Happy Family	Weston & Co.
Hare	Rumbold & Co.
Hector	Crosbies & Co.
Jenny	Knight & Co.
John	Boats & Co.
John	Fisher & Co.
John	"Holingwh" & Co.
John	Hunt & Co.
John	Tarleton & Co.
Juno	T. Scott & Co.
Kildare	Blundell & Co.
Kitty	Ingram & Co.
Lancaster	Ingram & Co.
Lark	Barber & Co.
Latham	Rt. Green & Co.
Liberty	Case & Co.
Little Will	James & Co.
Lively	Knight & Co.
Lottery	Forde & Co.
Maddock	Green & Co.
"Mars Granby"	Crosbies & Co.
Martin	Barber & Co.
Matthew	Dobson & Co.
Matty	Brown & Co.
Mentor	Higginson
Molly	Pownall & Co.
Nancy	Blundell & Co.
Nancy	Boats & Co.

Vessel	Owner
Nancy	S. Shaw
Nelly	Boats & Co.
Oak	Jam. Gildart
Phoenix	Crosbies & Co.
Polly	Dingman & Co.
Pr[ince] of Wales	Gregson & Co.
Rainbow	Rumbold & Co.
Ranger	Clemens & Co.
Renown	Brown & Co.
Revenge	Bacon
Richmond	Barber & Co.
Richmond	Boats & Co.
Robert	Hunt & Co.
Rose	Barber & Co.
Rose	T. Foxcroft & Co.
Rumbold	Rumbold & Co.
St. Domingo	Campbell & Heys
Sam	Clements & Co.
Sawrey	Dobson & Co.
Society	Savage & Co.
Thomas	Green & Co.
Trimmer	James & Co.
True Blue	Parr & Co.
Union	Davenport & Co.
Vine	Rumbold & Co.
William	Crosbie & Co.
William	Gregson & Co.

SOURCE: *Lloyd's Register 1764* (London: Gregg Press, n.d.).

IV. Slave Imports and Exports

TABLE I

Slave Imports Recorded by the Naval Office in Jamaica, 1719-1806

	Slaves on Vessels Owned by Non-Jews	Slaves on Vessels Owned by Jews	Other*
6/24/1719– 6/25/1720 (Q4)	3,643	295	455
9/29/1742– 12/25/1742 (Q1)	2,299	200§	0
3/25/1743– 3/25/1744 (Q4)	8,064+	0	0
3/25/1744– 12/25/1744 (Q3)	6,359+	0	4
12/25/1744– 12/24/1745 (Q4)	3,730	0	101
12/27/1745– 12/24/1746 (Q4)	4,698	0	0
12/29/1746– 12/25/1747 (Q4)	9,757+	0	0
12/25/1747– 3/25/1748 (Q1)	1,316	0	0
3/25/1748– 3/24/1749 (Q4)	10,886	0	210
3/25/1749– 6/25/1749 (Q1)	1,521	0	0
12/25/1751– 12/25/1752 (Q4)	6,011	0	0
12/25/1752– 12/25/1753 (Q4)	7,689	35	0
12/25/1753– 12/25/1754 (Q4)	9,459	0	0
12/25/1754– 12/25/1755 (Q4)	12,499+	55	0
12/25/1755– 12/25/1756 (Q2)	6,822	0	0
12/25/1756– 6/25/1757 (Q2)	4,580	0	0
12/25/1761– 12/25/1762 (Q4)	6,894	0	0
12/25/1762– 12/26/1763 (Q4)	7,718+	0	0
12/25/1763– 12/25/1764 (Q4)	10,498	0	0
12/25/1764– 12/25/1765 (Q4)	10,525	80	0

	Slaves on Vessels Owned by Non-Jews	Slaves on Vessels Owned by Jews	Other*
12/25/1765– 12/29/1766 (Q3)	9,919	142	0
12/29/1766– 12/29/1767 (Q4)	3,063	153	0
3/29/1768– 9/29/1768 (Q2)	3,077	0	0
3/29/1769– 12/29/1769 (Q2)	1,341	0	0
12/29/1781– 12/29/1782 (Q4)	6,167	0	0
9/29/1783– 12/29/1783 (Q1)	4,354	0	600
12/29/1783– 12/29/1784 (Q4)	15,238	0	0
12/29/1784– 12/29/1785 (Q4)	11,410	0	0
12/30/1785– 12/29/1786 (Q4)	5,655	0	0
12/29/1786– 12/29/1787 (Q4)	5,976	0	0
12/29/1787– 6/29/1788 (Q2)	2,668	0	0
12/29/1795– 12/29/1796 (Q3)	4,532	0	0
12/29/1796– 12/29/1797 (Q2)	7,201	0	0
12/29/1797– 9/29/1798 (Q2)	5,972	0	0
12/29/1801– 12/29/1802 (Q4)	8,444+	0	386
12/29/1802– 12/29/1803 (Q4)	5,395+	0	0
12/29/1803– 12/29/1804 (Q4)	5,064	0	0
12/29/1804– 12/29/1805 (Q4)	4,726	0	0
12/29/1805– 12/29/1806 (Q4)	7,989	0	377
12/29/1806– 6/29/1807 (Q2)	6,965	0	261
Totals	260,124+	960	2,394

*Names of vessel owners either not given or their religious affiliation not known

§Returned from the Spanish Coast

+Total higher but cannot be determined because of defective manuscripts

(Q1) One quarter of reporting year recorded

(Q2) Two quarters of reporting year recorded

(Q3) Three quarters of reporting year recorded

(Q4) All quarters of reporting year recorded

SOURCES: PRO, CO 142/15–142/24.

TABLE 2

Slave Exports Recorded by the Naval Office in Jamaica, 1719-1806

	Slaves on Vessels Owned by Non-Jews	Slaves on Vessels Owned by Jews	Other*
6/24/1719– 6/25/1720 (Q4)	21	0	12
9/29/1742– 12/25/1742 (Q1)	274	0	0
3/25/1743– 12/23/1743 (Q3)	815	8	0
12/25/1743– 12/24/1744 (Q4)	1,542	50	0
1/3/1745– 12/24/1745 (Q4)	595+	220+	0
12/30/1745– 12/26/1746 (Q4)	960	180	0
12/25/1746– 3/25/1748 (Q5)	2,654+	278	0
3/25/1748– 3/24/1749 (Q4)	2,681+	260	0
3/25/1749– 6/25/1749 (Q1)	278	0	0
12/25/1751– 12/25/1752 (Q4)	1,038	0	0
12/25/1752– 12/25/1753 (Q4)	939+	0	0
12/25/1753– 12/25/1754 (Q4)	1,592+	68	0
12/25/1754– 12/25/1755 (Q4)	652	0	0
12/25/1755– 12/25/1756 (Q2)	1,260	0	0
12/25/1756– 6/25/1757 (Q2)	738	0	0
12/25/1761– 12/25/1762 (Q4)	40	0	0
12/25/1762– 12/25/1763 (Q4)	1,502	0	0
12/25/1763– 12/25/1764 (Q4)	3,023	0	0

	Slaves on Vessels Owned by Non-Jews	Slaves on Vessels Owned by Jews	Other*
12/25/1764– 12/25/1765 (Q4)	2,275	4	6
12/25/1765– 12/29/1766 (Q3)	625	40	0
12/29/1766– 12/29/1767 (Q4)	544+	90	0
3/29/1768– 9/29/1768 (Q2)	73+	220	0
3/29/1769– 12/29/1769 (Q2)	99	105	0
12/29/1781– 12/25/1782 (Q4)	0	0	0
9/29/1783– 12/29/1783 (Q1)	0	0	0
12/29/1783– 12/29/1784 (Q4)	757	280	0
12/29/1784– 12/29/1785 (Q4)	904	349	0
12/29/1785– 12/29/1786 (Q4)	347	342	0
12/29/1786– 12/29/1787 (Q4)	473	12	32
12/29/1787– 6/29/1788 (Q2)	216	12	0
12/29/1795– 12/29/1796 (Q3)	1,122	52	23
12/29/1796– 12/29/1797 (Q2)	1,850	10	0
12/29/1797– 12/29/1798 (Q3)	393	50	83
12/29/1801– 12/29/1802 (Q4)	572	50	0
12/29/1802– 12/29/1803 (Q4)	863	36	0
12/29/1803– 12/29/1804 (Q4)	322	13	200
12/29/1804– 12/29/1805 (Q4)	182+	0	0
12/29/1805– 12/29/1806 (Q4)	106	0	0
12/29/1806– 6/29/1807 (Q2)	87	0	60
Totals	32,414+	2,729+	416

*Names of vessel owners either not given or their religious affiliation unknown

+Total higher but cannot be determined because of defective manuscripts

(Q1)One quarter of reporting year recorded

(Q2) Two quarters of reporting year recorded

(Q3) Three quarters of reporting year recorded

(Q4) All quarters of reporting year recorded

(Q5) Five quarters recorded

SOURCES: PRO, CO 142/15–142/24.

TABLE 3

Slave Exports from Jamaica on Vessels
Owned by Jews, 1742–1806

	Year	Destination	No. of Slaves
Bonito, A. M. & Co.	1784	St. Thomas	60
	1784	St. Thomas	26
	1784	St. Thomas	32
	1784	St. Thomas	50
	1785	St. Thomas	3
	1785	St. Thomas	50
	1785	St. Thomas	53
	1785	St. Thomas	62
	1785	St. Thomas	59
	1786	St. Thomas	60
Bravo, David	1745	Spanish Coast	220
	1746	Cuba	180
	1748	Spanish Coast	200
	1748–49	Spanish Coast	210
	1748–49	Spanish Coast	50
Bravo, Jacob	1754	Spanish Main	60
Da Costa, Isaac Mendes & Co.	1744	South Keys (Cuba)	50
Ferro, Moses & Co.	1784	Curaçao	30
Flamengo, Jacob & Co.	1765	Honduras	4
	1768	Curaçao	48
Franks, Jacob	1743	Ríohacha	8
Furtado, David Orobio	1745	Spanish Coast	*
Henriques, A. N. & Co.	1786	Mosquito Coast	6
	1787	Cartagena	12
	1788	Cartagena	8
Henriques, Jacob Gabay	1754	Curaçao	8

	Year	Destination	No. of Slaves
Lamera, Aaron & Co.	1747	Porto Bello	62
	1747	Porto Bello	16
Lindo, A. A. & Co.	1796	Jérémie	24
	1797	Jérémie	10
Lopez, Aaron & Co.	1767	Honduras	3
	1767	Honduras	2
Mendes, Issac & Co.	1768	Curaçao	59
Mendes, Jacob & Co.	1769	Hispaniola	25
Mendes, Moses & Co.	1745	Spanish Coast	*
Monis, Isaac & Co.	1766	Curaçao	40
	1767	Curaçao	20
	1767	Curaçao	15
	1767	Curaçao	50
	1768	Curaçao	32
	1768	Curaçao	41
	1769	Hispaniola	40
Myer, Isaac	1796	Havana	5
Pereira, Benjamin & Co.	1769	Curaçao	40
Pereira, I. M. & Co.	1784	Curaçao	50
	1785	Curaçao	50
	1785	Curaçao	47
	1786	Curaçao	3
	1786	Curaçao	4
Phillips, Judah & Co.	1788	Grand Cayman	4
	1796	Caymans	9
	1796	Caymans	14
	1798	Caymans	30
	1798	Caymans	20
	1802	Caymans	7
	1802	Caymans	25
	1802	Caymans	6
	1802	Caymans	12
	1803	Caymans	20
	1803	Caymans	4
	1803	Caymans	12
	1804	Caymans	7
	1804	Caymans	6

	Year	Destination	No. of Slaves
Seixas, D. M.	1786	Charleston	147
	1786	New Providence	72
	1786	Turks Island	18
Thalavera, Isa. *[sic]* Gomez	1768	Curaçao	40
Ximenes, Daniel	1784	Curaçao	32
	1785	St. Thomas	25
	1786	St. Thomas	32

*Number not entered in manuscript

SOURCE: PRO, CO 142/15–142/24.

TABLE 4

Slave Imports Recorded by the Naval Office in Barbados, 1728-1806*

	Slaves on Vessels Owned by			
	Non-Jews	Jews	*Jewish/Non-Jewish* Partners	Other**
6/25/1728– 12/25/1728 (Q2)	2,581	0	0	0
12/25/1728– 12/25/1729 (Q4)	4,794	0	0	0
6/25/1730– 9/25/1730 (Q1)	608	0	0	0
12/25/1730– 6/25/1731 (Q2)	3,212	0	0	0
4/13/1733– 10/13/1733 (Q2)	1,358	0	0	0
3/25/1735– 12/25/1735 (Q3)	2,760	0	0	0
12/25/1735– 12/25/1736 (Q4)	4,849	0	0	60
12/25/1736– 12/25/1737 (Q4)	1,467	0	0	0
12/25/1737– 3/25/1738 (Q1)	1,838	0	0	0
4/14/1747– 9/25/1747 (Q2)	319	0	0	0
9/25/1752– 12/25/1752 (Q1)	2,157	0	0	0
12/25/1752– 3/25/1753–(Q1)	775	0	0	0

	Slaves on Vessels Owned by			
	Non-Jews	Jews	Jewish/Non-Jewish Partners	Other**
1/1/1764– 4/1/1764 (Q1)	2,079	0	0	0
12/25/1772– 1/5/1774 (Q4)	764	0	0	0
1/5/1774– 1/5/1775 (Q4)	1,984	0	0	0
1/6/1775– 1/5/1776 (Q4)	1,035	0	0	0
1/5/1777– 1/5/1778 (Q4)	312	0	0	0
12/25/1778– 1/5/1780 (Q4)	0	0	0	0
11/11/1781– 2/10/1782 (Q1)	0	0	0	0
2/11/1782– 5/10/1782 (Q1)	550	0	0	0
7/1/1786– 1/1/1787 (Q2)	251	0	0	0
1/1/1787– 1/1/1788 (Q4)	688	0	0	0
1/1/1788– 4/1/1788 (Q1)	564	0	0	0
4/1/1797– 12/31/1797 (Q3)	2,597	0	0	0
1/1/1798– 12/31/1798 (Q3)	2,224+	0	128	0
1/1/1799– 12/31/1799 (Q4)	1,800	0	0	0
1/1/1800– 12/31/1800 (Q2)	670	0	0	0
4/1/1801– 12/31/1801 (Q3)	8	0	0	0
1/1/1802– 9/30/1802 (Q3)	95	0	0	0
2/1/1803– July 1803 (Q2)	1,005	0	0	0
8/1/1804– 1/31/1805 (Q2)	532	0	0	0
2/1/1805– 1/31/1806 (Q4)	1,348	0	0	0
Totals	45,224+	0	128	60

*Slaves imported between January 1, 1784 and July 1, 1786 not included here; no vessel owners listed in the nine quarters recorded by the Naval Office in that period

**Religion of vessel owner not known, or owner not listed
+Total higher; cargo size for one delivery not listed
(Q1) One quarter of reporting year recorded
(Q2) Two quarters of reporting year recorded
(Q3) Three quarters of reporting year recorded
(Q4) All quarters of reporting year recorded
SOURCES: PRO, CO 33/16–33/18, 33/21–33/22; PRO, T 64/48–64/49.

TABLE 5
Slave Exports Recorded by the Naval Office in Barbados, 1781-1806

| | Slaves on Vessels Owned by | | | |
	Non-Jews	Jews	Jewish/Non-JewishPartners	Other*
11/11/1781– 5/10/1782 (Q2)	467	0	0	0
7/1/1786– 1/1/1787 (Q2)	105	0	0	0
1/1/1787– 11/13/1787 (Q3)	9+	0	0	0
1/1/1788– 4/1/1788 (Q1)	155	0	0	0
4/1/1797– 12/31/1797 (Q3)	1,673	0	36	0
1/1/1798– 12/31/1798 (Q3)	900	0	101	100
1/1/1799– 12/31/1799 (Q4)	1,101	0	154	0
1/1/1800– 12/31/1800 (Q2)	373	0	0	0
4/1/1801– 12/31/1801 (Q3)	0	0	0	0
1/1/1802– 9/30/1802 (Q3)	10	0	0	0
2/1/1803– 7/26/1803 (Q2)	189	0	0	0
8/1/1804– 1/31/1805 (Q2)	53	0	0	0
2/1/1805– 1/31/1806 (Q4)	302	0	0	0
Totals	5,337+	0	291	100

*Religion of vessel owner uncertain
+Total higher; number missing for one shipment
(Q1) One quarter of reporting year recorded

(Q2) Two quarters of reporting year recorded
(Q3) Three quarters of reporting year recorded
(Q4) All quarters of reporting year recorded
SOURCES: PRO, CO 33/18, 33/20–33/22.

TABLE 6

Slave Imports Recorded by the Naval Office in New York,
1715-65

	Number of Slaves on Vessels Owned by		
	Non-Jews	Jews	Jewish/Non-Jewish Partners
6/24/1715– 12/25/1715 (Q2)	53	0	0
12/25/1715– 12/25/1716 (Q4)	65	0	1
12/25/1716– 12/12/1717 (Q4)	226+	0	102
12/25/1717– 12/25/1718 (Q4)	504+	6	33
12/25/1718– 12/25/1719 (Q3)	99	0	3
12/25/1719– 12/25/1720 (Q4)	76	0	0
12/25/1720– 12/25/1721 (Q4)	88	0	117
12/25/1721– 12/25/1722 (Q4)	89	1	0
12/25/1722– 12/25/1723 (Q4)	102	0	0
12/25/1723– 12/25/1724 (Q4)	61	0	0
3/25/1725– 12/25/1725 (Q3)	207	1	0
12/25/1725– 12/12/1726 (Q4)	161	2	2
12/25/1726– 12/25/1727 (Q4)	199	13	5
12/25/1727– 12/25/1728 (Q4)	128+	1	0
12/25/1728– 12/25/1729 (Q4)	167	4	38
12/25/1729– 9/29/1730 (Q3)	159	0	3
3/25/1731– 12/25/1731 (Q3)	291	1	4

	Number of Slaves on Vessels Owned by		
	Non-Jews	Jews	Jewish/Non-Jewish Partners
12/25/1731– 12/25/1732 (Q4)	135	1	0
12/25/1732– 12/25/1733 (Q4)	258	0	0
12/25/1733– 12/25/1734 (Q4)	51	0	0
12/25/1734– 12/25/1735 (Q4)	118	0	3
12/25/1735– 6/24/1736 (Q2)	14	1	0
3/25/1737– 12/25/1737 (Q3)	96	0	1
3/25/1738– 12/25/1738 (Q3)	103+	0	10
12/25/1738– 12/25/1739 (Q4)	80	0	18
12/25/1739– 12/25/1740 (Q4)	72	0	2
12/25/1740– 12/25/1741 (Q4)	55	0	0
12/25/1741– 12/25/1742 (Q4)	11	0	3
12/25/1742– 6/24/1743 (Q2)	4	1	0
3/25/1748– 9/29/1748 (Q2)	9	0	0
9/29/1751– 3/25/1752 (Q2)	0	0	0
10/10/1753– 1/5/1754 (Q1)	0	0	0
1/5/1754– 1/5/1755 (Q4)	65	0	0
1/5/1755– 10/10/1755 (Q3)	0	0	0
1/5/1763– 1/6/1764 (Q4)	205	0	0
1/5/1764– 1/5/1765 (Q4)	35	0	0
Totals	3,986+	32	345

+Total higher, but cannot be determined because of defective manuscripts

(Q1) One quarter of reporting year recorded

(Q2) Two quarters of reporting year recorded

(Q3) Three quarters of reporting year recorded

(Q4) All quarters of reporting year recorded

SOURCES: PRO, CO 5/1222–5/1228.

V. The Jewish Population of Port Royal, Jamaica

TABLE 1
Jewish Inhabitants of Port Royal, 1680

Name	No. of Whites	No. of Slaves
Alvarez, David	8	4
"Cars" [Cardozo], Moses Jesurun	2	4
Coheen [Cohen], Abraham	2	2
Coutinho, Isaac	2	2
Da Costa, Joseph	7	6
Da Costa, Matthias	1	
Da Silva, Abraham	3	2
Da Silva, Joseph	5	4
De Castro, Do[cto]r Jacob	2	3
Gabay, Abraham	5	3
Gavay [Gabay], David	5	4
Gutteres, Jacob Mendes	2	3
Lucena, Abraham De	3	2
Lucena, David	1	
Lucena, Moses De	7	2
Lucena, Rachel	3	1
Narbona [Narbonne], David Lopez	3	1
Rodrigo, Esther	2	1
Torres, David De	4	1
Torres, Jacob De	8	3
Religion Not Certain:		
Costa, Joane	2	
—— [ms. blank], Francisco	1	2
—— [ms. torn], Philip	[ms. torn]	[ms. torn]
——, —— [ms. torn]	[ms. torn]	[ms. torn]

SOURCE: PRO, CO 1/45, 96–107.

TABLE 2
Jewish Inhabitants of Port Royal, 1738–40

	Inhabitant, 1738	Poll Tax, 1740	Slaves Owned, 1738	1740
Aflalo, Samuel	*	*		10
Aguilar, Esther, and Rachel	*	*	6	7
Baruch, Aaron Lousada+			9	
Brandon, Sarah		*		
Cardozo, Jacob Yesm		*		20
Delapenha, Jacob, and Rebecca	*	*	4	5

	Inhabitant, 1738	Poll Tax, 1740	Slaves Owned, 1738	1740
De Leon, Abraham Roderigo	*	*		
De Silva, Mordecai		*		5
De Souza, Abraham Henriques	*	*	8	11
Dias, Abraham, and Esther	*	*	5	5
Ferro, Jacob	*		6	
Ferro, Moses, and Fetta	*	*	11	11
Lopez, Isaac		*		
Lopez, Rebecca		*		
Mendes, David, and Rachel	*		11	
Mesquita, Abraham Fernandez, and Rachel	*	*	2	2
Nunes, Widow+		*	15	8
Olivarsa, Moses Vere	*			
Pinto, Isaac, and Rachel	*	*	13	15
Pinto, Jacob+			1	
Salzada [Sarzedas], Abraham	*			
Suero, Daniel	*	*	4	4
Torres, Abraham+		*	2	1
Torres, David		*		
Torres, Isaac Lopez, and son	*	*	24	27
Torres, Jacob		*		5
Torres, Jacob Lopez, and Sarah	*	*		
Touro, Aaron+			2	
Religion Not Certain:				
Bravil, Widow+		*	14	9
Jacobs, Esther		*		5
Jacobs, Jacob		*		
Jacobs, Joshua		*		
Peralta, Anthony+			5	
Perriere, Antonio	*			
Rialto, Anthony		*		4

+Listed as slaveowners in 1738 but not as inhabitants

SOURCES: JA, 2/19/1, List of Slaves Taxed by the Parish of Port Royal, August 22, 1738; List of White Inhabitants of Port Royal Parish, October, 1738; and Poll Tax for Port Royal, 1740.

VI. The Jewish Population of Kingston, Jamaica

TABLE I

Jewish Households and Companies in Kingston, 1745

Name	No. of Slaves
Aboab, Isaac	2
Aboab, Isaac	2
Aguilar, Esther	6
Alvarenga, Isaac Da Costa	9
Alvina [Alvin], Judith	11
Almeyda, Daniel	1
Almeyda, Esther	18
Almeyda, Isaac Campos	8
Andrade, Mrs.	
Azevedo, David D'	3
Azevedo, Moses D'	
Barrios, Es[the]r Levy	6
Barrios, Mrs.—shop	
Barrow, Aaron	12
Brandon, Esther, and Abigail	13
Brandon, Isaac Pereira, Jr.	3
Brandon, Isaac Pinto	4
Brandon, Jacob Rodrigues	2
Bravo, David	23
Bravo, David—store	
Bretto [Britto], David	3
Brown, Abraham Torres	3
Campos, Abraham, Sr.	1
Campos, Isaac Henriques	4
Campos, Jacob	15
Campos, Jacob—store	
Cardozo, Abraham	19
Cardozo, Abraham Rodrigues	3
Cardozo, Jacob	13
Cariell, Solomon	8
Carvalho, Sarah	7
Cohen, Abraham	4
Cohen, Nathan	17
Correa, Isaac	3
Correa, Moses	7

Name	No. of Slaves
Costa, Jacob Lopez	2
Cunha, Isaac Henriques	8
Cunha, Isaac Mendes	9
Da Costa, Abraham Nunes	5
[Da Costa], Daniel Albuquerque	3
Da Costa, Daniel Mendes	16
Da Costa, Daniel Nunes	8
Da Costa, David Rodrigues	4
Da Costa, Jos. Rodrigues	1
De Castro, Leah	18
De Lara, Abraham Cohen, Jr.	
De Lara, Isaac Cohen, Sr.	15
De Lara, Joseph Cohen	3
De Lara, Moses Cohen	33
De Leon, Abraham "Lodreq"	17
De Leon, Jacob Rodrigues	4
De Leon, Dr. Jno.	9
De Leon, Widow Leah	
De Leon, Moses	15
De Leon, Moses Rodrigues	4
De Mattos, Moses	1
De Miranda, Abraham, and son	2
De Miranda, David	7
De Pass, Aaron Lopez	4
De Pass, Isaac	6
De Pass, Rebecca Lopez	5
De Silva, Jacob	9
De Silva, Judith	
De Silva, Samuel	
Devalle, Jacob	2
Devalo, Jacob	2
De Veiga, Isaac	4
Dias, Aaron & Co.	15
Dias, Messrs. & Co.—store	
Fernandez, Abraham	2
Fernandez, Benjamin Dias	12
Fernandez, Jacob	4
Fernandez, Moses Dias	7
Fernandez, Moses Dias	

Name	No. of Slaves
Ferro, Jacob	2
Frois, David Nunes	1
Furtado, David	6
Furtado, David Orobio	15
Furtado, Isaac	16
Furtado, Isaac Ch.	
Furtado, Isaac Henriques	13
Furtado, Moses	4
Furtado, Moses	5
Gideon, Moses	2
Gideon, Moses	
Gonzalez, Abraham	53
Gonzalez, Isaac	6
Gonzalez, Rebecca	7
Gonzalez & Pereira	
Gutteres, Joseph	1
Gutteres, Judith	44
Gutteres, Sarah	14
Henriques, Abraham Lopez	9
Henriques, Isaac	15
Henriques, Isaac Jesurun	7
Henriques, Jacob, "and Mo"	8
Henriques, Moses Lopez	9
Henriques, Moses Mendes	2
Henriques, Rebecca	5
Henriques, Samuel Cohane	5
Israel, Henry—shop	19
Ladesma, Abraham	7
Laguna, Abraham	2
Laguna, Jacob	11
Laguna, Jacob	
Laguna, Rebecca	
Laguna, Sarah	20
Lamera, "Mos. and AA"	24
Letob, ———— Gabay	
Levy, Michael—store	3
Lopez, Esther Rodrigues	1
Lopez, Moses	2
Lopez, Rachel	22
Lousada, Aaron Barrow—store	

Name	No. of Slaves
Lyon, Jacob	8
Mendes, Ab., and Is.	7
Mendes, Jacob Pereira	24
Mendes, Jacob Pereira—2 stores	
Mendes, Jacob Pereira	
[M]endes, Moses	23
Mendes, Rachel Pereira	4
Mendes, Samuel Pereira	20
Mesquita, Abraham Pereira	35
Mesquita, Sarah	1
Mesquita, Sarah	
Mesquita & Wood—wharf*	
Miranda, Aaron Nunes	1
Miranda, Abraham Nunes	3
Miranda, Isaac	7
Miranda, Moses Nunes	5
Miranda, Rebecca	
Modea, Abraham Rodrigues	2
Moinpast, Isaac Mendes	
[M]orais, Samuel	5
Netta, Rachel Nunes	12
Netta, Rachel Nunes	
Nunes, Abigail, and son	1
Nunes, Abraham Rodrigues	5
Nunes, Esther	8
Nunes, Esther	
Nunes, Joshua	16
Nunes, Judith	30
Nunes, Rebecca, and Rachel Gomez Castro	7
Nunes, Sarah	9
Pereira, Aaron	7
Pereira, Abigail	12
Pereira, Benjamin	10
Pereira, Isaac Fernandez	10
Pereira, Joseph	17
Pereira, Judith, Jr.	11
Pereira, Judith, Jr.	3
Pereira, Moses	14
Pereira, Moses	
Pereira, Samuel Lopez	4

Name	No. of Slaves
Pereira, Sarah	1
Pereira, Sarah	16
Pereira, Sarah	1
Pinheiro, Jacob	14
Pinheiro, Jacob—shop	
Pinheiro, Sl. Lopez	2
Pinto, Daniel	4
Pinto, David	2
Pinto, David	2
Pinto, Esther	7
Polander, Joseph	20
Polander, Joseph—store	
Portello, Sarah	1
Quixano, Abraham Henriques	10
Riz, Daniel	21
Riz, Han., and Is. Gz. Silva	5
Riz, Moses	5
Riz, Moses—shop	
Rodrigues, Is. Raphael	6
Salome, Samuel	2
Sarzedas, Abraham	10
Seruca, Abigail	5
Silva, Mordecai Da Costa	4
Silva, Rachel Gomez	12
Silvera, Isaac	16
Silvia, Daniel	6
Solas, Isaac Mendes	1
Tavares, David	21
Tavares, David—"st[ore]"	
Torres, Jacob Lopez	20
Touro, Rebecca	6
Touro, Rebecca	
Vizew [Vizea], Jacob Nunes	2
Ydana, Isaac	8
Religion Not Certain:	
Brown, Abraham	4
Brown, Moses	2
Casheire, ——	5
David, Ezekiel	3
Des[torn], David, and —— Gutteres	2

Name	No. of Slaves
Fernard, Esther	
Gabon, Rachel	
Mallena, Moses	1
Marks, ———	12
Marks, Levy	
Maso, David	3
Momfort, Joshua	6
Mon———, Simon	15
[Name torn]	3
[Name torn; landlord: Cavelier]	8
[Name torn]	4
[Name torn]	9
[Name torn]	2
[Name torn; landlord: Brown]	3
[Name torn]	2
[Name torn]	7
[Name torn; landlord: Dallas]	14
[Name torn]	2
[Name torn; landlord: Stringer]	1
[Name torn; landlord: Stringer]	7
[Name torn]	1
[Name torn; landlord: Pereira]	9
[Name torn; landlord: Henriques]	
[Name torn; landlord: Lynch]	
[Name torn; landlord: Henriques]	
[Name torn]	
[Name torn; landlord: Tirle]	
[Name torn]	5
[Name torn; landlord: Gregory]	
[Name torn; landlord: Dallas]	7
[Name torn; landlord: Atkins]	
[Name torn; landlord: Atkins]	
[Name torn; landlord: Farmary]	3
[Name torn; landlord: Inness]	1
[Name torn; landlord: A. De Leon]	
[Name torn; landlord: Coleman]	1
[Name torn; landlord: De Leon]	1
[Name torn; landlord: De Leon]	5
[Name torn]	1

Name	No. of Slaves
[Name torn]	10
[Name torn]	
[No name; landlord: Curtis]	6
[No name; landlord: Lopez]	11
Pestana, Sampson	2
Phillips, ——	7
Sa—na, Abraham, and son	7
Ser[torn], Dr. Thos.	38
Shop; landlord: Dallas	
Store; landlord: Garthwaite	
Store; landlord: Gandy	
Store; landlord: Vanbrough	
Store; landlord: Knight	
Store; landlord: Sharp	
Store; landlord: Gordon and Bright	2
Store; landlord: Welsh	
Store; landlord: Crymble	
Wharf; landlord: Furnell	

* Jewish/Non-Jewish partnership
SOURCE: JA, 2/6/1.

TABLE 2
Jewish Households and Companies in Kingston, 1769*

Name	No. of Slaves	Trade Tax	Comment
Aboab, Joshua			
Aflalo, David	14	1–0–0	
Aguilar, Abraham		4–0–0	
Aguilar, Widow	19		
Almeyda, Abraham			
Almeyda, Daniel	46	3–0–0	
Alvarenga, Jacob	10	3–0–0	
Alvis, Daniel Lopez	3	2–0–0	
Alvis, Isaac Rodrigues*	3	0–7–6	
Azevedo, David	8		
Bared, Anthony Da Costa			
Baretto, Dr.*	2		

Name	No. of Slaves	Trade Tax	Comment
Belphante [Belinfante], Solomon Cohen	6		
Brandon, Isaac*			
Brandon, Isaac	10		
Brandon, Isaac Pereira		1–0–0	
Brandon, Isaac Pereira	11		
Brandon, Moses			
Brandon, Moses Pinto			
Bravo, Jacob	30		
Bravo, Moses			Poor
Bravo, Rachel	16		
Campos, ——			
Cardozo, Abraham Rodrigues	8	6–0–0	
Cardozo, Daniel Rodrigues			
Cardozo, Esther*	10		
Cardozo, Rachel	2		
Carranza, Aaron Lopez			
Castro, Rachel			Poor; demented
Cespedes, Daniel			
Cohen, Sarah*			Poor
Cohen, Widow			Poor
Cordova, ——			
Coutinho, Isaac	9	1–10–0	
Coutinho, Isaac Dias		1–10–0	
Cunha, Widow			
Da Costa, Aaron Rodrigues			
Da Costa, Abraham Rodrigues	4		
Da Costa, David Henriques	5	0–10–0	
Da Costa, Esther Rodrigues			
Da Costa, —— Nunes	4		
Da Costa, Isaac Nunes	18	0–15–0	
Da Costa, Isaac Nunes			
Da Costa, Isaac Rodrigues*	8	0–5–0	
Da Costa, Jacob Nunes	14		
Da Costa, Leah Rodrigues	5	0–10–0	
Da Costa, Moses Rodrigues, Sr.	4	1–0–0	
Da Costa, Rachel Rodrigues	4		
Da Costa, Rebecca Pereira			
Da Costa, Solomon Rodrigues	15	1–10–0	
Da Veiga, Samuel Baretto	3		

Name	No. of Slaves	Trade Tax	Comment
Da Vilda, Jacob	7		
De Campos, Abraham			
De Castro, ———			
De Cordova, Jacob			
De Cordova, Joshua	4		
Delapenha, Abraham			
De Leon, Abraham			
De Leon, Abraham de Moses	10		
De Leon, Abraham de Moses			
De Leon, Jacob			
De Leon, Mrs.			
De Mendoza, Abraham Soares	8		
De Pass, Samuel	10	4–0–0	
De Silva, Rebecca			
Fernandez, Benjamin Dias	19	6–0–0	
Fernandez, Isaac Dias	5	1–0–0	
Fernandez, Moses			
Ferraro, Jacob Rodrigues			
Ferro, Isaac	4	1–0–0	
Ferro, Moses			
Flamengo, Benjamin	3		
Flamengo, Jacob Nunes	10	1–0–0	
Fonseca, Moses			
Franco, Rebecca			
Furtado, David Pinheiro	12	1–0–0	
Furtado, Isaac	34	3–0–0	
Furtado, Isaac of Jacob, Jr.			
Furtado, Jacob	12	3–0–0	
Furtado, Jacob Orobio	2	1–0–0	
Furtado, Sarah Pinheiro	3	0–10–0	
Furtado, Widow	5		
Furtado, Widow Henriques	29		
Gabay, Solomon	16	0–10–0	
Gideon, Sampson			
Gomez, Isaac Levy			
Henriques, Aaron Nunes			
Henriques, Abraham			
Henriques, Jacob Nunes	12		

Name	No. of Slaves	Trade Tax	Comment
Henriques, Joseph	5	2–0–0	
Henriques, Joseph	6		
Henriques, Moses	10	2–0–0	
Laguna, Esther*			
Lameza, Moses			
Lara, Jacob			
Linder [Lindo], Alexander [Alexandre]			
Lopez, ———			
Lopez, Mordecai Rodrigues	12	2–0–0	
Lopez, Moses	6	1–0–0	
Lousada, Aaron B.	6		Deceased
Lousada, Emanuel Barrow		4–0–0	
Lousada, Rachel Barrow	5		
Massias, Isaac			
Mattos, Isaac Da Costa			
Mattos, Moses	5	0–10–0	
Melhado, Jacob			
Melhado, Rachel			
Mella, Abraham [De]	3	2–0–0	
Mella, Widow [De]	6	1–10–0	
Mendes, ———*			
Mendes, Abraham	18		
Mendes, Abraham of Jacob Pereira	10		
Mendes, Benjamin Pereira	9	1–0–0	
Mendes, David			
Mendes, David Pereira	9	0–10–0	
Mendes, Isaac	15	1–0–0	
Mendes, Isaac Rodrigues*			Poor
Mendes, Leah Pereira			
Mendes, Rachel Pereira	9		
Mendes, Rachel Pereira			
Mendes, Simha	21		
Mendes, Widow			
Mendes, Widow Pereira	15		
Mercado, Jacob			
Mesquita, Daniel	6		
Mesquita, Moses	10	2–0–0	
Mesquita, Sarah			
Moheda, Abraham			

Name	No. of Slaves	Trade Tax	Comment
Monis, Isaac	3	1–0–0	
Monteiro, Moses Cardozo			Poor
Morais, Widow			Poor
Morenu, Aaron Levy	14	3–0–0	
Nabarro, Abraham Nunes	7	0–10–0	
Netto, Mrs.			
Netto, Rachel Nunes			
Nunes, Abraham Cardozo	6		
Nunes, Jacob Rodrigues	10	1–10–0	
Nunes, Joshua			Poor
Nunes, Moses, Jr.		4–0–0	
Nunes, Moses, Jr.	4		
Nunes, Moses Rodrigues		1–0–0	
Nunes, Rachel			Poor
Nunes, Rebecca Rodrigues	4		
Nunes, Solomon			
Pass, Mrs.			Poor
Pereira, ———			
Pereira, Benjamin	44	10–0–0	
Pereira, Benjamin of Joseph	34		Deceased
Pereira, Daniel			
Pereira, Daniel Mendes	41	3–0–0	
Pereira, Daniel Mendes			
Pereira, Emanuel			
Pereira, Esther			Poor
Pereira, Isaac and Samuel Mendes	18	5–0–0	
Pereira, Isaac and Samuel Mendes		2–0–0	
Pereira, Isaac Mendes		1–0–0	
Pereira, Jacob Mendes	20		
Pereira, Manasseh			
Pereira, Manasseh			
Pereira, Rachel			Poor
Pereira, Samuel Mendes	9	1–10–0	
Pereira, Widow		5–0–0	
Pessoa, Dr.	13	1–0–0	
Pinto, Isaac			Poor
Pixota [Peixoto], ———	10		
"Poor Hebrews" (+)			
Quixano, Sarah Henriques	17		
Riz, ———			Poor

Name	No. of Slaves	Trade Tax	Comment
Riz, Daniel Lopez	14		
Riz, Widow			
Rodrigues, Abraham			
Saldana, Jacob Carillo			
Salom, Widow			
Salome, Aaron			
Sanches, Abraham			
Sanches, Dr.			
Sanches, Isaac			Poor
Sanches, Isaac			
Sequeira, ———			
Sequeira, Daniel	3	0–10–0	
Sequeira, Jacob	14		
Silva, Aaron Gomez			
Silva, David	9		
Silva, Isaac			Poor
Silva, Jacob Gomez	9		
Silva, Joshua Gomez	4	0–10–0	
Silva, Moses Gomez			
Silva, Moses Gomez	4	1–0–0	
Silva, Moses Lopez			
Silvera, Mrs.			
Silvera, Mrs.			
Souza, Sarah	10		
Tavares, Sarah			
Thalavera, Jacob Gomez	5		
Torres, Abraham Lopez	14	2–0–0	
Torres, David Lopez	15	4–0–0	
Torres, Sarah Lopez	8		
Religion Not Certain:			
Benan [Bonan?], Solomon			Poor
Bere, Noah			
Bernard, Jacob, and Abraham			
Brown, Alexander	10		
Carvalio, William			
Carvalio, William			Poor
De Miguel, Mrs.			Poor
G[torn] [landlord: White]	6		
Joseph, Aaron			

Name	No. of Slaves	Trade Tax	Comment
Joseph, Abraham	23	4–0–0	
Lyon, Benjamin			
Manrique, Abraham			
Marks, Joseph & Co.	5	1–0–0	
Martin, David			
Martin, George			
Mathias, Martin	10		
Montfort, —ol	2	0–10–0	
Montfort, Joshua			Poor
[Name torn; landlord: Stevens]	4		
[Name torn; landlord: Sims]			
[Name torn; landlord: self]			
[Name torn; landlord: Wyllington]			
[No name; landlord: D'Luskie]	11		
[No name; landlord: Neil]	3	1–0–0	
[No name; landlord: Barry]			Poor
[No name; landlord: Barry]			Poor
[No name—yard and stables; landlord: Turner]			
Poor people			
Poor people			
Poor people [landlord: Netto]			
Poor people [landlord: Fernandez]			
Poor people [landlord: Fernandez]			
Poor people [landlord: Pereira]			
Poor people [landlord: Henriques]			
Poor people [landlord: De Leon]			
Poor people [landlord: De Leon]			
Poor people [landlord: De Leon]			
Poor woman [landlord: George]			
Rubalcavo, Emanuel			
Tora, Roanna			
Valentine, Mrs.			
———, Sarah [landlord: Darby]			
———, Lydia [landlord: Tittle]			
———, Emanuel [landlord: Gilbert]			

*Information for King St., East Division, missing for 1769; derived from 1770 poll-tax list
(+) Occupied two lots on Peter Lane, one of which belonged to the synagogue

TABLE 3
Jewish Households and Companies in Kingston, 1795

Name	No. of Slaves	Trade Tax
Aaron, Lazarus	2	0–13–9
Adolphus, Jos.		
Aguilar, Joseph	25	5–0–0
Aguilar, Jos.	15	
Alexander, Lazarus	6	2–10–0
Alexander, Reuben	2	0–13–9
Almeyda, Rebecca	6	
Alvarenga, Abraham Da Costa	7	1–7–6
Alvarenga, Isaac Da Costa	6	0–13–9
Barnett, Josh. [Joseph]	1	0–13–9
Baretto, Dr. Samuel	3	1–7–6
Benaim, Abraham	12	
Bonito, Isaac Ms.	6	1–17–6
Bonito, Solomon Ms.	10	2–1–3
Bonito, Widow	8	
Brandon, Abraham		
Brandon, Hannah	4	
Bravo, David	7	3–2–6
Bravo, Isaac	2	0–13–9
Bravo, Jacob	50	
Bravo, Moses	25	2–12–6
Bravo & Furtado		3–15–0
Cardozo, Daniel Rodrigues	8	2–10–0
Cardozo, Isaac		
Cohen, Henry	5	1–17–6
Cohen, Hyman		
Cohen, Hyman	6	2–12–6
Cohen, Isaac	1	0–13–9
Cohen, Judah	2	1–5–0
Coitini [Coutinho], Moses		
Corinaldi, David	7	1–17–6
Corinaldi, Jacob	5	
Cunha, Abraham Ms.	4	1–1–3
Cunha, Isaac Ms., Jr.	4	0–13–9
Cunha, Simha Ms.	5	0–13–9
Da Costa, Abraham Pa.	4	
Da Costa, David Rodrigues	6	1–17–6
Da Costa, Isaac Gs.	6	0–13–9

Name	No. of Slaves	Trade Tax
Da Costa, Isaac Rodrigues	10	1–7–6
Da Costa, Jacob Rodrigues	6	1–7–6
Da Costa, Moses	2	0–13–9
Da Costa, Solomon, and Moses Gomez	4	2–10–0
Da Costa & Alves	2	1–6–3
Da Costa & De Pass	15	2–1–3
De Campos, Abraham		
De Campos, Moses	1	0–13–9
De Cordova, Reverend Joshua His.	20	
Delapenha, Moses	6	
Delapenha, Moses	1	1–5–0
Delapenha, Solomon	10	1–12–6
De Leon, Nathan	2	0–13–9
De Lisser, Aaron	2	0–18–9
De Lisser, Ellis	1	0–13–9
De Lisser, Matthew	2	0–13–9
De Paz, Jacob		
De Souza, ———		0–13–9
Elkin, Solomon	6	3–2–6
Ezekiel, Joseph	6	0–13–9
Ezekiel, Jos.	8	1–17–6
Fernandez, Daniel Dias	2	3–15–0
Fernandez, Daniel Dias		
Fernandez, Isaac Dias	14	3–2–6
Fernandez, Sarah Dias	15	3–15–0
Fernandez, Sarah Dias	15	
Ferreira, Isaac Rodrigues	10	
Ferro, Abraham Silva	6	
Ferro, Judith	10	
Flamengo, Esther Nunes	20	1–7–6
Flamengo, Solomon Nunes	1	1–7–6
Franks, Isaac		
Furtado, David	20	
Furtado, David & Co.	1	2–1–3
Furtado, Isaac	19	3–15–0
Furtado, Leah	7	
Furtado, Rachel Hs.	12	2–10–0
Gabay, Isaac	6	1–5–0
Gabay, Solomon, Jr.	6	0–18–9

Name	No. of Slaves	Trade Tax
Garcia, David	10	1–5–0
Garcia, David	1	1–5–0
Gompertz, Eleazer Ms.—first shop	2	0–13–9
Gompertz, Eleazer Ms.—second shop	2	0–13–9
Gordozo [Cardozo?], Abigail Ab.		
Hadida, Jos.	2	0–18–9
Hart, Levy		1–7–6
Hatchwell, Isaac	2	0–18–9
Henriques, Aaron Nunes	8	2–10–0
Henriques, Aaron Nunes, Jr.	2	0–13–9
Henriques, Abraham of David Nunes	10	
Henriques, Bathsheba Nunes	10	1–5–0
Henriques, Jacob	4	
Henriques, Jacob		1–7–6
Henriques, Joseph	18	2–12–6
Henriques, Lunah Nunes	14	2–10–0
Henriques, Dr. Moses Nunes	2	1–7–6
Henriques & Belisario	2	7–10–0
Hyem, David	1	0–13–9
Hyhem [sic], David	2	0–13–9
Isaac, Joel		0–13–9
Isaacs [sic], Joel	2	1–17–6
Isaacs, Moses B.	10	1–7–6
Jacobs, Jacob		1–7–6
Jacobs, Jacob	8	2–12–6
Jacobs, Henry		
Lazarus, Mr.		
Lazarus, Isaac—two shops	1	1–17–6
Leoni, Mr. [Lyon, Myer]	4	
Levein, ——	2	0–13–9
Levein, Solomon	5	1–17–6
Leveins & Wolfe	3	5–0–0
Levy, Aaron		1–7–6
Levy, Isaac		1–7–6
Levy, Isaac	2	2–1–3
Levy, Jacob	8	2–10–0
Levy, Michael		0–13–9
Levy, Solomon	7	
Levy, Solomon		3–15–0
Lindo, Alexandre—"N[egro] yard"		
Lindo, Alexandre—wharf	20	7–10–0
Lindo, Alexandre	30	

Name	No. of Slaves	Trade Tax
Lindo, Son & Co.	6	22–10–0
Lindo & Lake*	2	12–10–0
Lombroso, Mrs.		
Lousada, Emb. [Eml.?] B.	25	5–0–0
Lousada, Eml. B.		
Lucas, Sampson	4	2–12–6
Mendes, Abigail Pa.	8	1–7–6
Mendes, David Pa.	10	2–1–3
Mendes & Tavares	5	1–5–0
Mercado, Mr.		
Monsanto, E. M.—estate	5	2–0–0
Morais, Moses		1–17–6
Morais, Moses	10	
Morais, Samuel		0–13–9
Morales, Abraham	3	
Morales, Esther		
Morales, Isaac		
Morales, Solomon		
Morao, Mos. Sanches	4	0–13–9
Moreno, David	12	1–5–0
Moreno, Leah	3	
Penha, Jacob	1	0–13–9
Pereira, Antonio		
Pereira, Jacob	21	
Pereira, Jacob & Co.—shop		3–2–6
Pereira, Miss	2	1–7–6
Pereira, Samuel Ms. & Co.	3	3–18–9
Pessoa, Isaac	8	0–13–9
Pessoa, Jacob	1	0–13–9
Phillips, Hyman	2	0–13–9
Phillips, Judah	2	2–12–6
Pinheiro, Isaac Alves	2	0–13–9
Ribeiro, Dr. Nunes	2	0–13–9
Ribeiro, David Nunes	2	0–13–9
Riz, Moses		
Rodrigues, Fernandez	1	0–16–3
Sanguinette, Jacob	8	1–6–3
Silva, David Rs.	6	1–7–6
Silvera, Aaron	8	1–7–6

Name	No. of Slaves	Trade Tax
Solas, Aaron		0–13–9
Solomon, Nathan	2	1–7–6
Tavares, Benjamin		
Tavares, Emanuel	14	1–7–6
Torres, ——— Lopez—estate		
Van Offen, Jacob		0–13–9
Vaz, Jacob Nunes		
Wolfe, Ellis	2	0–13–9
Wormes, Lion	2	0–16–3
Religion Not Certain:		
Benjamin, Abraham		1–17–6
Benjamin, Jos. [Joseph]	3	0–13–9
Berlindino, David, Jr.	18	3–15–0
Emanuel, George—estate	5	
Emanuel, Jos.	21	1–5–0
Freedland, Isaac	4	1–5–0
Hart, John	4	
Martin, Mr.	2	0–13–9
Martin, Mrs.		
Myer, Henry	2	0–13–9
Phillips, ———		0–13–9
Phillips, Judith	3	
Ricardo, Mr.	3	
Silva, Francisco	1	0–13–9
Silva, Francisco	2	0–13–9
Singer, Alexander	1	0–16–3
Solomon, Francis		0–13–9
Wolfe, Mrs.	2	

*Richard Lake, Alexandre Lindo's partner, was not Jewish.
SOURCE: JA, 2/6/105.

TABLE 4

Jewish Households and Companies in Kingston, 1819

Name	No. of Slaves	Trade Tax
Aarons, Jacob	7	2–5–0
Abraham[s], Isaac	4	
Abrahams, Henry	9	0–15–0
Abrahams, S[amuel]	13	1–5–0
Adolphus, Jacob (Princess St.)	13	0–15–0
Adolphus, Jacob (Princess St.)		
Adolphus, Jacob—"Crawle" (West St.)		0–10–0
Alberga, David	7	1–0–0
Alberga, Jacob (Harbour St.)	1	1–0–0
Alberga, Jacob (King St., East Division)	18	
Alberga, Judah	6	0–5–0
Alexander, David	4	1–0–0
Alexander, Joseph	2	
Alexander, Lazarus	4	0–15–0
Alvarenga, Isaac D.	4	1–15–0
Alves, B. Lopez	8	0–15–0
Barned, Levi (Oxford St.)		
Barned, Levi (West Queen St.)	8	1–0–0
Barrow, Isaac		
Bassan, Judith	12	
Belinfante, R.	2	0–15–0
Benaim, I.	6	
Bonita, Moses	6	
Bonita, Sarah Mendes	18	
Bonito, Isaac M.	8	0–5–0
Brandon, Joseph	10	1–0–0
Brandon, Man[asse]h	2	
Brandon, Moses—shop (Tower St.)		0–15–0
Brandon, Moses—house (Tower St.)	2	
Bravo, Abraham (King St., West Division)		
Bravo, Abraham (White St.)		
Bravo, Abraham (Orange St.)		
Bravo, David	20	2–5–0
Bravo, Dr. David	1	
Bravo, Judith (Orange St.)	21	
Bravo, Judith (Church St.)	8	
Bravo, Moses	41	2–15–0
Bravo, Dr. Moses	10	1–0–0

Name	No. of Slaves	Trade Tax
Bravo, Sarah	7	
Carvalho, S. N. (Harbour St.)	1	1–15–0
Carvalho, S. N. (East St.)	19	
Castello & Montefiore	4	3–5–0
Cespedes, Jacob	8	0–10–0
Cohen, Hyman, Jr. (Hanover St.)	6	
Cohen, Hyman, Jr. & Co. (Port Royal St.)	2	3–5–0
Cohen, Joseph	2	
Cohen, Judith Hyman	4	
Cohen, Moses	16	1–0–0
Cohen Brothers	2	5–10–0
Correa, Aaron	14	
Correa & Benaim	2	1–10–0
Coutinho, Moses		
Cunha, Dr.	7	
D'Aguilar, Hananel—pen	10	
Da Costa, ——— (Harbour St.)		
Da Costa, Abraham	4	0–15–0
Da Costa, Abraham R. (Orange St.)	14	
Da Costa, A. R. (Harbour St.)	2	1–15–0
Da Costa, D., Jr.	19	
Da Costa, Dr.	2	
Da Costa, Isaac, Jr.	4	
Da Costa, I. N. (White St.)	2	0–5–0
Da Costa, I. N. (King St., East Div.)	8	
Da Costa, I. N. (Duke St.)	2	
Da Costa, I. N. & Co. (King St., East Div.)	1	1–15–0
Da Costa, Joshua	1	0–15–0
Da Costa, Ralph	14	
Da Costa & Co.		
De Leon, Abigail	34	
De Leon, I. M.	11	0–15–0
De Leon, Rachel	12	
Delgado, Isaac	11	
Delgado, Moses (Harbour St.)	5	0–15–0
Delgado, Moses (King St., East Div.)	1	0–15–0
De Mercado, I. [J.?]	10	0–15–0
De Pass, I. H.	5	
De Pass, Solomon	6	0–10–0
De Souza, ———		

Name	No. of Slaves	Trade Tax
De Souza, Abraham H.	3	
De Souza, Emanuel	3	
De Souza, Solomon (Knight St.)	6	
De Souza, Solomon (Harbour St.)		
Dias, B., Jr.	2	1–0–0
Duke, Lewis	28	0–15–0
Elkin, Solomon	6	2–5–0
Emanuel, Em[anue]l (Harbour St.)		0–10–0
Emanuel, Emanuel (White St.)	6	0–15–0
Fernandez, D. D.	2	2–5–0
Fernandez, E. D.	16	0–15–0
Flamengo, Esther N.	6	1–0–0
Fonseca, E. Lopez	3	0–15–0
Furtado, I. [J.?], O.	5	
Furtado, Isaac D. (Orange St.)		0–15–0
Furtado, Isaac D. (White St.)	7	
Furtado, Jacob D. (Mordaunt Lane)	10	
Furtado, Jacob D. (Harbour St.)	1	2–0–0
Gabay, Moses	2	
Gabay, Rebecca	16	1–0–0
Garcia, Dr. Aaron	4	
Garcia, D[avid] H[enry]	1	
Gates, Elias (Princess St.)	5	
Gates, Elias (Princess St.)		
Gompertz, Marcus (Orange St.)	1	0–10–0
Gompertz, Marcus (King St., East Div.)	4	
Gompertz, Rachel	4	
Hart, Mrs. Rachel	32	
Henriques, Abraham D. N.	28	0–15–0
Henriques, D.	11	
Henriques, David	1	1–15–0
Henriques, Joseph	24	1–15–0
Henriques, Moses	11	
Henriques, S., and sister	16	1–0–0
Henriques, Sarah	3	
Hyams, Marcus A.	12	0–15–0
Hyman, Levy (Orange St.)	4	
Hyman, Levy (Harbour St.)	2	5–10–0
Isaacs, Henry	9	0–10–0
Isaacs, Joseph	2	

Name	No. of Slaves	Trade Tax
Isaacs, Moses	6	
Isaacs, S.	8	
Isaacs, Solomon & Co.	1	1–15–0
Jacobs, Abraham	1	
Jacobs, Daniel		
Jacobs, Rachel (Hanover St.)	9	0–15–0
Jacobs, Rachel (King St., West Div.)	17	
Joseph & Rodrigues		
Josephs, Barnet (Harbour St.)	2	2–15–0
Josephs, Barnet (Bourdon St.)	12	
Josephs, Isaacs & Co.	2	2–5–0
Labatt, Joseph	4	0–10–0
Lazarus, Eleazer	18	0–15–0
Lazarus, Samuel	7	
Lazarus, Solomon	5	
Levein, Joseph	8	0–15–0
Levy, H.	5	
Levy, Henry	4	
Levy, I., Sr.	2	
Levy, Isaac	9	0–15–0
Levy, John		0–5–0
Levy, Judah P.	3	1–5–0
Levy, Leah	5	
Levy, Moses, Jr.	4	1–5–0
Levy, Moses, Sr.	10	1–5–0
Levy, Sarah	20	0–10–0
Levy, Solomon	9	1–0–0
Lewis, Sophia Levy	17	0–10–0
Lindo, Abraham A[lexandre]		2–0–0
Lipman, Lewis (Harbour St.)	2	1–15–0
Lipman, Lewis (Church St.)	7	
Lopez, I.		
Lyon, A. (Knight St.)		
Lyon, Asher (King St., West Div.)	2	
Magnus, Ebenezer		
Magnus, Eliza	1	
Marchalleck, Joseph	8	0–10–0
Martin, M[ordecai] N[unes]	4	0–10–0
Melhado, Daniel (Orange St.)	25	
Melhado, D. & Co. (Harbour St.)		2–5–0

Name	No. of Slaves	Trade Tax
Mendes, ——		
Mendes, David P.	12	1–15–0
Mendes, Isaac	12	0–10–0
Mendes, Samuel P[ereira]	8	0–10–0
Mercado, E. D.	3	
Mesquita, A. G.	2	0–15–0
Mesquita, Isaac		
Montefiore, Moses	1	
Morais, Abraham	5	0–15–0
Morales, Moses	8	0–15–0
Moravia & Co.	3	5–10–0
Mordecai, Mark	7	0–10–0
Morea [Moreno?], Emanuel & Co.		1–0–0
Moreno, A. L.		0–10–0
Moreno, Abraham	6	
Myers, Solomon	4	
Naar, Joshua Ab[raha]m	3	0–10–0
Naar & Delgado	1	2–0–0
Nunes, Abraham I.	7	1–0–0
Nunes, David	18	
Pacifico, Isaac—"N[egro] Y[ar]d"		
Palache, Alexander	16	
Peixoto, A. C. (Orange St.)	5	
Peixoto, A. C. (Harbour St.)	1	0–10–0
Peixoto, A. C. (White St.)	5	
Pereira, A. Mendes	21	0–10–0
Pereira, Jacob (Princess St.)	1	1–0–0
Pereira, Jacob (Church St.)	26	
Pereira, Ralph F.	7	
Pessoa, Jacob	10	1–0–0
Pinto, Abraham (Bourdon St.)		0–10–0
Pinto, Abraham (Bourdon St.)	11	
Quellor, Aaron		
Ribeiro, A. N.	2	1–0–0
Rodrigues, I.	4	
Samuels, Michael (Orange St.)	12	0–15–0
Samuels, Michael (Port Royal St.)		
Sanguinette, Moses	5	
Seixas, S. M.	14	1–10–0
Sequeres [Sequeira?], L. G.	10	1–10–0

Name	No. of Slaves	Trade Tax
Shannon, Mashod	2	1–10–0
Solas, David	2	
Solomon, Isaac		0–10–0
Spyer, Lawrence	8	
Stine, Jacob		0–10–0
Tavares, A. L.	18	
Tavares, Judith	10	
Treves, David	3	
Treves, Jacob (Orange St.)	1	
Treves, Jacob (Harbour St.)	1	1–10–0
Vaz, Esther N.	6	
Wolfe, David	10	
Wolfe, E.—estate	2	
Ynfanson, I. F. [?]	2	5–10–0
Jewish/Non-Jewish Partnerships:		
Henriques & Jure (Harbour St.)		1–0–0
Henriques & Jure (East Queen St.)	20	0–15–0
Pacifico, Isaac & Dixon, Joseph	12	0–15–0
Religion Not Certain:		
Abrahams, Mr.		
Abrahams, I. C.	1	
Asher, Frances	10	0–15–0
Bana [Barra?] & Phillips	7	1–0–0
Barnett, Robert	4	
Barrow, Mary	12	
Benjamin, Joseph	17	0–10–0
Bennett, Sarah	1	
Berry, Samuel L.	5	
Bicca, M. & Co. (Port Royal St.)		0–10–0
Bicca, Manuel (Princess St.)		1–0–0
Bofill, Buento	4	0–10–0
Brown, Ann	13	
Brown, Fanny	3	
Cohen, James		0–15–0
Delcastello, M.	3	0–10–0
Delvalle, Aaron	3	1–0–0
Ferres, Joseph		
Forsythe, James's inmate [tenant]		0–10–0

Name	No. of Slaves	Trade Tax
Garcia, Juan		
Garcia, Vincent	2	
Gonzales, Rosalia	24	
Josephs, Jack	4	
Judah, Andrew	21	0–15–0
Leon, Paulina		
Leon, Thomas	12	1–0–0
Leon & Isaacs	1	2–5–0
Lessa, W. H. (Harbour St.)		0–10–0
Lessa, Wolfe H. (Orange St.)	4	
Levy, Philip	4	1–5–0
Lucas, Frederic	8	1–5–0
Lucas, Micholls & Co.	3	3–5–0
Lucas & Isaacs	1	2–5–0
Malachie, Mord[eca]i	12	
Malloch, David (Golden St.)	8	
Malock, David (Harbour St.)		0–15–0
Manuel, George		
Martin, Priscilla	10	
Michell, Joseph	1	0–10–0
Mitchell, James	6	
Mitchell's—"crawl"		
Montoya, Juan A.		
Nelson, James (Harbour St.)	20	0–15–0
Nelson, James—pen	46	
Phillips, John	6	
Phillips, Josh [sic]	5	
Pinto, Juan	1	5–10–0
Pinto, Manuel	4	
Saleidea, Raphael	2	
Samuels, Mary	6	
Sanches, Domingo		2–10–0
Solomon, Matthew	1	0–15–0
Staines, Jacob (White St.)	4	0–10–0
Staines, Jacob (Bourdon St.)		

SOURCE: JA, 2/6/106.

VII. The Jewish Population of the Parish of St. Catherine, Jamaica

TABLE I

Jewish Households and Companies in Spanish Town, 1772

Name	No. of Slaves	Trade Tax
Abrahams, Samuel		
Abrahams, Solomon	36	
Adolphus, Isaac, Jr.	3	1–0–0
Adolphus, Isaac, Sr.		
Adolphus, Jacob	7	5–0–0
Adolphus, Moses		
Adolphus, Sarah	10	0–5–0
Aflalo, Mordecai		1–10–0
Aflalo, Moses	29	6–0–0
Almeyda, M., and D.	25	7–10–0
Almeyda, Widow		
Alvarez, Esther	9	6–0–0
Belefante [Belinfante], S.C.	1	
Carvalho, M. Nunes	2	10–0–0
Chavis, Mordecai		5–0–0
Cohen, Abigail	10	
Cordova, Jacob		12–0–0
Correa, Abraham	13	0–10–0
Correa, David		
Cortisos, Benjamin		6–0–0
Da Silva, Isaac Henriques	21	8–0–0
De Castro, Leah	20	
De Cordova, Moses	6	13–0–0
De Cordova, Raphael	2	20–0–0
Delapenha, Solomon	1	2–0–0
De Leon, Isaac Pa.		
De Leon, Isaac & Sons	10	
De Leon, Jacob (deceased)	20	
De Leon, Joseph	6	6–0–0
De Leon, Rebecca		6–0–0
De Leon, Rebecca Rodrigues	2	8–0–0
De Lucena, Jacob (deceased)	2	
De Pass, Aaron		6–0–0

Name	No. of Slaves	Trade Tax
Devalle, Jacob		2–0–0
Feyreia [Ferreira?], David Henriques	10	10–0–0
Franks, Simon		
Gabay, Abraham	21	
Gutteres, Isaac M. (deceased)		
Gutteres, Isaac Mendes	62	2–0–0
Gutteres, Joseph	6	
Gutteres, M., and Isaac	6	
Gutteres, Widow	6	
Henriques, David	6	
Henriques, David Nunes	6	
Henriques, Jacob (deceased)	30	
Henriques, Moses Nunes	10	
Isaacs, Isaac (deceased)	8	
Levein, Gotchal	3	4–0–0
Lopez, Abraham Rodrigues	2	
Martin [Martins], Isaac	22	3–0–0
Martin [Martins], [Isaac], Jr.	4	
Martin [Martins], Jacob	3	
Martin [Martins], Moses (deceased)	6	
Martin [Martins], Solomon		2–0–0
Mendes, Joshua		
Mendes, Mrs.	2	3–0–0
Mendes, Solomon	8	
Minis, Philip	1	5–0–0
Morales, Jacob		6–0–0
Nunes, Moses, Jr.		1–10–0
Nunes, Rebecca Rodrigues		6–0–0
Nunes, ——— Vaz		20–0–0
Quiros, Isaac Mendes		6–0–0
Quiros, Jacob Mendes	1	6–0–0
Quiros, Moses Mendes		6–0–0
Ramalho, Leah, and Emanuel	24	
Raphael, Jacob Rodrigues		0–10–0
Rodrigues, Moses		0–10–0
Soares, Joseph	1	
Soares, Leah		6–0–0
Solas, Isaac De Silva		1–0–0
Souza, Abraham	7	

Name	No. of Slaves	Trade Tax
Tavares, Eleanor Nunes		6–0–0
Tavares, Rebecca		
Vaz, Mordecai		4–0–0
Ydania, Samuel	5	
Religion Not Certain:		
Caneo, David, and Esther	2	
Carteni, Esther		5–0–0
Jacobs, Barn[.]	4	
Martin, Ann	2	
Massias, Abraham	2	3–0–0
Nathan, Joseph	1	

SOURCE: JA, 2/2/22.

TABLE 2

Jewish Households and Companies in St. Catherine, 1820

Name	No. of Slaves	Trade Tax
Adolphus, Rachel		
Alberga, David	10	1–5–0
Benjamin, Isaac	3	5–0–0
Bernal, Isalr [Israel]	24	2–0–0
Da Costa, Jos. G.	5	10–0–0
Da Silva, Solomon	22	
De Campos, Sarah	11	
De Cordova, Rachel	3	5–0–0
De Leon, Joseph C.	48	10–0–0
De Leon, Judith C.	6	
De Leon, R. S.	5	
De Pass, Ralph	8	
Fonseca, Elias	1	5–0–0
Gutteres, Judith (deceased)		
Henriques, A. Q., and brother	1	16–0–0
Henriques, Abraham Mendes	1	2–10–0
Henriques, Benjamin	11	
Henriques, Joseph	30	
Levy, Asher	6	10–0–0
Levy, Isaac	3	5–0–0

Name	No. of Slaves	Trade Tax
Lopez, Yehiel	5	4–0–0
Martins, Moses	4	2–10–0
Melhado, Elias	16	
Melhado, Elias, and Daniel		12–10–0
Melhado, Emanuel	6	5–0–0
Mendes, Abigail (deceased)	22	
Mendes, Esther	38	
Mendes, Rachel	16	2–10–0
Mendes, Samuel N.	1	
Rivers, Isaac	3	7–10–0
Sanguinette, Jacob	9	7–10–0
Soares, R., and David	22	5–0–0
Religion Not Certain:		
Aaron, ———		
Alexander, Elizabeth	14	
Alexander, Mary	4	
Alves, Jane F.	8	
Franks, William	18	
Lyon, Ias. [Jas.?] H.	10	
Marcus, George	6	
Myers, William	5	
Sanches, William	16	
Walters, Isaac	8	

SOURCE: JA, 2/2/19.

VIII. Jewish Slaveowners in Montego Bay, Jamaica, 1774

Name	Profession	Family Members	No. of Slaves
Bernal, Abram	Merchant	None	5
Fonseca, Isaac [Da Silva] (deceased)	Merchant	Orphans	12
Furtado, David Orobio	Merchant	4	12
Jacob, Moses	Shopkeeper	1	5
Mesquita, Moses	Shopkeeper	3	7
Silva, Jacob G.	Shopkeeper	None	5
Religion Not Certain:			
Philips, Abram	Shopkeeper	1	9

SOURCES: BL, Long Papers, Add. Ms. 12,435, 3–4. For Isaac Da Silva Fonseca's profession, see IRO, Wills, XXXVI, 181.

IX. Jewish Landowners in Jamaica, 1754

Name	Acres	Parish
Adolphus, Joseph	1,048	St. John
Aflalo, Moses	618	St. John
Aguilar, Joseph	269	St. Catherine
Aguilar, Joseph *[sic]*	269 *[sic]*	St. Catherine *[sic]*
Aguilar, Rebecca	200	St. Catherine
	100	St. John
Bravo, Jacob	122	St. James
Bravo, Jacob *[sic]*	122 *[sic]*	St. James *[sic]*
Bravo, Moses	300	St. Andrew
Cardozo, Jacob Jesurun—estate	100	St. Andrew
	405	St. Thomas-in-the-East
Correa, Jacob—estate	624	St. John
De Lara, Jos. Cohen	150	St. Mary
De Souza, Abraham Hen[riques]	100	St. Catherine
Dias, Abraham	300	Clarendon
Fernandez, Aaron Dias	300	St. James
Fernandez, Benjamin Dias	300	St. James
Fernandez, Daniel Alvarez	300	St. Andrew
Fernandez, Moses Dias	300	St. James
Fernandez, Sol. Dias	300	St. James
Furtado, Isaac	912	St. Andrew
	900	St. James
Gabay, Isaac	499	St. Thomas-in-the-Vale
Gabay, Samuel	300	St. Elizabeth
	105	St. John
	83	St. Catherine
Gabay, Solomon—estate	407	St. Thomas-in-the-Vale
Gutteres, Isaac Mendes	535	St. Dorothy
	500	St. John
	2,134	St. Thomas-in-the-Vale
Gutteres, Jacob	300	St. Catherine
	273	St. John
Gutteres, Moses—estate	420	St. Elizabeth
	460	St. Andrew
Henriques, Jacob	221	St. Catherine
	550	St. John
	200	St. Thomas-in-the-Vale

Name	Acres	Parish
Lousada, Aaron Barrow	140	St. John
Mendes, Solomon	320	St. John
	420	St. John
	90	St. Mary
	32	St. Catherine
	1,000	St. Mary
Mesquita, Ab. Pereira	20	St. John
Mesquita, Solomon	320	St. John
Miranda, Moses	47	Hanover
Nunes, Judith, and Sarah	210	St. Catherine
Pinto, Jacob	44	Hanover
Quixano, Abra. Henriques	300	Westmoreland
Ramalho, Isaac	300	St. Catherine
	100	St. John
Riz, Daniel Lopez	300	St. George
Riz, Moses, and Aaron Lopez	220	St. Andrew
Silva, Isaac Gomez	1,186	St. James
Silva, Joshua Gomez	300	St. James
Silvera, Abraham	1,007	St. Andrew
Torres, Isaac Lopez	102	St. Andrew
	96	Vere
Torres, Isaac Lopez & Co.	250	Clarendon
	101	Vere
Ydana, Abraham	250	St. Thomas-in-the-Vale
Ydana, Isaac—estate	185	St. Catherine
Jewish/Non-Jewish Partnerships:		
Pinto & Chambers	500	Hanover
Polander & Wilson	1,279	St. James
Religion Not Certain:		
Abrahams, Nathaniel	40	St. Catherine
Brown, Abraham	200	St. John
Brown, Abraham [sic]	200 [sic]	St. John [sic]
Delion, Elizabeth	250	St. Mary
Harris, Barrow	600	St. Mary
	900	St. Elizabeth
	194	St. Dorothy
	677	St. John
Hart, Solomon	1,085	St. Dorothy

Name	Acres	Parish
Israel, Abraham	720	Clarendon
	11	Vere
Israel, Abraham [sic]	11 [sic]	Vere [sic]
	570	Clarendon
Israel, Robert	547	Clarendon

SOURCE: IJ, MS 1987, List of the Landholders in the Island of Jamaica in 1754 (Original at PRO, CO 142/31).

X. Jewish Inhabitants of Bridgetown, Barbados, 1798–1818

Name	1798	1810	1815	1818
Aarons, Judah		*	*	*
Abarbanel, Simha	*	*		
Abady, Abigail	*			
Aboab, David	*			
Aboab, Hannah			+	+
Abrahams, Myer		*	*	
Barrow, Jacob	*			
Barrow, Joseph	*			
Barrow, Sarah				*
Barrow, Mrs. Sarah of Hm	*	*	*	
Barrow, Mrs. Sarah I.		*		
Barrow, Simon	*	*	*	*
Belinfante, ——		*		
Brandon, Abraham	*	*		
Brandon, Abrm R.	*	*	*	*
Brandon, Bathsheba	*			+
Brandon, Mrs. Bathsheba		*	+	
Brandon, Isaac Lopez			*	*
Burgos, Esther	+			
Burgos, Mrs. Judith		*	*	
Buzaglo, Abraham	*			
Buzaglo, Salom	*			
Carvalho, Abrm	+			
Castello, Abraham			*	
Castello, R. N.	+			
Cohen, Abm.		*		
Cohen, Judah	*	*		*
Cohen, Lewis			*	
Cohen, Mehir, A.		*		
Cortissos, Isaac	*			
Da Costa, Daniel	*			
Da Costa, Isaac				*
Da Costa, J. H.			*	
Da Costa, Moses Mendes		*	*	*
D'Azevedo, Moses A'Cohen				*

221

Name	1798	1810	1815	1818
De Crasta, Lebonah	*			
De Lima, Rachel				+
De Lima, Reynah	+	+		
De Piza, Emanuel	*	*		
De Piza, Jacob	*	*	*	
De Piza, Jacob			+	+
De Piza, Moses	*			
Elkin, Benjamin		*	*	*
Elkin, Mozley			*	*
Fonseca, Isaac	+			
Fonseca, Lunah	+	+		
Fonseca, Moses	+			
Garcia, Esther	+	+	+	+
Gomez, Raphael	*	*		
Hart, Joseph			*	*
Hart, Nathan	*			
Israel, Abraham			*	
Keys, Abraham I.				*
Lealtad, Hannah	+			
Lealtad, Isaac		*	*	*
Levi, Isaac		*	*	*
Levi, Jacob Joseph	*	*	*	*
Levi, Joshua			*	*
Levi, Judah Eliezer		*	*	*
Levi, Walter Jacob			*	*
Lindo, Abraham		*	*	*
Lindo, David	*	*	*	*
Lindo, Isaac		*	*	*
Lobo, Sarah			+	+
Lopez, Isaac	*	*		
Lopez, Moses	*			
Lousada, Jeremiah Bk.	*			
Lousada, Rachel Bh.	*			
Lousada, Rachel of Bk.	*			
Lousada, Rebecca Bh.	*	*		
Luria, Abm.		*		
Luria, Beliah			*	*
Massiah, Abigail	*		+	+
Massiah, Angel		+		

Name	1798	1810	1815	1818
Massiah, Esther	*			
Massiah, Isaac D.	*		*	
Massiah, Isaac De Piza		*		*
Massiah, Jacob	*			
Massiah, Judah	*		+	
Massiah, Mordy B.	*			
Massiah, Mrs. Reb.		*		
Massiah, Sarah	+	+	+	+
Massiah, Sarah			+	+
Massiah, Sarah of Dd.	*			
Mocatta, Elias	*			
Montefiore, Eleazer	*	*	*	*
Nunes, I. I.			*	
Nunes, Isaac	+	+		
Nunes, Isaac Pl. [?]	*			
Nunes, Jacob	+			
Nunes, Jael		+	+	+
Nunes, Phineas/Pinhas	*	*	*	*
Nunes, Rachel	+			
Nunes, Reba.	+			
Paris, Isaac		*		
Pinheiro, Miss Jael		*	*	*
Pinheiro, Joseph		*		
Pinheiro, Miss Lunah		*	*	*
Pinheiro, Moses	*	*	*	*
Pinheiro, Rachel	*	*	*	*
Ramos, Rebecca	+			
Rus, Joseph				*
Salom, Ab.		*		
Sarafty, Rebecca	+			
Valverde, Abraham	*	*	*	* (deceased)
Valverde, Isaac	*	*	*	*
Valverde, Jacob		*	*	*
Valverde, Simha			*	*

*Paid congregational *finta* (assessment)
+Pensioner

SOURCE: Spanish and Portuguese Jews' Congregation (London), Mss. 328, 331, 333.

XI. Jewish Slaveowners in St. Michael, Barbados, 1729

Name	No. of Slaves
Registered Their Slaves:	
Aboab, David	23
Barrow, Aaron	6
Barrow, Solomon	7
Baruch, David	11
Brandon, Abraham	8
Brandon, Rachel	3
Burgess [Burgos], David	9
Burgess [Burgos], Mordecai	15
Burgess [Burgos], Rachel	3
Carvalho, Jacob Dias	4
Castello, Ephraim	7
Castello, Judith	9
Da Costa, David	11
De Campos, Rebecca	8
Delion [De Leon], David	2
De Piza, David	3
De Piza, Hester	4
De Piza, Sarah	3
Frances, Moses	11
Frances, Rebecca	19
Franco, Isaac	5
Franco, Moses	24
Frois, Jacob	7
Letob, Deborah	2
Letob, Leah	5
Lindo, David	7
Lindon, Jacob	8
Lopez, Hester	3
Lopez, Moses Henriques	5
Marquez, Hester	2
Marquez, Rachel	11
Massiah, Daniel	13
Massiah, Jacob	7
Massiah, Jeremiah	2
Massiah, Simeon	12

Name	No. of Slaves
Mendes, Abraham (deceased)	10
Mendes, Lebanna	3
Mendes, Moses	8
Monsanto, Jacob Nunes	1
Nemais [Nahamias], Sarah	5
Nunes, Abigail	5
Nunes, Benjamin	10
Nunes, David	10
Nunes, Deborah	10
Nunes, Moses	2
Pentiero [Pinheiro?], Moses	12
Pereira, Isaac De Campos	3
Pereira, Moses	3
Valverde, David	10
Valverde, Jacob	30
Villoa, Hester	1

Did Not Register Their Slaves:
Abarbanel, Joseph
D'Azevedo, Abraham
Dias, David
Letob, Rebecca
Lope[z], Abraham
Mendes, Rachel
Motta, Abraham
Nunes, Abraham
Nunes, Abraham Israel
Pacheco, Hezekiah
Peixoto, Joshua
Pereira, Aaron
Rodrigues, Isaac
Rodrigues, Raphael
Valverde, Elias

Religion Not Certain:
  Registered Their Slaves:
Roldon, Abraham Lopenz *[sic]*   2
  Did Not Register Their Slaves:
Barrow, Rachel

SOURCE: PRO, CO 28/21, 104–9, 165–209.

XII. Slave Registers, 1817

TABLE I
Barbados, 1817: Jewish Slaveholders

Name	No. of Slaves
Aarons, Judah	1
Aarons, Leonora	3
Aboab, Hannah	8
Abrahams, Meyer	1
Barrow, Joseph (deceased)	1
Barrow, Rebecca	3
Barrow, Sarah	8
Baru[c]h, Amelia	5
Belasco, Moses	2
Brandon, Abraham R[odrigues]	168
Brandon, Jos. J.	10
Burgos, Judith	1
Cohen, Lewis	6
Da Costa, Isaac	3
Da Costa, Jacob	59
Da Costa, Leah	4
Da Costa, Moses M[endes]	7
D'Azevedo, M. C.	4
De Crasto, Lebanah (deceased)	1
De Piza, Rachel	2
De Piza, Rachel	7
Elkin, Benjamin	1
Elkin, Mozley	3
Gomez, Rebecca (deceased)	4
Lealtad, Isaac	16
Levi, Isaac	4
Levi, Joshua	3
Levi, Walter I.	2
Lindo, Abraham	3
Lindo, David	11
Lousada, Aaron B.	1
Lousada, Jacob Barrow (deceased)	4
Lousada, Rachel B. (deceased)	1
Massiah, I. D.	19
Massiah, Isaac	1

Name	No. of Slaves
Massiah, Sarah	9
Montefiore, Eliezer	1
Montefiore, John	4
Nunes, Benjamin I.	7
Nunes, Deborah	4
Nunes, Esther	12
Nunes, Lunah	1
Nunes, Phineas	20
Pinheiro, Hannah	4
Pinheiro, Jael	1
Pinheiro, Jael	14
Pinheiro, Lunah	13
Pinheiro, Moses	11
Pinheiro, Rachel	15
Valverde, Simha	13
Religion Not Certain:	
Abarbanel, Frances	1
Alvis, Sarah	2
Barrow, Auba, and Mimba Barrow	3
Barrow, Samuel (deceased)	5
Barrows, Julius	3
Barrows, Samuel	1
Brandon, Benjamin, and Isaac Cohen	1
De Piza, Deborah	3
De Piza, Esther	9
De Piza, Rachel	2
De Piza, Sarah (deceased)	10
De Piza, Susanna	19
Lindo, Hester	7
Lindo, Nancy	2
Massiah, Debby Ann	3
Massiah, Eleanor C.	6
Massiah, Elizabeth	2
Massiah, Hannah	4
Massiah, Isaac H.	13
Nunes, Phelinah	5
Paris, Jas. B.	3

SOURCE: PRO, T 71/520–71/523.

TABLE 2
Jamaica, 1817: Jewish Slaveholders

Kingston	No. of Slaves
Aaron, Samuel	2
Aarons, Esther	2
Aarons, Jacob	9
Abendanon, Rebecca	4
Aboab, Rachel	1
Abraham, Isaac	4
Abrahams, Abraham	3
Abrahams, Abraham's children	9
Abrahams, Esther	2
Abrahams, Henry	10
Abrahams, Henry, Marie, Louise, and John	2
Abrahams, Samuel	13
Adolphus, Jacob	9
Adolphus, Dr. Jacob, Esq.	5
Adolphus, Joseph	10
Adolphus, Leah	2
Adolphus, Rebecca	3
Aflalo, Abigail	1
Aflalo, David	11
Aflalo, Joseph	4
Aguilar, Joseph	3
Alberga, David	8
Alberga, Jacob	24
Alberga, Judah	6
Alexander, Amelia, Belvidera, Jacob, Judith, and Frances	16
Alexander, Catherine	2
Alexander, David	2
Alexander, George	1
Alexander, Joseph	1
Alexander, Lazarus	4
Alvarenga, Abraham	1
Alvarenga, Daniel Da Costa (in right of his wife)	2
Alvarenga, Dr. Isaac	11
Alvarenga, Isaac Da Costa	8
Alvarenga, Isaac Da Costa (deceased)	2
Alvarenga, Jacob Da Costa (deceased)	1
Alvarenga, M. D[a] C[osta] (in right of his wife)	2

Kingston (cont.)	No. of Slaves
Alvarenga, Rebecca Da Costa	13
Alvarenga, Rebecca Da Costa	2
Alvarez, Esther Mendes's grandchildren	3
Alvarez, Rachel Mendes	3
Alves, Benjamin Lopez	8
Alves, Benjamin Lopez	1
Alves, Benjamin Lopez, and Daniel Lopez Alves	1
Alves, Daniel Lopez	1
Barned, Levi	32
Barnett, Joseph	7
Barnett, Widow Judith	4
Basan, Jacob (deceased)	20
Belinfante, Myer	1
Belinfante, R. C.	1
Belisario, Abraham Mendes	5
Belisario, Moses (in right of his wife)	8
Benaim, Isaac	8
Benaim, Jacob	1
Benaim, Jam [sic]	1
Bonito, Abraham Mendes	9
Bonito, Isaac Mendes	2
Bonito, Isaac Mendes	11
Bonito, Moses Mendes	5
Bonito, Sarah Mendes (tenant for life)	5
Bonito, Sarah Mendes	17
Brandon, Abigail	2
Brandon, Isaac (in right of his wife)	4
Brandon, Joseph	7
Brandon, Judith	1
Brandon, Judith	18
Brandon, Judith Pereira	1
Brandon, Manasseh	3
Brandon, Moses	2
Bravo, Mr. Abraham	1
Bravo, Bernard	2
Bravo, David	22
Bravo, Judith	23
Bravo, Judith of Isaac	19
Bravo, Leah	9
Bravo, Mrs. Luna	17

Kingston (cont.)	No. of Slaves
Bravo, Moses	3
Bravo, Dr. Moses	10
Bravo, Moses, Esq.	43
Bravo, Miss Sarah	3
Bravo, Simha	1
Brown, Rachel	4
Cardozo, Abigail Aboab	4
Cardozo, Daniel Rodrigues (deceased)	2
Cardozo, Esther Nunes	2
Cardozo, Rebecca Nunes	1
Carvalho, Daniel Riz (in right of his wife and children)	10
Carvalho, Samuel Nunes	25
Castello, Catherine	2
Castello, David	2
Cespedes, Jacob	16
Cespedes & Ribeiro	1
Chaves, Joseph	1
Cohen, Hyman, Jr.	2
Cohen, Judah	3
Cohen, Judah (part-owner)	4
Cohen, Marcus Solomon	1
Cohen, Moses	21
Cohen, Moses	3
Cohen, Rachel	2
Cohen, Rebecca	1
Cohens, Isaacs & Henriques	2
Corinaldi, Esther, Rachel, and Samuel	24
Correa, Aaron	13
Correa & Benaim	2
Cortissos, Widow Esther	5
Cortissos, Rebecca	6
Coutinho, Moses	2
Cunha, Isaac Mendes	11
Cunha, Isaac Mendes (deceased)	4
Cunha, Moses Mendes	2
Cunha, Moses Mendes	3
Cunha, Rachel Mendes	5
Da Costa, Abraham Rodrigues	13
Da Costa, David	1
Da Costa, David (in right of his wife and children)	14

Kingston (cont.)	No. of Slaves
Da Costa, David, Jr.	20
Da Costa, Mrs. Esther	4
Da Costa, Gomez	4
Da Costa, Isaac	2
Da Costa, Isaac Nunes	7
Da Costa, Isaac Nunes	6
Da Costa, Jacob Nunes	1
Da Costa, Jacob Rodrigues	19
Da Costa, Jacob Rodrigues	13
Da Costa, Joseph Pereira	3
Da Costa, Judah Cardozo	1
Da Costa, Judith Pereira	1
Da Costa, Moses Nunes	1
Da Costa, Moses Pereira, Jr.	3
Da Costa, Ralph	10
Da Costa, Raphael Pereira	5
Da Costa, Raphael Pereira, Jr.	3
Da Costa, Rebecca Pereira	11
Da Costa, Samuel Gomez (London merchant)	3
Da Fonseca, Esther Lopez	4
D'Aguilar, Hannah	5
D'Aguilar, Rebecca	2
Da Silva, Isaac (deceased)	1
Da Silva, Leah (deceased)	6
Da Silva, Solomon Mendes	1
Da Silva, Thellamount	1
D'Azevedo, Moses Cohen	1
De Campos, Jacob	2
De Cordova, Abraham Hisqueha	5
De Cordova, Moses	7
De Cordova, Rachel	11
De Cordova, Raphael	12
De Crasto, Abigail	2
De Crasto, Elizabeth	5
Delapenha, Widow Esther (owner for life, only)	6
Delapenha, Widow Esther	2
Delapenha, Jacob	2
Delapenha, Rebecca (spinster)	1
De Leon, Abigail	15
De Leon, Em[anuel]l M.'s children	6

Kingston (cont.)	No. of Slaves
De Leon, Esther	1
De Leon, Isaac M., Sr.	7
De Leon, Joseph Morache	2
De Leon, Rachel	12
De Leon, Sarah	1
Delgado, Isaac	14
Delgado, Moses	6
Delgado, Rachel	3
Delisser, Aaron (deceased)	4
Delisser, Abigail	7
De Mercado, Esther	3
De Mercado, Esther [sic]	3 [sic]
De Mercado, Manasseh	3
De Pass, Daniel	2
De Pass, David Garcia	4
De Pass, Hannah	1
De Pass, Isaac	11
De Pass, Jacob (deceased)	13
De Pass, Judith	9
De Pass, Rebecca Garcia	11
De Pass, Solomon	7
De Paz, Jacob Garcia	3
De Souza, Emanuel (in right of his wife)	3
De Souza, Isaac	3
De Souza, Isaac (in right of his wife)	40
De Souza, Sarah, Louisa, and Rebecca	3
De Souza, Solomon	8
Dias, Benjamin, Jr.	2
Dias, Jacob	2
Dolphy, Rebecca	5
Duke, Lewis	29
Elkin, Abraham	1
Elkin, Solomon	8
Emanuel, Emanuel	3
Ezekiel, Rachel	8
Ezekiel, Rachel, and Esther	4
Fernandez, Daniel Dias	1
Fernandez, David Dias	1
Fernandez, Esther Dias	20
Ferreira, Rebecca	5

Kingston (cont.)	No. of Slaves
Ferro, Jacob	6
Ferro, Judith	1
Ferro, Widow Judith	14
Ferro, Leah Silva	10
Ferro, Rebecca S.	5
Flamengo, Esther Nunes	6
Flash, Alexander	4
Flash, Alexander, Jacob, and Judith	13
Flash, Solomon	6
Flores, John	1
Flores, Sipporah	4
Fonseca, Emanuel Lopez	3
Fonseca, Esther	6
Franco, Moses (of London)	1
Furtado, David	1
Furtado, David Orobio	1
Furtado, David, and Rachel	5
Furtado, Esther	3
Furtado, Isaac	12
Furtado, Isaac David	2
Furtado, Isaac David's children	7
Furtado, Isaac O[robio]	2
Furtado, Jacob	6
Furtado, Jacob David	5
Furtado, Jacob David (in right of his wife)	1
Furtado, Jacob O[robio]	6
Furtado, Leah	2
Furtado, Leah (deceased)	3
Gabay, Moses	1
Gabay, Rebecca	12
Garcia, Aaron	4
Garcia, David Henry	1
Garcia, Isaac	4
Garcia, Jacob Louis (deceased)	3
Gates, Elias	3
Gomez, Joseph	1
Gompertz, Rachel	5
Hadida, Joseph	2
Hart, Daniel, Philip, and Jonas	7

Kingston (cont.)	No. of Slaves
Hart, Rachel	5
Hart, Rachel (owner for life, only)	16
Hart, Rachel (owner for life, only)	15
Hatchwell, Isaac (London merchant)	7
Hendricks, Herman [Harmon]	4
Henriques, Aaron Nunes (deceased)	5
Henriques, Abigail	11
Henriques, Abigail Gabay (spinster)	2
Henriques, Abigail Gabay (owner for life, only)	4
Henriques, Abraham David Nunes (in right of his wife)	26
Henriques, David	6
Henriques, David N.	1
Henriques, David Y., and Abraham	1
Henriques, David Y. (in right of his wife and children)	5
Henriques, Eliza Gabay	2
Henriques, Esther	3
Henriques, Esther Nunes	3
Henriques, Isaac	8
Henriques, Isaac Cohen	1
Henriques, Isaac, and Solomon	2
Henriques, Joseph	10
Henriques, Joseph Gutteres	6
Henriques, Leah	3
Henriques, Leah	10
Henriques, Louisa	6
Henriques, Mary Ann, Franco, Rachel, and Esther Belisario	1
Henriques, Matilda	1
Henriques, Moses	6
Henriques, Moses Cohen	5
Henriques, Dr. Moses Nunes	13
Henriques, Rebecca	20
Henriques, Rebecca	1
Henriques, Rebecca Cohen (deceased)	4
Henriques, Rebecca Jesurun	1
Henriques, Sarah	4
Henriques, Sarah Nunes	11
Henriques, Sarah Nunes, and Esther Nunes	3
Hyams, Marcus Abraham	11
Hyams, Marcus Abraham (in right of his wife)	12
Hyman, Joseph	1

Kingston (cont.)	No. of Slaves
Hyman, Levy	8
Hyman, Moses	2
Isaacs, Abraham	1
Isaacs, Bathsheba	4
Isaacs, Esther	1
Isaacs, Esther, and Rachel	4
Isaacs, Henry	7
Isaacs, Joseph	1
Isaacs, Judith	1
Isaacs, Sipporah	1
Isaacs, Solomon	10
Jacobs, Daniel	1
Jacobs, Rachel	12
Jacobs, Rachel	17
Jesurun, Rebecca	7
Joseph, Barnett	17
Joseph, Joseph	6
Labat, Sarah Cohen	3
Ladesma, Esther	2
Lazarus, Eleazer	13
Lazarus, Isaac	2
Lazarus, Samuel	7
Lazarus, Solomon	5
Levein, Joseph (owner for life, only)	1
Levy, Elizabeth	1
Levy, Henriette	1
Levy, Henry	5
Levy, Hyman	6
Levy, Isaac	9
Levy, Isaac, Sr.	1
Levy, Levy	12
Levy, Moses, Jr.	3
Levy, Moses, Sr.	10
Levy, Rachel	1
Levy, Sarah	22
Levy, Solomon	9
Lewis, Sophia Levi	18
Lindo, Abraham Alexandre	10
Lindo, Abraham Alexandre, and John Campbell	3

Kingston (cont.)	No. of Slaves
Lindo, Ann	1
Lindo, Ann	1 [sic]
Lindo, Jacob	21
Lindo, Sarah	1
Lindo, Sarah (owner for life, only)	3
Lipman, Lewis	10
Lopez, Abigail	2
Lopez, Isaac	3
Lousada, Mrs. Esther Baruch	1
Lucas, Louis	5
Madoure, Ann	1
Magnus, Eleazer	1
Magnus, Simeon [Simon?]	1
Martin, Mordecai Nunes	7
Melhado, Daniel	18
Melhado, Daniel (in right of his wife)	4
Melhado, Jacob Aaron	3
Melhado, Rachel	1
Mendes, Abraham Pereira	3
Mendes, David Pereira	12
Mendes, Esther	11
Mendes, Isaac	12
Mendes, Jacob Pereira (owner for life, only)	1
Mendes, Samuel Pereira	9
Mendes, Samuel Pereira	1
Mesquita, Abraham Gomez	2
Mesquita, Daniel	1
Mesquita, Esther Gomez	9
Miranda, Leah	3
Monis, Charlotte	4
Montefiore, Moses	1
Montefiore, Moses, and David Castillo [Castello]	3
Morais, Abraham	5
Morais, Abraham (in right of his son)	2
Morais, Joshua	3
Morais, Leah	10
Morais, Moses	1
Morais, Moses (in right of his wife)	9
Morales, Abigail	2
Morales, Benjamin	1

Kingston (cont.)	No. of Slaves
Morales, Esther	4
Morales, Moses	9
Moravia, George	2
Moravia & Palache	3
Mordecai, Mark	7
Moreno, Aaron	3
Moreno, Abraham	2
Moreno, Bl. [sic] (daughter of Abraham Moreno)	2
Moreno, Emanuel	1
Moreno, Leah Levy	3
Moses, Abigail	1
Moses, Elkin	2
Myers, Moses	1
Myers, Sarah, Solomon, Mordecai, and Abram Israel	4
Naar, Joshua	1
Naar, Joshua, and Isaac Delgado	2
Naar, Joshua of Abraham	3
Nabarro, Abraham	1
Nunes, Abram Israel	10
Nunes, David (in right of his wife)	4
Nunes, David's children	5
Nunes, Deborah	2
Nunes, Esther Rodrigues	1
Nunes, Rebecca Rodrigues, and Judith Rodrigues Nunes	3
Nunes, Sarah	2
Nunes, Widow Sarah	17
Nunes, Widow Sarah (owner for life, only)	7
Pacifico, Isaac (in right of his wife)	37
Pacifico, Lewis	1
Palache, Alexander	10
Palache, Mordecai	12
Palache, Rachel, Judith, and Sarah	6
Peixoto, Abraham Cohen	11
Peixoto, Moses Cohen	1
Pereira, Esther Mendes	6
Pereira, Jacob (in right of his wife)	28
Pereira, Raphael Fernandez	7
Pereira, Rebecca	1
Pereira, Samuel Mendes (deceased)	12

Kingston (cont.)	No. of Slaves
Pessoa, Esther	1
Pessoa, Jacob	10
Pinto, Abraham	11
Pinto, Isaac (in right of his wife)	8
Pinto, Moses	4
Pinto, Rachel	5
Pinto, Raphael, and Joshua	2
Pinto, Rebecca	2
Quello, Aaron	2
Ramos, Sarah (owner for life, only)	2
Ribeiro, Aaron Nunes	2
Ribeiro, Aaron Nunes	2
Ribeiro, Esther Nunes	8
Ribeiro, Judith Nunes	1
Ribeiro, Leah Bonner	3
Rietti, Abraham	6
Rietti, Sarah	1
Rodrigues, Anna	2
Rodrigues, Moses	3
Rodrigues, Sarah	2
Sabbath, Abraham	2
Salas, Mrs. Simha	2
Salom, Judith	1
Salom, Sarah	2
Samuel, Michael	20
Sanguinette, Moses	5
Sanguinette, Rebecca	6
Seixas, Samuel Mendes	13
Sequeira, Bienvenida, Judith, Emanuel, and Jacob	6
Sequeira, Jacob Henriques	2
Serffeyete [Sarfaty?], Mimi	1
Shannon, John's children (entrusted to their uncle, Mashod Shannon)	3
Shannon, Mashod	2
Silva, Esther Gomez (deceased)	5
Silva, Grace	2
Silva, Joseph	1
Silvera, Benjamin (deceased)	4
Silvera, Judith (deceased)	1
Skiffington, Jacob	1

Kingston (cont.)	No. of Slaves
Soares, Isaac	1
Soares, Phineas	2
Soares, Ralph	1
Soares, Rebecca	3
Solas, David Mendes	2
Spyer, Joseph, and Solomon	1
Spyer, Lawrence	12
Stein, Jacob	3
Tavares, Abraham, Aaron, Rachel, Hannah, and Simha	16
Tavares, Abraham Lopez	7
Tavares, Daniel (in right of his wife and children)	8
Tavares, Emanuel	2
Tavares, Esther	2
Tavares, Isaac	7
Tavares, Jacob, Jr.	3
Tavares, Widow Judith	10
Tavares, Moses	3
Tavares, Rebecca	4
Tavares, Simah	10
Treves, Abigail	1
Treves, David	3
Treves, Jacob	1
Vaz, Widow Abigail Nunes (in right of her children)	7
Vaz, Esther Nunes	1
Vaz, Esther Nunes	9
Ulloa, Jacob	2
Wolfe, David	7
Wolfe, Ellis (deceased)	5
Wolfe, Solomon	1

Clarendon	
Bravo, Moses	226
Levy, Isaac	4

Hanover	
Costa, Rebecca	9
Dias, Benjamin	1

Hanover (cont.)	No. of Slaves
Dias, Hetty	3
Dias, Joseph	2
Dias, Rebecca	6
Dias, Sarah	10
Furtado, Isaac O[robio]	2
Gabay, Joseph A.	7
Garcia, Esther	2
Isaacs, Jacob	3
Isaacs, Lyon	1
Levy, Daniel	1
Levy, Jacob	27
Levy, Moses	5
Levy, Moses (in right of his wife)	5

Manchester	
Abrahams, Alexander	5
Abrahams, Alexander, and Abraham	2
Albuquerque, Esther	9
Embden [Emden], Joseph	5
Hendricks, Herman [Harmon]	88
Morais, Grace	2
Morais, Sarah	1

Port Royal	
Basan, Jacob (deceased)	41
Da Costa, Raphael Pereira	1
De Pass, Caleb	2
De Pass, Henry, Sarah, and Elvira	6
Ezekiel, Rachel	2
Gadjie, Joseph Saul	1
Lindo, Abraham Alexandre	242
Moreno, Leah Levy	3
Rodrigues, Daniel	9
Serano, Moses Mendes	3

St. Andrew	No. of Slaves
Bravo, David	7
Cardozo, Abigail Rodrigues	8
Cardozo, Abigail Rodrigues (deeded in trust to David Da Costa)	3
Cardozo, Abigail Rodrigues (deeded in trust to David Da Costa and Joseph Aguilar, Jr.)	8
Da Costa, Abraham Pereira	25
Levy, Hyman	45
Lindo, Abraham Alexandre	312
Lindo, Abraham Alexandre	102
Lindo, Abraham Alexandre	354
Lindo, Abraham Alexandre	125
Pereira, Samuel Mendes (deceased)	21
Seixas, David	1
Seixas, David, and Samuel Mendes Seixas	6
Shannon, Mashod	11
Shannon, Mashod (in right of his wife)	2
Silvera, Abraham, Jr.	16
Silvera, Abraham, Sr.	7
Silvera, Benjamin (deceased)	12
Silvera, Benjamin of A. Silvera	4
Silvera, Eliza Ann	1
Silvera, Isaac	27
Silvera, M[oses]	2
Silvera, Robert, and George	2

St. Ann	
Da Silva, Isaac (deceased)	9
Da Silva, Jacob	3
Da Silva, Leah (deceased)	4
Da Silva, Solomon Mendes	119
Henriques, Benjamin B.	30
Henriques, Isaac	65
Lemon, Israel	1
Lemon, Israel, and Solomon	4
Lemon, Solomon	1
Lousada, Ms. *[sic]* B., Emanuel Lousada, Esq., and David Lousada, Esq.	122

St. Catherine	No. of Slaves
Adolphus, Rachel	12
Aflalo, Isaac Millas	1
Aflalo, Mordecai	4
Benjamin, Miss Hannah	2
Benjamin, Isaac	3
Bernal, Isaac Rodrigues	2
Bernal, James Rivers	19
Correa, Aaron	9
Correa, Esther	17
Da Costa, Joseph Gomez	19
D'Aguilar, Rebecca	2
Da Silva, Solomon Mendes	17
Da Silva, Solomon Mendes (in right of his wife)	2
De Campos, Sarah	16
De Cordova, Jacob (deceased)	1
De Cordova, Rachel	3
De Leon, Abraham Cohen	2
De Leon, Brancha [sic] Cohen	5
De Leon, Joseph Cohen	6
De Leon, Judith Cohen	6
De Leon, Judith Cohen's daughter	1
De Leon, Sarah Rodrigues	7
De Mattos, David	1
De Mattos, David (tenant by parole)	1
De Pass, Ralph	11
Fonseca, David	2
Henriques, Abraham Quixano (of London)	11
Henriques, Benjamin	5
Henriques, Jacob	17
Henriques, John Gabay	1
Henriques, Joseph	16
Isaacs, Solomon	3
Levy, Asher	5
Levy, Isaac	2
Lopez, Yehiel	9
Lynn, Sarah	3
Martins, Emanuel Mendes, Esq. (deceased)	18
Martins, Moses	7
Melhado, Elias	14

St. Catherine (cont.)	No. of Slaves
Melhado, Emanuel	15
Melhado, Jacob Aaron, Sarah, and David	3
Mendes, Abigail	43
Mendes, Abraham	6
Mendes, Abraham (in right of his wife)	7
Mendes, Daniel	1
Mendes, Esther	45
Mendes, Samuel Pereira	1
Mendes, Simha, Rebecca, and Rachel	6
Morales, Simah	1
Morao, Abigail Sanches	15
Rios, Daniel Nunes	2
Rivers, Isaac	2
Sanguinette, Jacob, Sr.	7
Soares, David Jacob	9
Soares, Rebecca	11
Vaz, Moses	3
Vaz, Rachel	1
Vaz, Rebecca	2
Vaz, Rebecca, Abraham, Rachel, and David	3

St. David	
Phillips, Joseph	10
Phillips, Julie (entrused to Joseph Phillips)	2

St. Dorothy	
Bravo, Moses, Esq.	55
Mendes, Samuel Pereira, Esq.	27

St. Elizabeth	
Adolphus, Jacob	4
Cardozo, Isaac	1
Cohen, Daniel Abraham's heirs	3
Hart, Elizabeth	1
Hart, Nathan	2

St. Elizabeth (cont.)	No. of Slaves
Hart, Rebecca	2
Hart, Rebecca, Ann, Sarah, and Elizabeth	48
Hendricks, Herman [Harmon]	10
Hyam, Matthew Azuly	2
Hyams, Michael (deceased)	2
Hyman, Lazarus	65
Isaacs, Elizabeth	1
Morais, Abraham	5
Morais, Emanuel	1
Myers, Abraham (deceased; entrusted to Louisa Myers)	42
Myers, Louisa	8
Myers, Louisa (in right of Rachel Smith)	3
Myers, Moses	8
Tavares, Elizabeth	12
Tavares, Isaac	6
Tavares, Jane (deceased)	8
Tavares, Sarah	5
Vaz, Isaac Nunes	8

St. James	
Cohen, Rebecca	2
Corinaldi, Emily	1
Corinaldi, Horatio	1
Corinaldi, Jacob Portello (in right of his wife)	7
Fernandez, Ben [sic] Dias	2
Furtado, Abraham O[robio]	4
Furtado, David Orobio	4
Furtado, Elizabeth	1
Furtado, Isaac O[robio]	1
Furtado, Jacob O[robio], Jr.	2
Gedelia, Isaac	2
Gedelia, Moses	7
Gedelia, Solomon	2
Isaacs, Henry Isaac	11
Jacobs, Jacob	21
Levy, John	1
Marks, Solomon	4
Simon, Isaac	11

St. James (cont.)	No. of Slaves
Solomon, Jacob	11
Wetzlar, Noe Daniel	8

St. John	
Adolphus, Rachel	13
Da Silva, Isaac (deceased)	5
Da Silva, Isaac (deceased)	5
Da Silva, Solomon Mendes, Esq.	16
Da Silva, Solomon Mendes, Jacob Henriques, and Joseph Henriques	21
Gutteres, Judith (deceased)	15
Mendes, Widow Abigail	18
Mendes, Esther	10
Vaz, David	3

St. Thomas-in-the-East	
Aguilar, Dias, et al.	361

St. Thomas-in-the-Vale	
Henriques, Jacob, Esq.	151

Trelawny	
Arnold, Solomon	5
Da Costa, Elizabeth	4
Nathan, Jacob Philip	2
Nunes, Esther	1
Solomon, Lazarus	12

Vere	
Bravo, Moses, Esq.	132

Westmoreland	No. of Slaves
Cardozo, Elias	3
Polack, Abraham David	4

Religion Not Certain:

Kingston	No. of Slaves
Almeyda, Sarah Turner	3
Amader, Juan Adios	4
Arnold, Charlotte	1
Arnold, Charlotte	1
Arnold, Mary	20
Arubla, Pedro	1
Asher, Francis	11
Aves, Esther	2
Barnett, William	1
Belindina, Esther	1
Benjamin, Joseph	17
Bennett, Augustin	2
Bennett, Sarah	2
Bernal, Mary Ann (tenant by parole of Ralph Bernal)	3
Bicca, Manuel	1
Brown, Charlotte	1
Brown, Edward James	6
Brown, Fanny	4
Brown, Hugh William	8
Brown, Jane	2
Brown, Rosanna	7
Burgo, Françoise	1
Chayon, Seme, Esther, and Gracey	2
Cohen, Clara	2
Del Castillo, Manuel	4
De Leon, Ann	10
Delvaille, Aaron, Sr.	2
De Sosser [De Souza?], Edward	1
Edwards, Solomon Wolfe	2
Emanuel [also Manuel], Joseph	2
Ferrier, David	3

Kingston (cont.)	No. of Slaves
Ferro, Ann	1
Garcia, Vincente	1
Gonzalez, Manuel (deceased)	10
Gonzalez, Rosalia	14
Hart, Mary	1
Jacobs, Ann	1
Jacobs, Robert	1
Jacobs, Mary	5
Joseph, Jack	5
Julian, Louis	5
Kessler, Charlotte	7
Kessler, Eugene	3
King, Charlotte	1
King, Sarah	9
Lessa, Wolfe Henry	5
Levien, Elizabeth	4
Levison, Charles	1
Lopez, George	2
Lucas, Frederick	8
Lyon, David	5
Malloch, David	6
Marks, Sophia	1
Marquez, Remigro	1
Martins, Esther	4
Massias, Joshua	1
Mattos, Mary Walker	1
Melhado, Cabey	2
Mendes, Samuel Peeke	1
Michel, Joseph	4
Myers, Elizabeth	1
Myers, Sarah	7
Narvaez, Juan Salvador	4
Navarre, Francis	1
Nelson, James	56
Perez, Paula	1
Phillips, Abraham	10
Phillips, Benjamin	9
Phillips, Charles	2
Phillips, Clarissa	5

Kingston (cont.)	No. of Slaves
Phillips, Elizabeth	1
Phillips, John	17
Phillips, John	1
Phillips, Mary	8
Phillips, Rachel	6
Pinto, Juan	1
Pinto, Manuel	4
Raphael, Abraham	1
Reales, Sophie	1
Ricardo, Sarah	1
Sabzedo, Raphael	1
Samuels, Mary	7
Sanches, Caroline	17
Sanches, John	2
Silva, Jane	4
Simons, Rebecca	13
Solomon, Matthew	1
Solomon, Phoebe	1

Clarendon	
Gottshalk, John (deceased)	47
Henry, Elizabeth	2
Phillips, John	5

Hanover	
Cerdova [Cordova?], Judith	2
Lyon, Isaac (in right of his wife, Judith)	3
Lyon, Jacob	32
Lyon, Sarah	7

Manchester	
D'Aguilar, Moses (William Kerr D'Aguilar, attorney)	32
D'Aguilar, William Kerr	1
Levys, Henriette	18
Levys, Philip	108
Nelson, Lewis	52
Sampson, James	71
Wolff, Maximillian Joseph, and Henry Cerf	20

Portland	No. of Slaves
Arnold, William	2

Port Royal	
Barnett, Jonathan	9
Benjamin, Sarah, and Elizabeth Taws Hewit (Isaac Benjamin, guardian)	2
Frank, William	7
Phillips, Abraham	100
Phillips, Elizabeth	10

St. Andrew	
Davila, Manuel	11
Josephs, Jacob	4
Josephs, Widow Judith	6
Lubin, Lewis Alexander (deceased)	165
Lucas, Frederick	17
Raphael, Johanna Innes	2
———, ——— (Joseph Henriques and Solomon Mendes Silva, trustees)	24

St. Ann	
Cohen, Michael J. [I.?]	12
Ferrara, Francis, and wife	11
Gonzalez, Alexander (deceased)	4
Israel, Henry	8
Martin, Edward	1
Martin, Elizabeth	16
Phillips, Elizabeth	1
Phillips, George	4
Phillips, Jonathan	15

St. Catherine	
Adolphus, Charles	1
Alexander, Mary	1
Alves, Jane Frances	6
Barnett, Eliza	1
Bennett, Edward	19
Cowan, Isaac	4
Elishur, Elizabeth	6

St. Catherine (cont.)	No. of Slaves
Israel, Widow Elizabeth	1
Lewis, Sarah	16
Lyon, David	22
Lyon, James Henry	5
Marcus, George	5
Martin, Anna	1
Mitchell, Ann	2
Mitchell, Elizabeth	5
Mitchell, John	10
Myers, Mrs. Sarah	5
Myers, Thomas (deceased)	2
Sanches, William	5
Sanches, William, and Elizabeth	3

St. David	
Jacob, John	15

St. Dorothy	
Gabriel, Sarah Elise	3

St. Elizabeth	
Abrahams, Ruthy	3
Cohen, A. S.	3
Cohen, Catherine, and Elizabeth Bowes	3
Cohen, David	8
Cohen, James Benstead	4
Hart, Thomas	12
Isaacs, John Powell, Mary, and Ann (entrusted to their mother, Abigail)	3
Isaacs, Joseph (entrusted to his mother, Sarah Clarke)	1
Levy, Benjamin	15
Levy, Jane Margaret (entrusted to Benjamin Levy)	1
Levy, William Benjamin (entrusted to Benjamin Levy)	2
Moies, Ja[me]s	60
Restivo, Mary Hannah (deceased)	2
Rize [Riz?], Moses	1
Samuda, David, and Mrs. Deborah Hewitt	70
Samuda, David, and Mrs. Deborah Hewitt	265

St. Elizabeth (cont.)	No. of Slaves
Simons, Rebecca	1
Solomons, Eve	23

St. George	
Ash, John	1
Bernea [Berneas?], Joseph	1
Myers, John	6

St. James	
Brown, Judith	6
Brown, William	33
Jacobs, Abraham	1
Leah, Roderigo	2
Levi, Rebecca, and Elizabeth (Rebecca Hewitt, their estate administrator)	6
Marks, Rebecca	1
Pulies, Isaac	2
Pulies, Moses	9
Pulies, Sarah Hall	1
Rodriguiz [Rodrigues?], Leonora	1
Samuells, Jane	12

St John	
Mendes, John	2

St. Mary	
Henry, Charlotte	1
Myers, Thomas (deceased)	56

St. Thomas-in-the-East	
Ash, Sarah (owner for life, only)	3
Franks, Mrs., Samuel Prado, Esq., et al.	243
Jacobs, Elizabeth	7
Mattas [Mattos?], Margaret	1
Mattos, Mary	3

St. Thomas-in-the-Vale	No. of Slaves
Leon, Thomas	22
Martin, Benjamin	2

Trelawny	
Benjamin, Henry	7
Flash, William	2
Harris, Sarah Lydia	1
Lyon, David, Esq.	186
Lyon, David, Esq.	190
Lyon, David, Esq.	42
Pareira [sic], Mary	1
Phillips, Ann	10
Samuells, Mary	6

Westmoreland	
Pessoa, Jacob	1
Samuda, Benjamin's children	38

SOURCES: PRO, T 71/1, 71/13, 71/19, 71/25, 71/33, 71/43, 71/51, 71/57, 71/65, 71/74–71/79, 71/119, 71/125, 71/139, 71/145, 71/151, 71/158, 71/164–71/166, 71/178, 71/190, 71/201–71/204, 71/224–71/229.

XIII. *Jewish Burghers and Slaves in St. Eustatius, 1781*

Name	No. of Slaves
Abendanon, Abram	5
Abendanon, David	3
Abendanon, Haim	6
Abendanon, Joseph	3
Abrahams, Levi	
Alberga, Abram	1
Almeyda, David	2
Azevedo, Abram	
Benjamin, Benjamin	
Benjamin, Judah	2
Benjamin, Solomon	2
Brandon, Gomez	
Cotinos, Isaac Henriques	
Cotinos, Moses	
Coutinho, Abram Dias	2
Da Costa, Michiel [sic] Andrade	
Da George, Solomon	
De Fonseca, Moses	
De Leon, David	14
De Leon, Emanuel	
De Leon, Judah	
De Leon, Solomon	
De Noble at Lindos	
De Solas, Isaac	1
Furtado, Isaac	
Gabriel, ———	
Garcia, Isaac	
Garcia, Jacob	3
Gomez, A., Jr.	
Gomez, Louis	
Hart, Naphtali	
Henriques, Isaac, Sr.	1
Henriques, Joseph	
Hoheb, Abm.	
Hoheb, Joseph	1

Name	No. of Slaves
Hoheb, Samuel	3
Jacobs, Leon	2
Jacobs, Solomon	4
Kann, Leon	
Levi, Abrahams [sic]	
Levi, Solomon	12
Lobo, David Jesurun	1
Lopez, Abram	4
Mendes, David	4
Mendes, Joshua Gideon	1
Meyers, Moses	
Moses, Philip	
Nathan, Bernard	1
Olivier, Jacob	
Pimentel, David Henriques	
Polock, Jacob	
Robles, Jacob	
Rodrigues, ——	
Samuel, Nathan	
Solas, Isaac	
Suasso, Eleazer	
Vais [Vaz?], Gomez	1
Van Praag, Philip David	
Waag, Moses	
Welcome, Benjamin	3
Welcome, Isaac	3
Welcome, Jacob	1

SOURCE: PRO, CO 318/8, 61–82.

Notes

Notes to the Introduction

1. For discussions during the last fifteen years of the volume of the slave trade as well as summaries of earlier estimates, see, for example, Paul Lovejoy, "The Volume of the Atlantic Slave Trade: A Synthesis," *Journal of African History* 23 (1982): 473–501; David Richardson, "Slave Exports from West and West-Central Africa, 1700–1810: New Estimates of Volume and Distribution," *Journal of African History* 30 (1989): 1–22; David Richardson, "The Eighteenth-Century British Slave Trade: Estimates of Its Volume and Coastal Distribution in Africa," *Research in Economic History* 12 (1989): 151–95; and Joseph E. Inikori and Stanley L. Engerman, "Introduction: Gainers and Losers in the Atlantic Slave Trade," 5–6, in Joseph E. Inikori and Stanley L. Engerman, eds., *The Atlantic Slave Trade: Effects on Economies, Societies, and Peoples in Africa, the Americas, and Europe* (Durham: Duke University Press, 1992). Inikori and Engerman suggest that the total carried from Africa to the Americas will in all likelihood prove to have ranged from twelve million to more than twenty million.
2. James A. Rawley, *The Transatlantic Slave Trade: A History* (New York: W. W. Norton, 1981), 269–81. For a powerful autobiographical account by an eighteenth-century African who was kidnapped, marched overland, and eventually sold into slavery, see [Olaudah Equiano], *The Interesting Narrative of the Life of Olaudah Equiano* (1791; Boston: St. Martin's Press, 1995).
3. Rawley, *Transatlantic Slave Trade,* passim, for the roles of Portugal, Holland, England, and France; and 51–70 for how Spain procured its empire's supply of slaves.
4. Simon Cohen, tr., Jacob R. Marcus and Stanley F. Chyet, eds., *Historical Essay on the Colony of Surinam, 1788* (Cincinnati and New York:

American Jewish Archives and Ktav, 1974), 44, 55, 58–59, 65, 67–68, 70, 86–87, 96–97, 99–101, 104, 129. For the author of this work, see R. Bijlsma, "David De Is. C. Nassy, Author of the *Essai Historique sur Surinam*," in Robert Cohen, ed., *The Jewish Nation in Surinam: Historical Essays* (Amsterdam: S. Emmering, 1982), 65–73. For the most recent examination of the Jews in Suriname, see Robert Cohen, *Jews in Another Environment: Surinam in the Second Half of the Eighteenth Century* (Leiden: E. J. Brill, 1991), with references to Jews who owned slaves at 76–77, 125–26, 139, 159. Cohen's work is especially valuable because of its examination of how the Jewish community dealt with mulatto offspring who wished to affiliate with it.

    Johannes Menne Postma reports that, in 1695, taxes were paid on 4,618 slaves in all of Suriname; *The Dutch in the Atlantic Slave Trade, 1600–1815* (Cambridge: Cambridge University Press, 1990), 185. According to Postma, the underreporting of slaves for tax purposes was only an occasional occurrence.

5. Salo Wittmayer Baron, *A Social and Religious History of the Jews*, 17 vols.; 2d ed., rev. and enl. (New York and Philadelphia: Columbia University Press and Jewish Publication Society of America, 1952–80), XV, 69, 275, 297–98, 355, 448.

6. Isaac S. Emmanuel and Suzanne A. Emmanuel, *History of the Jews of the Netherlands Antilles*, 2 vols. (Cincinnati: American Jewish Archives, 1970), I, 41, 49–50, 66, 74–80, 142, 228, 364; II, 622–77, 1036–45. See also Isaac S. Emmanuel, *Precious Stones of the Jews of Curaçao: Curaçaon Jewry, 1656–1957* (New York: Bloch Publishing Company, 1957), 92, 175, 208, 211–12, 249, 304, 306, 325, 404, 440–41.

7. There was a total of 551 entries, of which 392 (71.1 percent) were Christian, and 159 (or 28.8 percent) were Jewish. Almost all entries were of individual owners; a few, however, were of partners who owned slaves or of several children who owned slaves together. Emmanuel and Emmanuel generalized that, during the eighteenth century, the Jews amounted to 50 percent of the white population and owned about 25 percent of the colony's slaves; *Jews of Netherlands Antilles*, I, 226–27.

8. David De Sola Pool, *Portraits Etched in Stone: Early Jewish Settlers, 1682–1831* (New York: Columbia University Press, 1952), 223, 226, 229, 236, 280, 286, 454, 465, 468.

9. Lee M. Friedman, "Wills of Early Jewish Settlers in New York," *Publications of the American Jewish Historical Society* 23 (1915): 147–61; Leo Hershkowitz, ed., "Wills of Early New York Jews (1704–1740)," *American Jewish Historical Quarterly* 55 (1965–66): 319–63; Leo Hershkowitz, ed., "Wills of Early New York Jews (1743–1774)," *American Jewish Historical Quarterly* 56 (1966–67): 62–122; and Leo

Hershkowitz, ed., "Wills of Early New York Jews (1784–1799)," *American Jewish Historical Quarterly* 56 (1966–67): 163–207.

10. Leo Hershkowitz, ed., *Wills of Early New York Jews (1704–1799)* (New York: American Jewish Historical Society, 1967).

11. Wilfred S. Samuel, "A Review of the Jewish Colonists in Barbados in the Year 1680," *Transactions of the Jewish Historical Society of England* 13 (1932–35): 53–63, 71–90, 92–93; Bertram Wallace Korn, "Barbadian Jewish Wills, 1676–1740," in Bertram Wallace Korn, ed., *A Bicentennial Festschrift for Jacob Rader Marcus* (Waltham and New York: American Jewish Historical Society and Ktav Publishing House, 1976), 303–15.

12. Jacob R. Marcus, *The Colonial American Jew, 1492–1776*, 3 vols. (Detroit: Wayne State University Press, 1970), II, 532–33, 639, 697–705; Stanley F. Chyet, *Lopez of Newport: Colonial American Merchant Prince* (Detroit: Wayne State University Press, 1970), 64, 67–73.

13. Bertram W. Korn, "Jews and Negro Slavery in the Old South, 1789–1865," *Publications of the American Jewish Historical Society* 50 (1960–61): 151–201; the quotation is at 198–99. The essay was subsequently republished at least three times: as a monograph; in the 1970 paperback edition of Korn's *American Jewry and the Civil War* (New York: Atheneum, 1970); and in Leonard Dinnerstein and Mary Dale Palsson, eds., *Jews in the South* (Baton Rouge: Louisiana State University Press, 1973), 89–134.

14. Solomon Grayzel, *A History of the Jews: From the Babylonian Exile to the Present*, 2d ed. (Philadelphia: Jewish Publication Society of America, 1968), 628. The text enjoyed eighteen impressions between its publication in 1947 and 1967. The second edition was published in 1968, with three impressions by 1977.

15. *Encyclopaedia Judaica* (Jerusalem: Keter Publishing House, 1971), XIV, 1660–64.

16. AJHS, I, 1, Records of the American Jewish Historical Society, Correspondence of A. Kanof, 1960; *New York Times,* December 4, 1960, I, 154, and December 9, 1960, 20; and Isidore S. Meyer, ed., *The American Jew in the Civil War: Catalog of the Exhibit of the Civil War Centennial Jewish Historical Commission* (New York: American Jewish Historical Society, 1962), 285–88. The organizations that comprised the Jewish Historical Commission were the American Jewish Archives; the American Jewish Historical Society; the American Jewish History Center; B'nai B'rith Committee on Jewish Americana; Conference of Jewish Social Studies; the Jewish Museum of the Jewish Theological Seminary of America; Jewish War Veterans of the United States of America; and YIVO Institute for Jewish Research.

17. *The Secret Relationship between Blacks and Jews: Volume One* (Chicago: Nation of Islam, 1991), vii, 18–19, 37, 41ff, 46, 55–56, 67–68, 77, 83–85, 89–90, 94, 176–81, 196ff.
18. *New York Times*, August 9, 1991, A26; August 13, 1991, A17; August 25, 1991, IV, 14.
19. *New York Times*, February 4, 1994, A1, A13. The statement was impossible on its face, in view of the very small number of Jews in the South, almost none of whom engaged in agriculture or owned plantations.
20. Henry Louis Gates, Jr., "Black Demagogues and Pseudo-Scholars," *New York Times*, July 20, 1992, A15.
21. *New York Times*, August 7, 1991, B4; James Traub, *City on a Hill: Testing the American Dream at City College* (Reading: Addison-Wesley Publishing Company), 265.
22. For the smaller traders from Denmark, Sweden, and Brandenburg (in Germany), see Rawley, *Transatlantic Slave Trade*, 98ff.
23. Gates, op. cit.
24. By 1983 at the latest, the Sons of Liberty of Metairie, Louisiana, a white supremacist Christian organization, distributed a rabidly anti-Semitic pamphlet entitled *Who Brought the Slaves to America [?]* (N.p.: N.p., n.d.), which asserted that the Anti-Christ, the "sons of the devil—the Jews," were responsible. The Anti-Christ label appears passim, and the quotation at 19. The photographic service department of the New York Public Library filmed the tract in May 1983, thereby establishing that it preceded *The Secret Relationship* by at least eight years.
25. Harold Brackman, *Farrakhan's Reign of Historical Error: The Truth behind The Secret Relationship between Blacks and Jews* (N.p.: Simon Wiesenthal Center, 1992); Harold Brackman, *Ministry of Lies: The Truth behind the Nation of Islam's "The Secret Relationship between Blacks and Jews"* (New York: Four Walls Eight Windows, 1994); Nat Trager, *Empire of Hate: A Refutation of the Nation of Islam's "The Secret Relationship between Blacks and Jews"* (Fort Lauderdale: Coral Reef Books, 1995); Mark Caplan, *Jew-Hatred as History: An Analysis of the Nation of Islam's "The Secret Relationship between Blacks and Jews"* (N.p.: Anti-Defamation League, 1993); Winthrop D. Jordan, "Slavery and the Jews," *Atlantic Monthly*, September 1995, 109–14; Edward Conlon, "The Uses of Malice," *American Spectator*, April 1995, 38–42; Ralph A. Austen, "The Uncomfortable Relationship: African Enslavement in the Common History of Blacks and Jews," *Tikkun*, March–April 1994, 65ff; David Brion Davis, "Jews in the Slave Trade," *Culturefront*, Fall 1992, 42–45; David Brion Davis, "The Slave Trade

and the Jews," *New York Review of Books,* December 22, 1994, 14–16; David Brion Davis, "Jews in the Slave Trade," in Jack Salzman and Cornel West, eds., *Struggles in the Promised Land: Toward a History of Black-Jewish Relations in the United States* (New York: Oxford University Press, 1997), 65–72; Seymour Drescher, "The Role of Jews in the Transatlantic Slave Trade," *Immigrants and Minorities* 12 (1993): 113–25; and Selwyn R. Cudjoe, "Time for Serious Scholars to Repudiate Nation of Islam's Diatribe against Jews," *Chronicle of Higher Education,* May 11, 1994, B3. On the genesis of the statement by the Council of the American Historical Association, see *Chronicle of Higher Education,* February 17, 1995, A15.

26. David Richardson has estimated that total slave exports from Africa's west coast between 1700 and 1809 numbered 6,680,000, of which the British carried 3,120,000, or 46.7 percent. French exports were 1,052,000 (15.7 percent); Portuguese exports were 1,903,000 (28.4 percent); Dutch exports were 352,000 (5.2 percent); Danish exports were 51,000 (seven-tenths of 1 percent); and American exports were 208,000 (3.1 percent). British vessels carried 150,000 slaves between 1700 and 1709, exceeded only by Portuguese slave traders, who shipped 156,000. Between 1710 and 1719, the British transported 201,000 slaves, far surpassing Portugal's 126,000. See Richardson, "Slave Exports," 9–11.

27. Rawley, *Transatlantic Slave Trade,* 94, 165. For Richardson's figures for the British and Dutch between 1700 and 1809, with the British, again, far in the lead, see the preceding note.

28. Robert Louis Stein, *The French Slave Trade in the Eighteenth Century: An Old Regime Business* (Madison: University of Wisconsin Press, 1979), 159–60. Stein wrote that Jewish "participation was on a small scale and had slight impact." Only two Jewish firms, Gradis and Mendes, each sent out more than a single slave ship, and of more than three thousand French slaving ventures to Africa, only fourteen belonged to Gradis, the larger of the two. Ibid., xiii, 232, n. 15.

29. See Appendix I, infra, for discussion of the sources that, in addition to surnames, have been utilized for identifying the Jewish individuals studied here.

Notes to Chapter 1

1. Cecil Roth, *A History of the Marranos* (Philadelphia: Jewish Publication Society of America, 1932), 258–66; Todd M. Endelman, *The Jews of Georgian England, 1714–1830: Tradition and Change in a Liberal So-*

ciety (Philadelphia: Jewish Publication Society of America, 1979), 15–21; David S. Katz, *The Jews in the History of England, 1485–1850* (Oxford: Clarendon Press, 1994), 108–38.

2. Lucien Wolf, "The Jewry of the Restoration. 1660–1664," *Transactions of the Jewish Historical Society of England* 5 (1902–5): 20; A. S. Diamond, "The Community of the Resettlement, 1656–1684: A Social Survey," *Transactions of the Jewish Historical Society of England* 24 (1970–73): 134–36, 145–46; Haim Beinart, "The Jews in the Canary Islands: A Re-evaluation," *Transactions of the Jewish Historical Society of England* 25 (1973–75): passim.

3. The history of the persecutions in Spain and Portugal has frequently been told; the elements repeated here may be followed in, among many others, Roth, *History of the Marranos*; Haim Beinart, "The *Converso* Community in 15th Century Spain," in *The Sephardi Heritage: Essays on the History and Cultural Contributions of the Jews in Spain and Portugal*, ed. R. D. Barnett (London: Vallentine, Mitchell, 1971), 425–56; Alexandre Herculano, *History of the Origin and Establishment of the Inquisition in Portugal*, tr. John C. Branner (1926; New York: AMS Press, 1968); C. R. Boxer, *The Portuguese Seaborne Empire, 1415–1825* (New York: Alfred A. Knopf, 1969), 266–72 ; and Yitzhak Baer, *A History of the Jews in Christian Spain*, 2 vols. (Philadelphia: Jewish Publication Society of America, 1966), particularly Volume II.

4. Salo Wittmayer Baron, *A Social and Religious History of the Jews*, 17 vols., 2d ed., rev. and enl. (New York and Philadelphia: Columbia University Press and Jewish Publication Society of America, 1952–80), XV, 21, 23. For somewhat different numbers—one hundred households in 1610 and three thousand individuals at midcentury—see Violet Barbour, *Capitalism in Amsterdam in the 17th Century* (1950; Ann Arbor: University of Michigan Press, 1976), 25; Jonathan I. Israel, "The Economic Contribution of Dutch Sephardi Jewry to Holland's Golden Age, 1595–1713," *Tijdschrift voor Geschiedenis* 96(1983): 505, 513; Jonathan Israel, *The Dutch Republic: Its Rise, Greatness, and Fall, 1477–1806* (Oxford: Clarendon Press, 1995), 1, 369, 377, 476, 658, 708, 1026.

5. R. G. Fuks-Mansfeld, "Problems of Overpopulation of Jewish Amsterdam in the 17th Century," *Studia Rosenthaliana* 18 (1984): 142.

6. Moses A. Shulvass, *From East to West: The Westward Migration of Jews from Eastern Europe during the Seventeenth and Eighteenth Centuries* (Detroit: Wayne State University Press, 1971), 11–43; Albert M. Hyamson, *The Sephardim of England: A History of the Spanish and Portuguese Jewish Community, 1492–1951* (London: Methuen, 1951), 71; Cecil Roth, *The Great Synagogue, London 1690–1940* (London:

Edward Goldston and Son, 1950), 9–10, 12, 16–17; Arthur P. Arnold, "A List of Jews and Their Households in London Extracted from the Census Lists of 1695," *Miscellanies of the Jewish Historical Society of England* 6 (1962): 73–77.

7. H. S. Q. Henriques, "Proposals for Special Taxation of the Jews after the Revolution," *Transactions of the Jewish Historical Society of England* 9 (1918–20): 44–45. For the commerce conducted by London's Jewish merchants with India and their leading position in the diamond trade, see Gedalia Yogev, *Diamonds and Coral: Anglo-Dutch Jews and Eighteenth-Century Trade* (N.p.: Leicester University Press, 1978), 67ff. Yogev's excellent study illuminates many other facets of the economic activities of England's Jews in the late seventeenth and eighteenth centuries.

8. Jonathan I. Israel, *Dutch Primacy in World Trade, 1585–1740* (Oxford: Clarendon Press, 1989), 271–73.

9. George Frederick Zook, "The Company of Royal Adventurers Trading into Africa," *Journal of Negro History* 4 (1919): 134–231; K. G. Davies, *The Royal African Company* (1957; New York: Atheneum, 1970), 41–44, 57–60, 90–91, 97, 363.

10. Baron, *Social and Religious History*, XV, 188, 226.

11. "Slavery," *Encyclopaedia Judaica* (Jerusalem: Keter Publishing House, 1971), XIV, 1655–59; David Brion Davis, *Slavery and Human Progress* (New York: Oxford University Press, 1984), 21–22, 84–88.

12. Joseph Caro, *Shulhan Arukh*, "Yoreh De'ah," Section 267; and "Hoshen Mishpat," Section 196.

13. Johannes Menne Postma, *The Dutch in the Atlantic Slave Trade, 1600–1815* (Cambridge: Cambridge University Press, 1990), 10; Israel, "Economic Contribution of Dutch Sephardi Jewry," 512, 528; Robert Cohen, *Jews in Another Environment: Surinam in the Second Half of the Eighteenth Century* (Leiden: E. J. Brill, 1991), 305, n. 38.

14. Arnold Wiznitzer, *Jews in Colonial Brazil* (New York: Columbia University Press, 1960), 58–59, 130, 139–42; Wilfred S. Samuel, "A Review of the Jewish Colonists in Barbados in the Year 1680," *Transactions of the Jewish Historical Society of England* 13 (1932–35): 12–13.

15. Wiznitzer, *Jews in Colonial Brazil*, 67–73.

16. Between 1630 and 1651, or almost the entire time that Jews resided in Brazil, the Dutch West India Company imported a total of 26,286 slaves into Brazil; Postma, *Dutch in the Atlantic Slave Trade*, 21. Assuming that Jewish middlemen handled them all (and there is no reason to make such an assumption), this would represent the maximum extent of their involvement. During the seventeenth century alone, Brazil received approximately 560,000 slaves. Between 1760 and 1830, at least 1,750,000

slaves were brought there by Portuguese and Brazilian slave traders. For these figures, see James A. Rawley, *The Transatlantic Slave Trade: A History* (New York: W. W. Norton, 1981), 34, 45.

17. Wiznitzer, *Jews in Colonial Brazil,* 150.

18. Arnold Wiznitzer, "The Minute Book of Congregations Zur Israel of Recife and Magen Abraham of Maricia, Brazil," *Publications of the American Jewish Historical Society* 42 (1952–53): 238, 244, 271.

19. Robert Cohen, "The Egerton Manuscript," *American Jewish Historical Quarterly* 62 (1972–73): 334–35, 342, 346–47.

20. Simon Cohen, tr., Jacob R. Marcus and Stanley F. Chyet, eds., *Historical Essay on the Colony of Surinam, 1788* (Cincinnati and New York: American Jewish Archives and Ktav, 1974), 183–88; Isaac S. Emmanuel and Suzanne A. Emmanuel, *History of the Jews of the Netherlands Antilles,* 2 vols. (Cincinnati: American Jewish Archives, 1970), II, 774. Those who actually went to Essequibo either returned to Amsterdam or went to Cayenne.

21. *Historical Essay on the Colony of Surinam,* 24–25, 187.

22. Ibid., 25.

23. Ibid., 30–31; R. A. J. Van Lier, "The Jewish Community in Surinam: A Historical Survey," in Robert Cohen, ed., *The Jewish Nation in Surinam: Historical Essays* (Amsterdam: S. Emmering, 1982), 19.

24. *Historical Essay on the Colony of Surinam,* 34; J. H. Hollander, ed., "Documents Relating to the Attempted Departure of the Jews from Surinam in 1675," *Publications of the American Jewish Historical Society* 6 (1897): 17. For a more recent study, claiming that there were only two Jewish emigrants and thirty-three slaves, see L. L. E. Rens, "Analysis of Annals Relating to Early Jewish Settlement in Surinam," in Cohen, ed., *Jewish Nation in Surinam,* 29–43.

25. *CSP,* IX (1675–76, Also Addenda, 1574–1674), 284. The Jewish emigrant with 33 slaves was Gabriel De Solis; the Yearworth family transported the 15 slaves who belonged to Aaron De Silva. De Solis was accompanied by an overseer named Isaac De La Parr, who, if his family name was actually Pereira, may have also been Jewish. For an Isaac Pereira in Suriname, see ibid., 352, where the names of the other Jews reported to London early in 1676 are also listed.

26. *Historical Essay on the Colony of Surinam,* 30, 34, 44, 63, 148–49, 193–94. For Jews as slaveowners in Suriname, see the Introduction, supra, at n. 4.

27. Emmanuel and Emmanuel, *Jews of the Netherlands Antilles,* I, 37, 39–41, 45–46, 49–50, 75.

28. C. R. Boxer, *The Dutch Seaborne Empire: 1600–1800* (New York: Alfred A. Knopf, 1965), 24–25, 49, 87; C. R. Boxer, *The Dutch in*

   Brazil, 1624–1654 (Oxford: Clarendon Press, 1957), 6–8; Postma, *Dutch in the Atlantic Slave Trade*, 11, 14–17.
29. Postma, *Dutch in the Atlantic Slave Trade*, 19–21, 25–27, 35.
30. Ibid., 23–24, 36.
31. Boxer, *Dutch in Brazil*, 10–11.
32. Herbert I. Bloom, "A Study of Brazilian Jewish History 1623–1654, Based Chiefly upon the Findings of the Late Samuel Oppenheim," *Publications of the American Jewish Historical Society* 33 (1934): 49–50.
33. Baron, *Social and Religious History*, XV, 37.
34. Barbour, *Capitalism in Amsterdam*, 43, 45.
35. Israel, "Economic Contribution of Dutch Sephardi Jewry," 510.
36. Cecil T. Carr, ed., *Select Charters of Trading Companies*, Publications of the Selden Society, 28 (London: Bernard Quaritch, 1913), xli and n. 9 there, 175, 180; Endelman, *Jews of Georgian England*, 23–24.
37. For the names of the stockholders in all three years, see Elizabeth Donnan, ed., *Documents Illustrative of the History of the Slave Trade to America*, 4 vols. (Washington, D.C.: Carnegie Institution of Washington, 1930–35), I, 169–72. Davies, *Royal African Company*, 44, 63–64, describes shareholders as members of the royal family, the peerage, the court, and, by 1665, "a number of prominent London merchants."
38. Carr, *Select Charters*, 190, at the asterisked footnote there.
39. PRO, T 70/185, 1–5.
40. PRO, T 70/185, 12–16.
41. PRO, T 70/185, 70/186, 70/187, passim.
42. PRO, T 70/186, passim.
43. PRO, T 70/187, 9, 12, and, for James's sale, the insert between 33–34.
44. Alvaro Da Costa led the way, investing in the East India Company on August 5, 1668 and subsequently, during the 1670s, buying and selling shares; Ethel Bruce Sainsbury, *A Calendar of the Court Minutes Etc. of the East India Company*, 11 vols. (Oxford: Clarendon Press, 1907–38), VIII, 398; X, 396, 398–400, 404, 407, XI, 202, 333, 336. Ensuing investments were made in 1683 by Peter and "Pierra" Henriques, Anthony Gomez Serra, Alphonso Rodrigues, and Francis De Lis; in 1685 by Antonio Da Costa and Abraham Bueno Henriques; in 1687 by Antonio Rodrigues Marqueza; in 1688 by Moses Israel Nunes, Joshua Bueno Henriques, and Jno. Mendes Da Costa; in 1689 by Simon Rodrigues; and in 1690 by Jacob Gabay. All are in BL, Records of the East India Company, Court Books, B/37, 158, 166, 190; B/38, 85, 115; and B/39, 79, 128–30, 200, 260.
45. Davies, *Royal African Company*, 54.
46. Ibid., 59, 71–72, 81.

47. PRO, T 70/187, 57, for Da Costa's initial stock purchase. For his life and activities, see Norma Perry, "Voltaire and the Sephardi Bankrupt," *Transactions of the Jewish Historical Society of England* 29 (1982–86): 41–43; Maurice Woolf, "Foreign Trade of London Jews in the Seventeenth Century," *Transactions of the Jewish Historical Society of England* 24 (1970–73): 50–51; William A. Shaw, ed., *Letters of Denization and Acts of Naturalization for Aliens in England and Ireland, 1603–1700*, Publications of the Huguenot Society of London, 18 (Lymington: N.p., 1911), 99; Lionel D. Barnett, tr., *El Libro de los Acuerdos, Being the Records and Accompts of the Spanish and Portuguese Synagogue of London from 1663 to 1681* (Oxford: The University Press by John Johnson, 1931), xv; D. Bueno De Mesquita, "The Historical Associations of the Ancient Burial-Ground of the Sephardi Jews," *Transactions of the Jewish Historical Society of England* 10 (1921–23): 242–43; Lionel D. Barnett, *Bevis Marks Records Being Contributions to the History of the Spanish and Portuguese Congregation of London. Part I* (Oxford: The University Press by John Johnson, 1940), 19; and Jonathan I. Israel, *European Jewry in the Age of Mercantilism* (Oxford: Clarendon Press, 1985), 178.

For the heightened activity in stocks in general, see Davies, *Royal African Company*, 80–81; and K. G. Davies, "Joint-Stock Investment in the Later Seventeenth Century," 2d ser., *Economic History Review* 4 (1951–52): 292.

48. For examples of Jews in London who delayed circumcision and attended Mass in the homes of the Spanish and Venetian ambassadors, see Beinart, "Jews in the Canary Islands," 62.

49. As the Spanish consul in Amsterdam opined in 1655, "The president of the Synagogue signs his name Cortez instead of Corticos, which is his real name. . . . It is a custom among the members of his nation to assume as many names as they please, either for purposes of deceit or in order not to jeopardize their relatives who still bear their [true] name in Spain." Cited by Baron in *Social and Religious History*, XV, 58. Examples of aliases in the London Jewish community in addition to Da Costa's are Isaac Rodrigues Sequeira's Alfonso Rodrigues; Isaac Israel Henriques's Pedro Henriques, Jr.; Jacob Aboab Osorio's Jacob Jenes Osorio; and Jacob Lopez De Lis's Francisco De Lis, Jr., all in Lionel D. Barnett, ed., *Bevis Marks Records Being Contributions to the History of the Spanish and Portuguese Congregation of London. Part II: Abstracts of the Ketubot or Marriage-Contracts of the Congregation from Earliest Times until 1837* (Oxford: The University Press by Charles Batey, 1949), 65–66; and Barnett, *El Libro de los Acuerdos*, xi, n. 3. Other examples are Jacob Berahel and Diego Rodrigues Marquez, respectively known

also as Francisco De Lis and José De La Fuente; in Diamond, "Community of the Resettlement," 145–46, 149. See also Beinart, "Jews in the Canary Islands," 58–59, 62, n. 113, for Diego Rodrigues Arias's Abraham Rodrigues Arias and Francisco Vaez De Leon's Abraham Cohen Henriques; as well as Hyamson, *Sephardim of England,* 68, for David Penso, alias Alexander Felix.

50. Barnett, *El Libro de los Acuerdos,* xv; Hyamson, *Sephardim of England,* 33, 99; Barnett, *Bevis Marks Records . . . Part II,* 65–66, for the marriages of one of his sons and three of his daughters.

51. Sainsbury, *Calendar of the Court Minutes,* as cited at n. 44, supra.

52. For Da Costa's later purchases, see PRO, T 70/187, 63, 77. Still later acquisitions by him in the summer of 1691 are listed at PRO, T 70/188, 21–24, 32. The three new investors were Benjamin Levy, Jacques Gonzalez, and Samuel Sasportas; PRO, T 70/188, 4–5, 8–10, 26, 30, 33, 38. Sasportas's name is usually spelled "Suportas" in the Company's records. For Levy, who subsequently became the leading figure in the creation of the London Ashkenazi congregation, see Roth, *Great Synagogue,* 5–6, 16–17, 23. Roth incorrectly dated Levy's ownership of Royal African Company stock to 1688.

53. PRO, T 70/188, 113–21. Jews who held shares as individuals were Joseph Almanza (£1,200), Alvaro Da Costa (£3,150), John Mendes Da Costa (£4,550), Jacques Gonzalez (£400), Peter Henriques, Jr. (£4,000), Benjamin Levy (£1,900), Moses Israel Nunes (£1,600), and Isaac De Valencia (£1,100). The partnership was that of Simon and Alphonso Rodrigues (£1,200). The estate belonged to Samuel "Suportas" (£400), who was listed as deceased. For Samuel Sasportas's death in 1692, see R. D. Barnett, tr., "The Burial Register of the Spanish and Portuguese Jews, London, 1657–1735," *Miscellanies of the Jewish Historical Society of England* 6 (1962): 7.

54. PRO, T 70/189, 1–119, for the stock as it stood on March 25, 1699, valued overall at £1,101,050 (ibid., 164). The Jewish shareholders recorded there were Manuel De Almanza, Jacob Adolph, Aaron Alvarez, Abraham Bernal, Moses Carrion, Isaac Pereira Coutinho, Alvaro Da Costa, John Mendes Da Costa, Joseph Nunes Da Costa, Moses Telles Da Costa, Jacques Gonzalez, Isaac Senior Henriques, Peter Henriques, Jr., Peter Henriques, Sr., Benjamin Levy, Elias Lindo, Jacob Teixeira De Mattos, Moses De Medina, Solomon De Medina, Isaac Lopez Mellado, Jacob De Paz Morenu, Isaac Fernandez Nunes, Moses Israel Nunes, David Penso, Alphonso Rodrigues and Simon Rodrigues (in partnership), Samuel Sasportas (deceased), Phineas Gomez Serra, and Isaac De Valencia.

55. They are listed in Appendix II, Table 1. The additional possibility is

William Veiga, whose religion is not known. For Veiga, see the discussion infra at n. 57.

56. Arnold, "List of Jews and Their Households in London," 73, 77. The 185 families and 114 single lodgers amounted to between 751 and 853 individuals.

57. The general survey of Jewish investors in the Bank of England is in J. A. Giuseppi, "Sephardi Jews and the Early Years of the Bank of England," *Transactions of the Jewish Historical Society of England* 19 (1955–59): 53–63. For Giuseppi's annotated list of the stockholders, see "Early Jewish Holders of Bank of England Stock (1694–1725)," *Miscellanies of the Jewish Historical Society of England* 6 (1962): 143–74.

Giuseppi indicated in the latter (at 143) that he preferred to err on the side of inclusion rather than omission, writing that those he listed were "*almost entirely* [italics added] of known Jewish origin." However, seven of the individuals he included have been excluded from the numbers reported here and in the list in Appendix II, Table 1, infra, either because it is clear that they were not Jewish or because evidence regarding their religion is lacking.

Those among the seven who are known not to have been Jewish are Sir Jacob Jacobsen and Theodore Jacobsen. The Jacobsens were Protestants; P. G. M. Dickson, *The Financial Revolution in England: A Study in the Development of Public Credit, 1688–1756* (London: Macmillan, 1967), 114. For Sir Jacob Jacobsen, see also John Carswell, *The South Sea Bubble* (Stanford: Stanford University Press, 1960), 280; and for Theodore Jacobsen, see *Dictionary of National Biography*.

Those whose religion is not known include Jacques Dirquez and Abraham Duez, neither of whom appear in any of the sources for the Jewish inhabitants of London for the seventeenth and early eighteenth centuries, and who therefore were probably not Jewish. Three more, Abraham Martins, Philip Martins, and William Veiga, are entirely problematic. As a Jewish name, Martins (also, Martin) was interchangeable with the more obviously Sephardic Martinez (see Barnett, *Bevis Marks Records . . . Part II*, 150–51). An Abraham Vaes Martinez appears among the Sephardic synagogue's contributors in 1700–1702; Moses Gaster, *History of the Ancient Synagogue of the Spanish and Portuguese Jews* (London: N.p., 1901), 73. Whether he was the same as the Abraham Martins included in Giuseppi's list is not known, for Martin/Martins was also an English as well as a French Huguenot name. Moreover, there was an Abraham Martin who was naturalized in 1709; see [William Minet and Susan Minet], *A Supplement to Dr. W. A. Shaw's Letters of Denization and Naturalization*, Publications of the Huguenot Society of London, 35 (Frome: Butler and Tanner, 1932), 13. As a candidate for naturalization, Abraham Martin would have sworn an oath as a Christian and taken Communion. As for Veiga (also, Vega), no William appears in the relevant Jewish sources, although Samuel Da Vega and Benjamin Vega frequently do (e.g., Gaster, *History of the Ancient Synagogue,* 11–12, 17, 73), as does a Jacob de Abraham Da Vega (Barnett, *Bevis Marks Records . . . Part II,* 64) and an Aaron De Vega (Woolf, "Foreign Trade of London Jews," 55). Whether one of these used William as an alias is not known.

58. See Appendix II, Table 1. The ten additional investors during the period 1694–1701 included five Bank of England stockholders listed by Giuseppi whose religion is in fact not at all clear—Jacques Dirquez, Abraham Duez, Abraham Martins, Philip Martins, and William Veiga—as described in the preceding footnote. Another five individuals were Jewish, but are identified by Giuseppi as stockjobbers (brokers who handled Bank stock) without clarifying whether they themselves owned stock or not: Ephraim Abarbanel, David D'Avila, John Mendes Da Costa, Jr., Moses Hart, and Solomon Mendes. Did they also own stock as did such other stockjobbers identified by Giuseppi as Alvaro Da Costa, Isaac Da Costa Alvarenga, and Moses Barrow?

59. The discussion here excludes Samuel Sasportas, who died in 1692, two years before the Bank was established, and who therefore cannot be included when comparing investors in the Royal African Company with those in the Bank of England.

60. Dickson, *Financial Revolution in England,* 253–54, 259. The two newcomers in the East India Company were Benjamin Levy and Solomon De Medina. William Veiga, if Jewish, would have been a third. BL, Records of the East India Company, Court Books, B/40, 72–73, 212.

61. Davies, *Royal African Company,* 46, 85 (for the quotation), 113, 314, 337, 346.

62. PRO, CO 388/10, H 108, for the Company accountant's report; and Davies, *Royal African Company,* 363. For Davies's cautions, see 361–62.

63. Davies, *Royal African Company,* 143.

64. PRO, CO 137/8, 96.

65. For the 1708 investors, see Appendix II, Table 3. Investors with credits "to the General Stock" in January 1713 are at PRO, T 70/196. The sixteen investors then were Ephraim Abarbanel, Isaac Alvarez, Abraham Bernal, Abraham Da Costa, Anthony Da Costa, Jr., Phineas Gomez Serra, Isaac Gomez, Moses Hart, Jacob Teixeira De Mattos, Moses De Medina, John Mendes, Jr., Moses Mocatto, Isaac Portello, Joseph Rodrigues, Fernando Silva, Jr., and Rodrigo Ximenes. Their stock totaled £56,000. Isaac Senior Henriques may still have been an investor at the

end of 1712, raising the number of investors to seventeen, but his account is problematic. He is not listed with assets "to the General Stock" in January 1713, yet appears to have still owned stock; he apparently sold £8,900 worth on April 14, 1713.

66. Dickson relied on Giuseppi for the names of Jewish investors (Dickson, *Financial Revolution in England*, 259, n. 2) but there is no indication that he excluded individuals from his computations who were clearly not Jewish or whose religious identity is not known. For the need to do so see the discussions at ns. 57 and 69.

The number of Jewish investors in the East India Company is revised downward here from Dickson's 65 to 62; for them, see Appendix II, Table 4, infra.

67. Using Dickson's data, the factors are 4.083 for the Bank of England subscription; 3.615 for Bank of England stock; 2.875 for 1707 Annuities; and 2.837 for East India Company stock. The factor for the Royal African Company is 1.409.

68. See Appendix II, Table 2. In some cases, however, they were not entirely new to the world of investment, having acquired stock between 1691 and 1701 in one of the two companies. Later, between 1702 and 1712, they did so in the other enterprise, thereby warranting inclusion among the eighty-six discussed here. Examples include Moses Barrow, Isaac Gomez, Isaac Portello, and Benjamin Del Sotto.

69. Listed in Appendix II, Table 2. As before, identification of the Bank of England's Jewish stockholders is by Giuseppi in "Early Jewish Holders of Bank of England Stock." As before, as well, seven individuals listed by Giuseppi have been eliminated in arriving at the numbers presented here. Paul Heusch was definitely not Jewish. Born in Hamburg, Heusch (also Hensch) was naturalized in England in 1700. To qualify for naturalization, he submitted a certificate attesting that he had taken the Sacrament "according to the usage of the Protestant Church"; Shaw, *Letters of Denization*, 297. In the case of Simeon Julien, Giuseppi noted that he was "sometimes advocate in the Sovereign Court of Judicature of Grenoble in Dauphine," which makes a Jewish identification for him entirely dubious. Moreover, no Simeon Julien appears in the contemporary Anglo-Jewish sources. Nor does Solomon De La Creuze. Philip Martines, Isaac Martins, Jr., and Jacob Martins had names that could have been English, Huguenot, or Jewish; see n. 57 for the problem of identifying the religion of individuals surnamed Martin. Finally, Joseph Benjamin, Jr., whom Giuseppi includes on a 1712 dividend list, had a name that renders religious and ethnic identification impossible.

Another six individuals—Jacob Alvarez, Jr., Jacob Henriques Julian,

Alvaro Mendes, Jacob Roiz Mendes, Lewis Mendes, and Jacob Da Silva—may also have been Bank of England investors between 1702 and 1712. Giuseppi, however, describes them as stockjobbers only.

70. First-time investors in the Royal African Company between 1702 and 1712 who had invested in the Bank of England in the earlier period and continued to hold its stock, as demonstrated by their receipt of dividends in 1709 or 1712, were Isaac Alvarez, Moses Barrow, Isaac De Castro, Joseph De Castro, Isaac Gomez, Francis (or Francisco) Pereira, and Benjamin Del Sotto. The two who had invested earlier in the Bank and may have continued to hold its stock—they do not appear on the 1709 and 1712 dividend lists—were Anthony Da Costa, Sr. and Isaac Portello. The five who were first-time purchasers of RAC stock between 1702 and 1712 who did not own Bank stock in either period were Ephraim Abarbanel, Jacob Mendes Da Costa, Jacob Gabay, John Mendes, Jr., and Moses Mocatto. For the dividend lists of 1709 and 1712, see Giuseppi, "Early Jewish Holders of Bank of England Stock," 166–69.

71. The description of the Company is Davies's; in *Royal African Company*, 80–85, 90–91, 95, 346. (The quotations are at 85 and 95.) For the default, see BL, Records of the South Sea Company, Add. Ms. 25,564, 138.

72. The Jewish stockholders in the East India Company on March 25, 1709 are listed in Appendix II, Table 4.

73. Elizabeth Donnan, "The Early Days of the South Sea Company, 1711–1718," *Journal of Economic and Business History* 2 (1929–30): 422–28.

74. Dickson, *Financial Revolution in England*, 272, 536.

75. *A List of the Names of the Corporation of the Governor and Company of Merchants of Great Britain Trading to the South-Seas, and Other Parts of America, and for Encouraging the Fishery* (N.p.: John Barber, [1714]). The date is supplied at the beginning of the list of names.

76. Donnan, "Early Days of South Sea Company," 447ff; John G. Sperling, *The South Sea Company: An Historical Essay and Bibliographical Finding List* (Boston: Baker Library, 1962), 2, 7.

77. See Appendix II, Table 5, for the names of the Jewish shareholders, as well as for the two whose religion is not known.

78. For voting qualifications, see Sperling, *South Sea Company*, 17.

79. House of Lords Record Office, Main Papers, 17 February 1699 [1700]. The petitioners requested relief from regulations for certifying that imported "wrought silks" and certain other products were carried to Africa and not returned to England. The signatories described themselves as

traders not only to Africa but also to the "Plantations," Britain's overseas colonies. For Abraham Mendes's participation in trade with Africa, see the discussion infra.

80. Woolf, "Foreign Trade of London Jews," 48; Yogev, *Diamonds and Coral,* 25–49, 60–64, 69–70.

81. For the names of known interlopers, see Chapter Two, infra, n. 51.

82. Davies, *Royal African Company,* 134–51. The Company's record book of ten-percent payments on imports demonstrates that enforcement of the act continued until July 8, 1712; PRO, T 70/1198.

83. For Martin (also, Martinez) as a Jewish name, see n. 57, supra. For Jose Nunes Martinez's marriage, see Barnett, *Bevis Marks Records . . . Part II,* 69. For the non-Jewish Joseph Martin, see Carswell, *South Sea Bubble,* 282.

84. The value of all exports is derived from Davies, *Royal African Company,* 373.

85. BL, East India Company Records, B/36, B/37, B/38, B/39, B/40, B/41, B/43, B/44, passim. Indexes to the names that appear in these records of the General Court and the Courts of the Committees facilitate location of entries in which Jewish shareholders appear.

86. Rawley, *Transatlantic Slave Trade,* 36, 93–94, 111, 131, 137, 155, 208, 224.

87. PRO, CO 388/25, S39. The signers were "Hum Morice, Francs Chamberlayne, Rd Harris, Rando. Knipe, W. Gemish, Edward Byam, Tho Truman, Sam Bonham, Rowd. Frye, Davy Breholt, Sam. Wragg, Rich Splatt, Jacom Satur, James Fitter, Steph. Godin, Tho. Butler, Jr., Robert Atkyins, Robert Greene, Thomas Lane, Edward Dod, Preston [?], Geo. Arnold, Daniel Fox, Robt. Lidderdale, Jos Macham, Wm Hunt, Jos. Windham, David Miln, Wm. Coleman, Jno. Merewether, Samuel Travers, Mard Beline, Patrick Jeffreys, Francis Melmoth, S. Bethell, Jno. Radburne, Joseph Lowe, Benja. Weale, John Blackwood, John Heron, Benja. Curtis, Pr Delamotte, Dd Godin, George Smith, Wm Bassnett, Robt Brooke, John Spillett, Thomas Salter." Many of these owned slave ships in the same year, some of them several; see Appendix III, Table 3.

88. PRO, CO 324/34, 198–202. The seven were Aaron Lamego, Jacob Gutteres, Jacob Nunes, Moses Nunes Gonzalez, Daniel Dias Fernandez, Abraham Mendes, Sr., and Isaac Mendes. If Jewish, Jacob Martins would have been an eighth.

89. PRO, CO 137/22, 30–32. The Jewish signatories were "Aron Lamego, Fran Pereira, Benjamin Mendes da Costa, Fran Salvador, Alvero Lopes Suassa, Pinheiro, Anthony da Costa, Abraham Dafonseca, Fra. Salvador, Jun., Rodrigo Pacheco, Miguel Vianna, Jacob Fernandes Nunes, Abraham Franco, Miguel Pacheco Da Schuer[?], Alivo Dafonseca, Jac Men-

des da Costa, Jacob Abenator, C Pimentel, Moses Lameza, Solomon Mendez, Elias Paz, Moses Hart, Isaac Mendes Da Costa, Sr., Jacob Franco, Anthony Mendes, Danl. Dias Fernandez, Jac Israel Bernal, James Mendes, Lewis Mendes, Moses Espinola, Jac Belmonte Ergas, Jac Gomes Serra, Abra Osorie, Jacob Da Cort, Abra Alvares Corilof, Jon Mendes da Costa, Jr., David Lopez Perreyra, Isaac S[e]ranna, Benjn Bravo, Aaron Franks, A Bravo."

The religion of two of the other signatories—"Ruben" Solomons and Gabriel "Hedsmag"—is not certain.

90. Yogev, *Diamonds and Coral*, 39, 41.
91. As Gedalia Yogev has written, "Documents intended to point out the value of Jewish business activity for England's international trade are a very good source for estimating the comparative importance of the Jews in its various branches, since nothing was omitted which might strengthen the author's argument." Yogev, *Diamonds and Coral*, 44 (for the quotation from the pamphlet), 61.
92. *Further Considerations on the Act to Permit Persons Professing the Jewish Religion to Be Naturalized by Parliament. In a Second Letter from a Merchant in Town to His Friend in the Country* (London: R. Baldwin, 1753), 35–36, 44–51. On the probable author of the pamphlet, see Edgar R. Samuel, "The Jews in English Foreign Trade—A Consideration of the 'Philo Patriae' Pamphlets of 1753," in John M. Shaftesley, ed., *Remember the Days: Essays on Anglo-Jewish History Presented to Cecil Roth* (London: Jewish Historical Society of England, 1966), 123ff. On the controversy in 1753, see Endelman, *Jews of Georgian England*, 24–26, 59, 88–91; and Thomas W. Perry, *Public Opinion, Propaganda, and Politics in Eighteenth-Century England: A Study of the Jew Bill of 1753* (Cambridge, Mass.: Harvard University Press, 1962).

Opponents of the Jew Bill did their best to minimize the importance of Jewish merchants to England's trade, an interesting twist in view of the more usual allegations that they were crafty merchants who engrossed a great deal of trade at the expense of Christian merchants. See *An Answer to a Pamphlet, Entitled, Considerations on the Bill to Permit Persons Professing the Jewish Religion to Be Naturalized; Wherein the False Reasoning, Gross Misrepresentation of Facts, and Perversion of Scripture, Are Fully Laid Open and Detected*, 2d ed. ([London]: N.p., 1753), 54–55. The author averred that "There are not above ten *Jews* Houses in *London*, which carry on any large foreign Trade. . . . The *Jews* in their mercantile Character are very inconsiderable." He praised Sir John Barnard, a major figure in the City and a Lord Mayor ("No Man understands Trade better. . . ."), for bringing their insignificant commercial role to light.

93. *A Letter from a Merchant of the City of London, to the R — t H — ble W — P — Esq.: Upon the Affairs and Commerce of North America, and the West Indies; Our African Trade* (London: J. Scott, 1757), 48–54.

94. Ibid., 49–53.

95. *A List of the Company of Merchants Trading to Africa (Established by an Act of Parliament, Passed in the 23d Year of His Present Majesty, Intituled, An Act for Extending and Improving the Trade to Africa) Distinguishing Their Places of Abode* (N.p.: N.p., [1758]). A copy may be found at PRO, T 70/1508–1509.

96. *A List of the Company of Merchants Trading to Africa, Established by an Act the 23d. Year of George II, Intitled An Act for Extending and Improving the Trade to Africa* (N.p.: N.p., 1787). The eleven Jews were Isaac Bernal, Joshua Mendes Da Costa, Abraham Aboas [Aboab] Fonseca, Moses Aboas [Aboab] Fonseca, Abram Lara, Lewis Mendes, Hannanias Modigliani, Nathan Modigliani, David Samuda, Levy Samuel, and Isaac Sierra. The religion of three other individuals is not certain: David Martin, Richard Martin, and William Barrow. The personal names of the last two, occcuring as they did in the late eighteenth century, suggests that more than likely they were non-Jewish.

97. *Lloyd's Register 1776* (London: Gregg Press, n.d.) lists the *Judith* as belonging to M. Samuda; and the *Withywood, Susannah, Esther, George Booth*, and *Princess Royal* as the property of Samuda & Co. All sailed between London and Jamaica. Modigliani & Co. owned the *Fanny/Empress of Russia*, which traveled between London and Venice. M. Da Costa (not the same Da Costa who appeared on the 1787 list of the Company of Merchants Trading to Africa) owned the *Hananel* (a Hebrew name), which traveled between London and the Straits. Fonseca owned the *Rebecca*, traveling between London and Maryland.

   Lloyd's Register 1790 (London: Gregg Press, n.d.) included H. Da Costa's *Esther* and Samuda's *Fonseca* and *Withywood*. All three voyaged between London and Jamaica; the last also traveled between Memel and London.

   Use of *Lloyd's Register* to determine whether vessel owners traded with Africa does not, however, yield results that are conclusive in the absolute. The Francos of London owned the *Diamond* in 1764 (*Lloyd's Register 1764* [London: Gregg Press, n.d.]) and the *New Diamond* in 1776, the former voyaging between London and Italy and the latter between London and the Straits. In 1767, their firm sent a cargo to Africa, exchanging it for slaves who were transported to Puerto Rico; Yogev, *Diamonds and Coral*, 43. Similarly, the register for 1764 lists a vessel, the *Industry*, owned by Aaron Lopez of Newport, Rhode Island, sailing between London and Rhode Island, while the register for 1776 includes three ships that belonged to "A. Lopus" or "Aar. Lopus" (the *Flora*, the *Nancy*, and the *Minerva*), whose destinations were Rhode Island, London, and Jamaica. Lopez, however, also participated in the African slave trade; see the discussion in Chapter Six, infra.

98. *A Treatise upon the Trade from Great-Britain to Africa; Humbly Recommended to the Attention of Government* (London: R. Baldwin, 1772), 37–39. The statement that this was "By an African Merchant" appears on the title page.

99. Yogev, *Diamonds and Coral*, 36. Non-Jews also handled slaves for Portugal's Royal Guinea Company. In June 1699, Stephen Evance, Kt., Jeffry Jeffrys, Esq., John Stafford, and William Richardson, all London merchants, contracted to carry slaves for it to Spain's colonies; PRO, CO 138/9, 334–35.

The hazards of association with Jews to holders of the asiento were evident even earlier in the case of the Dutch house of Coymans, which obtained the contract in February 1685. The Coymans firm encountered hostility in Spain because they were Protestants, but their connections to two Jewish diplomats, Francisco Schoenberg and Baron Manuel de Belmonte, proved deadly. The Spanish government relieved Coymans of the asiento in April 1689. Israel, *Dutch Primacy in World Trade*, 320–22.

100. CSP, XXI (1702–3), 242.

101. PRO, CO 142/14, entries for June 24–September 29, 1719; BL, Records of the South Sea Company, Add. Ms. 25,497, 25, which clarifies that the Mendes in question was Abraham; and Donnan, *Documents Illustrative*, II, 196, 204. The *King Solomon* also delivered 296 slaves to St. Christopher in March 1721, and headed again for Africa in August to procure slaves for transport to Jamaica, but whether Mendes still owned it is not known. By August 1721 the Royal African Company may have; it certainly did so by the beginning of 1723. Ibid., II, 244–47, 259, 284, 298–99, 302.

102. Donnan, *Documents Illustrative*, II, 195. Nunes had four votes in the Company on December 25, 1714, indicating that he was among the top group of stockholders, those who owned at least £10,000 worth of shares; infra, Appendix II, Table 5. Jews did not serve as elected officers of the Company, but they did on rare occasion serve on committees to count ballots, and Nunes did so on March 16, 1721, December 12, 1721, and January 26, 1728, together on the last occasion with Abraham Da Fonseca, another Jewish shareholder; BL, Records of the South Sea Company, Add. Ms. 25, 505, at the dates indicated.

103. PRO, CO 5/1222, 5/1224, 5/1225, and 5/1226, passim. For details regarding Pacheco's life, see Leo Hershkowitz and Isidore S. Meyer,

eds., *The Lee Max Friedman Collection of American Jewish Colonial Correspondence: Letters of the Franks Family (1733–1748)* (Waltham: American Jewish Historical Society, 1968), 16, n. 4.

104. Entry of the *Crown Galley* of London to New York in the quarter between March 25 and June 24, 1721 is listed in the Naval Office records for New York at PRO, CO 5/1222. The non-Jews in the partnership were R[ichar]d Janeway of London and William Walton of New York.

105. Correspondence between Diego and Abraham Gonzalez of Port Royal, Jamaica, and Simson in London places Simson there in the summer of 1722. On May 19, 1726, the two Gonzalezes wrote from Kingston, Jamaica, to Mrs. Simson in London with condolences for her husband's death. PRO, C 104/13 and 104/14.

106. A. S. Diamond, "Problems of the London Sephardi Community, 1720–1733—Philip Carteret Webb's Notebooks," *Transactions of the Jewish Historical Society of England* 21 (1962–67): 52–53; Yogev, *Diamonds and Coral*, 30–31; Richard D. Barnett, "Diplomatic Aspects of the Sephardic Influx from Portugal in the Early Eighteenth Century," *Transactions of the Jewish Historical Society of England* 25 (1973–75): 217–18, where the affair is characterized as "a rather shady deal in slaves . . . with a seedy and impoverished Portuguese aristocrat of little reputation. . . ."

107. David Richardson, ed., *Bristol, Africa and the Eighteenth-Century Slave Trade to America*, 4 vols. (Volumes 38, 39, 42, and 47 of the Bristol Record Society's Publications) (Gloucester: Alan Sutton Publishing, 1986–96), IV, 140, 144. For the banking activity of London's West Indian firms and the relationship of the colonial factors to them, see S. G. Checkland, "Finance for the West Indies, 1780–1815," 2d ser., *Economic History Review* 10 (1957–58): 461, 466–67; Richard B. Sheridan, "The Commercial and Financial Organization of the British Slave Trade, 1750–1807," 2d ser., *Economic History Review* 11 (1958–59): 254 ff.; and Richard B. Sheridan, *Sugar and Slavery: An Economic History of the British West Indies, 1623–1775* (Baltimore: Johns Hopkins University Press, 1973), 292ff. On Alexandre Lindo, see the discussion in Chapter Five, infra.

108. JA, Records of the Court of Chancery, 1A/3/200, 44, 51–52, 258, 299, 301, 303, 305, 306, 323. These references appear in the suit brought by Lindo in 1803 against Richard Lake, his former partner in Lindo, Lake & Co.

109. Rawley, *Transatlantic Slave Trade*, 228–29.

110. PRO, CO 388/25, S37 for Bristol; S44 for Liverpool; and S74 for London. The capacity of two of the London vessels was not recorded.

111. See Appendix III, Table 3. For the largest of London's slave-ship owners in the 1720s, see J. A. Rawley, "Humphry Morice: Foremost London Slave Merchant of His Time," in Serge Daget, ed., *De la Traite à l'Esclavage: Actes du Colloque International sur la Traite des Noirs, Nantes 1985*, 2 vols. (Nantes: Centre de Recherche sur l'Histoire du Monde Atlantique, 1988), I, 269–81.

112. Lucy S. Sutherland, *A London Merchant, 1695–1774* (N.p.: Oxford University Press, 1933), 82, 153–56; Rawley, *Transatlantic Slave Trade*, 182–83, 210, 215; Richardson, *Bristol, Africa and Eighteenth-Century Slave Trade*, I, xxi.

113. Maurice Woolf, "Eighteenth-Century London Jewish Shipowners," *Miscellanies of the Jewish Historical Society of England* 9 (1970–73): 198–99, 201–4. Woolf used the records of letters of marque preserved at PRO. The value of this source for information regarding slaving ventures to Africa is evident from David Richardson's reliance on it for documentation of the Bristol slave fleet after 1770; Richardson, *Bristol, Africa and Eighteenth-Century Slave Trade*, IV, x.

114. Samuel, "Jews in English Foreign Trade," 134–35.

115. All Naval Office records are at PRO. For New York: CO 5/1222, 5/1223, 5/1224, 5/1225, 5/1226, 5/1227, and 5/1228; for Barbados: CO 33/18, 33/19, 33/20, 33/21, and 33/22; and for Georgia: CO 5/709 and 5/710. For the exceptions in New York, see the discussion, supra, at ns. 103 and 104, and Chapter Six, infra.

116. Rawley, *Transatlantic Slave Trade*, 234.

117. See Appendix III, Table 4, infra. For the register of 1764 as the first printed one, see C. E. Golding and D. King-Page, *Lloyd's* (New York: McGraw-Hill, 1952), 175.

118. See Appendix III, Tables 5 and 6. The 1776 register is not entirely complete; the first two pages for ships whose names began with the letter G are missing, and parts of the pages for the letter Y are torn. For 1790, another four vessels trading between Africa and London are listed (the *Betsy*, the *Mercury*, the *Royal*, and the *Union*), but the names of their owners are not. The *Royal* may have been owned by Daws & Co.

119. Rawley, *Transatlantic Slave Trade*, 179–80, 229.

120. Richardson, *Bristol, Africa and Eighteenth-Century Slave Trade*, I, 197–200; II, 152–54.

121. The names of two of the Bristol merchants and shipowners, Lewis Casamajor and Samuel Jacob, might be mistaken as Jewish. Casamajor was a Huguenot; W. E. Minchinton, ed., *The Trade of Bristol in the Eighteenth Century*, Vol. 20 of the Bristol Record Society's Publications (Bristol: J. W. Arrowsmith Ltd., 1957), 9, n. 1. Samuel Ja-

cob, one of the port's leading organizers of its slaving ventures, was active well before Jews first settled there; Richardson, *Bristol, Africa and Eighteenth-Century Slave Trade*, I, xxi.

122. Cecil Roth, *The Rise of Provincial Jewry: The Early History of the Jewish Communities in the English Countryside, 1740–1840* (London: Jewish Monthly, 1950), 41; Katz, *Jews in the History of England*, 281. Crypto-Jews (Marranos) were to be found in Bristol during the first half of the sixteenth century, but they were expelled during the 1550s; Baron, *Social and Religious History*, XV, 126.

123. Richardson, *Bristol, Africa and Eighteenth-Century Slave Trade*, III, 241–44.

124. Ibid., IV, passim, and especially 274–76.

125. Rawley, *Transatlantic Slave Trade*, 180, 193.

126. Ibid., 194, 210; Roth, *Rise of Provincial Jewry*, 82; Katz, *Jews in the History of England*, 281; David Hudaly, *Liverpool Old Hebrew Congregation, 1780–1974* (Liverpool: Liverpool Old Hebrew Congregation, 1974), 9; Bertram B. Benas, "A Survey of the Jewish Institutional History of Liverpool and District," *Transactions of the Jewish Historical Society of England* 17 (1951–52): 23–24.

127. The Liverpool members of the Company of Merchants Trading to Africa in 1752 were listed in Malachy Postlethwayt, *The Universal Dictionary of Trade and Commerce*, 2 vols., 4th ed. (London: W. Strahan, 1774), I, under the entry for England.

128. For Liverpool's slave fleet in 1752, see Donnan, *Documents Illustrative*, II, 496–98. The city's slave ships in 1764 are listed in Appendix III, Table 7, infra.

129. Gomer Williams, *History of the Liverpool Privateers and Letters of Marque with an Account of the Liverpool Slave Trade* (London: William Heinemann, 1897), 679; *Report of the Lords of the Committee of Council Appointed for the Consideration of All Matters Relating to Trade and Foreign Plantations*, in House of Commons, *Sessional Papers of the Eighteenth Century, Reports and Papers, 1789, Slave Trade*, LXXI, 210–18, for "Account of the Vessels and Amount of their Cargoes, now employed by the Merchants of Liverpool in the African Slave Trade—3d March 1790." The latter states that the total was 139 vessels; correctly added, the list comes to 141.

In the year that began on January 5, 1798, three slave vessels belonging to A. Joseph, "Mozley" (also "Mozely") & Co., and two others belonging to R. Abram & Co., sailed from Liverpool. Whether these three entrepreneurs were Jewish or not is not known. In all, their five ventures transported 1,619 slaves, or 3 percent of the 52,557 slaves shipped on Liverpool's 150 slave vessels that year; Williams, *Liverpool Privateers*, 681–85.

130. Based on a close reading of the Naval Office records listed under Manuscript Sources in the Bibliography, infra, and of those for Virginia in Walter E. Minchinton, Celia King, and Peter Waite, eds., *Virginia Slave-Trade Statistics, 1698–1775* (Richmond: Virginia State Library, 1984).

Notes to Chapter 2

1. Charles M. Andrews, *The Colonial Period of American History*, 4 vols. (New Haven: Yale University Press, 1934–38), II, 245, 251, 253; Richard S. Dunn, *Sugar and Slaves: The Rise of the Planter Class in the English West Indies, 1624–1713* (Chapel Hill: University of North Carolina Press, 1972), 85; James A. Rawley, *The Transatlantic Slave Trade: A History* (New York: W. W. Norton, 1981), 150, 156; Richard B. Sheridan, *Sugar and Slavery: An Economic History of the British West Indies, 1623–1775* (Baltimore: Johns Hopkins University Press, 1973), 247. Sheridan estimated that 262,000 slaves were imported into Jamaica, Barbados, and the Leeward Islands between 1627 and 1700, with 139,700 going to Barbados.

2. Wilfred S. Samuel, "A Review of the Jewish Colonists in Barbados in the Year 1680," *Transactions of the Jewish Historical Society of England* 13 (1932–35): 10, 12; Richard Ligon, *A True & Exact History of the Island of Barbadoes* (London: Peter Parker and T. Guy, 1673), 42, 85; Jonathan I. Israel, *Dutch Primacy in World Trade, 1585–1740* (Oxford: Clarendon Press, 1989), 206; Robert H. Schomburgk, *The History of Barbados* (1848; London: Frank Cass and Co., 1971), 97; and E. M. Shilstone, "The Jewish Synagogue Bridgetown, Barbados," *Journal of the Barbados Museum and Historical Society* 32 (1966–68): 5–6.

Dutch Jews remained a factor in the development of the Jewish community at Barbados, although the colony's governor reported in 1676 that there were "not above thirty Jew families of Dutch extraction from Brazil." In *CSP*, IX (1675–76, Also Addenda, 1574–1674), 422.

3. Samuel, "Jewish Colonists in Barbados," 95; "Quaker Records," *Journal of the Barbados Museum and Historical Society* 15 (1947–48): 82.

Endenization conferred fewer rights and privileges on aliens than full naturalization, but Jews who were denizens could engage in colonial trade; Andrews, *Colonial Period*, IV, 74–75, and Todd M. Endelman, *The Jews of Georgian England, 1714–1830: Tradition and Change in a*

Liberal Society (Philadelphia: Jewish Publication Society of America, 1979), 25.

A petition for endenization submitted by Elias Paz and Solomon De Paz of London in 1714 explained its value. "Your Petrs are merchants of the Jewish Religion," they wrote, "& labour under many Difficulties in their several Stations for want of being free Denizons [sic] of your Majties Dominions. The want of which Denization . . . maketh them incapable of being Owners of Shipping, & several other Inconveniencys they lye under in their Trades and Business upon the Import and Export of Goods & Merchandize. . . ." At AJHS, Samuel Oppenheim Collection, Box 4, Mordecai Gomez folder.

4. Samuel, "Jewish Colonists in Barbados," 6–7; *CSP,* IX (1675–76, Also Addenda, 1574–1674), 422; *CSP,* XI (1681–85), 102; Isaac S. Emmanuel, *Precious Stones of the Jews of Curaçao: Curaçaon Jewry, 1656–1957* (New York: Bloch Publishing Company, 1957), 218–19.

5. PRO, CO 1/21, 335b–336. Entitled "Some observations on the Island [of] Barbados," the document is not dated, but the PRO has assigned it to 1667 on the basis of internal evidence, including a reference to the year 1666. For the 1681 complaint, see *CSP,* XI (1681–85), 69.

6. Aaron Baruch, David Baruch, Joseph Bueno, Abraham Burgos, Moses Burgos, David Da Costa, Samuel De Leon, Moses De Lucena, David Raphael De Mercado, Luis Dias, David Gabay, Abraham Cohen Lobatto, Jacob Lopez, David Namias, Moses Namias, Aaron Nabarro, Abraham Nabarro, Isaac Nabarro, Samuel Nabarro, Jacob Pacheco, Isaac Rezio, Anthony Rodrigues, and Jeronimo Rodrigues; Hispanic Society of America, A Coppie Journall of Entries Made in the Custom House of Barbados Beginning August ye 10th 1665 continued in two distinct accotts to ye 24th Aprl [sic] 1667 & containes Ye accott Currant of 2 yeares 8 1/2 months, passim.

7. See the discussion at ns. 17, 18, and 19, infra, and the sources cited there.

8. The two who apparently did not reside in towns were Benjamin Bueno De Mesquita, an inhabitant of the parish of Christ Church, and David De Acosta, who resided in the parish of St. Thomas; Samuel, "Jewish Colonists in Barbados," 13–15, 90–91. The estimate of about 260 Jews was provided by the governor in June 1681; *CSP,* XI (1681–85), 72.

9. According to P. F. Campbell, "The Merchants and Traders of Barbados—1," *Journal of the Barbados Museum and Historical Society* 34 (1971–74): 95, "only one or two isolated instances are known of a Jew owning a plantation." For the three Jewish settlers who owned agricultural lands in 1680, see the discussion, infra, at n. 20. A list entitled The Jews Plantations and houses in Jamaica and Barbados submitted to the

Crown in 1692 provides the names of nine individuals in Barbados who owned "houses and plantations," along with the notation that "severall others" did too; PRO, CO 37/2. The nine were Mrs. Gratia De Mercado, Joseph Mendur [*sic*; Mendes?], Abraham Baruch Henriques, Luis Dias, "Roel" [Rowland] Gideon, Abraham Gomez, Abraham Bueno De Mesquita, Fernandez Nunes, and Luis Camacho. (For Gideon's first name, see Samuel, "Jewish Colonists in Barbados," 37–38.)

10. Herbert Friedenwald, "Material for the History of the Jews in the British West Indies," *Publications of the American Jewish Historical Society* 5 (1897): 63. For the animosities of non-Jewish merchants toward their Jewish counterparts in Barbados and Jamaica, see Stephen Alexander Fortune, *Merchants and Jews: The Struggle for British West Indian Commerce, 1650–1750* (Gainesville: University Presses of Florida, 1984), passim.

11. "The Lucas Manuscript Volumes in the Barbados Public Library," *Journal of the Barbados Museum and Historical Society* 14 (1946–47): 91, 94.

12. P. F. Campbell, "The Barbados Vestries 1627–1700—Part II," *Journal of the Barbados Museum and Historical Society* 37 (1983–86): 177–78, 182–83, 189–90. Campbell notes, however, that, despite protests against the assessments imposed on them in 1670 and 1698 by the St. Michael's vestry, there is no conclusive evidence that the Jewish population was taxed more heavily, although the amounts levied in some years do appear to have been unreasonably high.

13. Friedenwald, "Material for History of Jews in British West Indies," 96; *CSP*, XI (1681–85), 99; "Lucas Manuscript Volumes," 85–88.

14. *CSP*, X (1677–80), 446.

15. Richard Hall and Richard Hall, *Acts Passed in the Island of Barbados. From 1643, to 1762, Inclusive* (London: Richard Hall, 1764), 119, 166. The islanders may have had good reason to fear rebellion when they enacted the prohibition of 1688, for in 1692 a projected slave uprising was detected; Melville J. Herskovits, *The Myth of the Negro Past* (1941; Boston: Beacon Press, 1990), 94.

16. "Lucas Manuscript Volumes," 94; Hall and Hall, *Acts Passed in the Island of Barbados,* 166.

17. For the text of the census, see John Camden Hotten, ed., *The Original Lists of Persons of Quality; Emigrants; Religious Exiles; Political Rebels; Serving Men Sold for a Term of Years; Apprentices; Children Stolen; Maidens Pressed; and Others Who Went from Great Britain to the American Plantations 1600–1700* (Reprinted from 2d ed., New York, 1880; Baltimore: Genealogical Publishing Co., 1962), 438–507; and James C. Brandow, ed., *Omitted Chapters from Hotten's Original*

Lists of Persons of Quality (Baltimore: Genealogical Publishing Co., 1983), 3–17, 26–29, 33–49, 57–63, 68–72, 76–84.

The total number of slaves reported here was arrived at by recalculating all slave totals given in the original census. In his analysis of the census, Richard S. Dunn reported that the total was 38,782 after he recalculated the total for Bridgetown but accepted as accurate all other totals provided by the census's compiler. In fact, they are all incorrect, save for the total given for the parish of St. Lucy. Dunn, *Sugar and Slaves*, 88–89.

18. For the names of the Jewish owners and their holdings, see Samuel, "Jewish Colonists in Barbados," 13–15, 51, 63–65.

Simon Ffretto of St. Peter's parish, the owner of four slaves, is not included in the computations presented here. Although identified by Samuel as Jewish, he appears not to have been so, in view of the fact that a child named Katherine Ffretto was baptized in St. Peter's in 1678 or 1679; Brandow, *Omitted Chapters*, 86. For Simon Ffretto as a witness to a non-Jewish will in 1719 in St. Peter's, see Joanne Mcree Sanders, *Barbados Records: Wills and Administrations*, 3 vols. (Houston: Sanders Historical Publications, 1979–81), III, 157.

19. The data for Speightstown are part of the returns for St. Peter, but are not distinguished from the parish's rural areas. The census included the number of acres owned by each returnee, but none of the Jewish inhabitants was credited with land, making it apparent that they all resided in the parish's town.

20. Daniel Boyna, owner of 10 acres and 14 slaves in St. Michael (and 11 slaves in Bridgetown); David Namias, owner of 20 acres and 12 slaves in Christ Church (and 5 slaves in Bridgetown); David De Acosta, owner of 41 acres and 61 slaves in St. Thomas; and Benjamin Bueno De Mesquita, the owner of 1 slave in Christ Church.

21. The analysis provided here differs slightly from that offered by Dunn, *Sugar and Slaves*, 106–7, because of a different procedure in computing the average number of slaves per household. Dunn's results, however, yield an identical picture of Jewish participation in slaveowning in Bridgetown.

22. For the fourteen Jewish households (excluding Simon Ffretto, as explained at n. 18, supra) and the number of slaves in each, see Samuel, "Jewish Colonists in Barbados," 51. For the entire parish, see Brandow, *Omitted Chapters*, 76–84.

23. Sheridan, *Sugar and Slavery*, 247, 487–89; Rawley, *Transatlantic Slave Trade*, 166.

24. Michael Pawson and David Buisseret, *Port Royal, Jamaica* (Oxford: Clarendon Press, 1975), 20–36; Curtis Nettels, "England and the Span-

ish-American Trade, 1680–1715," *Journal of Modern History* 3 (1931): 6, 9, 16; Nuala Zahedieh, "Trade, Plunder, and Economic Development in Early English Jamaica, 1655–89," 2d ser., *Economic History Review* 39 (1986): 205–22.

25. Nettels, "England and Spanish-American Trade," 13–16, 19–20, 29; Nuala Zahedieh, "The Merchants of Port Royal, Jamaica, and the Spanish Contraband Trade, 1655–1692," 3d ser., *William and Mary Quarterly* 43 (1986): 582; Gedalia Yogev, *Diamonds and Coral: Anglo-Dutch Jews and Eighteenth-Century Trade* (N.p.: Leicester University Press, 1978), 46–48.

26. Jacob A. P. M. Andrade, *A Record of the Jews in Jamaica from the English Conquest to the Present Time* (Kingston: Jamaica Times, 1941), 2, 39; PRO, CO 1/28, no. 27, 57. The haham in 1683 came from Curaçao; M. Kayserling, "The Jews in Jamaica and Daniel Israel Lopez Laguna," Original ser., *Jewish Quarterly Review* 12 (1900): 711.

27. In 1688, 213 ships entered at Port Royal, 102 at Barbados, and 226 at all of New England's ports, and Port Royal's share therefore amounted to approximately 40 percent; Zahedia, "Merchants of Port Royal," 570. Zahedia (at 588) also observes that "trading gains may have made Port Royal the richest merchant community in English North America."

28. IJ, John Taylor, Multum in Parvo. Or Taylor's Historie of his Life, and Travells in America and other Parts, II, 499, 515–16.

29. PRO, CO 37/2, a petition in which the Jews of Jamaica protested against efforts by the colony's non-Jewish merchants to deprive them of the right to keep shops and engage in retail trade, in the course of which they mentioned the poverty of some of their contemporaries. The petition was submitted at the end of August, almost three months after the great earthquake of June 7, 1692, which may account for their condition. For the estate inventories, see Dunn, *Sugar and Slaves*, 183.

30. Friedenwald, "Material for History of Jews in British West Indies," 73–75.

31. Crown officials later ordered its repeal; *CSP*, XI (1681–85), 609–10, 614.

32. *CSP*, XIII (1689–92), 594. In 1695, the colony's governor echoed the Council's words when he reported to the Lords of Trade and Plantations that "the English think that the Jews eat out their trade. . . ."; *CSP*, XIV (1693–96), 455.

33. Samuel J. Hurwitz and Edith Hurwitz, "The New World Sets an Example for the Old: The Jews of Jamaica and Political Rights, 1661–1831," *American Jewish Historical Quarterly* 55 (1965–66): 39.

34. Anthony Rodrigues in 1664; Benjamin Mesquita Bueno in 1665, Abraham Rodrigues, Solomon Gabay, David Gomez, and Abraham Lucana

[Lucena?] in 1669. In the 1670s: Solomon Faro Gabay, Abraham Spinosa, Moses Jesurun Cardozo, Abraham Pereira, Jacob De Leon, Abraham Jacob Gabay, David Gabay, Abraham David Gabay, Joseph Ydana, Abraham Cohen, Solomon De Leon, Moses De Leon Cohen, Abraham Cohen De Leon, Joseph Da Costa Alvarenga, and Isaac Fonseca; in Andrade, *Jews in Jamaica,* 136–41.

35. The Jews Plantations and houses in Jamaica and Barbados, cited supra at n. 9. The Jamaican names were: Mr. Narbona; Solomon Gabay; Joseph Hidana [Ydana]; Solomon Adon; Abraham Gabay; Benjamin Carvalho; Moses Jesurun Cardozo; Joseph Corla [Da Costa] Alvarenga; David Alvarez; Jacob Mendes Gutteres; Jacob De Torres; and Sarah Gabay.

36. *CSP,* XVIII (1700), 225.

37. AJA, Collection of Jamaica Wills, Microfilm Reel 140, for the will of Solomon De Leon in 1696; Joseph De Leon in 1702; Joseph Ydana in 1704; and David Lopez Narbonne in 1707. Solomon De Leon left his plantation to his son, Joseph. The latter indicated in his will that he resided in Port Royal, but identified his brother, Elias De Leon, as a planter in St. Thomas-in-the-Vale. Joseph Ydana appears on the 1692 list of plantation owners presented to the Crown in 1692 (supra, at n. 35), while the Mr. Narbona on that list may well be the David Lopez Narbonne cited here.

38. Ibid., for the wills of David Alvarez in 1693, who owned a share in a ship called the *Joseph*; Joseph Da Costa Alvarenga in 1700, who owned five houses in Port Royal; and Moses Jesurun Cardozo in 1726, who identified himself as a Port Royal merchant.

39. PRO, CO 1/45, 96–107. The totals reported in the manuscript—2,086 whites and 845 slaves, for a grand total of 2,931—have been set aside in favor of the recomputed figures reported here, a difference of 48 individuals.

40. For the Jewish householders and the slaves they owned, see Appendix V, Table 1. Four households, or less than 1 percent, cannot be classified on the basis of their religion either because of defects in the manuscript or the indeterminacy of their names.

41. Zahedieh, "Trade, Plunder, and Economic Development," 212, provides the total number of slaves in the colony in 1680.

42. K. G. Davies, *The Royal African Company* (1957; New York: Atheneum, 1970), 294–97, with the quotation at 296–97; Rawley, *Transatlantic Slave Trade,* 157.

43. The Jamaica factor in May 1675 was Mr. Francis Man, when two others were appointed to join him: Mr. Andrew Langley and Mr. John Panden; PRO, T 70/76, 42b. Later factors in Jamaica were Hender

Molesworth, William Beeston, John Balle, Charles Penhallow, Walter Ruding, and Rowland Powell, while Stephen Gascoigne, Benjamin Skutt, Edwin Stede, and Giles Heysham served in Barbados; Davies, *Royal African Company*, 297–98.

44. PRO, T 70/936–49, passim. These volumes bear the notation "Invoice Book[s] Homewards." The Jewish purchasers were Abraham Alvarez, David Alvarez, Jacob Alvarez, Solomon Arrie [Arias], Moses Jesurun Cardozo, Benjamin Carvalho, Moses Cohen, Jacob Correa, "Da." Coutinho, Isaac Coutinho, Abraham Da Costa, Isaac Da Costa, Joseph Da Costa, Elias Da Cunha, Joseph Da Silva, Benjamin Franks, Abraham David Gabay, David Gabay, Solomon Gabay, Jacob Mendes Gutteres, Moses Gutteres, Abraham Pereira, Isaac Da Fonseca, Mordecai Da Silva, David Cohen De Lara, Jacob De Leon, Moses De Leon, Solomon De Leon, Jacob De Torres, Jacob Lopez, Abraham Lucena, David Lucena, Moses Lucena, Samuel Lucena, Issac Marquez, Daniel Nahar, David Lopez Narbona, Isaac Narvais, David Lopez Torres, and Jacob Lopez Torres. The partnerships were those of Walter Ruding & Moses Jesurun Cardozo; "Christ. Fleir" & Mordecai Da Silva; and Richard Westcomb & Diego Luis Gonzalez.

The total number of slaves delivered to Jamaica by the Company during the period indicated exceeded the 16,636 reported here. The latter does not include slaves paid to ships' captains as their commissions; slaves applied to freight charges (i.e., reimbursements to the owners of the vessels); slaves who went unsold because they died or were too sickly to fetch a price; or slaves who were sold for "Cash." In the last instance, the invoice lists did not include the names of the purchasers. In nearly all such cases, slaves sold for "Cash" were very few in number, minimizing the distortion that arises by not knowing who made the purchases.

45. Ibid. The Jewish purchasers were Phineas Abarbanel, Isaac Aboab, Isaac Athias, Aaron Baruch, Abraham Baruch, Rachel Baruch, Abraham Bueno, Abraham Burgos, David Da Costa, Moses Coutinho, Jacob Da Fonseca, Philip De Mesquita, Abraham Da Silva, David De Mercado, Moses De Mercado, Luis Dias, Jacob Franco, Abraham Gomez, Abraham Baruch Henriques, David Israel, Isaac Israel, David Latob, Abraham Mendes, Isaac Mendes, Joseph Mendes, Solomon Mendes, Joseph Mercado, David Namias, Samuel Nabarro, Abraham Pacheco, Hannah Pacheco, Jacob Pacheco, Moses Pacheco, Anthony Rodrigues, Joseph Senior, Isaac Silva, and Jacob Da Fonseca Valle. The partnerships were those of Peter Baxter & Abraham Baruch Henriques; John Stewart, Abraham Baruch & Co.; John Stewart, Aaron Baruch & Co.; and John Millington & Abraham Baruch.

The comment in the preceding note regarding the total number of slaves delivered to Jamaica applies to Barbados.

46. In Jamaica, the major Jewish purchasers were Abraham Alvarez and Moses Jesurun Cardozo. In Barbados, they were Aaron Baruch, Abraham Baruch, Abraham Baruch Henriques, Joseph Mendes, and Solomon Mendes.

47. "Refuse" purchases were made by Abraham Alvarez and/or Moses Jesurun Cardozo in 1676, 1677, 1678, 1680, 1683, and 1694.

48. Elizabeth Donnan, ed., *Documents Illustrative of the History of the Slave Trade to America*, 4 vols. (Washington, D.C.: Carnegie Institution of Washington, 1930–35), I, 370–71; Nettels, "England and Spanish-American Trade," 5; *CSP*, XIII (1689–92), 106; *CSP*, XIV (1693–96), 633–34.

49. Zahedieh, "Merchants of Port Royal," 591–92.

50. A letter from the governor and Council to the Lords of Trade in 1700, in *CSP*, XVIII (1700), 225–26, provides the fullest statement of what non-Jewish Jamaicans found objectionable about the colony's Jews. The latter, the writers alleged, refused to comply with the terms of their immigration, which required that they settle on the land as planters. Becoming merchants instead, they undersold English merchants, engrossed much of the island's commerce, particularly the wholesale trade, and refused to accept non-Jewish children as apprentices in their businesses. They induced slaves to steal from their masters. Except for occasional service as constables, they were not liable for service in civil or military office or for the charges arising therefrom.

51. Interlopers known to have operated at Barbados between 1675 and 1677 were Morris, Fowell, James Vaughan, Chief Justice Colonel William Sharpe, John Worsam, Major John Hallet, Philip Cheeke, Commissioner of Customs Roger Cowley, Richard Bate, John Thornborough, Leonard Woodfine, Barnard Schenckingh, and Arthur Middleton; in 1684, Peirson, Thomas Briscoe, John Bradley, Thomas Curtin, Eliathim Tolman, Samuel Whillett, and Mr. Richard Walter; in 1686, Beeston, Waterhouse, Nathaniel Hickes, and Colonel Samuel Barry; at Jamaica in 1686, Col. Freeman and Mr. Kelly; and at Nevis in 1680, Thornebury. In addition to the foregoing there were a Captain John Gribble in 1676, Captain Elton in 1678, whose vessel was owned by the Duke of Ormond, a Mr. Rany and a Captain Daniell in 1681, Captain Bell in 1693, and, in Africa, Captain Charles Plumer in 1680 and Captain Ford in 1698. *CSP*, IX (1675–76, Also Addenda, 1574–1674), 278; X (1677–80), 93–94, 579; XII (1685–88), 157; Donnan, *Documents Illustrative*, I, 200, 203, 222, 224–25, 236, 259, 261, 271, 325, 333–35, 391, 418–19.

52. Vere Langford Oliver, ed., *Caribbeana Being Miscellaneous Papers Relating to the History, Genealogy, Topography, and Antiquities of the British West Indies*, 6 vols. (London: Mitchell, Hughes and Clarke, 1909–19), III, 27–35, 70–81. The "Jewes," four men, one woman, and three children, are listed at 35.

53. PRO, T 70/936–49 passim. The Jewish purchasers were Moses Burgos, Anthony Correa, Abraham Bueno De Mesquita, Rowland Gideon, Abraham Lobatto, Jacob Lobatto, Sarah Lobatto, Daniel Mendes, Abraham Nunes, Isaac Pinheiro, and Abraham Rezio. A Daniel Cohen also purchased slaves, but whether he was Jewish or not is not known. The comment at n. 44 regarding the total number of slaves delivered to Jamaica applies to Nevis.

Notes to Chapter 3

1. Michael Pawson and David Buisseret, *Port Royal, Jamaica* (Oxford: Clarendon Press, 1975), 120–23.

2. Jacob A. P. M. Andrade, *A Record of the Jews in Jamaica from the English Conquest to the Present Time* (Kingston: Jamaica Times, 1941), 40, 46; Colin G. Clarke, *Kingston, Jamaica: Urban Development and Social Change, 1692–1962* (Berkeley: University of California Press, 1975), 5, 18. The will of Benjamin Henriques of the parish of Kingston, written in 1697 and enrolled in 1702, pinpoints what may have been the earliest settlement by a Jewish individual in Kingston; AJA, Jamaica Wills, Microfilm Reel 140. The map of Kingston drawn in 1702 shows that such Jewish settlers as David Da Silva, M. Da Silva, S. I. De Leon, S. Flamengo, D. Nahar, and S. L. Narbona, among others, had either acquired land or built homes; PRO, MPG 1067, A Plan of Kingston.

3. By entry is meant primarily a household or a business firm; see the discussion, infra, in the present chapter.

4. Edward Long, *The History of Jamaica. Or, General Survey of the Antient and Modern State of That Island*, 3 vols. (London: T. Lowndes, 1774), II, 28. The rest of Spanish Town's population, according to Long, was made up of 1,116 other whites, 800 free blacks, and 1,960 slaves. Outside the town in the rural areas of St. Catherine, Spanish Town's parish, another 50 Jews, 308 Christian whites, 100 free blacks, and 5,348 slaves resided.

Spanish Town's Jewish population in the early 1770s probably exceeded New York's; see the discussion in Doris Groshen Daniels, "Colonial Jewry: Religion, Domestic and Social Relations," *American Jewish Historical Quarterly* 66 (1976–77): 380. It presumably also exceeded that of Bridgetown, Barbados; for the decline of the Jewish community there during the eighteenth century, see Chapters Four and Five, infra.

5. *CSP,* XXI (1702–3), 226–27. This figure apparently included single men who resided separately, for, three years before, in a statement prepared at the behest of the governor, the community described itself as "not surpassing Eighty persons including Married men, Batchelors, Widows, & the poor maintained upon Charity." By "persons" the 1700 authors must have meant households, for "Married men" encompassed wives and children, since women were otherwise counted only as "Widows." For the 1700 version, see Frank Cundall, "The Taxing of the Jews in Jamaica in the Seventeenth Century," *Publications of the American Jewish Historical Society* 31 (1928): 245.

6. PRO, CO 137/22, 34; *The North-American and the West-Indian Gazetteer* (London: G. Robinson, 1776), entry for "Jamaica."

7. BL, Add. Ms. 12,418–12,419, James Knight, The Natural, Moral, and Political History of Jamaica, and the Territories thereon depending; From the first Discovery of the Island by Christopher Columbus, to the Year 1746, II, 74b. For Knight and the origins of his work, never published despite the author's intention to do so, see K. E. Ingram, *Sources of Jamaican History, 1655–1838: A Bibliographical Survey with Particular Reference to Manuscript Sources,* 2 vols. (Zug: Inter Documentation Company, 1976), I, 196–99.

8. Long, *History of Jamaica,* II, 18, 28–29, 295–96. On Long, see Elsa V. Goveia, *A Study on the Historiography of the British West Indies to the End of the Nineteenth Century* (Washington, D.C.: Howard University Press, 1980), 53ff, 74.

9. As the members of the Assembly wrote in 1741, "If some of them have purchased houses in the Towns, no great benefit accrues to the public, by such purchases; and it is notorious they were made, for the greatest part, with a view of defeating their creditors, houses having never, or until very lately, been extended or sold in this island for debt. . . ." In George Fortunatus Judah, "The Jews' Tribute in Jamaica. Extracted from the Journals of the House of Assembly of Jamaica," *Publications of the American Jewish Historical Society* 18 (1909): 173.

10. Knight, History of Jamaica, II, 74b–75b. The allegation about the purchases of homes had been voiced even earlier by Richard Mill, president of the Council. In 1738, he wrote that "they are great owners of Houses in the several Towns, most of which I believe were bought or built, to avoid payment of their creditors." In PRO, CO 137/56, 115b.

11. Long, *History of Jamaica,* II, 295. In an appeal to the Crown in 1721 against a law barring Jews, Catholics, and Nonconformists from receiving incentive payments designed to attract white settlers to the island,

Jamaica's Jews noted that they had "with the greatest readiness according to their Duty taken up Arms against the French at the time they invaded the said Island, where severall of them were kill'd wounded and taken Prisoners." In PRO, CO 137/14, 51.

12. Long, *History of Jamaica*, II, 18, 30, 293, 296, 459.

13. Albert M. Hyamson, *The Sephardim of England: A History of the Spanish and Portuguese Jewish Community, 1492–1951* (London: Methuen, 1951), 136–38. A proposal to impose a special tax on the Jewish population was the other major reason for the appeal to London for intervention with the new governor.

14. Long, *History of Jamaica*, I, 556–58, 570, 573.

15. Knight, *History of Jamaica*, II, 75.

16. Long, *History of Jamaica*, II, 459–60, 491. For the slave rebellion of 1760, see Orlando Patterson, *The Sociology of Slavery: An Analysis of the Origins, Development and Structure of Negro Slave Society in Jamaica* (London: MacGibbon and Kee, 1967), 271.

17. *CSP*, XVIII (1700), 226.

18. PRO, CO 137/56, Reasons Relating to the Jews. 1738, 118; Knight, History of Jamaica, II, 75; Long, *History of Jamaica*, II, 487.

19. The Maroons were the descendants of Spanish slaves who had established themselves in the island's interior after the English seized Jamaica in 1655. For the Maroon rebellion between 1725 and 1740, which attracted runaway slaves, see Patterson, *Sociology of Slavery*, 269–71.

20. *CSP*, XL (1733), 172–73, 216; PRO, CO 137/56, 118; Knight, History of Jamaica, II, 75b, 224. Knight had written that the Jews were suspected "of holding a Correspondence with the Negroes in the Mountains, when they were in Rebellion, and even of furnishing them with Powder and Arms." An unidentified reviewer whom he had asked to comment on the accuracy of his manuscript wrote that "You mencon a suspicion of the Jews holding a Corispondance with the Wild Neg[roe]s. Since their Coming in, Capt. Cajo and all the rest of the Wild Neg[roe]s. have been Strictly Examined upon that Head, & have all declar'd, that never had any Corispondance with the Jews upon any head wh[at]soever." Accepting the correction, Knight subsequently drew a line through the offending sentence.

21. BL, Shelburne Papers, XLIV, 813–14, for John Mereweather to the South Sea Company; PRO, CO 137/56, 115a, for Richard Mill to Governor Trelawny, July 14, 1738.

22. Assembly of Jamaica, *Journals of the Assembly of Jamaica,* 14 vols. (Jamaica: Alexander Aikman, 1811–1829), IV, 238, 246–47, 249. For Sanches's effort at enfranchisement, as well as for how and when the Jewish population obtained the right to vote, see Samuel J. Hurwitz and

Edith Hurwitz, "The New World Sets an Example for the Old: The Jews of Jamaica and Political Rights, 1661–1831," *American Jewish Historical Quarterly* 55 (1965–66): 42–45.

23. PRO, CO 137/22, 34, and CO 137/56, 115a–b; Knight, History of Jamaica, II, 74b; Long, *History of Jamaica*, II, 229.

24. IJ, MS 1987, List of the Landholders in the Island of Jamaica in 1754, passim, and 71 for the total acreage. (The original of this document, transmitted to England by Governor Knowles at the end of 1754, is at PRO, CO 142/31.) See Appendix IX, infra, for Jewish landowners on the list and for those whose religion is not certain. For an analysis of the landholding patterns revealed by this source, see Richard B. Sheridan, *Sugar and Slavery: An Economic History of the British West Indies, 1623–1775* (Baltimore: Johns Hopkins University Press, 1973), 219.

25. The Jewish merchant Benjamin Bravo wrote in 1736 that "many Jews . . . are owners of lands and houses in the towns of Kingston, Spanish Town, and Port Royal, as well as other parts of the island"; PRO, CO 137/22, 34. "They are great owners of Houses in the several Towns," wrote Richard Mill in 1738; PRO, CO 137/56, 115b. James Knight concurred in the mid-1740s: "[A] Great part of the Houses and Ware Houses at Port Royall, and Kingston, belong to them." In Knight, History of Jamaica, II, 74b.

26. Willemstad, Curaçao's capital, is another location that could conceivably qualify for the leading position.

27. Many copies of the wills of eighteenth-century Jamaican Jews can be conveniently examined at AJA, but the collection there is by no means complete; for others, see the originals at IRO. For examples of the occasional individuals between 1700 and 1780 who did not identify themselves as shopkeepers or merchants, see the wills at AJA of Isaac Da Costa Alvarenga, doctor; Isaac Lopez Alvin, fisherman, mentioned in the will of Isaac Henriques Alvin; Abraham De Lyon, "house keeper"; Moses Henriques, goldsmith, mentioned in the will of Moses Gabay Faro; Abraham Rodrigues, distiller; Solomon Saldana, goldsmith; and Daniel Suero, goldsmith. For planters, see the wills of Judith Baruch Alvarez for Jacob Mendes Gutteres; Benjamin Bravo; Jacob Correa; Moses Gabay Faro; David Gabay; Isaac Gabay; and Jacob Narbona.

28. PRO, CO 137/14, 51, and CO 137/56, 118; Knight, History of Jamaica, 74b; Long, *History of Jamaica*, II, 28–29. Long's description of the Jewish market in Spanish Town was not flattering. After noting that most of the Jewish shopkeepers dealt in salted butter, herring, beef, cheese, and train oil, he wrote that "their shops may be scented at a great distance; and, in what is called the Jew-market in this town, a

whole street of their houses reeks incessantly with these abominable odors."

29. PRO, C 104/13C and C 104/14, Nathan Simson Papers: Benjamin Pereira to Nathan Simson, May 6, 1715 and July 20–August 24, 1715. Diego and Abraham Gonzalez to Nathan Simson, July 31, 1719, August 27, 1719; July 26–August 3, 1722, December 20, 1722; January 4, 1722 [1723], June 15, 1723, September 25, 1723, September 26, 1723; October 9, 1724; May 26, 1725. Abraham Gonzalez to Nathan Simson, April 26, 1724. Diego and Abraham Gonzalez to Nathan Simson, Isaac Levy, and Samuel Levy, January 28, 1722. Diego and Abraham Gonzalez to Mrs. Nathan Simson, May 19, 1726.

30. PRO, CO 137/17, 88a.

31. PRO, CO 137/56, 115a, for Mill's statement; and Judah, "Jews' Tribute in Jamaica," 172, for the Assembly's remark.

32. PRO, CO 137/19, Part Two, 2.

33. PRO, CO 137/22, 30–32, for the petition, and 35–36, for William Wood's letter to Allured Popple, Esq., February 18, 1735 [1736]. Wood's language has been modernized here. For the London Jewish merchants who signed the petition, see Chapter One, supra, at n. 89.

34. Eli Faber, *A Time for Planting: The First Migration, 1654–1820* (Baltimore: Johns Hopkins University Press, 1992), 21–23, 42–51.

35. PRO, C 104/14, Simson Papers, Diego and Abraham Gonzalez to Nathan Simson, July 26–August 3, 1722, and January 4, 1722 [1723]. Diego Luis Gonzalez mentioned his brother at Bayonne in his will; AJA, Jamaica Wills. (That Diego Gonzalez and Diego Luis Gonzalez were one and the same is apparent in a letter from him to Nathan Simson on May 26, 1725, in which he signed his full name.)

Perhaps it had been "Needful att presentt" for Moses Lamego to go to London because of charges that he was one of seven individuals at Port Royal, including the Marquis De Quesne, commander of the fort, who had traded illegally with Dutch and French vessels calling there under pretense of obtaining legal refreshment. In addition to the Marquis, three non-Jewish parties—John Drudge, Captain Lauderdale, and a Bonfils, Jr.—and three Jewish parties—Isaac Lopez, Widow Silvera, and a Lamego whose personal name is not known—stood accused. See *The State of the Island of Jamaica* (London: H. Whitridge, 1726), 72–77.

36. AJA, Jamaica Wills, for the wills of Judith Baruch Alvarez, Moses Levy Alvarez, Isaac Pereira Brandon, Jacob Brandon, Benjamin Bravo, David Bravo, Isaac Bravo, Moses Yesurun Cardozo, Daniel Carvalho, Asher Cohen, Jacob Correa, Isaac Mendes Da Costa, Daniel Nunes Da Costa,

Jacob Ferro, Solomon Franco, Benjamin Henriques, Mordecai Rodrigues Lopez, Abraham Nahar, Daniel Pachexe [Pacheco], Isaac Nunes, Benjamin Pereira, Isaac Pereira, Abraham Mendes Quixano, and Moses Mendes Quixano.

37. For the synagogue, see "The Earliest Extant Minute Books of the Spanish and Portuguese Congregation Shearith Israel in New York, 1728–1786," *Publications of the American Jewish Historical Society* 21 (1913): 3, 25–35; Jacob R. Marcus, "The Oldest Known Synagogue Record Book of Continental North America, 1720–1721," in Jacob R. Marcus, *Studies in American Jewish History: Studies and Addresses* (Cincinnati: Hebrew Union College Press, 1969), 47; Hyman B. Grinstein, *The Rise of the Jewish Community of New York, 1654–1860* (Philadelphia: Jewish Publication Society of America, 1947), 206; Henry J. Cadbury, "An Account of Barbados 200 Years Ago," *Journal of the Barbados Museum and Historical Society* 9 (1941–42): 82. For instruction in Spanish in New York's synagogue school, see "Earliest Extant Minute Books," 72.

For wills written in Portuguese during the eighteenth century, see Wilfred S. Samuel, "A Review of the Jewish Colonists in Barbados in the Year 1680," *Transactions of the Jewish Historical Society of England* 13 (1932–35): 79–80, 83, 93; and Bertram Wallace Korn, "Barbadian Jewish Wills, 1676–1740," in Bertram Wallace Korn, ed., *A Bicentennial Festschrift for Jacob Rader Marcus* (Waltham: American Jewish Historical Society, 1976), 312. Tombstones with Spanish or Portuguese inscriptions are recorded in Vere Langford Oliver, ed., *The Monumental Inscriptions in the Churches and Churchyards of the Island of Barbados, British West Indies* (1915; San Bernadino: Borgo Press, 1989), 197–206, and in E. M. Shilstone, tr., *Monumental Inscriptions in the Burial Ground of the Jewish Synagogue at Bridgetown, Barbados* (N.p.: N.p., n.d.). In Jamaica, Portuguese inscriptions are known for 342 tombstones, Spanish inscriptions for 92; Richard D. Barnett and Philip Wright, *The Jews of Jamaica: Tombstone Inscriptions, 1663–1880* (Jerusalem: Ben Zvi Institute, 1997), 202.

The papers of Aaron Lopez include many letters to Lopez at Newport in Spanish and Portuguese. See, for examples, AJA, Aaron Lopez Papers, Microfilm Reel 1,212, Isaac Da Costa at Charleston, South Carolina, to Lopez on January 11, 1763 and July 19, 1764, and Joseph Obediente, Jr., at Curaçao to Lopez on September 11, 1773; and in the Aaron Lopez Papers at AJHS, Daniel Gomez at New York to Lopez on October 30, 1752, Jacob Franks at New York to Lopez on January 30, 1753, Isaac Fernandez at Barbados to Lopez on May 20, 1753, and Daniel Torres at Providence, Rhode Island, to Lopez on October 6, 1754. That

Franks wrote in Portuguese demonstrates that Ashkenazic Jewish merchants also employed it in commercial correspondence.

In New York in 1741, a member of the Gomez family served as interpreter in the trials of five Spanish slaves implicated in the alleged slave conspiracy to burn the city and kill its white inhabitants; Daniel Horsmanden, *The New York Conspiracy, or a History of the Negro Plot with the Journal of the Proceedings against the Conspirators at New-York in the Years 1741–2* (1810; New York: Negro Universities Press, 1969), 222.

38. Knight, History of Jamaica, 74b. Examples of wills include Abraham Alvarez's (1693) in Spanish, and Daniel Lopez Laguna's translated from the Spanish (1723); at AJA, Jamaica Wills. Both versions of Isaac De Mella's will are at IRO, XXXVIII, 36.

39. Long, *History of Jamaica,* II, 295.

40. Ibid., II, 116: "The Jews are numerous in this town, being possessed of the greatest share in the Spanish trade."

Examples of Jews who participated in the Spanish trade are provided by the suits brought against David Dias Arias in 1743 and Isaac Mendes in 1773. Arias was supercargo (consignee and sales agent) for Matthias Philp and Alexander Campbell, both of whom were non-Jewish merchants in Kingston, and for Aaron Lopez Riz, a Jewish merchant there. The three accused him of fraud regarding the amount of their merchandise he actually sold on the Spanish Coast. In the second case, in which only Jewish individuals were involved, Jacob Carillo Saldana and Joshua Mendes, the complainants, had transported goods belonging to Simha, Isaac, and Jacob Mendes to Havana. Unable to sell the merchandise there because of a glut in the market, Saldana and Mendes arranged for a prominent Havana merchant to ship the goods to the Mississippi River. The suits against Arias are at JA, Records of the Court of Chancery, 1A/3/12, 453–56, and 1A/3/13, 222–23, 228–31; the case of *Saldana and Mendes v. Mendes* is at ibid., 1A/3/63, 254–77. These lawsuits are of great interest because they demonstrate that Jewish merchants ventured directly into Spanish territory at a time when the presence of Jews was prohibited there. A letter from Jacob Mendes at Kingston to Saldana and Joshua Mendes at Havana in 1763, part of the evidence submitted to the court, demonstrates that the two did not employ aliases while they were in Cuba.

41. PRO, CO 137/9, 79. They were "Jno. Lynch, Jno. Wyllys, John Canelier, J. Morris, Deane Poyntz, Edward Pratter, Jos. Carpenter, Panceft Miller, John Lewis, Anthony Major, Thomas Hacker, Harrington Gibbs, John Major, Samuel Andrew, William Leaver, Alget Pestell, Gervase Brough, William Attwood, Chris. Feake, W. Herneley, James Knight,

Hn. Crawford, Charles Vincent, Robert Elbridge, Pat Miln, Walter Chapman, James Moon, Richard Basnett, Thomas Colbey, Will Lodge, Thomas Perkin, W. Morris, Will White, Robert Howard, Samuel Clarke, Wll [*sic*] Hayman, Thomas Grey, Henry Smithson, William Puckle, D. Brinitrot [?], John Eastwick, and Leopold Stapleton."

42. The three were Mr. Aaron Portello, Mr. Isaac Carvellio [Carvalho], and Mr. Dias Fernandez; *A Defence of the Observations on the Assiento Trade, As It Hath Been Exercised by the South-Sea Company, &c.* (London: H. Whitridge, 1728), 45–46. Supercargoes were agents for other merchants, but they usually also carried goods that they themselves owned; Sheridan, *Sugar and Slavery*, 320.

43. PRO, CO 142/15, for clearances out during the period indicated. The Jewish owners were Moses Mendes, Cardozo-Nunes, and Moses Lamego & Co. The combined tonnage of their vessels was 90 (average 30); that of the non-Jewish owners was 1,270 (average 45.3).

44. PRO, CO 137/56, 115a, 118; Judah, "Jews' Tribute in Jamaica," 171–72.

45. PRO, CO 142/13, 176ff. The two vessels owned exclusively by Jews, followed by their owners' names in parentheses, were the *John and Thomas* (Isaac Lopez Torres) and the *Three Brothers* (Isaac Lopez Torres, Jacob Nunes, and Isaac Lamego). The two owned by Jews and non-Jews in partnership were the *John and Thomas,* a venture different from the aforementioned vessel of the same name (Roger Morgan, Isaac Lopez Torres, Jacob Nunes, and Isaac Lamego) and the *Thomas and Elizabeth* (John Burton, Thomas Douglass, and Jose De Torres).

46. PRO, CO 142/14. Entries are given for all four quarters of the year in Kingston's case, and for three of the four quarters in Port Royal's. The two New Yorkers were Mordecai Gomez, whose vessel's name was not given, and Moses Levy, who owned the *Abigail.* The third Jewish entry was Mendes & Co., owner of the *King Solomon* of London, regarding which see the discussion in Chapter One, supra, at n. 101. The owner whose religion cannot be determined was Jacobs & Co. of New York. A Jewish individual named Abraham Jacobs resided in New York in 1727; see Leo Hershkowitz, ed., *Wills of Early New York Jews (1704–1799)* (New York: American Jewish Historical Society, 1967), 36, n. 1.

47. PRO, CO 142/15, for entries between December 25, 1744 and December 24, 1745. The non-Jamaican owners, both of New York, were Jacob Franks, owner of the *Griffin* and the *Abigail,* and Mordecai Gomez & Co., whose vessel's name was not entered. The vessel whose owner's place of residence is not known belonged to Isaac Mendes Da Costa & Co. Aaron Lamera & Co. (the *Olive Branch*) and David Tavares & Co.

were the Jamaicans. Both appear on Kingston's poll tax for 1745; see Appendix VI, Table 1.
48. PRO, CO 142/16, for all entries between December 25, 1754 and December 25, 1755. The *Camelion* [*sic*] belonged to Naphtali Hart of Newport, Rhode Island. The vessels that were owned apparently by Jews of Jamaica were the *Young Jacob*, belonging to Jacob Mendes & Co.; the *Ann and Mary*, property of Isaac Mendes; and the *King David*, owned by Moses Mendes, which entered the port three times during the year.
49. PRO, CO 142/18, for entries between December 25, 1764 and December 25, 1765. The *Osprey* and the *Wheel of Fortune* belonged, respectively, to Naphtali Hart and to Isaac Elizer of Newport, Rhode Island. The remaining vessels were the *King George*, owned by Jacob Flamengo; the *Good Intent*, which entered twice, property of Isaac Nunes Netto; and the *Esther*, belonging to Solomon Levy & Co. The results reported here for 1745, 1755, and 1765 are listed in Appendix III, Table 1, along with data for 1785–1805.
50. PRO, CO 142/15, clearances for January 3–December 24, 1745. Three vessels belonged to Moses Mendes & Co.; 2 to Aaron Lamera & Co.; 2 to Jacob Franks of New York; and 1 each to David Bravo and to Da[vid] "Urabia" [Orobio] Furtado.
51. PRO, CO 142/16, for clearances between December 25, 1754 and December 25, 1755. The Jewish owners were Naphtali Hart & Co. of Rhode Island, owner of the *Osprey*, sailing to London, and the *Camelion*, bound for Rhode Island; Moses Mendes (two voyages on the *King David*, the first to Curaçao, the second to the Bay of Honduras); and Isaac Mendes (the *Ann & Mary*, going to Curaçao).
52. PRO, CO 142/18, clearances for December 25, 1764–December 25, 1765. The vessels were owned by Isaac Nunes Netto (the *Good Intent*, clearing out from Kingston twice for Curaçao); Jacob Flamengo, whose vessel sailed for Honduras; Naphtali Hart of Rhode Island (the *Osprey*, sailing to Rhode Island); and Isaac Elizer & Co., another Rhode Islander, whose *Wheel of Fortune* also sailed to Rhode Island.
53. [Edward Trelawny], *An Essay Concerning Slavery, and the Danger Jamaica Is Expos'd to from the Too Great Number of Slaves* (London: Charles Corbett, [1745]), 34; and Bryan Edwards, *The History, Civil and Commercial, of the British Colonies in the West Indies*, 2 vols. (1793; New York: Arno Press, 1972), II, 134. On the issue generally, see Richard B. Sheridan, *Doctors and Slaves: A Medical and Demographic History of Slavery in the British West Indies, 1680–1834* (Cambridge: Cambridge University Press, 1985), 146–47, 185, 247–48.

54. PRO, CO 388/11, no. 11.
55. *Report of the Lords of the Committee of Council Appointed for the Consideration of All Matters Relating to Trade and Foreign Plantations,* in House of Commons, *Sessional Papers of the Eighteenth Century, Reports and Papers, 1789, Slave Trade,* LXIX, 262–63, 296; LXX, 278, 288. For its figures on slave imports to Jamaica, the Committee relied on the figures provided by Stephen Fuller, the colony's agent in London, available also in Patterson, *Sociology of Slavery,* 289–91, and in Sheridan, *Sugar and Slavery,* 502–4. Both these authorities provide figures that differ somewhat from the Parliamentary source cited here, as well as with each other, underscoring the impossibility of achieving absolute precision with eighteenth-century population data. Sheridan, ibid., 505, also presents figures for slaves imported into Barbados that, likewise, differ from the figures cited here, viz., 36,014 for 1723–34; 7,958 for 1756–58; and 38,682 for 1764–72. These differences do not detract from the point that Jamaica was preeminent as a slave-importing island.
56. Judah, "Jews' Tribute in Jamaica," 171. The Assembly's comments on Jews and slavery were embedded in a statement in which the lower house explained why it continued to impose special taxes on the Jewish population after the Crown forbade the practice. It is highly unlikely that the Assembly meant to suggest that only five or six paid the export tax but that other Jewish merchants avoided doing so by smuggling slaves off the island. The legislators invoked many other charges that painted the Jewish population in a bad light, including nefarious methods to avoid paying import duties on cocoa and indigo. Had Jews exported slaves by smuggling them, it is reasonable to assume that a very hostile Assembly would have said so. In sum, the statement can be taken to mean exactly what it says: that no more than five or six Jewish merchants were engaged in the export of slaves. For the range of allegations by the Assembly against the Jews, see ibid., 170–73.
57. For the history of the Naval Office, see Charles M. Andrews, *The Colonial Period of American History,* 4 vols. (New Haven: Yale University Press, 1934–38), IV, 180–91. On the records of the Naval Office, called the Shipping Returns, see David Richardson, ed., *Bristol, Africa and the Eighteenth-Century Slave Trade to America,* 4 vols. (Volumes 38, 39, 42, and 47 of the Bristol Record Society's Publications) (Gloucester: Alan Sutton Publishing, 1986–96), I, x–xi, II, ix–x; III, ix; IV, ix–x. For a discussion of the information supplied by the Naval Office records, see Walter E. Minchinton, "The British Slave Fleet, 1680–1775: The Evidence of the Naval Office Shipping Lists," in Serge Daget, ed., *De la Traite à l'Esclavage: Actes du Colloque International sur la Traite des Noirs, Nantes 1985,* 2 vols. (Nantes: Centre de Recherche sur l'Histoire

du Monde Atlantique, 1988), I, 395–425. The earliest records for Jamaica are at PRO, CO 142/13, but the earliest listings of owners are at CO 142/14.

58. *Report of the Lords of the Committee of Council,* LXIX, 262–63, for total imports between 1742 and 1769. For the Naval Office years and the total in each year, see Appendix IV, Table 1, infra. The number of imported slaves in the years covered by the Naval Office records was marginally higher, but faded manuscripts, as well as several omissions of the number of slaves on board, reduce the total to the figure of 149,705 reported here. The instances of missing data, however, are so few that, were they available, they would raise the total by very little. All missing data occur in connection with non-Jewish vessel owners; were the numbers available, the proportion of slaves imported on vessels owned by Jews would therefore be even smaller.

59. PRO, CO 142/16, under entries for September 29–December 25, 1753. For Massiah's tombstone, see Shilstone, *Monumental Inscriptions,* 167.

60. PRO, CO 142/16, entries for June 25–September 29, 1755; and CO 142/18, entries for December 25, 1764–March 25, 1765. For Newport's significance to the slave trade and the activity of Jewish merchants there in it, see Chapter Six, infra.

61. PRO, CO 142/17, entries for December 29, 1766–March 29, 1767. Lopez had a partner in the *Betty* and the *Africa,* his father-in-law, Jacob Rodrigues Rivera; Jay Coughtry, *The Notorious Triangle: Rhode Island and the African Slave Trade, 1700–1807* (Philadelphia: Temple University Press, 1981), 253, where Coughtry lists the *Betty* as the *Betsey.* Rivera's other activity in the slave trade is discussed in Chapter Six, infra.

62. PRO, CO 142/15, entries for September 29–December 25, 1742. For the later export record, see ibid., clearances out for January 3–December 24, 1745.

63. Long, *History of Jamaica,* I, 491.

64. PRO, CO 142/15. Home ports are assumed from the columns in the records of the Naval Office that list where bond was posted for each vessel. In the absence of such bond postings, other sources identify Henry Lascelles & Co. as a London firm (Sheridan, *Sugar and Slavery,* 59, 64, 296–97), and James Laroche & Co. as a Bristol company (Richardson, *Bristol, Africa and Eighteenth-Century Slave Trade,* II, 153). The six owners of vessels whose home ports are not given are Anthony Guther, James Pearce, Robert Brown & Co., Thomas Perkins & Co., Godfrey Malbone & Co., and John Perks & Co. The two vessels whose home port was Jamaica, presumably at Kingston, were both owned by non-Jews: John Curtin, whose ship brought ten slaves back from Carta-

gena; and Samuel Hurlock & Co., returning with thirty-six slaves from the same location. Both appear on the Kingston poll tax for 1745, John Curtin on Port Royal Street, Hurlock on Orange Street, and the firm of Hurlick [sic] & Parkinson on Port Royal Street. The 1745 poll tax is at JA, 2/6/1.

65. PRO, CO 142/15, entries under the dates indicated.
66. PRO, CO 142/16, under the dates indicated. All were owned by non-Jewish firms.
67. Sheridan, *Sugar and Slavery*, 292. The Kingston poll tax for 1769 is at JA, 2/6/5. The entry for the firm of Hibbert & Jackson is under Orange Street. The next highest amount, £10, was assessed on the firm of Taylor & Graham (Port Royal Street), on Lewis Cuthbert (Port Royal Street), and on Benjamin Pereira, a Jewish merchant (Peter Lane). For Hibbert & Jackson's prominence in factoring, see the discussion, infra, in the present chapter.
68. Knight, History of Jamaica, 74b. Sheridan, *Sugar and Slavery*, 318, described Knight as "a leading slave factor in Jamaica."
69. Long, *History of Jamaica*, II, 116, 295–96, 491–92.
70. The names of only two independent factor firms are known prior to 1750: Messrs. Bassnett, Tyms & Hyde; and Tyndall & Assheton. They are in Elizabeth Donnan, ed., *Documents Illustrative of the History of the Slave Trade to America*, 4 vols. (Washington, D.C.: Carnegie Institution of Washington, 1930–35), II, 380, 382, 387–88. The South Sea Company's agents at Jamaica in the mid-1720s were Edward Pratter and James Rigby; BL, Records of the South Sea Company, Add. Ms. 25,551, November 10, 1724. Rigby, unable to solicit anyone to serve as his security, was suspended by the Company early in 1732, as per the Committee of Correspondence on February 19, 1733; in Add. Ms. 25,554. John Mereweather was appointed in his stead; ibid., October 18, 1733. Edward Manning subsequently replaced Pratter; ibid., December 23, 1735. The agents' activity as factors who purchased slaves for the Company in Jamaica is apparent in the correspondence with them. On March 31, 1725, the Company wrote to them: "'Tis with regret we observe Your Complaints for want of Negroes which has put You under a Necessity of Buying them at very high prices for the Supply of our Factorys"; in Add. Ms. 25,564, 85–86. Late in 1729 and again in 1730, the South Sea Company advertised that it would purchase slaves at Jamaica to meet its obligations under the asiento; in Add. Ms. 25,504, December 3, 1731. On June 18, 1731, the Company wrote to Humphry Morice, a major slave-ship owner in London, to inform him that "they [the Company] have Resolved for some time past, to depend on the Jamaica Market for the provision of all such Negroes as their Agents

shall want for the supply of the Spanish West Indies, upon which En-
couragement, many Merchants as well from hence [London] as from
Bristol and Liverpoole, have dispatched their Ships to the Coast of
Guinea. . . . Our Agents buy of all Importers Indifferently as They want
and find Negroes for their purpose as to price and Goodness. . . ."; in
Add. Ms. 25,557, 119.

71. Richardson, *Bristol, Africa and Eighteenth-Century Slave Trade,* III, 40,
46, 50–53, 55–56, 58, 60–61, 64–66, 80, 142, 155, 157, 164, 167, 174,
177, 180–81, 204, 220, 230.

72. Donnan, *Documents Illustrative,* III, 225–27. Massachusetts Historical
Society, 7th ser., *Collections,* 9 (1914): 203, 205, 212–13; cited hereafter
as *Commerce of Rhode Island,* the title of Volumes 9–10. For the irre-
sponsible Abraham Pereira Mendes, see Stanley F. Chyet, *Lopez of
Newport: Colonial American Merchant Prince* (Detroit: Wayne State
University Press, 1970), 97–103.

73. Aaron Lopez's genealogy includes a different Abraham Lopez, who
arrived in Newport in 1767 and died there in 1775; Malcolm H. Stern,
First American Jewish Families: 600 Genealogies, 1654–1988, 3d ed.
(Baltimore: Ottenheimer, 1991), 175. Abraham Lopez of Savanna la
Mar in Jamaica lived until 1781. The *Royal Gazette* for August 18,
1781, Supplement, reported that he died at Flamstead, his estate in
Hanover Parish, adding that "he carried on a very considerable scene of
business at Savanna la Mar, for many years, and was universally respected."

74. AJHS, Aaron Lopez Papers, Abraham Lopez to Aaron Lopez, April 23,
1771, and June 21, 1772. For more on Aaron Lopez's "Proposels relative to the Guinea Concern" to Abraham Lopez, see AJA, Aaron Lopez
Papers, Microfilm Reel 1,215, Benjamin Wright to Aaron Lopez, February 21 and 29, 1772.

75. Donnan, *Documents Illustrative,* III, 211–13.

76. Ibid., III, 264–65, 272–73, 291. Ironically for Abraham Lopez, it was
he who had first introduced Benjamin Wright to Aaron Lopez, recom-
mending him for his "Honesty & Sobriety" and his skill as a businessman; AJA, Aaron Lopez Papers, Microfilm Reel 1,214, Abraham Lopez
to Aaron Lopez, April 30, 1767.

77. *Commerce of Rhode Island,* 9: 455, 461, 467; Donnan, *Documents
Illustrative,* III, 273–77.

78. Donnan, *Documents Illustrative,* II, 524–25; III, 297, 326–27; *Jamaica
Mercury and Kingston Weekly Advertiser* (later the *Royal Gazette*) in
the issues for May 22, Supplement; June 5, Supplement; June 12, Supplement; July 3, Supplement; and September 18, 1779, Supplement;
Proceedings of the Hon. House of Assembly of Jamaica, on the Sugar

and Slave-Trade, in a Session Which Began the 23d of October, 1792 (London: Stephen Fuller, 1793), 20; Richardson, Bristol, Africa and Eighteenth-Century Slave Trade, IV, 71; and JA, Records of the Court of Chancery, 1A/3/73, 7.

79. Coppells & Aguilar took delivery of 413 slaves shipped on the Molly in 1779; see Jamaica Mercury and Kingston Weekly Advertiser, May 15, 1779, Supplement. Aguilar's first name is known from a list of 150 merchants who in 1781 pledged to accept specified British and Spanish coin in an effort to relieve the colony's shortage of hard currency, and thereby prevent potential hardship on the island. The subscribers to the pledge included eight Jewish merchants and one company, viz, J. I. Bernal, Alexandre Lindo, Isaac Nunes Da Costa, Emanuel B. Lousada, Abraham Aguilar, Benjamin Dias Fernandez, A. M. Bonito, Abraham Bernal, and the firm of Dias, Tavares & Co. The non-Jewish subscribers included John and William Coppell, but whether one or both were Aguilar's partners in Coppells & Aguilar is not known. See Royal Gazette, October 27, 1781.

80. Two Reports (One Presented the 16th of October, the Other on the 12th of November, 1788) from the Committee of the Honourable House of Assembly of Jamaica on the Subject of the Slave-Trade (London: B. White and Son, 1789), 11, 20–21; Report of the Lords of the Committee of Council, LXIX, 262–63. For Hibbert & Jackson's activity during the 1760s as consignee of slaves imported on vessels from Bristol, see Richardson, Bristol, Africa and Eighteenth-Century Slave Trade, III, 142, 155, 157, 164, 167, 177, 180–81, 220, 230. On the Hibberts, see Richard B. Sheridan, "The Slave Trade to Jamaica, 1702–1808," in B. W. Higman, ed., Trade, Government and Society in Caribbean History, 1700–1920 (Kingston: Heinemann Educational Books, 1983), 10; and Richard B. Sheridan, "The Commercial and Financial Organization of the British Slave Trade, 1750–1807," 2d ser., Economic History Review 11 (1958–59): 255. Captain Peleg's remark is in Donnan, Documents Illustrative, III, 330.

81. Sheridan, "Commercial and Financial Organization," 255.

82. See Appendix VIII for data regarding the Jewish population of Montego Bay in 1774. The name of a deceased Jewish merchant who had resided there was also included in the census.

83. Donnan, Documents Illustrative, III, 302–3; Cornwall Chronicle, December 14, December 21, 1776; and March 15, May 3, 1777.

84. Donnan, Documents Illustrative, II, 382. For the incident in 1689, see the discussion in Chapter Two, supra, at n. 48.

85. Colin Palmer, Human Cargoes: The British Slave Trade to Spanish America, 1700–1739 (Urbana: University of Illinois Press, 1981), 62.

Prior to the episode described here, Furtado & Co. purchased 25 slaves early in 1723, "Messrs. Furtado & Torres" purchased 35 later that year, and Furtado & Bonfills purchased 75 in 1724, all from the Royal African Company; PRO, T 70/958, 41–42, 59–60, 185–86. For David Orobio Furtado's activity exporting slaves to the Spanish Coast in the 1740s, see the discussion, supra, at n. 62.

86. PRO, CO 137/45, no. 51. The writer was Gilbert Heathcote, a major West Indian trader; Curtis Nettels, "England and the Spanish-American Trade, 1680–1715," *Journal of Modern History* 3 (1931): 20.

87. Long, *History of Jamaica*, I, 506. For examples, see the clearing-out records at PRO, CO 142/15, entries for March 25, 1748–March 24, 1749, June 25–September 29, 1752; CO 142/16, December 25, 1753–March 25, 1754, March 25–June 25, 1755, March 25–June 25, 1757; CO 142/18, December 25, 1764–March 25, 1765, March 25–June 25, 1765, June 25–September 25, 1765; CO 142/17, June 29–September 29, 1767, June 29–September 29, 1768. North Carolina was a particularly frequent destination in North America.

88. BL, Records of the South Sea Company, Add. Ms. 25,552, 84–85. On the other hand, Isaac and Benjamin Bravo legally acquired a combined total of 176 slaves in three purchases from the Royal African Company at the beginning of 1723; PRO, T 70/958, 37–38, 41–42, 43–44.

89. Jean O. McLachlan, *Trade and Peace with Old Spain, 1667–1750: A Study of the Influence of Commerce on Anglo-Spanish Diplomacy in the First Half of the Eighteenth Century* (Cambridge: Cambridge University Press, 1940), 85.

90. *Report of the Lords of the Committee of Council,* LXIX, 262–63, for total exports between 1742 and 1769. For the Naval Office years and the total in each year, see Appendix IV, Table 2, infra. The number of exported slaves in the years covered by the Naval Office records was higher, but several omissions of the number of slaves on board reduce the total to the figure of 25,728 reported here. Missing data occur in connection with both non-Jewish and Jewish exporters, although in only two instances among the latter: Moses Mendes & Co., and David Orobio Furtado, both in 1745. The number of slaves for eight shipments on vessels owned by non-Jews is missing for the same year.

91. The four located in Jamaica were David Bravo, David Orobio Furtado, Aaron Lamera & Co., and Moses Mendes & Co. All appear on the Kingston poll tax for 1745. Jacob Franks was the New Yorker, while Isaac Mendes Da Costa & Co.'s location is not known. For the years and the known totals exported by each, as well as the destinations of their shipments, see Appendix IV, Table 3.

92. For discussion of the identification process, see Appendix I, infra.

93. Edwards, *History, Civil and Commercial*, I, 219.
94. [Trelawny], *Essay Concerning Slavery*, 18.
95. Long reported that 166,904 slaves resided in Jamaica in 1768; *History of Jamaica*, I, 57–58; II, 229. That his figure was based on poll-tax records is evident from the Long Papers at BL, Add. Ms. 12,435, 32, "An Estimate of the Number of Negroes . . . in Jamaica calculated from the Poll Tax Roll ariseing from the Law Pass'd in December 1768. . . ." (The total given there is 166,914.)
96. See n. 95 above.
97. For the poll-tax results, see the discussion at n. 3, supra. In 1776, Port Royal reportedly had 3 streets, 2 or 3 lanes, and about 200 houses; Kingston about 1,665 houses and 11,000 inhabitants; and Spanish Town around 20 streets and 4,000 inhabitants; *North-American and West-Indian Gazetteer*, entries for "Kingston," "Port Royal," and "Jago De La Vega, St." (i.e., Spanish Town). For Port Royal's meager Jewish population in the early nineteenth century, see Chapter Five, infra.
98. Long, *History of Jamaica*, II, 62, 188, for The Cross and Lacovia; and Andrade, *Record of the Jews in Jamaica*, 214–15, for Lucea and Savanna la Mar. The evidence for a synagogue at Lucea is in the wills of Issac Da Silva Fonseca (1767) and Jacob Lopez Torres (1768). The latter also mentions the synagogue at Savanna la Mar. Both wills may be consulted at AJA, Jamaica Wills.

     A Jewish shopkeeper, Emanuel Moreno, alias Browne, resided at Lacovia as early as 1699 and until his death in 1712; JA, Records of the Court of Chancery, 1A/3/6, 189–92. For others there between 1749 and 1803, see IJ, MS 1,896, Tombstone Inscriptions Compiled by Philip Wright, Jewish Tombstone Inscriptions, for Jacob Abraham, Isaac Frois, Sr., Isaac Frois, Jr., Rachel Lindo, and Abraham Tavares, Sr.
99. By the late 1760s, according to Long, *History of Jamaica*, II, 215, 140 vessels annually entered and cleared from Montego Bay, and it had emerged as an important center for the distribution of slaves.
100. BL, Long Papers, Add. Ms. 12,435, 3–4. The relevant data are reported in Appendix VIII, infra.
101. BL, Long Papers, Add. Ms. 12,435, 3–4, 7.
102. There were undoubtedly more households in Montego Bay (some of which may have been Jewish), for the town reportedly contained 146 houses in 1774 (55 more than the 91 slaveholding households); and the parish in its entirety had a small non-slaveholding white population of 120 men who could bear arms and 30 women and children. In BL, Long Papers, Add. Ms. 12,435, 3–4.

Notes to Chapter 4

1. Population estimates for 1715 are provided by Robert Cohen, "Early Caribbean Jewry: A Demographic Perspective," *Jewish Social Studies* 45(1983): 124. These numbers are indicative of little if any growth in the Jewish population since the late seventeenth century. In 1680, there had been seventy Jewish families; see Chapter Two, supra.

2. Spanish and Portuguese Jews' Congregation (London), Records of Congregation Nidhe Israel, Barbados, Ms. 328. The members and pensioners in 1798 are listed in Appendix X, infra.

3. Bryan Edwards, *The History, Civil and Commercial, of the British Colonies in the West Indies*, 2 vols. (1793; New York: Arno Press, 1972), I, 340; James C. Brandow, "A Young Virginian's Visit to Barbados, 1771–1772," *Journal of the Barbados Museum and Historical Society* 35 (1975–78): 75. Information about the fire of 1766, including the partial destruction of Swan Street, was reported in "An Address in Favour of the Sufferers at Barbadoes," *Gentleman's Magazine* 36 (1766): 425–26. The accompanying map of Bridgetown identifies Swan Street as "Swan Street or Jew Street." For Swan Street as the town's Jewish quarter, see Stephen Alexander Fortune, *Merchants and Jews: The Struggle for British West Indian Commerce, 1650–1750* (Gainesville: University Presses of Florida, 1984), 12, 160.

4. New York Public Library, Weather Almanac of Hugh Hall, Jr., Kept at Boston, Barbados, and in England, 1714–17, entries facing December 1717. Hall listed Speightstown by name but included Bridgetown under the designation "[Parish of] St. Michael's Levy." For population estimates in 1710, see "T. Walduck's Letters from Barbados, 1710," *Journal of the Barbados Museum and Historical Society* 15 (1947–48): 30. Jew Street in Speightstown is mentioned in the 1711 will of Ra[c]hel Mendes; Bertram Wallace Korn, "Barbadian Jewish Wills, 1676–1740," in Bertram Wallace Korn, ed., *A Bicentennial Festschrift for Jacob Rader Marcus* (Waltham and New York: American Jewish Historical Society and Ktav Publishing House, 1976), 311.

5. The incident began when a young non-Jewish guest attending a Jewish wedding was accused of theft and attacked by several Jews as he lay sick outside the festivities. He was bound over to court, but, as reported by the *New York Gazette,* the outraged citizens of Speightstown "rais'd a Mob," expelled the entire Jewish population from the town, and leveled the synagogue. See Samuel Oppenheim, "The Jews in Barbados in 1739. An Attack upon Their Synagogue. Their Long Oath," *Publications of the American Jewish Historical Society* 22 (1914): 197–98.

6. Richard Hall and Richard Hall, *Acts Passed in the Island of Barbados. From 1643, to 1762, Inclusive* (London: Richard Hall, 1764), 382.
7. Henry J. Cadbury, "An Account of Barbados 200 Years Ago," *Journal of the Barbados Museum and Historical Society* 9 (1941–42): 82. For examples of merchants and shopkeepers, see the following in the collection at AJA, Caribbean Jewry Commercial Documents, 1708–90: Benjamin Abarbanel, Joseph Abarbanel, Phineas Abarbanel, Baruch Barrow, Joseph Barrow, Mordecai Burgos, David Nunes Castello, Samuel De Campos, Isaac De Piza, Sr., Moses Franco, Abraham Gomez, Abraham Lindo, Jr., Simeon Massiah, Joseph Mendes, Jacob Monsanto, Eliezer Montefiore, David Nunes, Isaac Nunes, Moses Nunes, Phineas Nunes, Aaron Pereira, David Valverde, and Elias Valverde, all of whom were merchants. Jacob Arobus, David Burgos, and David Da Costa were shopkeepers. For the commercial activity of Mathias Lopez, see AJA, Microfilm Reel 1,687, Account Book of General Merchandise Kept by Mathias Lopez of Barbados [1779–89].

   For merchants and shopkeepers named in wills, see Korn, "Barbadian Jewish Wills," 305, 309, 313; and Wilfred S. Samuel, "A Review of the Jewish Colonists in Barbados in the Year 1680," *Transactions of the Jewish Historical Society of England* 13 (1932–35): 57, 59–60, 81–82, 85–88. Despite its title, the latter includes wills through 1739.
8. Residents of Barbados, followed by vessel names in parentheses, were Hezekiah Pacheco (*Dolphin* and *Goodspeed*, the latter owned in partnership with Moses Pacheco); Ephraim Castello (*New Rebecca*, entering and clearing five times, and *New Bob*); and Moses Franco and Jacob Valverde (*Friends Adventure*, entering and clearing twice, and owned with Mark Waters, a non-Jewish partner). Hezekiah Pacheco is known to have been an inhabitant of Barbados from the will of David Pachexe [*sic*] of Jamaica; in AJA, Jamaica Wills, 1692–1798, Microfilm Reel 140. He later owned the *Dolphin* in partnership with a non-Jew, Jacob Biddle. Ephraim Castello, Moses Franco, and Jacob Valverde resided in Barbados in the parish of St. Michael, where they owned slaves in 1729; PRO, CO 28/21, 165b, 166, 168.

   Jewish shipowners who did not reside in Barbados included Esther Pinheiro of Nevis, who owned the *Samuel* and the *Abigail*. Isaac Lopez of Boston, together with Joseph Lopez, owned the *Barnthy* [*sic*], a vessel registered in London. Alone, he owned the *J[o]s[e]p[h] and Isaac*, registered at Boston. Moses Levy, Samuel Levy, and Jacob Franks of New York owned the *Abigail*. For Pinheiro, see the discussion in this chapter, infra, and for the three New Yorkers, see Chapter Six, infra. For Isaac Lopez, see Jacob R. Marcus, *The Colonial American Jew, 1492–1776*, 3 vols. (Detroit: Wayne State University Press, 1970), I, 419; II, 660.

Vessels owned by Jews who did not reside in Barbados and in partnership with non-Jews included the *John and Elizabeth* of Connecticut, entering and clearing twice, which belonged to John Burrows and Abraham De Lucena; for the latter, a New Yorker, see Leo Hershkowitz, ed., *Wills of Early New York Jews (1704–1799)* (New York: American Jewish Historical Society, 1967), 33. Abraham Franco Nunes owned the *Elizabeth*, registered in London, with four non-Jewish partners, while Moses Levy, Samuel Levy, and Jacob Franks, already noted as residents of New York, owned the *Charlotte* with Henry Cuylers. The *Isaac and Rachel* of Connecticut was the property of John Wyard and Isaac De Medina, who resided first in New York and later at Hartford; Marcus, *Colonial American Jew*, I, 312, II, 544. De Medina and Wyard also owned the *Merchants Delight*, along with two other partners, Thomas Clark and William Wickham. The *Eagle*, which entered in and cleared out three times, belonged to Isaac Lopez of Boston, noted above, and Adino Bulfinch; the vessel was registered at Boston.

For the vessels and owners listed here, see PRO, CO 33/15, 66b, 67b, 68a, 68b, 70a, 72a, 73a, 73b, 74b, 84a, 87b, 91a, 91b, 95b, 97a, 100a, 100b, 102a, 103a, and 104a.

9. PRO, CO 33/16, listings for vessels that entered March 25–June 25, June 25–September 25, September 25–December 25, 1735, and December 25, 1735–March 25, 1736 (where the missing owner's vessel appears).

10. PRO, T 64/49 for the records of vessels that arrived January 5–April 5, April 5–July 5, July 5–October 10, 1774, and October 10, 1774–January 5, 1775. The *Flora, Gaspy [sic]*, and *Gasper [sic]* were owned by Aaron Lopez of Newport, Rhode Island, while the *Jacob* was owned by Lopez, his father-in-law Jacob Rodrigues Rivera, and Benjamin Wright, their non-Jewish associate and factor stationed at Savanna la Mar, Jamaica. For the latter, see Chapter Three, supra, at n. 76. For Lopez and Rivera, see Chapter Six, infra.

11. For all slave imports recorded by the Naval Office between June 25, 1728 and January 5, 1780, see Appendix IV, Table 4, infra. The sixty arrived on the *Margaret and Susannah*, registered in Barbados and owned by Jno. David, Ezekiel David, and Samuel De La Cruze; PRO, CO 33/16, entering-in, March 25–June 25, 1736. David was apparently a family name among Sephardic Jews, but there are no Davids among the Jewish tombstones in Barbados; Lionel D. Barnett, ed., *Bevis Marks Records Being Contributions to the History of the Spanish and Portuguese Congregation of London. Part II: Abstracts of the Ketubot or Marriage-Contracts of the Congregation from Earliest Times until 1837* (Oxford: The University Press by Charles Batey, 1949), 126, 128, 129,

and E. M. Shilstone, tr., *Monumental Inscriptions in the Burial Ground of the Jewish Synagogue at Bridgetown, Barbados* (N.p.: N.p., n.d.), passim. Also, there was a "Jon. David" whose daughter was baptized in St. Michael parish in 1720; Joanne Mcree Sanders, *Barbados Records: Baptisms, 1637–1800* (Baltimore: Genealogical Publishing Co., 1984), 64.

12. Elizabeth Donnan, ed., *Documents Illustrative of the History of the Slave Trade to America*, 4 vols. (Washington, D.C.: Carnegie Institution of Washington, 1930–35), II, 25–28.

13. PRO, CO 28/18, 321–25, Entitled "Barbadoes. Liste of Negroes imported into this Island from the 4th March 1707, to the 16th September 1726," the compilation did not list consignees between 1707 and 1712. Another copy is at PRO, CO 33/15, 4–8. Total imports reported by the governor for 1713–September 16, 1726, numbering 46,004, are 87.2 percent of the total of 52,731 for 1713–26 (inclusive) reported in Richard B. Sheridan, *Sugar and Slavery: An Economic History of the British West Indies, 1623–1775* (Baltimore: Johns Hopkins University Press, 1973), 505.

14. Burgos owned slaves in the parish of St. Michael in 1729; PRO, CO 28/21, 165. For his 1736 will, see Samuel, "Jewish Colonists in Barbados," 88.

15. For the sources, see Table 4.2.

16. The factors were Barrow & Rowe; Daniel & Lytcott; John Deverall; Hannington & Stritch; John Haslen; Jones & Ewing; David Minvielle & Co.; Smith & Dowling; Smith & Walker; Alexander Stevenson; Stevenson & Went; and John Thomas. All are in David Richardson, ed., *Bristol, Africa and the Eighteenth-Century Slave Trade to America*, 4 vols. (Volumes 38, 39, 42, and 47 of the Bristol Record Society's Publications) (Gloucester: Alan Sutton Publishing, 1986–96), III, 39, 41, 44, 71, 97, 169, 192, 202, 218, 226, 228; IV, 13, 55; and in Donnan, *Documents Illustrative*, III, 299.

17. Jacob Rodrigues Rivera and Aaron Lopez to Captain Nathaniel Briggs, July 4, 1770, examined at the gallery of Kenneth W. Rendell, Inc., New York City, December 8, 1995; and AJA, Aaron Lopez Papers, Microfilm Reel 1,213 for Daniel & Lytcott to Jacob Rodrigues Rivera and Aaron Lopez, February 19, 1771.

18. PRO, 33/16, 33/17, T 64/48, 64/49, passim.

19. See Chapter Three, supra, at n. 59.

20. Information supplied in April 1997 by the Department of Archives, Black Rock, St. James, Barbados.

21. PRO, CO 28/21, 104–9, 165–209. The list is of the levy imposed in 1729 for 1730.

22. Governor Worsley of Barbados to the Duke of Newcastle, December 4, 1729, in *CSP*, XXXVI (1728–29), 541. Noncompliance continued; on April 23, 1730, Worsley informed Newcastle that, for 1729, 689 slaveholders paid the levy and that 2,719 had not. In 1730, those who reported their holdings totaled 120, while 3,331 failed to report. See *CSP*, XXXVII (1730), 88–89.

23. See Appendix XI, infra, for all Jewish individuals, both those who reported and those who did not, as well as for parties whose religion is not certain.

24. The six were Abraham Carvalho, Lebanna De Leon, David Lopez, Moses Lopez, Deborah Ulloa, and Hester Ulloa; PRO, CO 28/21, 201–3. Simon Ffretto has not been counted as Jewish for reasons explained in Chapter Two, supra, at n. 18. Isaac Levine, despite his name, has also not been classified as Jewish; for Levine as a non-Jewish name on the island in the 1720s, see Sanders, *Barbados Records: Baptisms*, 334. Only 350 slaves were reported in all of St. Peter's; PRO, CO 28/21, 182.

     David Israel of the parish of St. Thomas (who failed to report his slaveholdings) was also not Jewish; Sanders, *Barbados Records: Baptisms*, 518–19.

25. *CSP*, XLI (1734–35), 90.

26. "List of the Inhabitants of Nevis with the Number of Their Slaves, 13 March 1707–8," in Vere Langford Oliver, ed., *Caribbeana Being Miscellaneous Papers Relating to the History, Genealogy, Topography, and Antiquities of the British West Indies*, 6 vols. (London: Mitchell, Hughes and Clarke, 1909–19), III, 173–79. The six were Isaac Lobatto (2 whites, 12 slaves); Hananiah Arobus (2 whites, 3 slaves); Isaac Pinheiro (6 whites, 9 slaves); Abraham Bueno De Mesquita (1 white, 8 slaves); Ralph Abendana (number of whites not given, 1 slave); and Solomon Israel (5 whites, 13 slaves).

27. Malcolm H. Stern, "A Successful Caribbean Restoration: The Nevis Story," *American Jewish Historical Quarterly* 61 (1971–72), 23. For the rise and decline in the general population, see Sheridan, *Sugar and Slavery*, 164.

     Archaeological investigation in the mid-1990s has led to the suggestion that the tombstone dated to 1768 may, in fact, have been erected in the 1680s. If so, the latest surviving Jewish tombstone on Nevis would date to 1730; *Caribbean Week*, December 7–20, 1996, 37. I am indebted to Horace Banbury for bringing this article to my attention.

28. Stern, "Successful Caribbean Restoration," 22–23, ns. 16, 17; Hershkowitz, *Wills of New York Jews*, 21–25.

29. PRO, CO 187/2, entering in for June 25–September 25, September 25–December 25, 1720, December 25, 1720–March 25, 1721, June 25–

December 25, 1721, June 25–September 25, 1722, March 25–June 25, 1723, March 25–June 25, 1724, December 25, 1724–March 25, 1725, September 25–December 25, 1725, December 25, 1726–March 25, 1727, June 25–September 25, 1727, March 25–June 25, 1728; clearing-out for June 25–September 25, 1720, March 25–June 25, 1721, September 25–December 25, 1721; and supra, n. 8.

30. Stern, "Successful Caribbean Restoration," 23.

Notes to Chapter 5

1. For the origins of the triennial registrations in the context of the anti-slavery movement, see B. W. Higman, *Slave Population and Economy in Jamaica, 1807–1834* (Cambridge: Cambridge University Press, 1976), 45–46.

2. Jacob A. P. M. Andrade, *A Record of the Jews in Jamaica from the English Conquest to the Present Time* (Kingston: Jamaica Times, 1941), 2, 45, 55. On disputes between the two groups, see Eli Faber, *A Time for Planting: The First Migration, 1654–1820* (Baltimore: Johns Hopkins University Press, 1992), 60–63.

3. The names of individuals who resided at Port Royal in the late 1700s and early 1800s appear in the congregational records of Kingston's two synagogues, copies and analyses of which are at AJA: Phyllis DeLisser, Analysed Register of Births & Marriages of the Ashkinazi Congregation 'Kahal Kodosh Shaanare Yosher Holy Congregation Gates of Right-eousness' English and German Jews, Kingston Jamaica; Phyllis DeLisser, Analysed Register of Births—Deaths—Marriages 1809–1907 of the Se-phardic Congregation 'Kaal Kadosh Shahar Ashamaim' 'Holy Congre-gation of Gate of Heaven' Founded 1693 Kingston Jamaica; and the photostat copies of the records of births and marriages at Jamaica in MSS Col 465, Box 1, Folder 1 and Folder 6.

4. Wolfe's marriage in 1805 is recorded in the photostats of Jamaica mar-riage records at AJA, MSS Col 465, Box 1, Folder 6.

5. Andrade, *Record of the Jews in Jamaica*, 39, 189. A census conducted in 1881 revealed that no Jews remained in Port Royal, while, of the island's 2,535 Jews, 1,087 resided in Kingston and 621 in St. Catherine, the parish in which Spanish Town is located; ibid., 279.

6. The assumption here is that all the Jews in the parish resided in Spanish Town. Their slaveholdings were generally not large enough to suggest residence on plantations outside the town; and Joseph C. De Leon, the Jewish individual with the largest number of slaves, forty-eight, also paid a trade tax, indicating that he was a merchant. The poll-tax list is

in JA, 2/2/19. For the Jewish entries and for entries whose religion is not certain, see Appendix VII, Table 2, infra.

7. The 1795 poll-tax list is at JA, 2/6/105. For all 167 Jewish entries and 18 entries whose religion is not certain, see Appendix VI, Table 3, infra.

8. Levi Sheftall of Savannah recorded the comings and goings of Jews from Jamaica in his diary during the 1780s; Malcolm H. Stern, ed., "The Sheftall Diaries: Vital Records of Savannah Jewry (1733–1808)," *American Jewish Historical Quarterly* 54 (1964–65): 252–55, 265. For Jamaican Jews who essayed life in New York during the 1790s because of disruptions to commerce caused by war between England and France, see Maxwell Whiteman, *Copper for America: The Hendricks Family and a National Industry, 1755–1939* (New Brunswick: Rutgers University Press, 1971), 69–71.

9. The poll-tax list for 1819 is in JA, 2/6/106. For the entries that were Jewish, for three firms that combined Jewish and non-Jewish partners, and for those whose religion is uncertain, see Appendix VI, Table 4, infra.

10. The total trade tax assessment in 1819 was 789–6–8. Of this, 625–11–8 was levied on 374 non-Jews; 130–10–0 on 104 Jews; 2–10–0 on three firms in which Jews and non-Jews were partners; and 30–15–0 on 25 entries whose religion is not certain. The average assessment for non-Jews was approximately 1–13–0, while that for Jews was lower, at 1–5–0.

11. For the 1769 figures, see Chapter Three, Table 3.2, supra.

12. For 1772, see Chapter Three, Table 3.2; for 1820, Appendix VII, Table 2, infra, for the trade tax assessments on the Jewish entries. Sixteen non-Jewish merchants and shopkeepers were assessed 74–10–0, averaging 4–13–0. Their nineteen Jewish counterparts were assessed 118–5–0, a more substantial average of approximately 6–4–0 each.

   The 1820 poll tax for St. Catherine did not distinguish between the inhabitants of Spanish Town and the rest of the parish. The assumption here is that all those who paid trade taxes resided in Spanish Town.

   The impact of the Jewish population on commerce in Kingston and Spanish Town is reflected in the annual almanacs published in the colony. They included calendars of the Jewish religious year with listings of major and minor holidays according to both the Hebrew and the secular calendars, as well as the dates of the Jewish calendar's lunar months. The holidays and the names of the months were printed in Hebrew letters and in English transliteration. The almanacs were probably useful not only to the Jewish population but also to non-Jews who patronized their businesses and wanted to know when they would be closed for religious observances. For examples, see, at BL, *An Almanack and Reg-*

ister for Jamaica for the Year of Our Lord 1776. Being Bissextile or Leap-Year (Jamaica: Joseph Thompson & Co., n.d.), and, at IJ, *The New Jamaica Almanack and Register* for 1796, 1798, and 1799.

13. The importance of Jamaica's Jewish merchants to the colony's trade with Spain's possessions in the western hemisphere long preceded the period examined here; see, supra, Chapter One at ns. 91 and 92 and Chapter Three at n. 40. Their continuing involvement with the Spanish trade predated Senior's arrival in Jamaica. Early in the 1800s, the firm of Da Costa & Co. at Kingston wrote to the firm of Moses Levy Newton in London that "commerce again seems to resume a buisy appearance, occaison'd by corresponding with the Spaniards (who are now coming in fast, & purchasing largely) . . . which induce us to trouble you . . . for a larger Scale than we usually write for. . . ."; PRO, C 114/41. Although the letter has no date, its context in this vast manuscript collection places it in the early 1800s.

Kingston's Jewish merchants were, however, hardly the only ones interested in the commerce that the colony enjoyed with the Spanish empire. When eighty-eight of the port's merchants protested early in 1805 to the vice admiral against the seizure of a Spanish vessel, citing the importance of the Spanish trade to the island's economy, eighty of them, or 90.9 percent, were non-Jewish. The eight Jewish firms were those of Lindo, Henriques & Lindo; Wolfe & Cohens; Cohen & Isaacs; Moses Bravo; Da Costa & Benaim; J. Aguilar, Jr.; Isaac Hatchwell; and Sol. G. Da Costa; *Royal Gazette,* February 9, 1805, Supplement.

14. A Retired Military Officer [Bernard Martin Senior], *Jamaica As It Was, As It Is, and As It May Be* (London: T. Hurst, 1835), preface, 16, 125–27.

15. DeLisser, Register of Births & Marriages of the Ashkinazi Congregation, for Aaron Samson at Alligator Pond (Manchester Parish) and Solomon Marks at Montego Bay; DeLisser, Register of Births—Deaths—Marriages 1809–1907 of the Sephardic Congregation, for Alexander Abrahams at Alligator Pond; and the AJA photostat file of Ashkenazic marriage records, Box 1, Folder 6, for Jewish households at Lucea, Falmouth, and Montego Bay, and in the parish of St. Elizabeth.

Jewish tombstone inscriptions for the entire island are at IJ, MS 1,896, Tombstone Inscriptions Compiled by Philip Wright. Publication of Wright's work occurred in 1997: Richard D. Barnett and Philip Wright, *The Jews of Jamaica: Tombstone Inscriptions, 1663–1880* (Jerusalem: Ben Zvi Institute, 1997).

Wills of Jews elsewhere on the island frequently provide the names of people other than the testators who also resided outside Kingston and Spanish Town. Examples include the wills of Noe Daniel Wetzlar, Benjamin Dias Fernandez, Alexander Dolphy, Nathan Hart, William Hendricks, and Anna Phillips; at IRO, XCV, 18; XCIX, 178; CV, 112; CXII, 156; CXVII, 174; and CXXII, 168.

For Jews outside Kingston and Spanish Town (parish of St. Catherine) in the 1817 slave register, see Appendix XII, Table 2.

16. PRO, C 114/40, for frequent letters from Solomon Arnold, and C 114/41 for correspondence from Samuel Solomon.

17. JA, 2/3/1, St. James Vestry Minutes, 1807–25, entry for the Vestry meeting of April 14, 1817. The nine Jewish merchants were Jacob P. Corinaldi, Isaac Gedelia, Moses Gedelia, Solomon Gedelia, Jacob Jacobs, Solomon Marks, Isaac Simon, Jacob Solomon, and Noe D. Wetzlar. Although they comprised 15.7 percent of the fifty-seven listed, they were assessed 9.8 percent of the entire levy (£15 out of £153).

18. [Senior], *Jamaica, As It Was*, 125.

19. N. Darnell Davis, "Notes on the History of the Jews in Barbados," *Publications of the American Jewish Historical Society* 18 (1909): 146, citing William Dickson, whose *Letters on Slavery* was published in London in 1789; Jerome S. Handler, ed., "Memoirs of an Old Army Officer: Richard A. Wyvill's Visits to Barbados in 1796 and 1806–7," *Journal of the Barbados Museum and Historical Society* 35 (1975–78): 29, n. 7.

20. Spanish and Portuguese Jews' Congregation, London, Records of Congregation Nidhe Israel, Barbados, Mss. 328, 329, 330, 331, and 333. For the names of all in the years indicated, see Appendix X, infra. Not all actually paid; some were "taken off," according to notations in the original records. For the Barbados community's gradual disappearance, see "Extracts from Various Records of the Early Settlement of the Jews in the Island of Barbados, W.I.," *Publications of the American Jewish Historical Society* 26 (1918): 252–55.

21. Lowell Joseph Ragatz, *The Fall of the Planter Class in the British Caribbean, 1763–1833* (1928; New York: Octagon Books, 1963), 145; Orlando Patterson, *The Sociology of Slavery: An Analysis of the Origins, Development and Structure of Negro Slave Society in Jamaica* (London: MacGibbon and Kee, 1967), 27.

22. *Report of the Lords of the Committee of Council Appointed for the Consideration of All Matters Relating to Trade and Foreign Plantations*, in House of Commons, *Sessional Papers of the Eighteenth Century, Reports and Papers, 1789, Slave Trade*, LXX, 181.

23. PRO, T 64/48, for returns for all four quarters in each of the years indicated.

24. Patterson, *Sociology of Slavery*, 291.

25. PRO, CO 142/19, entitled "An Account of all the Exports from the several Free ports in the Island of Jamaica, since their Establishment,"

and signed by the Inspector and Examiner of the Plantation Collector Accounts and by his clerk, who attested that the accounts of slaves going out of Kingston were complete. Exports of slaves were "specially mentioned by the Collectors in their Accounts," they explained, because such were "liable to a Duty," while other exports were, contrastingly, not as accurately reported.

26. Bryan Edwards, *The History, Civil and Commercial, of the British Colonies in the West Indies*, 2 vols. (1793; New York: Arno Press, 1972), I, 340; "The Autobiographical Manuscript of William Senhouse," *Journal of the Barbados Museum and Historical Society* 2 (1934–35): 200–208.

27. AJA, Aaron Lopez Papers, Microfilm Reel 1,212, Letter Book No. 625, David Pereira Mendes to Aaron Lopez, August 15, 1781. Mendes was the brother of Abraham Pereira Mendes, Lopez's floundering son-in-law. The letter was mailed to Leicester, Massachusetts, where Aaron Lopez resided after he fled from Rhode Island in 1777, likewise experiencing the effects of war; Stanley F. Chyet, *Lopez of Newport: Colonial American Merchant Prince* (Detroit: Wayne State University Press, 1970), 103, 156–58.

28. *Two Reports (One Presented the 16th of October, the Other on the 12th of November, 1788) from the Committee of the Honourable House of Assembly of Jamaica on the Subject of the Slave-Trade* (London: B. White and Son, 1789), 13–14; *Notes on the Two Reports from the Committee of the Honourable House of Assembly of Jamaica, Appointed to Examine into, and to Report to the House, the Allegations and Charges Contained in the Several Petitions Which Have Been Presented to the British House of Commons, on the Subject of the Slave Trade, and the Treatment of the Negroes* (London: James Phillips, 1789), 41.

29. See Chapter Two, supra, at n. 5; and Chapter Three, at n. 22.

30. *Jamaica Mercury and Kingston Weekly Advertiser* (later *Royal Gazette*), October 2, 1779, Supplement, 2–3; and November 20, 1779. Bernal, a naturalized British subject who originated in Bayonne, France, believed that his ordeal began because he had provided assistance to several French prisoners of war. Gomez was also, reputedly, a naturalized British subject.

31. John Hartog, "The Honen Daliem Congregation of St. Eustatius," *American Jewish Archives* 19 (1967): 61; Isaac S. Emmanuel and Suzanne A. Emmanuel, *History of the Jews of the Netherlands Antilles*, 2 vols. (Cincinnati: American Jewish Archives, 1970), I, 518–27.

32. Robert A. Selig, "The French Capture of St. Eustatius, 26 November 1781," *Journal of Caribbean History* 27 (1993): 130–31; J. Franklin

Jameson, "St. Eustatius in the American Revolution," *American Historical Review* 8 (1902–3): 685–88, 696–700; Barbara Tuchman, *The First Salute* (New York: Alfred A. Knopf, 1988), 97.

33. Jameson, "St. Eustatius," 684, for the island's very small sugar-growing capacity.

34. Ibid., 705, and n. 1 there.

35. *The Massachusetts Spy,* May 24, 1781, 4; and May 31, 1781, 2.

36. *Royal Gazette,* August 18, 1781, 521.

37. *Royal Gazette,* October 11, 1783, Supplement, 719; October 18, 1783, Supplement, 733.

38. R. C. Dallas, *The History of the Maroons from Their Origin to the Establishment of Their Chief Tribe at Sierra Leone,* 2 vols. (1803; London: Frank Cass and Co., 1968), I, 3–5.

39. Patterson, *Sociology of Slavery,* 291, as reported in England in the late 1780s. The figures recorded by the Naval Office in Jamaica were remarkably similar: 6,167 in 1782, 15,238 in 1784, and 11,410 in 1785; PRO, CO 142/19, 142/20, and 142/22.

40. PRO, CO 142/19, "Account of Exports."

41. Edwards, *History, Civil and Commercial,* I, 205.

42. See Chapter Three, supra, at ns. 49 and 50.

43. PRO, CO 142/22, entering in and clearing out for December 29, 1784–March 29, 1785, March 29–June 29, 1785, June 29–September 29, 1785, and September 29, 1785–December 29, 1785.

44. David Samuda, whose vessel, the *Hector,* arrived from London with plantation supplies, dry goods, and wine during the first quarter of 1785. The *Hector* returned to London with sugar, rum, logwood, fustic, and mahogany during the following quarter of 1785, as did a second vessel owned by Samuda & Co., the *Withywood,* carrying sugar and rum to London. A Samuda appears in *Lloyd's Register 1790* (London: Gregg Press, n.d.) as the owner of the *Withywood,* sailing between London-Memel and London-Jamaica, and as the owner of the *Fonseca,* described as a "constant Trader" between London-Jamaica. (Fonseca was a Sephardic family name.)

The Samudas had a long-standing trading relationship with Jamaica. "D. Samude" appears in *Lloyd's Register 1764* (London: Gregg Press, n.d.) as owner of the *Esther,* running between London-Jamaica. In *Lloyd's Register 1776* (London: Gregg Press, n.d.), M. Samuda is listed as owner of the *Judith,* London-Jamaica; and Samuda & Co. as owner of the *Withywood,* the *Susannah,* the *Esther,* the *George Booth,* and the *Princess Royal,* all of them sailing between London-Jamaica.

From London, David Samuda was involved in several suits in Jamaica's Court of Chancery during the last quarter of the eighteenth

century; see JA, Records of the Court of Chancery, 1A/3/67, 407; 1A/3/
134, 420; 1A/3/135, 356; 1A/3/138, 187; and 1A/3/199, 280.

By the late 1780s, David Samuda was a leader of London's Jewish
community. He established the company of David Samuda & Sons in
the early 1800s. Samuda died on January 30, 1824 at the age of fifty-
eight, and was identified in his obituary notice as a merchant. See *Gentleman's Magazine* 94 (1824): Part One, 189; and *The Jewish Encyclo-
pedia* (New York: Funk and Wagnalls, 1909), XI, 4.

45. Daniel Ximenes of Daniel Ximenes & Co, and Moses Franks. Ximenes
may well have resided in Kingston. In 1783 he married one of the Jewish
community's daughters, Abigail Lousada, the daughter of one of its
leading merchants; *Royal Gazette*, January 11, 1783, Supplement, lists
her father, Emmanuel Baruch Lousada, Esquire, as one of the three
largest Jewish contributors to a fund for English captives. The marriage
announcement is in ibid., November 29, 1783, Supplement. Moreover,
in 1785, Ximenes's vessel, the *Abigail*, his new wife's name, was registered at Kingston. It entered Jamaica on six occasions with flour, corn,
cotton, mahogany, and indigo from Hispaniola, and cleared out to St.
Thomas, three times in ballast and once with slaves.

Moses Franks, of Moses Franks & Co., owned the *Betsey*, registered
at Tortola, which cleared out one time from Jamaica for Philadelphia
with sugar and rum. For two possibilities for Moses Franks, one of
whom was not Jewish (because his mother was not), see Leo Hershkowitz and Isidore S. Meyer, eds., *The Lee Max Friedman Collection of
American Jewish Colonial Correspondence: Letters of the Franks Family
(1733–1748)* (Waltham: American Jewish Historical Society, 1968), xvi,
xxiv, 129, and the genealogical chart opposite 70. For yet another possibility, see the Moses Franks of Philadelphia described by Jacob Rader
Marcus, *United States Jewry, 1776–1985*, 4 vols. (Detroit: Wayne State
University Press, 1989–93), I, 58–59. Despite the uncertainty, Franks
has been counted here as Jewish because of the latter, who resided in
Philadelphia, the destination of the *Betsey* from Jamaica.

46. In addition to Lindo, the others were A. M. Bonito & Co., owner of the
Rachel and the *Kingston*, importing mahogany, cotton, and indigo from
Hispaniola, rice and shingles from Charleston, and exporting slaves to
St. Thomas; Isaac Mendes Pereira & Co., owner of the *Two Friends*,
importing mahogany, cotton, and indigo from Hispaniola and exporting
slaves, provisions, and dry goods to Curaçao; Aaron Nunes Henriques
& Co., owner of the *Friendship* and the *Fortune*, importing cotton and
indigo from Hispaniola, and mahogany and sarsaparilla from the Mosquito Coast; Moses Ferro, owner of the *Two Friends*, importing mahogany from the Spanish mainland; I. I. Bernal & Co., owner of the *Fortune*

and the *Friendship,* importing mahogany, shell, and sarsaparilla from the Mosquito Coast and sarsaparilla from St. Andreas; and Judah Phillips, owner of the *Rover,* importing mahogany and cotton from the Mosquito Coast, timber, cotton, tortoise shell, and deer skins from St. Andreas. That Phillips was Jewish is apparent from the diary of Levi Sheftall of Savannah, Georgia, who made a point of recording the arrivals and departures of Jewish individuals there. Accordingly, on June 7, 1788 he noted that "Judah Phillips and Moses Gabay returned to Jamaica, they came here a short time before in their own vessell." In Stern, "Sheftall Diaries," 255.

Lloyd's Register 1790 described the *Esther,* property of A. Lindo, and the *Esther Lindo,* owned by Lindo & Co., each as a "constant trader" on the London-Jamaica run. On May 28, 1790, the *Esther Lindo* cleared Jamaica for London laden with sugar, cotton, pimento, Nicaragua wood, coffee, ginger, rum, wine, silver plate, sweetmeats, tamarinds, balsam, copper, castor oil, and tortoise shell; *Daily Advertiser,* May 29, 1790.

A. M. Bonito, Isaac Mendes Pereira, Aaron Nunes Henriques, Moses Ferro, J. *[sic]* I. Bernal, and Alexandre Lindo all appear on the lists of Kingston merchants in the *Royal Gazette* issues of October 26, 1781, Supplement, and January 11, 1783, Supplement.

47. PRO, CO 142/23, for December 29, 1795–March 29, 1796, June 29–September 29, 1796, and September 29–December 29, 1796. Of the 587 vessels entering in, 548 (93.3 percent) were owned by non-Jews, and 27 (4.5 percent) had owners whose names were not listed or whose religion cannot be determined. Of the 699 that exited, 623 (89.1 percent) belonged to non-Jews, while 59 (8.4 percent) were either not listed or their religion cannot be ascertained.

48. PRO, CO 142/24, records for December 29, 1804–March 29, 1805, March 29–June 29, 1805, June 29–September 29, 1805, and September 29–December 29, 1805. Of the 788 that entered in, 739 (93.7 percent) belonged to non-Jews, and 40 (5 percent) had owners who were not listed or whose religion cannot be identified. Of the 861 clearing out, 792 (91.9 percent) belonged to non-Jews; 58 (6.7 percent) had owners who were not listed or whose religion cannot be determined.

49. The seven were A[braham] A[lexandre] Lindo & Co., owner of *L'Voltiguer* and *Hindostan*; Leon Worms & Co. *(Flying Fish)*; Judah Phillips *(Rover, Fortune, Margery,* and *Eliza)*; Levy Barned *(Chance)*; Solomon Flash *(Lady Nugent; Lion)*; Solomon Wolfe & Co. *(Hope)*; and M[ashod] Shannon & Co. *(Swift)*. All but Phillips and Wolfe appear in the vital records of the colony's two Jewish congregations at Kingston; see DeLisser, Register of Births & Marriages of the Ashkinazi Congre-

gation, and DeLisser, Register of Births—Deaths—Marriages 1809–1907 of the Sephardic Congregation, both passim. For Phillips, see n. 46, supra. Solomon Wolfe appears in the records of the Jewish firm of Moses Levy Newton of London between 1797 and 1799; PRO, C 114/97, LXXII, 1–2. For Abraham Alexandre Lindo, see the discussion, infra. Shannon (pronounced Sha-known) was a Sephardic family name; for Mashod Shannon's marriage to Rachel B. Tavares in 1813, Joseph Shannon's to Gidla P. Phillips in 1824, and the births of several Shannon children between 1825 and 1841, see the records of Kingston's Sephardic congregation.

50. The five were Moses Myers (owner of *Fame, Eliza, Paragon,* and *Emily,* all registered at Norfolk); Isaac Aguilar & Co. (*Jamaica Planter, Lady Penrhyn, Jackson Junior, Arethura,* and *Esther Lindo,* all registered at London); M. L. Newton & Co. and Moses Levy & Co. (*Enterprise,* registered at London); David Samuda & Co. (*Dorset,* registered at London); and Moses Franks (*Democrat,* registered at Philadelphia). The two uncertain cases were those of Isaac Meyer (*Liberty*); and Sol. D'Agu[i]lar (*Pellas,* registered at Liverpool).

For Moses Myers of Norfolk, Virginia, see Marcus, *United States Jewry,* I, 90, 143–45. According to the vital records of Kingston's two synagogues, Aguilars resided in Jamaica, but none was named Isaac or Sol[omon] in the late 1700s or early 1800s; for the full reference to the synagogue records, see n. 3, supra. *Lloyd's Register 1790* lists "Aguilr & Co." as the owner of not only the *Jamaica Planter* but also the *Alexandre* and the *Three Sisters,* where each of the three is described as a "constant trader" between London-Jamaica. Moreover, Isaac Aguilar was one of the 182 members of Lloyd's in 1790, according to the "List of the Members of the Society for 1790" included in the register. For the London firm of Lindo, Aguilar & Dias, later Aguilar, Dias & Son, see Chapter One, supra, at ns. 107 and 108. For David Samuda of London, see n. 44 in the present chapter. On Moses Franks, see n. 45, supra.

The *Enterprise,* which entered in and cleared from Jamaica for London in 1805, was listed variously as owned by Moses Levy & Co. and by M[oses] L[evy] Newton & Co., reflecting the evolution of the London firm's name. Newton and Levy were partners, but Levy took Newton's name after the latter died in 1800. Between 1800 and 1823, when Levy died, the company was therefore known as the firm of Moses Levy Newton; see K. E. Ingram, *Sources of Jamaican History, 1655–1838: A Bibliographic Survey with Particular Reference to Manuscript Sources,* 2 vols. (Zug: Inter Documentation Company, 1976), II, 899.

51. For the years and arrivals in each year for which Naval Office records survive between 1780 and mid-1807, see Appendix IV, Table 1, infra.

52. PRO, CO 142/19, 142/20, 142/22. For the number of exports in each year, see Appendix IV, Table 2. According to one set of figures submitted to the British government in the late 1780s, 14,447 slaves were exported from Jamaica in 1784–87, while according to a second set, the total was 15,224; *Report of the Lords of Committee of Council,* LXX, 197; LXXI, 207–8. The number in the Naval Office records for the same period of time is 3,496, or 24.1 percent of the first figure and 22.9 percent of the second.

53. PRO, CO 142/21, 142/23, 142/24. For the annual totals, see Appendix IV, Table 2.

54. The six during the 1780s who resided in Jamaica were A. M. Bonito & Co.; Isaac Mendes Pereira & Co.; Moses Ferro & Co.; Aaron Nunes Henriques & Co.; Judah Phillips; and D[aniel] M[endes] Seixas. For the first five, see n. 46, supra. "Messrs. Dan[iel] Mendes Seixas" appears among the Jewish merchants in the *Royal Gazette,* Supplement issue of January 11, 1783. The one who may have resided in Jamaica was Daniel Ximenes; see n. 45, supra. In the 1790s, A[braham] A[lexandre] Lindo & Co., and Isaac Meyer sent out small shipments. For the activity of all these exporters, see Appendix IV, Table 3, which lists destinations and the numbers of slaves shipped.

55. *Royal Gazette,* Supplement issues for June 2, September 15, and December 29, 1781. For Coppells & Aguilar's factoring activity in 1779, see Chapter Three, at n. 79. The partnership of Coppells & Aguilar ended sometime shortly before February 1, 1783; a notice in the Supplement issue of the *Royal Gazette* on that date announced that it had been dissolved for some time and that John Coppell intended to leave the island. Another notice in the same issue informed the public that Aguilar also planned to emigrate.

56. *Two Reports from the Committee of the Honourable House of Assembly of Jamaica,* 11–12, 25.

57. *Report, Resolutions, and Remonstrance, of the Honourable the Council and Assembly of Jamaica, at a Joint Committee, on the Subject of the Slave-Trade, in a Session Which Began the 20th of October 1789* (London: B. White and Son, 1790), 16; and *Daily Advertiser,* February 5, 1790. Reporting on a shipment on board the *King Pepple,* Lindo indicated that an "epidemic flux," traceable to unripe yams, had killed approximately 150 slaves during the Atlantic crossing, and that approximately 20 more had died after the vessel arrived at Jamaica.

58. *Jamaica Mercury and Kingston Weekly Advertiser,* April 29, 1780, Supplement; and *Royal Gazette,* July 21, 1781, Supplement.

The Lindo name was imprinted on Kingston in other ways. Major John Bennet Pechon's 1807 map of the city shows a Lindo Square, abutted by Lindo Street, on Kingston's northern side. The southwestern side contained "Kingston Pen The Property of A[braham] A[lexandre] Lindo," Alexandre Lindo's son. "Lower Lindos Street" was on the pen's south side. A copy of this map is at the New York Public Library, Map Division.

59. *Royal Gazette,* October 27, 1781, Supplement; January 11, 1783, Supplement, for thirty-four of the subscribers including Lindo; and February 1, 1783, Supplement, for the remaining two.

60. *Daily Advertiser,* January 1, 1790.

61. JA, 2/6/105, for the Kingston poll-tax list of 1793.

62. JA, 2/6/105 for Kingston's poll tax in 1795, when Lindo was assessed 7–10–0 in trade taxes for his wharf, and 22–10–0 for the firm of Lindo, Son & Co. In addition, he and Richard Lake were assessed 12–10–0 for their partnership. The next largest trade tax paid by members of the Jewish community was the 7–10–0 levied on the firm of Henriques & Belisario.

For entries of Jewish inhabitants and firms on the 1795 poll-tax list and for entries whose religion is uncertain, see Appendix VI, Table 3, infra.

63. AJA, Collection of Jamaica Wills, 1692–1798, Microfilm Reel 140. For Lousada, see n. 45, supra. His trade tax in 1795 was £5, the third highest assessed on Kingston's Jewish merchants. This amount was levied as well on two other Jewish entries: Joseph Aguilar, and the partnership of Leveins & Wolfe.

At his death in 1797, Lousada was reportedly memorialized in elegiac verse published by Jamaica's *Columbian Magazine, or Monthly Miscellany;* noted in *Publications of the American Jewish Historical Society* 25 (1917): 114.

64. For the sale of Lindo's effects, conducted by his attorneys Abraham Alexandre Lindo and A. M. Belisario, see *Royal Gazette,* August 8, 1795, Postscript. In 1803 Lindo sued his partner, Richard Lake, in Jamaica's Court of Chancery, at which time he testified that he resided in England in December 1796, and did not intend at that time to ever see Jamaica again. His growing belief in 1802 that Lake had mismanaged their partnership and had appropriated funds for his own use prompted Lindo to return to the colony. The lawsuit, cited hereafter as *Lindo v. Lake,* is at JA, Records of the Court of Chancery, 1A/3/200, passim.

65. The rendering is at PRO, MPH 512; reproduced here as Illustration 9. For reference to Lindo's London countinghouse, see *Lindo v. Lake*, 299. His will is at IRO, LXXXVI, 168–71, along with a codicil in LXXXIX, 77. For the inventory of his estate, which provides the details of his holdings in Jamaica, see JA, Inventories, CXXVII, 143b–51. A notice of his death is in *Gentleman's Magazine* 82 (1812): Part One, 394.

I am indebted to Ms. Jacqueline Ranston of Cooper's Hill, St. Andrew, Jamaica, for clarifying the relationship between Alexandre Lindo and Abraham Alexandre Lindo for me and for supplying the latter's year of birth, 1775. Ms. Ranston is the author of a forthcoming history of the Lindo family, tracing it from its origins on the Iberian Peninsula to the present in many parts of the world.

66. *Royal Gazette*, January 3, 1795, Supplement; November 14, 1795; May 31, 1800, Supplement; and October 18, 1800, Supplement; PRO, CO 142/23, entering in for December 29, 1795–March 29, 1796, September 29–December 29, 1796, and clearing out for December 29, 1795–March 29, 1796, June 29–September 29, 1796, and December 29, 1796–March 29, 1797. For the number of slaves exported, see Appendix IV, Table 3, infra. For Lindo's interest in the Spanish trade as a partner in Lindo, Henriques & Lindo, see n. 13, supra.

67. Lindo, Lake & Co. was created on December 20, 1796 by Alexandre Lindo, who by then had settled in England, and by Abraham Alexandre Lindo, Richard Lake, and Richard Lake, Jr., all of Jamaica; *Lindo v. Lake*, 44.

68. The wife of the Lieutenant Governor described the case as "the *grand* cause between Lindo and Lake," and was gratified that her husband, presiding in Chancery, was able to settle it to the satisfaction of both parties; Frank Cundall, ed., *Lady Nugent's Journal: Jamaica One Hundred Years Ago* (London: Adam and Charles Black, 1907), 189–90. *Lindo v. Lake* was no doubt viewed as a major case because of the firm's importance in the slave-factoring business. Events attending the case must have contributed as well to Lady Nugent's characterization of it. At one point, for example, the two antagonists raced one another to take possession of a plantation whose owner had suddenly died, leaving large unsecured debts for slave purchases owing to the firm of Lindo, Lake & Co. In the course of the contest to be the first to occupy the plantation, the men under Lake's command fired shots at Lindo. Lindo believed that Lake gave the order to shoot; see *Lindo v. Lake*, 42.

69. For the firm's participation in 1805 in the protest by Kingston's merchants against seizure of a Spanish vessel, see n. 13, supra. The wharf owned by Lindo, Henriques & Lindo is listed in the Kingston poll tax for 1805; JA, 2/6/105. In the same year, the firm owned the *Plover* and

the *Alexandre Lindo*, the latter sailing for Liverpool; *Royal Gazette*, February 23, 1805, Supplement, and August 3, 1805, Supplement.

70. *Daily Advertiser*, September 6, and September 7, 1790. For Hibbert, see, in addition to Table 5.4, Chapter Three, supra, at n. 80. "Messrs. Soln. Levy & Co. Jam." appears in the papers of the London firm of Moses Levy Newton; PRO, C 114/97, LXXII, 11–12, 168–69; C 114/99, Part 1, Letterbook LXX, Moses Levy to Soln. Levy, December 6, 1798.

71. *The Royal Gazette*, May 11, 1805, Supplement. All four members of this firm were Jewish, including Solomon Flash, who appears in the records of the Ashkenazic synagogue at Kingston; De Lisser, Register of Births & Marriages of the Ashkinazi Congregation. 67.

72. Montego Bay factors between 1781 and 1790 were Jo. & Ja. Wedderburn; John & Tho. Roberts; Birch & [James] Gibson; John Perry; James Wedderburn & Co.; Messrs. Barrett & Parkinson; John Cunningham; Francis Grant; and Mures & Dunlop. For the latter, see *Royal Gazette*, June 23, 1781. For the others, with the exceptions of Cunningham and Grant; see the Supplement issues of *Cornwall Chronicle* for December 1, 1781, December 8, 1781, January 5, 1782, January 11, 1783, February 3, 1787, February 10, 1787, September 6, 1788, September 13, 1788, December 13, 1788, December 20, 1788, January 3, 1789, January 10, 1789, December 5, 1789, and January 16, 1790. For Cunningham and Grant, see David Richardson, ed., *Bristol, Africa and the Eighteenth-Century Slave Trade to America*, 4 vols. (Volumes 38, 39, 42, and 47 of the Bristol Record Society's Publications) (Gloucester: Alan Sutton Publishing, 1986–96), IV, 167, 176, 182, 200, 203.

Factors at locations other than Montego Bay were John Cunningham, Andrew & James Fowler, Francis Grant, Alexander Macleod, Malcolm[s] & Barton, John Mitchell, Salmon & Gauntlett, John Perry, Thomas and William Salmon & Co., John Sharpe & Co., and John Vanheelen; ibid., IV, 125, 137–38, 150, 161, 164, 166, 175, 178, 181, 195, 197, 206, 215, 224, 231.

73. See Chapter Three, Table 3.6, supra.

74. See Chapter Three at n. 93, supra.

75. Higman, *Slave Population and Economy in Jamaica*, 46–47, 58–61, 255–56.

76. From 345,252 in 1817, the slave population declined to 310,707 in 1832, the year of the final registration; Higman, *Slave Population and Economy in Jamaica*, 256.

77. For all Jewish entries in the 1817 triennial register and for those whose religion is not certain, see Appendix XII, Table 2. Identifications have

been established not only on the basis of family names but also by relying on the extensive synagogue records for Kingston that begin in the late 1780s and continue through the nineteenth century, cited at n. 3, supra; the vast collection of wills of both Jews and non-Jews at IRO; Philip Wright's compilation of Jewish tombstone inscriptions at IJ, cited at n. 15, supra, as well as his published inscriptions of non-Jewish tombstones, *Monumental Inscriptions of Jamaica* (London: Society of Genealogists, 1966); and the papers of the London firm of Moses Levy Newton at PRO.

Individuals have been classified as of uncertain religion if their names could have been either Jewish or non-Jewish but they themselves are not identifiable in any of the above sources as having been Jewish (e.g., in Kingston: Charlotte Arnold, Joseph Benjamin, Clara Cohen, Solomon Wolfe Edwards, Louis Julian, and Esther Martins; in St. Andrew: Jacob Josephs; in Port Royal: Abraham Phillips; in Portland: William Arnold); if their family names appear to have been Jewish but their personal names do not (e.g., in Kingston: Sarah Turner Almeyda, Mary Walker Mattos, Cabey Melhado, Samuel Peeke Mendes, Juan Pinto, Caroline Sanches, and Jane Silva; in Manchester: William Kerr D'Aguilar, as well as Moses D'Aguilar, represented by the former as his attorney; in St. Catherine: Charles Adolphus; in St. John: John Mendes); or where crucial information is missing from the registry (e.g., in St. Andrew: an unnamed slaveowner, albeit one who was represented by Joseph Henriques and Solomon Mendes Silva, trustees, both of whom were Jewish; and in Westmoreland, Jacob Pessoa, who unlike Abraham Pessoa there, was not identified as a person "of colour").

David Samuda, partner of Mrs. Deborah Hewitt in the ownership of 335 slaves in the parish of St. Elizabeth, has been classified as of uncertain religion despite his name, because of the burial of one David Samuda, Jr., in a Christian cemetery in 1822 in Savanna la Mar; Wright, *Monumental Inscriptions,* 189. For David Samuda of London who, on the other hand, was clearly Jewish, see n. 44, supra. Owing to the resulting confusion, the children of Benjamin Samuda in the parish of Westmoreland, owners of 38 slaves, have also been classified as of uncertain religion.

Free people of color, identified as such in the register, who had Jewish family names and who owned slaves have been counted as non-Jews, in the absence of any evidence that they were regarded as members of the Jewish community.

For the process, in general, of identifying the individuals discussed throughout the course of this study, see Appendix I, infra.

78. Lindo owned Temple Hall with 312 slaves, Green Hall with 102, Constant Spring with 354, and Greenwich Park Pen with 125; in PRO, T 71/125.
79. Pleasant Hill Plantation; in PRO, T 71/119, 55–61.
80. Moses Bravo, Esq., with 226 in Clarendon, 55 in St. Dorothy, and 132 in Vere; Solomon Mendes Da Silva in St. Ann with 119; Harmon Hendricks in Manchester with 88 and St. Elizabeth with 10; Jacob Henriques, Esq., in St. Thomas-in-the-Vale with 151; Isaac Henriques in St. Ann with 65; Lazarus Hyman in St. Elizabeth with 65; Ms. B. Lousada, Emmanuel Lousada, Esq., and David Lousada, Esq., in St. Ann with 122; and Aguilar, Dias et al., with 361 slaves in the parish of St. Thomas-in-the-East. (The latter may have been the London firm of Aguilar, Dias & Son; see Chapter One, supra, at ns. 107 and 108.)

   Verification that Harmon Hendricks was Jewish comes from a letter that he wrote in 1808 from Black River, Jamaica, to Harmon Hendricks of New York, a member of one of that city's Jewish families, in which he identified himself as a cousin and as a successful merchant; New York Historical Society, Hendricks Papers, Case III, Folder 1801–9.
81. In Kingston, Abraham Alexandre Lindo owned 10, and 3 more in partnership with a non-Jewish individual, John Campbell; Harmon Hendricks owned 4; Moses Bravo, Esq., owned 43; and Solomon Mendes Da Silva owned 1. In St. Catherine, presumably in Spanish Town, Solomon Mendes Da Silva owned 19, and Jacob Henriques, Esq., owned 17. Da Silva owned 16 in St. John, and another 21 in that parish with Jacob Henriques, together with a third partner, Joseph Henriques.

   Isaac Henriques and Ms. B. Lousada are more problematic. In Kingston, an Isaac Henriques owned 8 slaves, an Isaac Cohen Henriques owned 1, and Isaac and Solomon Henriques owned 2 in partnership. Perhaps Ms. B. Lousada was the same as the Mrs. Esther Baruch Lousada who owned 1 slave in Kingston.
82. Higman, *Slave Population and Economy in Jamaica*, 144.
83. See Chapter Three, supra, Table 3.6.
84. Few slave-factor firms are known for Barbados after 1780, and none that have been identified was Jewish. They are Griffith & Applewhaite; Lytcott & Maxwell; Barton & Sibbald; and Richard Redwar. In *Barbados Gazette or General Intelligencer* for October 13 and December 29, 1787, February 13, March 22, June 14, and August 6, 1788; and *Barbados Mercury*, August 30, 1783.
85. PRO, CO 33/18, 33/19, 33/20, 33/21. For the annual totals, see Appendix IV, Table 4, infra.
86. Barrow was a name that Christians and Jews in Barbados shared, the latter deriving it from the Hebrew name Baruch, which Sephardic Jews

employed as a family name. Jacob Barrow and Joseph Barrow appear on the *finta* list of 1798, the year of the slave delivery in question; see Appendix X, infra. For other Barrows in Barbados who were Jewish, see E. M. Shilstone, tr., *Monumental Inscriptions in the Burial Ground of the Jewish Synagogue at Bridgetown, Barbados* (N.p.: N.p., n.d.), passim. Joseph Barrow of Bridgetown is identified as a merchant in a 1786 commercial record (along with Baruck *[sic]* Barrow); AJA, Caribbean Jewry Commercial Documents, 1708–90.

No non-Jewish Barrows named Jacob or Joseph appear to have resided in Bridgetown at the end of the eighteenth century, although a Joseph Barrow whose children were baptized in 1786, 1790, and 1798 resided in St. Lucy Parish; Joanne Mcree Sanders, *Barbados Records: Baptisms, 1637–1800* (Baltimore: Genealogical Publishing Co., 1984), 397–99.

The Barrows' non-Jewish associates were John Roach, Samuel LeGay, James B. Evans, Alexander Hall, and George Reed. The vessel arrived between October 1 and December 31, 1798; in PRO, CO 33/21.

87. PRO, CO 33/18, 33/19, 33/20, 33/21, 33/22. For the annual totals, see Appendix IV, Table 5, infra.

88. Eliezer Montefiore appears on the *finta* lists for 1798, 1810, 1815, and 1818, and Lewis Cohen on the list for 1815; see Appendix X, infra. Montefiore is identified as a merchant in a 1794 commercial document; AJA, Caribbean Jewry, Commercial Documents, 1708–90.

In addition to Thomas Ames, the other non-Jewish partners in these ventures were Jno. Roach, Samuel LeGay, James Evans, Alexander Hall, David Hall, George Hall, George Reed, Gabriel Jemmett, Nathaniel Phillips, James Woodruff, and Samuel Ames. During the same period of time as the five voyages in which Jewish partners joined with these men, Jemmett was partner in another six export ventures, Phillips in another five, Woodruff in another two, and LeGay Evans, and Samuel Ames each participated in one other.

For the exports in question, see April 1–June 30, 1797, January 1–March 31, 1798, and July 1–September 1, 1799 at PRO, CO 33/21.

89. B. W. Higman, *Slave Populations of the British Caribbean, 1807–1834* (Baltimore: Johns Hopkins University Press, 1984), 413.

90. For all Jewish owners and for those whose religion is not certain, see Appendix XII, Table 1, infra.

91. Abraham Rodrigues Brandon, with 168 slaves, and Jacob Da Costa, with 59.

Notes to Chapter 6

1. Ira Rosenswaike, "An Estimate and Analysis of the Jewish Population of the United States in 1790," *Publications of the American Jewish Historical Society* 50 (1960–61): 25, 27, and passim, supplemented by Malcolm H. Stern, "Some Additions and Corrections to Rosenswaike's 'An Estimate and Analysis of the Jewish Population of the United States in 1790,' " *American Jewish Historical Quarterly* 53 (1963–64): 285–88.

2. Jacob R. Marcus, *The Colonial American Jew, 1492–1776*, 3 vols. (Detroit: Wayne State University Press, 1970), I, 308.

3. The census is in E. B. O'Callaghan, ed., *The Documentary History of the State of New York*, 4 vols. (Albany: Weed, Parsons and Co., 1849–51), I, 611–24. For Jews on two assessments in 1703, one to maintain the minister and the poor, the second to pay the bellman and other public bills, see AJHS, Samuel Oppenheim Collection, Box 18. For Jamaica's population, see Chapter Three, supra, at n. 5.

The individuals on the two tax lists are Joseph Bueno, Moses Levy, Samuel Levy, Jacob De Porto, Abraham De Lucena "ye Jew," Isaac Fernandez (as well as the estate of Isaac Fernandez), Luis Gomez, Widow Robles, Isaac De Lara, Joseph Nunes, the widow of Saul Brown [Esther Brown], Isaac Gabay, Isaac Rodrigues Marquez, Mrs. Granada, and Mr. Solomon "the Jew." Joseph Isaacs appears on one of the lists, and Mr. Isaac, "the Jew," on the second, but whether they were one and the same is not known. Additional complications arise from the occurrence of Mr. Isaacs's estate and Widow Isaacs on one of them. How many "Isaacs" there were in the town and how many were Jewish cannot be ascertained with assurance. Individuals of uncertain religion on one of the lists are Simon Bonan and Abraham Hart.

For the households on the census, see the discussion below.

4. The six Jewish families and the number of slaves they owned were those of Joseph Isaacs (1); Moses Levy (2); "Yacob deportee" [Jacob De Porto]; "Delancena Jew" [Abraham De Lucena] (2); Widow Brown [Esther Brown]; and Luis Gomez (2). The five uncertain cases are those of Simon Bonan; Amon Bonan; Widow Solomon; and two more households surnamed Solomon, without personal names. (For Mr. Solomon, "the Jew," see n. 3, supra.) None owned slaves, with the exception of Amon Bonan who held one. For all, see O'Callaghan, *Documentary History*, loc. cit.

5. The commercial ledger of New York's Daniel Gomez illustrates the transatlantic trading interests of many. Gomez traded extensively with Jewish merchants in Barbados, Jamaica, and Curaçao, as well as with

other locations in the Atlantic region; AJHS, Ledger of Daniel Gomez, 1739–74.

6. For the slave trade at New York in general, see Edgar J. McManus, *A History of Negro Slavery in New York* (Syracuse: Syracuse University Press, 1966), 23ff; and James G. Lydon, "New York and the Slave Trade, 1700 to 1774," 3d ser., *William and Mary Quarterly* 35 (1978): 375–94.

7. PRO, CO 5/1222, 5/1223, 5/1224, 5/1225, 5/1226, 5/1227, and 5/1228. For individual years and the arrivals therein, see Appendix IV, Table 6, infra. The total reported here is slightly less than the 4,398 reported by Lydon, "New York and the Slave Trade," 382–83.

8. The dates of entry at New York for the fifteen undertakings from Africa owned by non-Jews were August 2, 1715; June 2, 1716; August 23, 1717; September 12, 1717; April 4, 1718; August 6, 1718; December 12, 1725; September 27, 1731; July 13, 1733; May 8, May 24, September 13, and September 16, 1754; the quarter between April 4, 1763 and July 5, 1763; and July 18, 1763.

An eighteenth venture, one owned by non-Jews, is not included here because of confusion in the record as to whether the two slaves it transported to New York originated in Africa or in Jamaica; it entered New York on October 24, 1723.

9. PRO, CO 5/1222, for the arrival of the *Postillion* in the quarter between June 24 and September 27, 1717.

10. PRO, CO 5/1222, for the arrival of the *Crown Galley* of London at New York during the quarter between March 25 and June 24, 1721. The path of the vessel from London to Madagascar and from there to Brazil, Barbados, New London, and finally New York, may be followed at PRO, Nathan Simson Papers, C 104/14, in the shipping orders to Captain Dennis Downing; the account of the sale of slaves at Brazil, February 17, 1721; Downing at Barbados to Walton and Simson in New York, April 19, 1721; Downing at New London to Walton and Simson in New York, May 25, 1721; and Janeway and Levy at London to Walton and Simson in New York, July 27, 1721. Part of the record of the sales of the slaves delivered at New York is reproduced here as Illustration 3.

11. New York State Archives, Manifest Books XXIV, XXV, XXVI, XXVII, XXXIV, XXXV, and Entry Books, X. The data for the thirteen are reported here in the following order: name of importer; volume and date, or number of entry; number of slaves. Peter Van Binghamton, Manifest Book XXIV, July 27, 1749, 38; William Beekman & Co., Manifest Book XXV, September 18, 1750, 52; Peter Livingston & Co., Manifest Book XXVI, May 20, 1751, 66; Jno. Livingston & Co., Man-

ifest Book XXVI, May 22, 1751, 13; Garrit Cousine & Co., Manifest Book XXVII, July 4, 1751, 20; Captain Thomas Grenell, Manifest Book XXVII, August 2, 1751, 10; John Troup & Co., Manifest Book XXXIV, July 22, 1758, and Entry Book X, no. 9,232, 70; Hugh Wallace & Co., Manifest Book XXXV, July 9, 1759, number of slaves destroyed; William and Jacob Walton & Co., Entry Book X, no. 3038, 1765?, 1; Thomas Crowell, Entry Book X, no. 3042, 1765, 4; John V. [sic] Cortland, Entry Book X, no. 3448, 1765, 12; Entry Book X, no. 3449, 1765, White [sic], 21; and Edmund Kelly, Entry Book X, no. 3450, 1765, 3.

12. Of the other 22, 14 were divided among Rhode Island, South Carolina, "Madeira and Jamaica," and Suriname, while the origins of 8 were not recorded in the Naval Office records.

13. In addition to his commerce with Barbados, Jamaica, and Curaçao known from the source cited at n. 5, supra, Daniel Gomez traded with England, Ireland, Holland, Madeira, Newport, Charleston, New Haven, and Philadelphia. For the commercial enterprise of the Levy-Franks group, see their correspondence in Leo Hershkowitz and Isidore S. Meyer, eds., *The Lee Max Friedman Collection of American Jewish Colonial Correspondence: Letters of the Franks Family (1733–1748)* (Waltham: American Jewish Historical Society, 1968). See also Chapter Three, supra, at ns. 46, 47, and 50 for trade with Jamaica by Mordecai Gomez, Moses Levy, and Jacob Franks.

14. Pacheco, who imported 21 slaves in partnership with non-Jews (1 of them also in partnership with Nathan Simson), and 4 on his own, returned to London, as noted in Chapter One, supra, at n. 103. For his importation of 5 slaves into South Carolina in 1731, see below in the present chapter at n. 43. The remaining 3 slaves were imported to New York by Abraham De Lucena.

15. The following are all that can be retrieved from the two badly damaged sources: Emanuel Rodrigues Campos—1 slave; Isaac Campos—1; Isaac Da Costa—1; Moses De Mattos—4; Benjamin Gomez—1; David Gomez—2; Mordecai Gomez—7; Mordecai and David Gomez—1; Asher Isaacs—1; Rachel Levy—1; David Machado—2; Judah Mears—2; Isaac Mendes—1; Jacob Serzea [sic] Mesquita—1; Mordecai Nunes—2; Menasseh Pereira—1; Rebecca Silva—2; Simha Torres—3; and Abraham Rodrigues Rivera, Jacob Rodrigues Rivera, and Moses Lopez, for whom see immediately below. Two other individuals may have been Jewish: John Mendes—3 slaves; and Matthew D. Hart—1 slave. For all, see Manifest Books, VI, May 9, 11, and 22, 1741; XI, July 29, 1742; XVIII, September 16, 1745; XIX, November 13, 1746; XXIII, April 14, 1749; XXV, November 23, 1749 and October 8, 1750; and Entry

Books, I, nos. 782, 1177; II, nos. 1329, 1452, 1516, 1766, 1793, 1846, 2185; IV, nos. 148, 172, 201, 262, 291, 313, 861, 867, 891.

16. For the relationships between the three, see Malcolm H. Stern, *First American Jewish Families: 600 Genealogies, 1654–1988,* 3d ed. (Baltimore: Ottenheimer, 1991), 175.

17. Entry Books, II, nos. 1452, 1513, and 1988.

18. Manifest Books, XIX, November 13, 1746; XX, October 5, 1747; and XXVII, November 8, 1751.

19. Stanley F. Chyet, *Lopez of Newport: Colonial American Merchant Prince* (Detroit: Wayne State University Press, 1970), 16–23, 62.

20. Eli Faber, *A Time for Planting: The First Migration, 1654–1820* (Baltimore: Johns Hopkins University Press, 1992), 36–37.

21. JA, Records of the Court of Chancery, 1A/3/17, 30–31. The others, all of them non-Jewish, were John Brown, Sr., John Brown, Jr., Thomas Coggerhall, and Benjamin Cranston, identified, with Hart, as the owners of the *King George.*

22. For Hart and Elizer, see Chapter Three, supra, at ns. 48, 49, 51, and 52. Lopez's extraordinary range of activity is amply documented by Chyet, *Lopez,* passim, but see also Virginia B. Platt, "Tar, Staves, and New England Rum: The Trade of Aaron Lopez of Newport, Rhode Island, with Colonial North Carolina," *North Carolina Historical Review* 48 (1971): 1–22. Vessels owned between 1765 and 1770 by Naphtali Hart (*Truelove*), Isaac Elizer (*Hope, Success, Wheel of Fortune, Swallow, Rhode Island, Freemason, Charlotte, Endeavor, Adventure, New Brig*), Moses Levy (*Greyhound*), Myer Polock (*Hope, Hero*), and Moses Hays (*Hope,* in partnership with Aaron Lopez, Jacob Rodrigues Rivera, and Myer Polock), as well as many owned by Lopez and Rivera, are in AJA, Aaron Lopez Papers, Microfilm Reel 323, Alphabet for Ship Book A.

23. For the early 1760s: Chyet, *Lopez,* 52. The thirteen families in 1774 were those of Isaac Elizer, Moses Michael Hays, Isaac Hart, Jacob Isaacs, Joseph Jacob [Jacobs], Aaron Lopez, Rebecca Lopez, Moses Levy, Myer Polock, Jacob Rodrigues Rivera, Catherine Sarzedas, Moses Seixas, and Abraham de Isaac Touro. The religion of nine other households is uncertain, viz., John "Garzia," Benjamin Hart, Jacob Hart, William Hart, "Stiam" Levy, Esther Morris, Samuel Moses, Jacob Myers, and Frances Polock. For all twenty-two, see *Census of the Inhabitants of the Colony of Rhode Island and Providence Plantations, Taken by Order of the General Assembly, in the Year 1774* (Providence: Knowles, Anthony & Co., 1858), 13, 15, 16, 18, 19, 21, 22, 23, 25, 28, 29, 32. Catherine Sarzedas's religion is known from her marriage as "Caty"

Hays to Abraham Sarzedas, while the Joseph Jacob in the census is assumed here to have been the same as Joseph Jacobs; Stern, *First American Jewish Families,* 104, 131, 262.

A comment by the Reverend Ezra Stiles in 1769 lends credence to the higher reading of the census. Stiles estimated that approximately twenty-five Jewish families resided in the town; Rosenswaike, "Estimate and Analysis of Jewish Population of the United States in 1790," 25.

24. Chyet, *Lopez,* 53–56, 58–60.

25. James A. Rawley, *The Transatlantic Slave Trade: A History* (New York: W. W. Norton, 1981), 359; Elaine Forman Crane, *A Dependent People: Newport, Rhode Island in the Revolutionary Era* (New York: Fordham University Press, 1985), 21.

26. Jay Coughtry, *The Notorious Triangle: Rhode Island and the African Slave Trade, 1700–1807* (Philadelphia: Temple University Press, 1981), 247. For the Vernons, see Rawley, *Transatlantic Slave Trade,* 372–77.

27. PRO, CO 142/16, under the entries for June 25–September 29, 1755.

28. Coughtry, *Notorious Triangle,* 250–61, with the exception of the *Ann* in 1774, for which Coughtry did not provide the owners' names. That it belonged to Lopez and Rivera is clear from Lopez's correspondence: AJA, Aaron Lopez Papers, Microfilm Reel 1,214, Charles Davis to Aaron Lopez and Jacob Rodrigues Rivera, November 27, 1774; William Moore, Jr., to Aaron Lopez and Jacob Rodrigues Rivera, November 27, 1774; and John Strange to Aaron Lopez, February 3, 1775.

29. Coughtry, *Notorious Triangle,* 251–52, 254; Chyet, *Lopez,* 67; and Chapter Three, supra, at ns. 60 and 61. Hart's ownership of the *Osprey* is not provided by Coughtry but by the records of the Naval Office for Jamaica; PRO, CO 142/18, entries for December 25,1764–March 25, 1765. Samuel Moses's religion is not certain; his partner was clearly Jewish.

30. Coughtry, *Notorious Triangle,* 241–61.

31. Ibid., 240, 246–61.

32. The Jewish merchants were Jacob Rodrigues Rivera, who on August 27, 1785 and again on August 14, 1786 launched ventures in the *Three Friends;* Coughtry, *Notorious Triangle,* 262; and Moses Seixas, who participated in five voyages between 1805 and 1807 with Edward Easton, John Price, and William Price; ibid., 278–79, 281–82, 284.

Coughtry identified Rodrigues & Co. and Nathaniel Briggs as partners in their second venture. Rodrigues's involvement in the first one, along with Jacob Rodrigues Rivera & Co. *[sic],* John Cooke, and Nathaniel Briggs as partners, is from a list of goods for shipment to Africa on the *Three Friends* dated August 22, 1785, examined on December 8, 1995 at the gallery of Kenneth W. Rendell, Inc., New York City. Voyages from Liverpool numbered 4,810 between 1698 and 1807, 2,200 from Bristol between 1698 and 1807, and approximately 2,100 from London between 1700 and 1807. Totals for the three ports are derived from the figures presented by David Eltis and David Richardson, "The 'Numbers Game' and Routes to Slavery," *Slavery and Abolition* 18 (1997): 4; and by Stephen D. Behrendt, "The Annual Volume and Regional Distribution of the British Slave Trade, 1780–1807," *Journal of African History* 38 (1997): 189. Adding the 935 known to have emanated from Rhode Island yields a total greater than 10,000.

33. AJA, Aaron Lopez Papers, Microfilm Reel 1,216, Shipping Book, 1771–73. The three ships to Africa in the lading book were the *Ann*, the *Africa*, and the *Cleopatra*, all of them in partnership with Jacob Rodrigues Rivera. All are included in Coughtry's list in *Notorious Triangle*, 259, as are the three others.

34. Virginia B. Platt, " 'And Don't Forget the Guinea Voyage': The Slave Trade of Aaron Lopez of Newport," 3d ser., *William and Mary Quarterly* 32 (1975): 616. Platt found that Lopez was involved in "well over" two hundred voyages, but attributed only fourteen slaving expeditions to him.

35. Jewish households with slaves were those of Isaac Elizer (2), Moses Michael Hays (2), Isaac Hart (3), Jacob Isaacs (2), Aaron Lopez (5), Rebecca Lopez (2), Moses Levy (1), Jacob Rodrigues Rivera (12), Catherine Sarzedas (4), Joseph Jacob [Jacobs] (3), and Moses Seixas (1). Slaveowning families of uncertain religion were those of John "Garzia" (1), Jacob Hart (1), "Stiam" Levy (1), Esther Morris (4), and Frances Polock (2). For all, see the locations in the census of 1774 cited at n. 23, supra. For the cumulative totals in the entire census, see *Census of Inhabitants of Rhode Island*, 239.

36. Darold D. Wax, "Negro Imports into Pennsylvania, 1720–1766," *Pennsylvania History* 32 (1965): 270, 272, 276; Faber, *Time for Planting*, 38–39.

An individual named Joseph Marks advertised slaves for sale on ten occasions between 1740 and 1761; Wax, op. cit., 274–76, 279–80, 282, 284. Despite his name, there is no evidence that Marks was Jewish; Edwin Wolf and Maxwell Whiteman, *The History of the Jews of Philadelphia from Colonial Times to the Age of Jackson* (Philadelphia: Jewish Publication Society of America, 1957), 33, 387.

37. Wax, "Negro Imports," 255–58.

38. Ibid., 284–85.

39. Ibid., 256, n. 9.
40. *Colonial Records of Pennsylvania,* 17 vols. (Harrisburg: Jo. Severns et al., 1851–53, 1860), VIII, 575–76, 578–79; Wax, "Negro Imports," 255–57.
41. "Proprietary Tax of the City of Philadelphia, 1769," in *Pennsylvania Archives,* 3d ser., XIV (1897): 149–220. Jewish entries, with the number of slaves for each, were for Israel Jacobs (2); Levi Marks (1); Benjamin Levy (1); Samson Levy (1); Barnard Gratz (1); and David Franks (2). Entries whose religion is not certain were for Samuel Simson (2); Jacob "Godshalk" (1); and Jacob Meyers (1). All are in loc. cit. at 156, 157, 164, 172, 184, 193, 196, 208, and 218.

    Slaves enumerated in the tax list appear under the heading "Servants." In a similar tax list for Philadelphia in 1783, the heading is "Negroes." See "Federal Supply Tax for the City of Philadelphia. For the year 1783," in *Pennsylvania Archives,* 3d ser., XVI (1898): 729–837.
42. PRO, CO 5/508, 5/509, 5/510, 5/511. Those whose religion is not known are Joshua Gabriel, G. Legate, and Nat. Brandden [Brandon?], importing 5 slaves from Barbados in the quarter between December 12, 1723 and March 25, 1724; 18 slaves from Montserrat, imported in the quarter ending on Lady Day in 1734, where the vessel owner's name is not known; and 1 slave from Barbados on a vessel whose owner was not entered in the records that arrived between March 25 and June 24, 1739.
43. PRO, CO 5/509, entering into South Carolina in the quarter between December 24, 1730 and March 3, 1731. For Pacheco, see Chapter One, supra, at n. 103; and in the present chapter supra, at n. 14.
44. PRO, CO 5/510, entering in between September 9, 1757 and January 1, 1758. For Lindo, an expert on the cultivation of indigo, see Charles Reznikoff and Uriah Z. Engelman, *The Jews of Charleston: A History of an American Jewish Community* (Philadelphia: Jewish Publication Society of America, 1950), 23–33.
45. As described above, at n. 28. The Naval Office record is at PRO, CO 5/510.
46. Rawley, *Transatlantic Slave Trade,* 415.
47. Elizabeth Donnan, ed., *Documents Illustrative of the History of the Slave Trade to America,* 4 vols. (Washington, D.C.: Carnegie Institution of Washington, 1930–35), IV, 314, 375, 381. The number of slaves reputedly advertised for the *Greyhound* is 160, but the figure in the records of the Naval Office is 134, as reported, supra, at n. 45. Donnan's compilation of newspaper advertisements in the colony for 1733–44, 1749–57, 1759–61, 1762–65, 1769, and 1771–74 is at 278–80, 296–

97, 301–2, 310–12, 314, 338, 365, 372, 375–76, 378, 380–81, 386, 411–13, 428–29, 438, 442, 453–54, and 467.

48. W. Robert Higgins, "Charles Town Merchants and Factors Dealing in the External Negro Trade, 1735–1775," *South Carolina Historical Magazine* 65 (1964): 205, 208, 210, 211, 214, 215, 216.

49. Faber, *Time for Planting*, 41.

50. PRO, CO 5/709, entering during the quarter between January 5 and April 5, 1763. For Isaac De Lyon, see Saul Jacob Rubin, *Third to None: The Saga of Savannah Jewry, 1733–1983* (Savannah: S. J. Rubin, 1983), 21. Naval Office records for the colony also survive at PRO CO 5/710.

51. PRO CO 5/710, under the entries for April 5–July 5, 1767. For Lucena, see Marcus, *Colonial American Jew*, I, 436; II, 605, 632–33, 701, 1021; III, 1241–42.

52. James William Hagy, *This Happy Land: The Jews of Colonial and Antebellum Charleston* (Tuscaloosa: University of Alabama Press, 1993), 91–92; Stern, "Some Additions and Corrections," 286, 288.

53. Stern, "Some Additions and Corrections," 285–88.

54. See n. 32, supra.

Bibliography

I. Original Sources: Manuscript

BRITISH LIBRARY (London)

1. Additional Mss.
   South Sea Company Papers
   25,494, 25,496–25,497, 25,504–25,505—Minutes of the Court of Directors
   25,544–25,545—Minutes of the General Court
   25,550–25,5054—Minutes of the Committee for Correspondence and Factorys [sic]
   25,556–25,558—Copies of Home Letters and Memorials
   25,560–25,561, 25,564–25,566—Correspondence of the Court of Directors

   12,418–12,419—James Knight, The Natural, Moral, and Political History of Jamaica, and the Territories Thereon depending; From the first Discovery of the Island by Christopher Columbus, to the Year 1746

   12,435—Long Papers—Papers on the Statistics of Jamaica, 1739–70

2. Shelburne Papers
   Volumes 43–44—Asiento Papers

3. East India Company Records
   Minutes of the General Court and of the Courts of the Committees
   B/36—Court Book, April 1680–April 1682
   B/37—Court Book, April 1682–April 1684
   B/38—Court Book, April 1684–April 1687
   B/39—Court Book, April 1687–March 1690
   B/40—Court Book, April 1690–19 April 1695
   B/41—Court Book, April 1695–April 1699

B/43—Court Book, 27 April 1699–27 April 1702
B/44—Court Book, April 1702–April 1705
Papers on the Unification of the Two Companies, 1702–9
B/50A—The Adventurers Names of the Old East India Company and shares in the Fund and Stock of the English Company amounting to £1581599–15–7

HOUSE OF LORDS RECORD OFFICE (London)

Main Papers
17 February 1699 [1700]—Petition to the House of Lords from Merchants and Others Trading to Africa and the Plantations

PUBLIC RECORD OFFICE (Kew)

1. Moses Levy Newton Papers
   C 114/40, 114/41, 114/97, 114/98, 114/99

2. Nathan Simson Papers
   C 104/13, 104/13A, 104/13B, 104/13C, 104/14

3. Naval Office Records
   Bahamas—
   CO 27/12, 27/13, 27/14

   Barbados—
   CO 33/13, 33/14, 33/15, 33/16, 33/17, 33/18, 33/19, 33/20, 33/21, 33/22; T 64/48, 64/49

   Bermuda—
   CO 41/6, 41/7, 41/8

   Dominica—
   CO 76/4, 76/5, 76/6

   Georgia—
   CO 5/709, 5/710

   Grenada—
   CO 106/1, 106/2, 106/3, 106/4

   Jamaica—
   CO 142/13, 142/14, 142/15, 142/16, 142/17, 142/18, 142/19, 142/20, 142/21, 142/22, 142/23, 142/24

   Nevis—
   CO 157/1, 187/2

New York—
CO 5/1222, 5/1223, 5/1224, 5/1225, 5/1226, 5/1227, 5/1228

South Carolina—
CO 5/508, 5/509, 5/510, 5/511

St. Christopher—
CO 243/1

St. Vincent—
CO 265/1

4. Records of the Royal African Company
CO 388/10, H121—An Accott of Exports made by Private Traders from 29 September 1702 to the 29 September 1704

CO 388/10, H122—An Account of Exports Made by Private Traders from the 29th September 1704 To the 29th September 1707

T 70/101—Minute Book of the General Court—1679–1720
T 70/185, 70/186, 70/187, 70/188, 70/189, 70/190, 70/191, 70/196-Stock Transfer Ledgers—1674–1713
T 70/646—Barbados Ledger—1662–64
T 70/869, 70/870, 70/871, 70/872—Jamaica Ledgers—1665–69, 1678, 1695ff
T 70/936, 70/937, 70/938, 70/939, 70/940, 70/941, 70/942, 70/943, 70/944, 70/945, 70/946, 70/947, 70/948, 70/949, 70/950, 70/951, 70/952, 70/953, 70/954, 70/955, 70/956, 70/957, 70/958, 70/959, 70/960, 70/961—Invoice Book[s] Homeward—1672/3–1729
T 70/1198—Inwards [Ten Percent Records]
T 70/1199—London Outwards. 10 Percent. From 2d Janry 1701 to 8th July 1712.

5. Slave Registers
Barbados, 1817—
T 71/520, 71/521, 71/522, 71/523

Jamaica, 1817—
T 71/1—St. Catherine
T 71/13—St. Dorothy
T 71/19—St. John
T 71/25—St. Thomas-in-the-Vale
T 71/33—St. Mary
T 71/43—St. Ann
T 71/51—Vere
T 71/57—Clarendon

T 71/65—Manchester
T 71/74, 71/75, 71/76, 71/77, 71/78, 71/79—Kingston
T 71/119—Port Royal
T 71/125—St. Andrew
T 71/139—St. David
T 71/145—St. Thomas-in-the-East
T 71/151—Portland
T 71/158—St. George
T 71/164, 71/165, 71/166—St. Elizabeth
T 71/178—Westmoreland
T 71/190—Hanover
T 71/201, 71/202, 71/203, 71/204—St. James
T 71/224, 71/225, 71/226, 71/227, 71/228, 71/229—Trelawny
6. Miscellaneous
CO 1/21—Some observations on the Island [of] Barbados, [1667]
CO 1/28—Thomas Lynch to the Council of Plantations, March 10, 1671/2
CO 1/30—Sir Peter Colleton to the Council of Trade, May 28, 1673
CO 1/45, 96–107—Port Royal Census, 1680
CO 28/18, 321–25—Barbadoes. Liste of Negroes imported into this Island from the 4th March 1707, to the 16th September 1726
CO 28/21, 104–9, 165–209—Barbados Slave Tax, 1729
CO 28/22, 26–28, 31–33, 45–46—Accounts of cash received and amounts bonded for the duty on slaves in the Treasury Office at Barbados
CO 28/25, 136–37, 139–40—Bonds posted in the Treasury Office at Barbados for the duty on slaves
CO 33/30—An Account of all such Ships & Vessells that have Imported New Negroes, in the Barbados Treasurer's Accounts of Excise from 8 Feb 1726–27 Nov 1728
CO 37/2—The Jews Plantations and houses in Jamaica and Barbados—1692
CO 137/8, 91–96—[List of] all vessels Arrived at The Island of Jamaica from the Coast of Africa from the . . . 1698 to the 14th of June 1708
CO 137/9, 79—Petition of Jamaica Merchants—1713
CO 137/14, 51—The Jews Case in Jamaica—1721
CO 137/17—Impost Accounts, Jamaica
CO 137/19, Part 2—Governor Hunter's Answers to Queries of the Board of Trade—1730
CO 137/22, 30–32, 34–36—The Humble Petition and Representation of several Traders to Jamaica and others in behalf of the Jews who are

Inhabitants of that Island; Answers provided by Benjamin Bravo; and William Wood to Alured Popple, Esq.—1736

CO 137/56, 114–18—Richard Mill et al. to Governor Edward Trelawny, 1738

CO 138/9, 334–35—Petition to the Lords Justice of England from Stephen Evance, Jeffry Jeffrys, and John Stafford—1699

CO 152/15, 332–33, 390–91—Slaves imported from 20 Dec. 1720–25 Dec. 1726, St. Christopher, Antigua, Montserrat, and Nevis

CO 318/8, 61–82—An Alphabetical Liest off all Burghers Resident in the Island of St. Eustatius—1781

CO 324/34, 198–206—Petitions from Merchants trading to and from Jamaica—1722

CO 388/10, H 105, H 108—Royal African Company's Accountant's Report of Slaves Delivered to the Colonies, 1698–1707

CO 388/25, S 39—Memorial to the Lords of Trade and Plantations from the Merchants of London Tradeing to Africa—1726

CO 388/25, S74—March the 30th 1726. An Account of Ships belonging to the Port of London that are Imployed in the Trade to the Coast of Africa

SPANISH AND PORTUGUESE JEWS' CONGREGATION (London)

Congregation Nidhe Israel, Bridgetown, Barbados—
328—Minute Book 5552 [1792]
329—Ledger
331—Minute Book, 1809–20
333—Ledger

JAMAICA ARCHIVES AND RECORD CENTER (Spanish Town)

1. Parish Records: Vital Statistics
1B/11/8/1/2—St. Andrew Baptisms, Marriages, Burials, 1807–26
1B/11/8/3/48—St. Catherine Baptisms, Marriages, Burials, 1764–1808
1B/11/8/8/1—St. James Baptisms and Marriages, 1774–1809
1B/11/8/9/14—Kingston Marriages, 1753–1814
1B/11/8/13/9—Port Royal Baptisms, 1791–1811, Marriages, 1804–24, Burials, 1799–1810

2. Parish Records: Vestry Minutes and Tax Records
1B/11/9/1—St. David Vestry Minutes, 1785–93
1B/11/9/5—St. David Vestry Minutes, 1814–20
2/1/1—St. Thomas-in-the-Vale Vestry Minutes, 1789–1802

2/2/19—St. Catherine Taxation Rolls, 1807–22
2/2/22—St. Catherine Poll-Tax Records, 1772–74
2/3/1—St. James Vestry Minutes, 1807–25
2/6/1—Kingston Vestry Minutes, 1744–49
2/6/5—Kingston Vestry Minutes, 1769–70
2/6/105—Kingston Poll Taxes, 1792–1805
2/6/106—Kingston Poll Taxes, 1819–35
2/6/155—Kingston Church Warden Accounts, 1722–59
2/7/1—Westmoreland Vestry Minutes, 1780–81, 1801–6
2/17/1—Manchester Vestry Minutes, 1816–24
2/19/1—Port Royal Vestry Minutes, 1735–41

3. Court of Chancery
   1A/3/1–1A/3/200, Records of the Court of Chancery—Libers I–IV, VI,
   VII–XVIII, XXI–XXII, XXV–XXVI, XXIX–XXX, XXXIX, XLII–
   XLIV, LVIV–LXIII, LXVI–LXXIV, CXVIII–CXXVII, CXXXIV–
   CXXXV, CXXXVIII–CXL, CLVI–CLXVII, CXCIX–CC- 1676–1803

4. Manumission Records
   1B/11/6/5—1747–55
   2/6/277—Kingston Register of Free Persons, 1761–95

ISLAND RECORD OFFICE (Spanish Town)

Wills—Libers XXI–CXXV—1737–1850

INSTITUTE OF JAMAICA (Kingston)

List of the Landholders in the Island of Jamaica in 1754
John Taylor, Multum in Parvo. Or Taylor's Historie of his Life, and
   Travells in America and other Parts. 3 vols.
Tombstone Inscriptions Compiled by Philip Wright

AMERICAN JEWISH HISTORICAL SOCIETY (Waltham, Massachusetts)

Aaron Lopez Papers
Gratz Family Papers
Ledger of Daniel Gomez, 1739–74
Records of The American Jewish Historical Society—Correspondence of
   A. Kanof
Samuel Oppenheim Collection

AMERICAN JEWISH ARCHIVES (Cincinnati)

Aaron Lopez Papers
Caribbean Jewry Commercial Documents, 1708–90

Jamaica Births and Marriages
Jamaica Wills—1692–1798 (Microfilm Reel 140)
Ledger of Mathias Lopez, 1779–89
Phyllis DeLisser, Analysed Register of Births—Deaths—Marriages 1809–1907 of the Sephardic Congregation 'Kaal Kadosh Shahar Ashamaim' 'Holy Congregation of Gate of Heaven' Founded 1693 Kingston Jamaica
Phyllis DeLisser, Analysed Register of Births & Marriages of the Ashkinazi Congregation 'Kahal Kodosh Shaanare Yosher Holy Congregation Gates of Righteousness' English and German Jews, Kingston Jamaica

NEW YORK PUBLIC LIBRARY (New York City)

Hugh Hall, Jr., Weather Almanac Kept at Boston, Barbados, and in England, 1714–17

NEW YORK HISTORICAL SOCIETY (New York City)

Harmon Hendricks Papers

NEW YORK STATE LIBRARY (Albany)

1. Customs Records—Manifest Books, VI–XI, XIII, XV, XVIII–XXI, XXIII–XXVII, XXX, XXXII, XXXIV–XXXVII, XXXIX—1740–62
2. Treasurer's Records—Entry Books, I–II, IV–X—1728–66

HISPANIC SOCIETY OF AMERICA (New York City)

A Coppie Journall of Entries Made in the Custom House of Barbados Beginning August ye 10th 1665 continued in two distinct accotts to ye 24th Aprl [sic] 1667 & containes Ye accott Currant of 2 yeares 8 1/2 months

II. Original Sources: Published

"An Account of His Majesty's Island of Barbados and the G'overnmt Thereof." *Journal of the Barbados Museum and Historical Society* 3 (1935–36): 44–57.
An Account of the Island of Jamaica; With Reflections on the Treatment, Occupation, and Provisions of the Slaves. Newcastle: S. Hodgson, 1788.
An Account of the Number of Negroes Delivered in to the Islands of Barbadoes, Jamaica, and Antego from the Year 1698 to 1708. N.p.: N.p., [1708].

"An Address in Favour of the Sufferers at Barbadoes." *Gentleman's Magazine* 36 (1766): 425–26.

An Almanack and Register for Jamaica for the Year of Our Lord 1776. Being Bissextile or Leap-Year. Jamaica: Joseph Thompson & Co., n.d.

An Answer to a Pamphlet, Entitled, Considerations on the Bill to Permit Persons Professing the Jewish Religion to Be Naturalized; Wherein the False Reasoning, Gross Misrepresentation of Facts, and Perversion of Scripture, Are Fully Laid Open and Detected. 2d ed. [London]: N.p., 1753.

Assembly of Jamaica. *Journals of The Assembly of Jamaica.* 14 vols. Jamaica: Alexander Aikman, 1811–29.

Atkins, John. *A Voyage to Guinea, Brasil, and the West-Indies.* London: Ceasar Ward and Richard Chandler, 1735.

Barnett, Lionel D., ed. *Bevis Marks Records Being Contributions to the History of the Spanish and Portuguese Congregation of London. Part II: Abstracts of the Ketubot or Marriage-Contracts of the Congregation from Earliest Times until 1837.* Oxford: The University Press by Charles Batey, 1949.

———, tr. *El Libro de los Acuerdos, Being the Records and Accompts of the Spanish and Portuguese Synagogue of London from 1663 to 1681.* Oxford: The University Press by John Johnson, 1931.

Barnett, R. D. *Bevis Marks Records Part IV: The Circumcision Register of Isaac and Abraham De Paiba (1715–1775).* Oxford: Spanish and Portuguese Jews' Congregation and the Jewish Historical Society of England: 1991.

———. "The Burial Register of the Spanish and Portuguese Jews, London, 1657–1735." *Miscellanies of the Jewish Historical Society of England* 6 (1962): 1–72.

Barnett, Richard D., and Philip Wright. *The Jews of Jamaica: Tombstone Inscriptions, 1663–1880.* Jerusalem: Ben Zvi Institute, 1997.

Brandow, James C., ed. *Omitted Chapters from Hotten's Original Lists of Persons of Quality.* Baltimore: Genealogical Publishing Co., 1983.

Bridges, George Wilson. *The Annals of Jamaica.* 2 vols. London: John Murray, 1828.

Browne, Patrick. *The Civil and Natural History of Jamaica.* London: N.p., 1789.

Byars, William Vincent, ed. *B. and M. Gratz: Merchants in Philadelphia, 1758–1798.* Jefferson City, Mo.: Hugh Stephens Printing Co., 1916.

Cadbury, Henry J. "An Account of Barbados 200 Years Ago." *Journal of the Barbados Museum and Historical Society* 9 (1941–42): 81–83.

Caribbeana. Containing Letters and Dissertations, Together with Political

Essays, On Various Subjects and Occasions. 2 vols. London: T. Osborne, 1741.

Carr, Cecil T., ed. *Select Charters of Trading Companies.* Publications of the Selden Society, 28. London: Bernard Quaritch, 1913.

The Case of the Jews Considered, with Regard to Trade, Commerce, Manufactries and Religion, &c. By a Christian. London: R. Richards, 1753.

Census of the Inhabitants of the Colony of Rhode Island and Providence Plantations, Taken by Order of the General Assembly, in the Year 1774. Providence: Knowles, Anthony & Co., 1858.

Cohen, Simon, tr., Jacob R. Marcus and Stanley F. Chyet, eds., *Historical Essay on the Colony of Surinam, 1788.* Cincinnati and New York: American Jewish Archives and Ktav, 1974.

Colonial Records of Pennsylvania. 17 vols. Harrisburg: J. Severns et al., 1851–53, 1860.

Commerce of Rhode Island. Massachusetts Historical Society, *Collections,* 7th ser., vols. 9–10. 1914–15.

Cooper, William Durrant. *Lists of Foreign Protestants and Aliens, Resident in England 1618–1688.* Camden Society, 82. Westminster: John Bowyer Nichols and Sons, 1862.

Cundall, Frank, ed. *Lady Nugent's Journal: Jamaica One Hundred Years Ago.* London: Adam and Charles Black, 1907.

———. "The Taxing of the Jews in Jamaica in the Seventeenth Century." *Publications of the American Jewish Historical Society* 31 (1928): 243–47.

Cundall, Frank, N. Darnell Davis, and Albert M. Friedenberg. "Documents Relating to the History of the Jews in Jamaica and Barbados in the Time of William III." *Publications of the American Jewish Historical Society* 23 (1915): 25–29.

Dallas, R. C. *The History of the Maroons from Their Origin to the Establishment of Their Chief Tribe at Sierra Leone.* 2 vols. 1803; London: Frank Cass and Co., 1968.

A Defence of the Observations on the Assiento Trade, As It Hath Been Exercised by the South-Sea Company &c. London: H. Whitridge, 1728.

Don John Further Display'd: Being A Supplement to Considerations on the American Trade. London: J. Roberts, 1740.

Donnan, Elizabeth, ed. *Documents Illustrative of the History of the Slave Trade to America.* 4 vols. Washington, D.C.: Carnegie Institution of Washington, 1930–35.

Douglass, William. *Summary, Historical and Political of the First Planting, Progressive Improvements, and Present State of the British Settlements in North-America.* 2 vols. Boston: Rogers and Fowle, 1749–51.

"The Earliest Extant Minute Books of the Spanish and Portuguese Congregation Shearith Israel in New York, 1728–1786." *Publications of the American Jewish Historical Society* 21 (1913): 1–171.

Edwards, Bryan. *The History, Civil and Commercial, of the British Colonies in the West Indies.* 2 vols. 1793; New York: Arno Press, 1972.

[Equiano, Olaudah]. *The Interesting Narrative of the Life of Olaudah Equiano,* ed. Robert J. Allsion. 1791; Boston: St. Martin's Press, 1995.

"Extracts from Various Records of the Early Settlement of the Jews in the Island of Barbados, W. I." *Publications of the American Jewish Historical Society* 26 (1918): 250–56.

Falconbridge, Alexander. *An Account of the Slave Trade on the Coast of Africa.* London: J. Phillips, 1788.

"Federal Supply Tax for the City of Philadelphia. For the year 1783." *Pennsylvania Archives,* 3d ser., XVI (1898): 729–837.

Friedenwald, Herbert. "Material for the History of the Jews in the British West Indies." *Publications of the American Jewish Historical Society* 5 (1897): 45–101.

Further Considerations on the Act to Permit Persons Professing the Jewish Religion to Be Naturalized by Parliament. In a Second Letter from a Merchant in Town to His Friend in the Country. London: R. Baldwin, 1753.

Gross, Charles. "Documents from the Public Record Office (London)." *Publications of the American Jewish Historical Society* 2 (1894): 165–70.

Hall, Richard, and Richard Hall. *Acts Passed in the Island of Barbados. From 1643, to 1762, Inclusive.* London: Richard Hall, 1764.

Handler, Jerome S., ed. "Memoirs of an Old Army Officer: Richard A. Wyvill's Visits to Barbados in 1796 and 1806–7." *Journal of the Barbados Museum and Historical Society* 35 (1975–78): 21–30.

Hershkowitz, Leo, ed. *Wills of Early New York Jews (1704–1799).* New York: American Jewish Historical Society, 1967.

Hershkowitz, Leo, and Isidore S. Meyer, eds. *The Lee Max Friedman Collection of American Jewish Colonial Correspondence: Letters of the Franks Family (1733–1748).* Waltham: American Jewish Historical Society, 1968.

Hollander, J. H., ed. "Documents Relating to the Attempted Departure of the Jews from Surinam in 1675." *Publications of the American Jewish Historical Society* 6 (1897): 9–29.

———. "The Naturalization of Jews in the American Colonies under the Act of 1740." *Publications of the American Jewish Historical Society* 5 (1897): 103–17.

Horsmanden, Daniel. *The New York Conspiracy, or a History of the Negro Plot with the Journal of the Proceedings against the Conspirators at New-*

York in the Years 1741–2. 1810; New York: Negro Universities Press, 1969.

Hotten, John Camden, ed. *The Original Lists of Persons of Quality; Emigrants; Religious Exiles; Political Rebels; Serving Men Sold for a Term of Years; Apprentices; Children Stolen; Maidens Pressed; and Others Who Went from Great Britain to the American Plantations 1600–1700*. Reprinted from 2d ed., New York, 1880; Baltimore: Genealogical Publishing Co., 1962.

House of Commons. *Sessional Papers of the Eighteenth Century, Reports and Papers, 1789, Slave Trade*. LXIX–LXXI: *Report of the Lords of the Committee of Council Appointed for the Consideration of All Matters Relating to Trade and Foreign Plantations*.

Houstoun, James. *The Works of James Houstoun, M.D.* London: N.p., 1753.

Jamaica Almanack. N.p.: N.p. [1787].

Judah, George Fortunatus. "The Jews' Tribute in Jamaica. Extracted from the Journals of the House of Assembly of Jamaica." *Publications of the American Jewish Historical Society* 18 (1909): 149–77.

Korn, Bertram Wallace. "Barbadian Jewish Wills, 1676–1740." In Bertram Wallace Korn, ed., *A Bicentennial Festschrift for Jacob Rader Marcus*, 303–15. Waltham and New York: American Jewish Historical Society and Ktav Publishing House, 1976.

[Leslie, Charles]. *A New History of Jamaica from the Earliest Accounts to the Taking of Porto Bello by Vice-Admiral Vernon. In Thirteen Letters from a Gentleman to his Friend*. 2d ed. London: J. Hodges, 1740.

A Letter from a Merchant of the City of London, to the R — t H — ble W — P — Esq.: Upon the Affairs and Commerce of North America, and the West Indies; Our African Trade. London: J. Scott, 1757.

Ligon, Richard. *A True & Exact History of the Island of Barbadoes*. London: Peter Parker and T. Guy, 1673.

A List of the Company of Merchants Trading to Africa, (Established by an Act of Parliament, Passed in the 23d Year of His Present Majesty, Intituled, An Act for Extending and Improving the Trade to Africa) Distinguishing Their Places of Abode. N.p.: N.p., [1758].

A List of the Company of Merchants Trading to Africa, Established by an Act the 23d. Year of George II, Intitled An Act for Extending and Improving the Trade to Africa. N.p.: N.p., 1787.

A List of the Names of the Corporation of the Governor and Company of Merchants of Great Britain Trading to the South-Seas, and Other Parts of America, and for Encouraging the Fishery. N.p.: John Barber, [1714].

Lloyd's Register 1764. London: Gregg Press, n.d.

Lloyd's Register 1776. London: Gregg Press, n.d.

Lloyd's Register 1790. London: Gregg Press, n.d.

Loker, Zvi. *Jews in the Caribbean: Evidence on the History of the Jews in the Caribbean Zone in Colonial Times.* [Jerusalem]: Misgav Yerushalaim, 1991.

Long, Edward. *The History of Jamaica. Or, General Survey of the Antient and Modern State of That Island.* 3 vols. London: T. Lowndes, 1774.

"The Lucas Manuscript Volumes in the Barbados Public Library." *Journal of the Barbados Museum and Historical Society* 14 (1946–47): 70–94.

Marcus, Jacob Rader. *American Jewry — Documents — Eighteenth Century.* Cincinnati: Hebrew Union College Press, 1959.

Memoirs of the First Settlement of the Island of Barbados, and Other of the Carribbee Islands, with the Succession of the Governors and Commanders in Chief of Barbados to the Year 1742. London: E. Owen, 1743. Reprinted Bridgetown, 1891.

Minchinton, W. E., ed. *The Trade of Bristol in the Eighteenth Century.* Bristol Record Society's Publications, 20. Bristol: J. W. Arrowsmith Ltd., 1957.

Minchinton, Walter E., Celia King, and Peter Waite, eds. *Virginia Slave-Trade Statistics 1698–1775.* Richmond: Virginia State Library, 1984.

[Minet, William, and Susan Minet]. *A Supplement to Dr. W. A. Shaw's Letters of Denization and Naturalization.* Publications of the Huguenot Society of London, 35. Frome: Butler and Tanner, 1932.

The New Jamaica Almanack and Register. Kingston: Thomas Stevenson & Co., [1788].

The New Jamaica Almanack and Register. St. Jago de la Vega: N.p., [1796].

The North-American and the West-Indian Gazetteer. London: G. Robinson, 1776.

Notes on the Two Reports from the Committee of the Honourable House of Assembly of Jamaica, Appointed to Examine into, and to Report to the House, the Allegations and Charges Contained in the Several Petitions Which Have Been Presented to the British House of Commons, on the Subject of the Slave Trade, and the Treatment of the Negroes. London: James Phillips, 1789.

O'Callaghan, E. B., ed. *The Documentary History of the State of New York.* 4 vols. Albany: Weed, Parsons and Co., 1849–51.

———. *Documents Relative to the Colonial History of the State of New York.* 11 vols. Albany: Weed, Parsons and Co., 1856–61.

Oliver, Vere Langford, ed. *Caribbeana Being Miscellaneous Papers Relating to the History, Genealogy, Topography, and Antiquities of the British West Indies.* 6 vols. London: Mitchell, Hughes and Clarke, 1909–19.

———. *The Monumental Inscriptions in the Churches and Churchyards of the Island of Barbados, British West Indies.* 1915; San Bernadino: Borgo Press, 1989.

[Postlethwayt, Malachy]. *The African Trade, the Great Pillar and Support of the British Plantation Trade in America.* London: J. Robinson, 1745.

Postlethwayt, Malachy. *The Universal Dictionary of Trade and Commerce,* 2 vols. 4th ed.; London: W. Strahan, 1774.

Proceedings of the Hon. House of Assembly of Jamaica, on the Sugar and Slave-Trade, in a Session Which Began the 23d of October, 1792. London: Stephen Fuller, 1793.

"Proprietary Tax of the City of Philadelphia, 1769." *Pennsylvania Archives,* 3d ser., XIV (1897): 149–220.

"Quaker Records." *Journal of the Barbados Museum and Historical Society* 15 (1947–48): 81–83.

Ramsay, James. *An Essay on the Treatment and Conversion of African Slaves in the British Sugar Colonies.* London: James Phillips, 1784.

Report, Resolutions, and Remonstrance, of the Honourable the Council and Assembly of Jamaica, at a Joint Committee, on the Subject of the Slave-Trade, in a Session Which Began the 20th of October 1789. London: B. White and Son, 1790.

Roth, C. "The Membership of the Great Synagogue, London, to 1791." *Miscellanies of the Jewish Historical Society of England* 6 (1962): 175–85.

Sainsbury, Ethel Bruce. *A Calendar of the Court Minutes Etc. of the East India Company.* 11 vols. Oxford: Clarendon Press, 1907–38.

Sainsbury, W. Noel et al., eds. *Calendar of State Papers, Colonial Series, America and West Indies.* 43 vols. London: H.M.'s Stationery Office, 1860–1963.

Sanders, Joanne Mcree. *Barbados Records: Baptisms, 1637–1800.* Baltimore: Genealogical Publishing Co., 1984.

———. *Barbados Records: Marriages, 1643–1800.* 2 vols. Houston: Sanders Historical Publications, 1982.

———. *Barbados Records: Wills and Administrations.* 3 vols. Houston: Sanders Historical Publications, 1979–81.

[Senhouse, William]. "The Autobiographical Manuscript of William Senhouse." *Journal of the Barbados Museum and Historical Society* 2 (1934–35): 61–79, 115–34, 191–209; 3 (1935–36): 3–19.

[Senior, Bernard Martin]. *Jamaica As It Was, As It Is, and As It May Be.* London: T. Hurst, 1835.

Shaw, William A., ed. *Letters of Denization and Acts of Naturalization for Aliens in England and Ireland, 1603–1700.* Publications of the Huguenot Society of London, 18. Lymington: N.p., 1911.

———. *Letters of Denization and Acts of Naturalization for Aliens in England and Ireland, 1701–1800.* Publications of the Huguenot Society of London, 27. Manchester: Sherratt and Hughes, 1923.

Shilstone, E. M., tr. *Monumental Inscriptions in the Burial Ground of the Jewish Synagogue at Bridgetown, Barbados*. N.p.: N.p., n.d.

The State of the Island of Jamaica. London: H. Whitridge, 1726.

Stern, Malcolm H., ed. "The Sheftall Diaries: Vital Records of Savannah Jewry (1733–1808)." *American Jewish Historical Quarterly* 54 (1964–65): 243–77.

[Thomas, Sir Dalby]. *An Historical Account of the Rise and Growth of the West-India Collonies and of the Great Advantages They Are to England in Respect of Trade*. 1690; New York: Arno Press, 1972.

A Treatise upon the Trade from Great-Britain to Africa; Humbly Recommended to the Attention of Government. London: R. Baldwin, 1772.

[Trelawny, Edward]. *An Essay Concerning Slavery, and the Danger Jamaica Is Expos'd to from the Too Great Number of Slaves*. London: Charles Corbett, [1745].

Two Reports (One Presented the 16th of October, the Other on the 12th of November, 1788) from the Committee of the Honourable House of Assembly of Jamaica on the Subject of the Slave-Trade. London: B. White and Son, 1789.

[Walduck, T.]. "T. Walduck's Letters from Barbados, 1710." *Journal of the Barbados Museum and Historical Society* 15 (1947–48): 27–51.

Wiznitzer, Arnold. "The Minute Book of Congregations Zur Israel of Recife and Magen Abraham of Maricia, Brazil." *Publications of the American Jewish Historical Society* 42 (1952–53): 217–302.

Wright, Philip. *Monumental Inscriptions of Jamaica*. London: Society of Genealogists, 1966.

III. Original Sources: Newspapers

Bridgetown, Barbados—*Barbados Gazette or General Intelligence*—June 30, 1787–February 14, 1789.

Bridgetown, Barbados—*Barbados Mercury*—April 5, 1783–May 29, 1784.

Kingston, Jamaica—*Daily Advertiser*—1790, August 14, 1793.

Kingston, Jamaica—*Jamaica Mercury and Kingston Weekly Advertiser*—May 1, 1779–April 29, 1780.

Kingston, Jamaica—*Royal Gazette*—1781, 1783, 1795, 1800, 1805.

Montego Bay, Jamaica—*The Cornwall Chronicle and Jamaica General Advertiser*—1776–90.

IV. Secondary Sources: Books

Andrade, Jacob A. P. M. *A Record of the Jews in Jamaica from the English Conquest to the Present Time.* Kingston: Jamaica Times, 1941.

Andrews, Charles M. *The Colonial Period of American History.* 4 vols. New Haven: Yale University Press, 1934–38.

Armytage, Frances. *The Free Port System in the British West Indies: A Study in Commercial Policy, 1766–1822.* London: Longmans, Green and Co., 1953.

Baer, Yitzhak. *A History of the Jews in Christian Spain.* 2 vols. Philadelphia: Jewish Publication Society of America, 1966.

Barbour, Violet. *Capitalism in Amsterdam in the 17th Century.* 1950; Ann Arbor: University of Michigan Press, 1976.

Barnett, Lionel D. *Bevis Marks Records Being Contributions to the History of the Spanish and Portuguese Congregation of London. Part I.* Oxford: The University Press by John Johnson, 1940.

Baron, Salo Wittmayer. *A Social and Religious History of the Jews.* 17 vols. 2d ed., rev. and enl. New York and Philadelphia: Columbia University Press and Jewish Publication Society of America, 1952–80.

Bean, Richard Nelson. *The British Trans-Atlantic Slave Trade, 1650–1775.* New York: Arno Press, 1975.

Beckles, Hilary McD. *White Servitude and Black Slavery in Barbados, 1627–1715.* Knoxville: University of Tennessee Press, 1989.

Blussé, Leonard, and Femme Gaastra, eds. *Companies and Trade: Essays on Overseas Trading Companies during the Ancien Régime.* N.p.: Leiden University Press, 1981.

Boxer, C. R. *The Dutch in Brazil, 1624–1654.* Oxford: Clarendon Press, 1957.

———. *The Dutch Seaborne Empire, 1600–1800.* New York: Alfred A. Knopf, 1965.

———. *The Portuguese Seaborne Empire, 1415–1825.* New York: Alfred A. Knopf, 1969.

Brackman, Harold. *Farrakhan's Reign of Historical Error: The Truth behind The Secret Relationship between Blacks and Jews.* N.p.: Simon Wiesenthal Center, 1992.

———. *Ministry of Lies: The Truth behind the Nation of Islam's "The Secret Relationship between Blacks and Jews."* New York: Four Walls Eight Windows, 1994.

Carswell, John. *The South Sea Bubble.* Stanford: Stanford University Press, 1960.

Chaudhuri, K. N. *The Trading World of Asia and the English East India Company, 1660–1760.* Cambridge: Cambridge University Press, 1978.

Chyet, Stanley F. *Lopez of Newport: Colonial American Merchant Prince.* Detroit: Wayne State University Press, 1970.

Clarke, Colin G. *Kingston, Jamaica: Urban Development and Social Change, 1692–1962.* Berkeley: University of California, 1975.

Cohen, Robert, ed. *The Jewish Nation in Surinam: Historical Essays.* Amsterdam: S. Emmering, 1982.

———. *Jews in Another Environment: Surinam in the Second Half of the Eighteenth Century.* Leiden: E. J. Brill, 1991.

Coughtry, Jay. *The Notorious Triangle: Rhode Island and the African Slave Trade, 1700–1807.* Philadelphia: Temple University Press, 1981.

Crane, Elaine Forman. *A Dependent People: Newport, Rhode Island in the Revolutionary Era.* New York: Fordham University Press, 1985.

Craton, Michael. *Sinews of Empire: A Short History of British Slavery.* Garden City: Doubleday, 1974.

Craton, Michael, and James Walvin. *A Jamaican Plantation: The History of Worthy Park, 1670–1970.* Toronto: University of Toronto Press, 1970.

Curtin, Philip D. *The Atlantic Slave Trade: A Census.* Madison: University of Wisconsin Press, 1969.

Davies, D. W. *A Primer of Dutch Seventeenth Century Overseas Trade.* The Hague: Matinus Nijhoff, 1961.

Davies, K. G. *The Royal African Company.* 1957; New York: Atheneum, 1970.

Davis, David Brion. *The Problem of Slavery in the Age of Revolution, 1770–1823.* Ithaca: Cornell University Press, 1975.

———. *The Problem of Slavery in Western Culture.* 1966; New York: Oxford University Press, 1988.

———. *Slavery and Human Progress.* New York: Oxford University Press, 1984.

Davis, Ralph. *The Rise of the English Shipping Industry in the Seventeenth and Eighteenth Centuries.* London: Macmillan, 1962.

Dickson, P. G. M. *The Financial Revolution in England: A Study in the Development of Public Credit, 1688–1756.* London: Macmillan, 1967.

Dunn, Richard S. *Sugar and Slaves: The Rise of the Planter Class in the English West Indies, 1624–1713.* Chapel Hill: University of North Carolina Press, 1972.

Elzas, Barnett A. *The Jews of South Carolina from the Earliest Times to the Present Day.* Philadelphia: Lippincott, 1905.

Emmanuel, Isaac S. *Precious Stones of the Jews of Curaçao: Curaçaon Jewry, 1656–1957.* New York: Bloch Publishing Company, 1957.

Emmanuel, Isaac S., and Suzanne A. Emmanuel. *History of the Jews of the Netherlands Antilles.* 2 vols. Cincinnati: American Jewish Archives, 1970.

Endelman, Todd M. *The Jews of Georgian England, 1714–1830: Tradition and Change in a Liberal Society.* Philadelphia: Jewish Publication Society of America, 1979.

Faber, Eli. *A Time for Planting: The First Migration, 1654–1820.* Baltimore: Johns Hopkins University Press, 1992.

Feurtado, W. A. *Official and Other Personages of Jamaica from 1655 to 1790.* Kingston: W. A. Feurtado's Sons, 1896.

Fortune, Stephen Alexander. *Merchants and Jews: The Struggle for British West Indian Commerce, 1650–1750.* Gainesville: University Presses of Florida, 1984.

Freund, Miriam K. *Jewish Merchants in Colonial America.* New York: Behrman's Jewish Book House, 1939.

Galenson, David W. *Traders, Planters, and Slaves: Market Behavior in Early English America.* Cambridge: Cambridge University Press, 1986.

Gaster, Moses. *History of the Ancient Synagogue of the Spanish and Portuguese Jews.* London: N.p., 1901.

Gemery, Henry A., and Jan S. Hogendorn, eds. *The Uncommon Market: Essays in the Economic History of the Atlantic Slave Trade.* New York: Academic Press, 1979.

Golding, C. E., and D. King-Page. *Lloyd's.* New York: McGraw-Hill, 1952.

Goslinga, Cornelis Ch. *The Dutch in the Caribbean and on the Wild Coast, 1580–1680.* Gainesville: University of Florida Press, 1971.

Goveia, Elsa V. *A Study on the Historiography of the British West Indies to the End of the Nineteenth Century.* Washington, D.C.: Howard University Press, 1980.

Grinstein, Hyman B. *The Rise of the Jewish Community of New York, 1654–1860.* Philadelphia: Jewish Publication Society of America, 1947.

Gutstein, Morris A. *The Story of the Jews of Newport: Two and a Half Centuries of Judaism, 1658–1908.* New York: Bloch, 1936.

Hagy, James William. *This Happy Land: The Jews of Colonial and Antebellum Charleston.* Tuscaloosa: University of Alabama Press, 1993.

Harlow, Vincent T. *A History of Barbados, 1625–1865.* 1926; New York: Negro Universities Press, 1969.

Hartog, J. *The Jews and St. Eustatius: The Eighteenth Century Jewish Congregation Honen Dalim and Description of the Old Cemetery.* N.p.: N.p., 1976.

Herculano, Alexandre. *History of the Origin and Establishment of the Inquisition in Portugal,* tr. John C. Branner. 1926; New York: AMS Press, 1968.

Herskovits, Melville J. *The Myth of the Negro Past.* 1941; Boston: Beacon Press, 1990.

Higman, B. W. *Slave Population and Economy in Jamaica, 1807–1834.* Cambridge: Cambridge University Press, 1976.

———. *Slave Populations of the British Caribbean, 1807–1834*. Baltimore: Johns Hopkins University Press, 1984.

Hudaly, David. *Liverpool Old Hebrew Congregation, 1780–1974*. Liverpool: Liverpool Old Hebrew Congregation, 1974.

Hurwitz, Samuel J., and Edith F. Hurwitz. *Jamaica: A Historical Portrait*. New York: Praeger, 1971.

Hyamson, Albert M. *David Salomons*. London: Methuen, 1939.

———. *The Sephardim of England: A History of the Spanish and Portuguese Jewish Community, 1492–1951*. London: Methuen, 1951.

Ingram, K. E. *Sources of Jamaican History, 1655–1838: A Bibliographic Survey with Particular Reference to Manuscript Sources*. 2 vols. Zug: Inter Documentation Company, 1976.

Inikori, Joseph E., and Stanley L. Engerman, eds. *The Atlantic Slave Trade: Effects on Economies, Societies, and Peoples in Africa, the Americas, and Europe*. Durham: Duke University Press, 1992.

Israel, Jonathan I. *Dutch Primacy in World Trade, 1585–1740*. Oxford: Clarendon Press, 1989.

———. *The Dutch Republic: Its Rise, Greatness, and Fall, 1477–1806*. Oxford: Clarendon Press, 1995.

———. *European Jewry in the Age of Mercantilism, 1550–1750*. Oxford: Clarendon Press, 1985.

Katz, David S. *The Jews in the History of England, 1485–1850*. Oxford: Clarendon Press, 1994.

Klein, Herbert S. *The Middle Passage: Comparative Studies in the Atlantic Slave Trade*. Princeton: Princeton University Press, 1978.

Lindo, E. H. *The History of the Jews of Spain and Portugal*. 1848; New York: Burt Franklin, 1970.

Mackenzie-Grieve, Averil. *The Last Years of the English Slave Trade: Liverpool 1750–1807*. 1941; New York: A. M. Kelley, 1968.

Marcus, Jacob R. *The Colonial American Jew, 1492–1776*. 3 vols. Detroit: Wayne State University Press, 1970.

———. *Early American Jewry*. 2 vols. Philadelphia: Jewish Publication Society of America, 1951–53.

———. *United States Jewry, 1776–1985*. 4 vols. Detroit: Wayne State University Press, 1989–93.

McLachlan, Jean O. *Trade and Peace with Old Spain, 1667–1750: A Study of the Influence of Commerce on Anglo-Spanish Diplomacy in the First Half of the Eighteenth Century*. Cambridge: Cambridge University Press, 1940.

McManus, Edgar J. *Black Bondage in the North*. Syracuse: Syracuse University Press, 1973.

———. *A History of Negro Slavery in New York.* Syracuse: Syracuse University Press, 1966.

Mintz, Sidney W. *Caribbean Transformations.* Baltimore: Johns Hopkins University Press, 1974.

Morgan, Kenneth. *Bristol and the Atlantic Trade in the Eighteenth Century.* N.p.: Cambridge University Press, 1993.

Palmer, Colin. *Human Cargoes: The British Slave Trade to Spanish America, 1700–1739.* Urbana: University of Illinois Press, 1981.

Pares, Richard. *War and Trade in the West Indies, 1739–1763.* 1936; London: Frank Cass and Co., 1963.

———. *A West-India Fortune.* 1950; Hamden: Archon, 1968.

Parkinson, C. Northcote. *The Rise of the Port of Liverpool.* Liverpool: University Press, 1952.

Patterson, Orlando. *The Sociology of Slavery: An Analysis of the Origins, Development and Structure of Negro Slave Society in Jamaica.* London: MacGibbon and Kee, 1967.

Pawson, Michael, and David Buisseret. *Port Royal, Jamaica.* Oxford: Clarendon Press, 1975.

Perry, Thomas W. *Public Opinion, Propaganda, and Politics in Eighteenth-Century England: A Study of the Jew Bill of 1753.* Cambridge, Mass.: Harvard University Press, 1962.

Pitman, Frank Wesley. *The Development of the British West Indies, 1700–1763.* 1917; N.p.: Archon Books, 1967.

Pool, David De Sola. *An Old Faith in the New World: Portrait of Shearith Israel, 1654–1954.* New York: Columbia University Press, 1955.

———. *Portraits Etched in Stone: Early Jewish Settlers, 1682–1831.* New York: Columbia University Press, 1952.

Postma, Johannes Menne. *The Dutch in the Atlantic Slave Trade, 1600–1815.* Cambridge: Cambridge University Press, 1990.

Rabinowicz, Oskar K. *Sir Solomon de Medina.* London: Jewish Historical Society of England, 1974.

Ragatz, Lowell Joseph. *The Fall of the Planter Class in the British Caribbean, 1763–1833.* 1928; New York: Octagon Books, 1963.

Rawley, James A. *The Transatlantic Slave Trade: A History.* New York: W. W. Norton, 1981.

Reznikoff, Charles, and Uriah Z. Engelman. *The Jews of Charleston: A History of an American Jewish Community.* Philadelphia: Jewish Publication Society of America, 1950.

Richardson, David, ed. *Bristol, Africa and the Eighteenth-Century Slave Trade to America.* 4 vols. Bristol Record Society's Publications, Volumes 38, 39, 42, 47. Gloucester: Alan Sutton Publishing, 1986–96.

Roth, Cecil. *The Great Synagogue, London 1690–1940*. London: Edward Goldston and Son, 1950.

———. *A History of the Marranos*. Philadelphia: Jewish Publication Society of America, 1932.

———. *The Rise of Provincial Jewry: The Early History of the Jewish Communities in the English Countryside, 1740–1840*. London: Jewish Monthly, 1950.

Rubin, Saul Jacob. *Third to None: The Saga of Savannah Jewry, 1733–1983*. Savannah: S. J. Rubin, 1983.

Schomburgk, Robert H. *The History of Barbados*. 1848; London: Frank Cass and Co., 1971.

Scott, William Robert. *The Constitution and Finance of English, Scottish and Irish Joint-Stock Companies to 1720*. 3 vols. Cambridge: Cambridge University Press, 1912.

The Secret Relationship between Blacks and Jews: Volume One. Chicago: Nation of Islam, 1991.

Sheridan, Richard B. *Doctors and Slaves: A Medical and Demographic History of Slavery in the British West Indies, 1680–1834*. Cambridge: Cambridge University Press, 1985.

———. *Sugar and Slavery: An Economic History of the British West Indies, 1623–1775*. Baltimore: Johns Hopkins University Press, 1973.

Shulvass, Moses A. *From East to West: The Westward Migration of Jews from Eastern Europe during the Seventeenth and Eighteenth Centuries*. Detroit: Wayne State University Press, 1971.

Solow, Barbara L., ed. *Slavery and the Rise of the Atlantic System*. Cambridge: Cambridge University Press, 1991.

Sperling, John G. *The South Sea Company: An Historical Essay and Bibliographical Finding List*. Boston: Baker Library, 1962.

Stein, Robert Louis. *The French Slave Trade in the Eighteenth Century: An Old Regime Business*. Madison: University of Wisconsin Press, 1979.

Stern, Malcolm H. *First American Jewish Families: 600 Genealogies, 1654–1988*. 3d ed. Baltimore: Ottenheimer, 1991.

Sutherland, Lucy S. *The East India Company in Eighteenth-Century Politics*. Oxford: Clarendon Press, 1952.

———. *A London Merchant, 1695–1774*. N.p.: Oxford University Press, 1933.

Thomas, Hugh. *The Slave Trade*. New York: Simon and Schuster, 1997.

Thornton, A. P. *West-India Policy under the Restoration*. Oxford: Clarendon Press, 1956.

Tuchman, Barbara. *The First Salute*. New York: Alfred A. Knopf, 1988.

Whiteman, Maxwell. *Copper for America: The Hendricks Family and a*

National Industry, 1755–1939. New Brunswick: Rutgers University Press, 1971.

Williams, Gomer. *History of the Liverpool Privateers and Letters of Marque with an Account of the Liverpool Slave Trade*. London: William Heinemann, 1897.

Wiznitzer, Arnold. *Jews in Colonial Brazil*. New York: Columbia University Press, 1960.

Wolf, Edwin, and Maxwell Whiteman. *The History of the Jews of Philadelphia from Colonial Times to the Age of Jackson*. Philadelphia: Jewish Publication Society of America, 1957.

Wolf, Lucien. *Essays in Jewish History*. London: Jewish Historical Society of England, 1934.

Yogev, Gedalia. *Diamonds and Coral: Anglo-Dutch Jews and Eighteenth-Century Trade*. N.p.: Leicester University Press, 1978.

V. Secondary Sources: Articles

Abrahams, Dudley. "Jew Brokers of the City of London." *Miscellanies of the Jewish Historical Society of England* 3 (1937): 80–94.

Abrahams, I. "Passes Issued to Jews in the Period 1689 to 1696." *Miscellanies of the Jewish Historical Society of England* 1 (1925): xxiv–xxxiii.

Anstey, Roger. "The Volume and Profitability of the British Slave Trade, 1761–1807." In Stanley L. Engerman, and Eugene D. Genovese, eds., *Race and Slavery in the Western Hemisphere: Quantitative Studies*, 3–31. Princeton: Princeton University Press, 1975.

Arnold, Arthur P. "A List of Jews and Their Households in London Extracted from the Census Lists of 1695." *Miscellanies of the Jewish Historical Society of England* 6 (1962): 73–141.

August, Thomas G. "Family Structure and Jewish Continuity in Jamaica since 1655." *American Jewish Archives* 41 (1989): 27–42.

Barnett, Richard D. "Anglo-Jewry in the Eighteenth Century." In V. D. Lipman, ed., *Three Centuries of Anglo-Jewish History*, 45–68. N.p.: Jewish Historical Society of England, 1961.

———. "The Correspondence of the Mahamad of the Spanish and Portuguese Congregation of London during the Seventeenth and Eighteenth Century." *Transactions of the Jewish Historical Society of England* 20 (1959–61): 1–50.

———. "Diplomatic Aspects of the Sephardic Influx from Portugal in the Early Eighteenth Century." *Transactions of the Jewish Historical Society of England* 25 (1973–75): 210–21.

Behrendt, Stephen D. "The Annual Volume and Regional Distribution of the British Slave Trade, 1780–1807." *Journal of African History* 38 (1997): 187–211.

Beinart, Haim. "The *Converso* Community in 15th Century Spain." In R. D. Barnett, ed., *The Sephardi Heritage: Essays on the History and Cultural Contributions of the Jews in Spain and Portugal*, 425–56. London: Vallentine, Mitchell, 1971.

———. "The Jews in the Canary Islands: A Re-evaluation." *Transactions of the Jewish Historical Society of England* 25 (1973–75): 48–86.

Benas, Bertram B. "A Survey of the Jewish Institutional History of Liverpool and District." *Transactions of the Jewish Historical Society of England* 17 (1951–52): 23–37.

Bloom, Herbert I. "A Study of Brazilian Jewish History 1623–1654, Based Chiefly upon the Findings of the Late Samuel Oppenheim." *Publications of the American Jewish Historical Society* 33 (1934): 43–125.

Brandow, James C. "A Young Virginian's Visit to Barbados, 1771–1772." *Journal of the Barbados Museum and Historical Society* 35 (1975–78): 73–86.

Brown, Malcolm. "Anglo-Jewish Country Houses from the Resettlement to 1800." *Transactions of the Jewish Historical Society of England* 28 (1981–82): 20–38.

Brown, Vera Lee. "The South Sea Company and Contraband Trade." *American Historical Review* 31 (1926): 662–78.

Burnard, Trevor. "European Migration to Jamaica, 1655–1780." 3d ser., *William and Mary Quarterly* 53 (1996): 769–96.

———. "Who Bought Slaves in Early America? Purchasers of Slaves from the Royal African Company in Jamaica, 1674–1708." *Slavery and Abolition* 17 (1996): 68–92.

Campbell, P. F. "The Barbados Vestries 1627–1700—Part II." *Journal of the Barbados Museum and Historical Society* 37 (1983–86): 174–96.

———. "The Merchants and Traders of Barbados—1." *Journal of the Barbados Museum and Historical Society* 34 (1971–74): 85–98.

Chaudhuri, K. N. "Treasure and Trade Balances: The East India Company's Export Trade, 1660–1720." 2d ser., *Economic History Review* 21 (1968): 480–502.

Checkland, S. G. "Finance for the West Indies, 1780–1815." 2d ser., *Economic History Review* 10 (1957–58): 461–69.

Christelow, Allan. "Contraband Trade between Jamaica and the Spanish Main and the Free Port Act of 1766." *Hispanic American Historical Review* 22 (1942): 309–43.

Cohen, Robert. "Early Caribbean Jewry: A Demographic Perspective." *Jewish Social Studies* 45 (1983): 123–34.

———. "The Egerton Manuscript." *American Jewish Historical Quarterly* 62 (1972–73): 333–47.

———. "Sampson and Jacob Mears, Merchants." *American Jewish Historical Quarterly* 67 (1977–78): 233–45.

Daiches-Dubens, Rachel. "Eighteenth Century Anglo-Jewry in and around Richmond, Surrey." *Transactions of the Jewish Historical Society of England* 18 (1953–55): 143–69.

Daniels, Doris Groshen. "Colonial Jewry: Religion, Domestic and Social Relations." *American Jewish Historical Quarterly* 66 (1976–77): 375–400.

Davies, K. G. "Joint-Stock Investment in the Later Seventeenth Century." 2d ser., *Economic History Review* 4 (1951–52): 283–301.

———. "The Origins of the Commission System in the West India Trade." 5th ser., *Transactions of the Royal Historical Society* 2 (1952): 89–107.

Davis, David Brion. "Jews in the Slave Trade." *Culturefront,* Fall 1992, 42–45.

Davis, N. Darnell. "Notes on the History of the Jews in Barbados." *Publications of the American Jewish Historical Society* 18 (1909): 129–48.

De Bethencourt, Cardozo. "Notes on the Spanish and Portuguese Jews in the United States, Guiana, and the Dutch and British West Indies during the Seventeenth and Eighteenth Centuries." *Publications of the American Jewish Historical Society* 29 (1925): 7–38.

De Mesquita, D. Bueno. "The Historical Associations of the Ancient Burial-Ground of the Sephardi Jews." *Transactions of the Jewish Historical Society of England* 10 (1921–23): 225–54.

Diamond, A. S. "The Community of the Resettlement, 1656–1684: A Social Survey." *Transactions of the Jewish Historical Society of England* 24 (1970–73): 134–50.

———. "Problems of the London Sephardi Community, 1720–1733 — Philip Carteret Webb's Notebooks." *Transactions of the Jewish Historical Society of England* 21 (1962–67): 39–63.

Donnan, Elizabeth. "The Early Days of the South Sea Company, 1711–1718." *Journal of Economic and Business History* 2 (1929–30): 419–50.

Drescher, Seymour. "The Role of Jews in the Transatlantic Slave Trade." *Immigrants and Minorities* 12 (1993): 113–25.

Dunn, Richard S. "The Barbados Census of 1680: Profile of the Richest Colony in English America." 3d ser., *William and Mary Quarterly* 26 (1969): 3–30.

Eltis, D. "The British Contribution to the Nineteenth-Century Transatlantic Slave Trade." 2d ser., *Economic History Review* 32 (1979): 211–27.

———. "The Traffic in Slaves between the British West Indian Colonies, 1807–1833." 2d ser., *Economic History Review* 25 (1972): 55–64.

Eltis, David. "The Total Product of Barbados, 1664–1701." *Journal of Economic History* 55 (1995): 321–38.

Eltis, David, and David Richardson. "The 'Numbers Game' and Routes to Slavery." *Slavery and Abolition* 18 (1997): 1–15.

"Extracts from Various Records of the Early Settlement of the Jews in the Island of Barbados, W.I." *Publications of the American Jewish Historical Society* 26 (1918): 250–56.

Farnie, D. A. "The Commercial Empire of the Atlantic, 1607–1783." 2d ser., *Economic History Review* 15 (1962): 205–18.

Fisher, H. E. S. "Review Article: Jews in England and the 18th-Century English Economy." *Miscellanies of the Jewish Historical Society of England* 12 (1978–80): 156–65.

Friedman, Lee M. "Wills of Early Jewish Settlers in New York." *Publications of the American Jewish Historical Society* 23 (1915): 147–61.

Fuks-Mansfeld, R. G. "Problems of Overpopulation of Jewish Amsterdam in the 17th Century. *Studia Rosenthaliana* 18 (1984): 141–42.

Galenson, David. "The Slave Trade to the English West Indies, 1673–1724." 2d ser., *Economic History Review* 32 (1979): 241–49.

[Giuseppi, J. A.] "Early Jewish Holders of Bank of England Stock (1694–1725)." *Miscellanies of the Jewish Historical Society of England* 6 (1962): 143–74.

Giuseppi, J. A. "Sephardi Jews and the Early Years of the Bank of England." *Transactions of the Jewish Historical Society of England* 19 (1955–59): 53–63.

Hartog, John. "The Honen Daliem Congregation of St. Eustatius." *American Jewish Archives* 19 (1967): 60–77.

Henriques, H. S. Q. "Proposals for Special Taxation of the Jews after the Revolution." *Transactions of the Jewish Historical Society of England* 9 (1918–20): 39–66.

Hershkowitz, Leo. "Some Aspects of the New York Jewish Merchant and Community, 1654–1820." *American Jewish Historical Quarterly* 66 (1976–77): 10–34.

Higgins, W. Robert. "Charles Town Merchants and Factors Dealing in the External Negro Trade, 1735–1775." *South Carolina Historical Magazine* 65 (1964): 205–17.

Hilfman, P. A. "Some Further Notes on the History of the Jews in Surinam." *Publications of the American Jewish Historical Society* 16 (1907): 7–22.

Hurwitz, Samuel J., and Edith Hurwitz. "The New World Sets an Example for the Old: The Jews of Jamaica and Political Rights, 1661–1831." *American Jewish Historical Quarterly* 55 (1965–66): 37–56.

Hyde, Francis E., Bradbury B. Parkinson, and Sheila Marriner. "The Nature and Profitability of the Liverpool Slave Trade." 2d ser., *Economic History Review* 5 (1953): 368–77.

Israel, Jonathan I. "The Economic Contribution of Dutch Sephardi Jewry to Holland's Golden Age, 1595–1713." *Tijdschrift voor Geschiedenis* 96 (1983): 505–35.

Jameson, J. Franklin. "St. Eustatius in the American Revolution." *American Historical Review* 8 (1902–3): 683–708.

Kayserling, M. "The Jews in Jamaica and Daniel Israel Lopez Laguna." Original ser., *Jewish Quarterly Review* 12 (1900): 708–17.

Kohler, Max J. "A Memorial of Jews to Parliament Concerning Jewish Participation in Colonial Trade, 1696." *Publications of the American Jewish Historical Society* 18 (1909): 123–27.

Korn, Bertram Wallace. "The Haham DeCordova of Jamaica." *American Jewish Archives* 18 (1966): 141–54.

———. "Jews and Negro Slavery in the Old South, 1789–1865." *Publications of the American Jewish Historical Society* 50 (1960–61): 151–201.

Krohn, Franklin B. "The Search for the Elusive Caribbean Jews." *American Jewish Archives* 45 (1993): 147–57.

Loker, Zvi. "Cayenne: A Chapter in Jewish Immigration and Settlement in the New World during the Seventeenth Century" (in Hebrew). *Zion* 48 (1983): 107–16.

———. "An Eighteenth-Century Plan to Invade Jamaica; Isaac Yeshurun Sasportas—French Patriot or Jewish Radical Idealist?" *Miscellanies of the Jewish Historical Society of England* 13 (1981–82): 132–44.

Lovejoy, Paul. "The Volume of the Atlantic Slave Trade: A Synthesis." *Journal of African History* 23 (1982): 473–501.

Ludlum, David M. "The Great Hurricane." *Journal of the Barbados Museum and Historical Society* 31 (1964–66): 127–31.

Lydon, James G. "New York and the Slave Trade, 1700 to 1774." 3d ser., *William and Mary Quarterly* 35 (1978): 375–94.

Marcus, Jacob R. "The Oldest Known Synagogue Record Book of Continental North America, 1720–1721." In Jacob R. Marcus, *Studies in American Jewish History: Studies and Addresses.* Cincinnati: Hebrew Union College Press, 1969.

Masur, Louis P. "Slavery in Eighteenth-Century Rhode Island: Evidence from the Census of 1774." *Slavery and Abolition* 6 (1985): 139–50.

McDonald, Roderick A. "Measuring the British Slave Trade to Jamaica,

1789–1808: A Comment." 2d ser., *Economic History Review* 33 (1980): 253–58.

Merrill, Gordon. "The Role of Sephardic Jews in the British Caribbean Area during the Seventeenth Century." *Caribbean Studies* 4 (1964): 32–49.

Minchinton, Walter E. "The British Slave Fleet, 1680–1775: The Evidence of the Naval Office Shipping Lists." In Serge Daget, ed., *De la Traite à l'Esclavage: Actes du Colloque International sur la Traite des Noirs, Nantes 1985,* 2 vols., I, 395–425. Nantes: Centre de Recherche sur l'Histoire du Monde Atlantique, 1988.

Molen, Patricia A. "Population and Social Patterns in Barbados in the Early Eighteenth Century." 3d ser., *William and Mary Quarterly* 28 (1971): 287–300.

Morgan, David T. "The Sheftalls of Savannah." *American Jewish Historical Quarterly* 62 (1972–73): 348–61.

Nasatir, A. P., and Leo Shpall. "The Texel Affair." *American Jewish Historical Quarterly* 53 (1963–64): 3–43.

Nelson, George H. "Contraband Trade under the Asiento." *American Historical Review* 51 (1945): 55–67.

Nettels, Curtis. "England and the Spanish-American Trade, 1680–1715." *Journal of Modern History* 3 (1931): 1–32.

Newman, Aubrey. "Anglo-Jewry in the 18th Century: A Presidential Address." *Transactions of the Jewish Historical Society of England* 27 (1982): 1–9.

Oppenheim, Samuel. "The Early History of the Jews in New York, 1654–1664. Some New Matter on the Subject." *Publications of the American Jewish Historical Society* 18 (1909): 1–91.

———. "An Early Jewish Colony in Western Guiana, 1658–1666, and Its Relation to the Jews in Surinam, Cayenne and Tobago." *Publications of the American Jewish Historical Society* 16 (1907): 95–186.

———. "Jewish Owners of Ships Registered at the Port of Philadelphia, 1730–1775." *Publications of the American Jewish Historical Society* 26 (1918): 235–36.

———. "The Jews in Barbados in 1739. An Attack upon Their Synagogue. Their Long Oath." *Publications of the American Jewish Historical Society* 22 (1914): 197–98.

Perry, Norma. "Voltaire and the Sephardi Bankrupt." *Transactions of the Jewish Historical Society of England* 29 (1982–86): 39–52.

Platt, Virginia B. " 'And Don't Forget the Guinea Voyage': The Slave Trade of Aaron Lopez of Newport." 3d ser., *William and Mary Quarterly* 32 (1975): 601–18.

———. "Tar, Staves, and New England Rum: The Trade of Aaron Lopez of

Newport, Rhode Island, with Colonial North Carolina." *North Carolina Historical Review* 48 (1971): 1–22.

Rawley, J. A. "Humphry Morice: Foremost London Slave Merchant of His Time." In Serge Daget, ed., *De la Traite à l'Esclavage: Actes du Colloque International sur la Traite des Noirs, Nantes 1985*, 2 vols., I, 269–81. Nantes: Centre de Recherche sur l'Histoire du Monde Atlantique, 1988.

Richardson, David. "The Eighteenth-Century British Slave Trade: Estimates of Its Volume and Coastal Distribution in Africa." *Research in Economic History* 12 (1989): 151–95.

———. "Slave Exports from West and West-Central Africa, 1700–1810: New Estimates of Volume and Distribution." *Journal of African History* 30 (1989): 1–22.

Roos, J. S. "Additional Notes on the History of the Jews in Surinam." *Publications of the American Jewish Historical Society* 13 (1905): 127–36.

Rosenbloom, Joseph R. "Notes on the Jews' Tribute in Jamaica." *Transactions of the Jewish Historical Society of England* 20 (1959–61): 247–54.

Rosenswaike, Ira. "An Estimate and Analysis of the Jewish Population of the United States in 1790." *Publications of the American Jewish Historical Society* 50 (1960–61): 23–67.

Roth, Cecil. "The Amazing Clan of Buzaglo." *Transactions of the Jewish Historical Society of England* 23 (1969–70): 11–21.

Samuel, Edgar Roy. "Anglo-Jewish Notaries and Scriveners." *Transactions of the Jewish Historical Society of England* 17 (1951–52): 113–59.

———. "The Jews in English Foreign Trade—A Consideration of the 'Philo Patriae' Pamphlets of 1753." In John M. Shaftesley, ed., *Remember the Days: Essays on Anglo-Jewish History Presented to Cecil Roth*, 123–43. London: Jewish Historical Society of England, 1966.

———. "Manuel Levy Duarte (1631–1714): An Amsterdam Merchant Jeweller and His Trade with London." *Transactions of the Jewish Historical Society of England* 27 (1978–80): 11–31.

———. "New Light on the Selection of Jewish Children's Names." *Transactions of the Jewish Historical Society of England* 23 (1969–70): 64–86.

Samuel, Wilfred S. "Anglo-Jewish Ships' Names." *Miscellanies of the Jewish Historical Society of England* 3 (1937): 103–5.

———. "The Jewish Oratories of Cromwellian London." *Miscellanies of the Jewish Historical Society of England* 3 (1937): 46–56.

———. "A Review of the Jewish Colonists in Barbados in the Year 1680." *Transactions of the Jewish Historical Society of England* 13 (1932–35): 1–111.

———. "Tentative List of Underwriting Members of Lloyd's (from some time prior to 1800 until the year 1901)." *Miscellanies of the Jewish Historical Society of England* 5 (1948): 176–92.

Samuel, Wilfred S., R. D. Barnett, and A. S. Diamond. "A List of Persons Endenizened and Naturalised 1609–1799." *Transactions of the Jewish Historical Society of England* 22 (1968–69): 111–44.

Selig, Robert A. "The French Capture of St. Eustatius, 26 November, 1781." *Journal of Caribbean History* 27 (1993): 129–43.

Sheridan, Richard B. "The Commercial and Financial Organization of the British Slave Trade, 1750–1807." 2d ser., *Economic History Review* 11 (1958–59): 249–63.

———. "The Slave Trade to Jamaica, 1702–1808," in B. W. Higman, ed., *Trade, Government and Society in Caribbean History, 1700–1920*. Kingston: Heinemann Educational Books, 1983.

———. "The Wealth of Jamaica in the Eighteenth Century." 2d ser., *Economic History Review* 18 (1965): 292–311.

———. "The Wealth of Jamaica in the Eighteenth Century: A Rejoinder." 2d ser., *Economic History Review* 21 (1968): 46–61.

Shilstone, E. M. "The Jewish Synagogue Bridgetown, Barbados." *Journal of the Barbados Museum and Historical Society* 32 (1966–68): 3–15.

Silber, Mendel. "America in Hebrew Literature." *Publications of the American Jewish Historical Society* 22 (1914): 101–37.

Stern, Malcolm H. "Some Additions and Corrections to Rosenswaike's 'An Estimate and Analysis of the Jewish Population of the United States in 1790.' " *American Jewish Historical Quarterly* 53 (1963–64): 285–88.

———. "Some Notes on the Jews of Nevis." *American Jewish Archives* 10 (1958): 151–59.

———. "A Successful Caribbean Restoration: The Nevis Story." *American Jewish Historical Quarterly* 61 (1971–72): 19–32.

Sutherland, Lucy. "Samson Gideon: Eighteenth Century Jewish Financier." *Transactions of the Jewish Historical Society of England* 17 (1951–52): 79–90.

Thomas, Robert Paul. "The Sugar Colonies of the Old Empire: Profit or Loss for Great Britain?" 2d ser., *Economic History Review* 21 (1968): 30–45.

Ville, Simon. "The Growth of Specialization in English Shipowning, 1750–1850." 2d ser., *Economic History Review* 46 (1993): 702–22.

Walton, Gary M. "Sources of Productivity Change in American Colonial Shipping, 1675–1775." 2d ser., *Economic History Review* 20 (1967): 67–78.

Ward, J. R. "The Profitability of Sugar Planting in the British West Indies, 1650–1834." 2d ser., *Economic History Review* 31 (1978): 197–213.

Wax, Darold D. "Negro Imports into Pennsylvania, 1720–1766." *Pennsylvania History* 32 (1965): 254–87.

Wiznitzer, Arnold. "Jews in the Sugar Industry of Colonial Brazil." *Jewish Social Studies* 18 (1956): 189–98.

Wolf, Lucien. "American Elements in the Resettlement." *Transactions of the Jewish Historical Society of England* 3 (1896–98): 76–100.

———. "Crypto-Jews under the Commonwealth." *Transactions of the Jewish Historical Society of England* 1 (1893–94): 55–88.

———. "The Jewry of the Restoration. 1660–1664." *Transactions of the Jewish Historical Society of England* 5 (1902–5): 5–33.

Woolf, Maurice. "Eighteenth-Century London Jewish Shipowners." *Miscellanies of the Jewish Historical Society of England* 9 (1970–73): 198–204.

———. "Foreign Trade of London Jews in the Seventeenth Century." *Transactions of the Jewish Historical Society of England* 24 (1970–73): 38–58.

———. "Joseph Salvador 1716–1786." *Transactions of the Jewish Historical Society of England* 21 (1962–67): 104–37.

Zahedieh, Nuala. "The Merchants of Port Royal, Jamaica, and the Spanish Contraband Trade, 1655–1692." 3d ser., *William and Mary Quarterly* 43 (1986): 570–93.

———. "Trade, Plunder, and Economic Development in Early English Jamaica, 1655–89." 2d ser., *Economic History Review* 39 (1986): 205–22.

Zook, George Frederick. "The Company of Royal Adventurers Trading into Africa." *Journal of Negro History* 4 (1919): 134–231.

Index

About the Author

Eli Faber is Professor of History at John Jay College of Criminal Justice, The City University of New York, and author of *A Time for Planting: The First Migration, 1654–1820,* the first volume in the five-volume *The Jewish People in America.*